MOZART AND HIS WORLD

THE BARD MUSIC FESTIVAL

LEON BOTSTEIN AND CHRISTOPHER H. GIBBS
SERIES EDITORS

MOZART
AND HIS WORLD

EDITED BY
SIMON P. KEEFE

THE UNIVERSITY OF CHICAGO PRESS
CHICAGO AND LONDON

The University of Chicago Press, Chicago 60637
The University of Chicago Press, Ltd., London

Published 2026
Printed in the United States of America

35 34 33 32 31 30 29 28 27 26   1 2 3 4 5

ISBN-13: 978-0-226-85536-3 (cloth)
ISBN-13: 978-0-226-85573-8 (paper)
ISBN-13: 978-0-226-85574-5 (ebook)
DOI: https://doi.org/10.7208/chicago/9780226855745.001.0001

This publication has been produced by the Bard College Publications Office:
Irene Zedlacher, project director
Karen Spencer, design
Text copy edited by Erin Clermont
Music typeset by Christopher Deschene
Indexed by Scott Smiley

This publication has been underwritten in part by a grant from Roger and Helen Alcaly.

Library of Congress Control Number: 2026937781

∞ This paper meets the requirements of ANSI/NISO Z39.48-1992 (Permanence of Paper).

Authorized Representative for EU General Product Safety Regulation (GPSR) queries:
Easy Access System Europe—Mustamäe tee 50, 10621 Tallinn, Estonia,
gpsr.requests@easproject.com
Any other queries: https://press.uchicago.edu/press/contact.html

Permissions and Credits

The following copyright holders, individuals, and institutions have graciously granted permission to reprint or reproduce the following materials:

Bärenreiter for Examples 4–8 in Waldoff, "Seduction and the (Mis) Representation of Love in Mozart's Da Ponte Operas"

The Schwarzenberg Archive at Český Krumlov for Figures 1 and 2 in Glatthorn, "Transcribing the Popular: *Harmonie* Arrangements and Opera Reception, ca. 1800"

The Metropolitan Opera for Figure 3 (photo by Erika Davidson) in Goehring, "A Reading of *The Magic Flute*"

Alamy Stock Photos for Figure 1 in Goehring, "A Reading of *The Magic Flute*," and Figures 1 and 2 in Botstein, "Understanding Mozart: The Claims of History and Philosophy"

Introduction

SIMON P. KEEFE

On first encountering Papageno early in *The Magic Flute*, Tamino asks him who he is, to which Papageno replies, "Who am I? Stupid question! A person [*Mensch*], like you are." In his own era, Mozart too was just an individual human being navigating the highs and lows, and the stresses, strains, challenges, triumphs, and joys of his personal and professional life. Much posthumous reception suggests otherwise, however, especially hyperbolic *bon mots* from eminent musicians and non-musicians alike, who either take him for a god-like figure, or gaze in awe at his accomplishments. Among a disparate group of the musical world's great and good, Hector Berlioz considered him a "celestial figure" to be "worshipped," Richard Wagner professed to "believe in God, Mozart, and Beethoven," Charles-François Gounod found that "before Mozart, all my ambition turns to despair," Georg Solti thought "Mozart makes you believe in God—more than going to church," and Hans Keller signaled Mozart's ear "as the only truly omniscient ear of which we know." Amid an even more varied coterie of non-musicians and musical amateurs, the author and illustrator Maurice Sendak understood that "designing an opera by Mozart [is] like doing something for God— . . . a labour of love," playwright Arthur Miller described Mozart's music as "happiness before it has gotten defined," and no less an authority on the universe than Albert Einstein, identifying Mozart as "the greatest composer of all," claimed that his music "is of such purity and beauty that one feels he merely 'found' it—that it has always existed as part of the inner beauty of the universe, waiting to be revealed."[1] Furthermore, and resonating with Mozart's own experiences of the therapeutic qualities of making music during his difficult trip to France and Germany in 1777–79,[2] artist Eugène Delacroix and literary critic Harold Bloom found Mozart good for their physical and mental well-being: Delacroix's excessive fatigue vanished on encountering a Mozart symphony, which displayed "perfection, that completeness, those delicate shadings, all that must be the despair of musicians who have any soul and any taste"; and Bloom explained that he goes "back to the

G-minor Quintet [K. 516] for comfort, sometimes when I am most desperate . . . helping me to bear myself in the despair of solitude."[3]

A little over twenty years ago, in an essay on twentieth-century Mozart reception, Jan Smaczny claimed that the collision of popular images of the composer—including myth-inducing ones related to the kinds of statements quoted above—and scholarly images was something that "the twenty-first century will have to sort out."[4] Indeed, Mozart scholars this century have often embraced a fact-fiction continuum in reception-related work, evaluating myths, legends, and fictions as positive rather than negative contributors to critical discourse.[5] Disquiet in some circles has arisen less for methodological and ontological reasons than as a result of the practical reality of Mozart losing his central position in musicological discourse usually taken for granted in earlier eras: he has to compete for air time these days with so many performers, composers, and other musicians in a wide range of genres and sub-disciplines, and in an intellectual climate and institutional culture that regularly works against placing him and his music center stage. Yet the fascination with Mozart endures, propelled by 200-plus years of reception—hyperbolic, fictional, critical, and scholarly alike—and stimulated by a belief that the more scholarship is carried out, the more there remains to be done. Few Mozart (indeed classical-music) lovers would disagree with Robert Schumann's famous rhetorical question: "Does it not seem as if Mozart's works become fresher and fresher the oftener we hear them?"[6] And all writers on Mozart surely aspire to an analogous condition for the development of Mozart scholarship, in the direction of ever greater color, vibrancy, and vigor.

Focusing on core areas of Mozart scholarship, including hermeneutic endeavor, contextual study, and reception, *Mozart and His World* accommodates the interests of readers wishing to proceed through the book from beginning to end as well as those choosing to focus more selectively on specific topics or subject areas. Covering perennially popular works and topics in original ways, as well as filling scholarly lacunae, the volume progresses from studies of instrumental music to the interpretation and reception of Mozart's operas, and finally to important documents, fully introduced and contextualized, from the decade or so after the composer's death.

In the first essay, Dorian Bandy views Mozart's chamber music and to a lesser extent operas through the lens of the "system," previously associated only with scientific and philosophical texts from the Enlightenment. Focusing on for example the violin and viola duos K. 423 and 424, the "Haydn" string quartets, the B-flat Violin Sonata, K. 454, the C-major String Quintet K. 515, the F-major Piano Sonata K. 533, and the Da Ponte operas, Bandy situates issues and ideas previously characterized as "coherence" and "unity" in their own specific intellectual climate. Next, Edward Klorman examines Mozart's set of string quartets K. 168–173 in light of stylistic continuities with later repertoire, rather than (as is standard practice) stylistic differences, thereby demonstrating the significance of these works in their own right. Traversing the worlds of instrumental music and opera, Austin Glatthorn expands and refines our knowledge and understanding of late eighteenth- and early nineteenth-century *Harmonien* (music for winds). He focuses on institutional collections and the work of practitioners such as Josef Triebensee, Johann Went, and Anton Schneider, explaining the varied nature of *Harmonie* ensembles and their diverse performances of operas and opera excerpts.

The next five essays comprise interpretations and studies of the reception of Mozart's operas, and of his music more generally. Edmund J. Goehring offers a wide-ranging, revisionist interpretation of *The Magic Flute*, linking it to the ethos of the Counter-Reformation and to a Baroque culture of ceremonial piety. Moving beyond ideas such as spectacle and ritual impeding Enlightenment, and conflict between rationality and irrationality existing at the opera's core, Goehring sheds light on heroism and sensibility among the main characters, and on Mozart's creation of Counter-Reformation music, in the process drawing parallels between Mozart and Dante. Jessica Waldoff considers seduction in Mozart's operatic repertory in relation to the broad category of late eighteenth-century love duets. She identifies Mozart's adaptations and alterations to the model for dramatic purposes in *La villanella rapita*, *Le nozze di Figaro*, *Don Giovanni*, and *Così fan tutte*, including his writing of "counterfeit" and "pretend" love duets. My own essay reevaluates the reception of the French parody of *The Magic Flute* as *Les mystères d'Isis* (Paris Opéra, 1801), by Étienne Morel de Chédeville and Ludwig Wenzel Lachnith. Initially revered then long reviled, this *grand opéra*'s complicated genesis and cultural environment in Napoleonic France, and its crucial role as a springboard for nineteenth-century reception of Mozart in France, demonstrate the power of publicly popular events and works to exert a profound influence on a wide range of reception-related activity. Martin Nedbal looks at the early Viennese reception of Mozart's *opera serie Idomeneo* and *La clemenza di Tito* up to 1811, before they disappeared from the stage for a substantial portion of the nineteenth century. He examines competition between the Theater an der Wien and Viennese Court Theater in German and Italian productions of *Tito* in 1801 and 1804, the "Germanization" of both *Idomeneo* and *Tito* at the Court Theater in the first two decades of the nineteenth century, and their status as masterworks by 1820. Finally, in a broad-ranging essay

Contents

(and as a "Coda" to the volume), Leon Botstein situates understandings of Mozart in historical, cultural, and philosophical contexts. Focusing on nineteenth- and twentieth-century ideas and trends, he examines inter alia parallels between Mozart and Raphael, nineteenth-century concepts of the Renaissance, Classicism, and modernity, Mozart's philosophical heritage (especially through Moses Mendelssohn), comparisons between Mozart and Beethoven, and Mozart and ethical truth.

The Documents section comprises new translations of a famous Mozart obituary and of six Mozart-related articles from early issues of the Leipzig-based *Allgemeine musikalische Zeitung*, which following its launch in 1798 quickly established itself as a leading source of highbrow critical discourse on music. Friedrich Schlichtegroll's 6,000-word obituary (1793) constitutes the first substantial biography of Mozart and de facto instigator of the Mozart biographical tradition, rooted in Schlichtegroll's close engagement—via a Salzburg intermediary, Albert von Mölk—with Mozart's sister Nannerl and a close family friend, Johann Andreas Schachtner. I preface the translation with an extended introductory essay, in which the reception and significance of the biography are contextualized and reevaluated in view of the interests and orientations of Schlichtegroll himself, and a rarely mentioned addendum to the biography from 1798 on Mozart's Requiem is translated and explained.

The articles included from the *Allgemeine musikalische Zeitung* are among this journal's most important and wide ranging on Mozart from the turn of the nineteenth century: a review of songs with piano accompaniment; an extended comparison between painter Raphael and Mozart; and reviews of Breitkopf & Härtel's complete works of Mozart (which ultimately remained incomplete), the first edition of the Requiem, a volume of cadenzas for Mozart's piano concertos written by Frankfurt-based pianist and composer P. C. Hoffmann, and a review of Ignaz Ferdinand Arnold's *Mozarts Geist* (Mozart's Spirit, 1803), an early landmark in the reception of the composer's music. As Lisa de Alwis points out in her introduction to the translations, lavish praise for Mozart does not preclude criticism of him.

Writing in the aftermath of the Second World War, two of Mozart's greatest scholarly advocates remind us why he remains so important to us. Edward J. Dent, at the end of the second edition of his study of Mozart's operas, explained that "more than ever now, in these times of turmoil and confusion . . . we need the profound and noble sincerity of *Idomeneo* and the serene spirituality of *The Magic Flute*."[7] Alfred Einstein, closing his Mozart biography as an exiled German Jew in the United States, regarded the composer and the absence of his "earthly remains" as the ideal antidote to the devastation of his own era: "It is as though the world-spirit wished to show that here is pure sound, conforming to a weightless cosmos, triumphant over all chaotic earthliness, spirit of the world-spirit."[8] In our own socially, politically, and environmentally troubled times, Mozart can continue to have a powerfully humane influence on our lives—as listeners, music lovers, writers, critics, and scholars. As one of his biggest nineteenth-century admirers, Pyotr Ilyich Tchaikovsky, once wrote, "To hear his music is to feel one has accomplished some good deed. It is difficult to say wherein this good influence lies, but undoubtedly it is beneficial."[9]

NOTES

1. See Joseph Solman, *Mozartiana: Two Centuries of Notes, Quotes, and Anecdotes about Wolfgang Amadeus Mozart* (New York: Walker & Company, 1990), 59, 62, 59, 82, 117, 82, 89, 94.

2. See Simon P. Keefe, "Mozart 'Stuck in Music' in Paris (1778): Towards a New Biographical Paradigm," in *Mozart Studies 2*, ed. Keefe (Cambridge: Cambridge University Press, 2015), 23–54, at 28–29.

3. Solman, *Mozartiana*, 106, 113–14.

4. Jan Smaczny, "Mozart and the Twentieth Century," in *The Cambridge Companion to Mozart*, ed. Simon P. Keefe (Cambridge: Cambridge University Press, 2003), 185–99, at 199.

5. In this respect, see for example Simon P. Keefe, *Mozart's Requiem: Reception, Work, Completion* (Cambridge: Cambridge University Press, 2012); and Adeline Mueller, "Mythmaking," in *Mozart in Context*, ed. Keefe (Cambridge: Cambridge University Press, 2019), 83–88. On positive aspects of mythmaking for composers in general, see Keefe, "Mythmaking and Hagiography," in *The Oxford Handbook of Music Biography and Life-Writing*, ed. Christopher Wiley and Paul Watt (New York: Oxford University Press, forthcoming).

6. As quoted in Friedrich Kerst, *Mozart: The Man and the Artist Revealed in His Own Words* (London: Geoffrey Bles, 1926), 11.

7. Edward J. Dent, *Mozart's Operas: A Critical Study*, 2nd ed. (London: Oxford University Press, 1947), 266.

8. Alfred Einstein, *Mozart: His Character, His Work* (1946), trans. Arthur Mendel and Nathan Broder (London: Panther Books, 1970), 487.

9. Modeste Tchaikovsky, *The Life and Letters of Peter Ilich Tchaikovsky*, vol. 2 (New York: Haskell House Publishers, 1970), 432–33.

PART I: ESSAYS

Systematic Mozart

DORIAN BANDY

This essay seeks to make headway into an understanding of the relationship between Mozart and his intellectual world. My touchstone will be the "system," a literary genre that flourished among authors of philosophical and scientific texts during the Enlightenment, and whose formal conventions find analogues in Mozart's instrumental music beginning around 1783. Eighteenth-century systems organized and advanced knowledge through the use of comprehensive yet parsimonious explanatory frameworks that enabled exploration of abstract and often counterintuitive intellectual terrain. Like the authors of literary systems, Mozart developed strategies that allowed him to invest particular works with the capacity for recursive self-criticism, whether by rigorously probing the affordances of local premises in individual movements or by using such premises to synthesize multiple movements or compositions into broader cycles that comment on their own musical contents. My purpose here is to explore Mozart's participation in a mode of conceptual investigation that characterized eighteenth-century thought at the broadest level. Even more, however, I hope to demonstrate that the compositions I discuss may be understood as part of the Enlightenment project to *know the world*—that is, I hope to show that they aim not only to offer aesthetic pleasure but to further a genuine process of learning and discovery. In the end, I will argue that Mozart's compositional persona embodies a degree of intellectual ambition that has largely been overlooked: one that both complements and transcends the performative virtuosity and dramatic sensibility for which he is celebrated.

My reading builds upon yet also challenges prevailing approaches to Mozart's place in the late eighteenth-century world of ideas. Over the past four decades, it has become increasingly common for scholars to ground Mozart's activities in contemporary currents, whether by adopting historically inflected modes of analysis or by interpreting his music in light of Enlightenment humanistic ideals, an approach reinforced by the many literary and philosophical references in his letters. Yet even as such historicism has become *de rigueur*, parallel developments have dismantled the foundations on which it rests. The embattled term "Enlightenment," once freely invoked in Mozart scholarship, has been subjected to sustained critique from numerous fields—"critiqued into near oblivion," as Robert Miles puts it.[1] Immanuel Kant, in his celebrated 1784 essay "Beantwortung der Frage: Was ist Aufklärung?," felt justified in asserting that he lived in an "Age of Enlightenment," but the meaning of his dictum has never seemed less self-evident. What was once treated as a unified cultural moment has splintered into competing regional and ideological strands: European Enlightenment, Postcolonial Enlightenment, and Democratic Enlightenment, to say nothing of Contested Enlightenment.[2] These historiographical shifts are compounded by mounting unease over the lives and views of key Enlightenment figures, a point from which Mozart is not exempt given critiques of the racial portrayals in more than one of his operas.[3]

Nonetheless, attempts have been made to rehabilitate the concept of Enlightenment by seeking unity on deeper, foundational levels. The physicist and philosopher David Deutsch has argued that despite the nuance brought about by recent historical studies, the many strands of Enlightenment all share an underlying "tradition of criticism," a cultural commitment to solving problems without appeals to authority.[4] More germane to my present purposes, the literary historians Clifford Siskin and William Warner characterize Enlightenment as "an event in the history of mediation," emphasizing that various concrete forms of knowledge organization—print media, scholarly societies, museums—can themselves shape intellectual development by enabling highly productive feedback loops in which the creation and dissemination of knowledge become mutually reinforcing.[5] In order to be useful, after all, knowledge must not only come into existence but be retrievable. Mediation sparked Enlightenment's ferment by organizing ideas in ways that were previously impossible, allowing widespread participation in a communal endeavor that swiftly shaped the intellectual terrain.

"System" is not merely one literary genre among many but the flagship technology of Enlightenment mediation. As Siskin documents in a wide-ranging historical study, system originated in the seventeenth and eighteenth centuries, overtaking competing forms such as the essay to become the premiere vehicle for communicating philosophical and scientific knowledge.[6] Beginning with Galileo's efforts to explain celestial motion (a legacy preserved in terms like the "solar system") and reaching maturity with Isaac Newton's *Principia* (known then as the "Newtonian

System") and Adam Smith's *The Wealth of Nations*, system "filled the Enlightenment with the work of writing."[7] The genre's success derived from three characteristics. First, systems are comprehensive. Galileo sought to explain not just Earth's orbit but those of all celestial bodies; Newton framed universal laws of motion; and Smith attempted to capture the full scope of human behavior both on the individual level (in his *Theory of Moral Sentiments*) and in society at large (in *The Wealth of Nations*). Second, systems aim for the highest possible ratio of parts to principles.[8] Many writers described their systems as "simple" precisely because those systems encompassed an enormous number of details without multiplying their premises. One interesting corollary of this high ratio of parts to principles is that, in Siskin's words, "systems talked to themselves, quieting discourse [such as criticism from peers] in favor of an internal conversation among parts."[9] This comes very close to Elaine Sisman's description of a musical opus as a collection of pieces in dialogue with one another—though, as I will argue below, opuses and systems diverge in important respects.[10] Finally, systems are scalable, crossing boundaries of size and abstraction. The laws explaining the relationship between a planet and its moons also explain the relationship between planets and the sun, and indeed the relationship between our sun and the galactic center of the Milky Way. This scalability enabled system's distinctive capacity for self-organization and recursive complexity.

Many of the systems Siskin discusses are scientific works. Yet other fields, too, spawned systems. Some musical texts, including Jean-Philippe Rameau's *Nouveau système de musique théoretique* (1726), used the word in their titles. Christoph Mizler, whom Leopold Mozart extols in the introduction to the *Violinschule*, refers to "system" repeatedly throughout his four-volume *Musikalische Bibliothek* (1736–54) when discussing subjects ranging from mathematical theory to musical composition.[11] Later authors, too, continued to describe their works in such terms. Augustus Frederic Christopher Kollmann's 1806 *New Theory of Musical Harmony, According to a Complete and Natural System of that Science*, for instance, identifies both his and Johann Kirnberger's earlier writings as systems:

> My first Theoretical work . . . was founded on Kirnberger's system. . . . But having since discovered cases in which that system is still incomplete, and imperfect, I have endeavoured to remove them.[12]

Writings described as "theories" also embodied elements of system—indeed, the two terms were largely interchangeable. Samuel Johnson defined theory as "a system yet subsisting only in the mind,"[13] and Smith, in his "History of Astronomy," treats theories and systems alike as "imaginary machine[s] invented to connect together in the fancy those different movements and effects" observed in external reality.[14] Thus, texts ranging from the *Theory of Moral Sentiments* to the writings of Heinrich Christoph Koch are also best understood as systems.

System in Eighteenth-Century Musical Composition

If system was a technology for Enlightenment knowledge work, the question arises whether its organizational principles might also govern other intellectual and cultural enterprises. Genre is substrate neutral, after all, and many contemporaries referred to system's characteristics when describing internal features of musical compositions. To be sure, not all sophisticated compositions are systems. Comprehensiveness alone, such as that embodied by Bach's *Das wohltemperierte Klavier* and many other baroque collections, does not itself ensure systematic thought in the sense I mean. Bach's collections more closely resemble a different literary genre, the eighteenth-century encyclopedia, as repositories collecting an enormous range of information without necessarily producing new theoretical insights through the interaction of their parts. Systematic composition, by contrast, requires premises that actively generate ongoing, internal cross-referential discourse.

System's advantageous ratio of parts to principles, in particular, finds clear analogues in eighteenth-century treatises on musical composition, where writers regularly refer to "premises" that composers could use to ensure coherence in their works. In his *Musicalischer-Trichter* of 1706, Martin Heinrich Fuhrmann describes the allemande as "the proposition in a musical suite, from which the [other movements] flow as parts," a framing later transmitted nearly verbatim by Johann Gottfried Walther and which harkens to the rhetorical practice of asserting an argument (*propositio*) and then dividing it into parts (*partitio*).[15] Later writers continued in this vein, with Koch defending the "unity" (*Einheit*) achieved by beginning with a *Hauptsatz* or *Thema*, effectively a premise, and letting all other ideas derive from it. The mechanism enabling such integration is variation, which lends itself readily to analogies with system both in the genre of the variation set (whose recursive engagement with a theme has long been understood as music-theoretical self-criticism directed at its own contents) and elsewhere, whenever disparate passages acquire significance through meaningful cross-referencing.[16] This link, too, was often made explicit. André Grétry, copies of whose music Mozart owned, stated that composing variations is "like supplying proofs to the propositions one has made at the outset," and Abbé Vogler identified variations with the rhetorical ploy in which a basic idea is spun out in all manner of florid turns—a point suggesting the device synecdoche ("many things realized from a part") and linking variation to Erasmus's influential rhetoric manual *De copia*.[17] Leopold Mozart, who studied formal rhetoric, almost certainly used such texts when educating his son; and outside the Mozart household too, variation was understood as a means of developing both local phrases and longer compositions.

Despite their grounding in technical elements of composition, such ideals were also espoused by philosophers of the time, not least in the writings of that great systematizer Adam Smith, whose probing essay "On the Nature of that Imitation which takes place in what are called the Imitative Arts" (published posthumously in 1795) argues that music derives expressive power by aspiring to the condition of system. In Smith's words, a "well-composed concerto of instrumental Music" presents an object

> so great, so various, and so interesting, that alone, and without suggesting any other object, . . . it can occupy, and as it were fill up, completely the whole capacity of the mind. . . . In the contemplation of that immense variety . . . into so complete and regular a system, the mind in reality enjoys not only a very great sensual, but a very high intellectual, pleasure, not unlike that which it derives from the contemplation of a great system in any other science.[18]

Kant, whose aesthetic theory was influenced by Smith, furthers a similar claim in his systematic *Kritik der Urteilskraft* (1790), where he describes the alignment and integration of many diverse components as being the hallmark of a successful artwork.[19] Such appraisals slot neatly among broader intellectual currents as well. Jean-Baptiste Robinet and Johann Wolfgang von Goethe drew analogies between the natural world and artworks, both of which exhibited, in David Montgomery's words, "fantastic transformational possibilities whereby highly varied and dissimilar life forms shared and evolved from a common germinal model invested with superabundant capacity and a powerful will."[20] Despite the infamously value-laden assumptions with which unity and organicism would later become entangled, the concepts were familiar among and lionized by eighteenth-century critics. A symphony by Christian Cannabich won praise from Daniel Schubart in 1791 for being "a musical whole whose parts, like spiritual emanations, again form a whole"—a statement that, as Carl Dahlhaus observes, anticipates E. T. A. Hoffmann's panegyrics to Beethoven.[21]

Even so, lest these accounts depict a musical culture single-mindedly in thrall to unity, systematic integration was by no means a foregone conclusion. Just as literary authors could choose between systems and other forms, musicians too had alternatives. Particularly conducive to looser treatment was the free fantasia, an essayistic genre championed by C. P. E. Bach and many contemporaries as a vehicle for direct, personal expression. Whereas systematic composition demanded methodical development of premises, the fantasia reveled in digression. When improvised, fantasias were thought to lay bare the performer's shifting emotions in real time, unmediated by planning or revision.[22] Even when composed in advance, fantasias were exploratory and episodic: soliloquys celebrated as revealing the innermost essence of those who wrote or played them. Because the fantasia is a genre, such associations were matters of convention. Systematic composition, by contrast, was not a genre but a set of priorities that composers could pursue in a range of generic contexts. A symphony could be written in as loose or systematic a style as a composer wished.

That freedom carried real weight. As Siskin emphasizes, writing a system was a deliberate choice requiring considerable commitment. For every author who grappled with system, many others pursued different genres, and reasonably so. Newton's work on his system involved extensive effort to discover, understand, and frame premises that could track reality and support further discovery. Systematic musical composition, too, presented challenges both during the creative process and in the reception a piece would receive. The music I examine here shows Mozart adopting systematic strategies—not simply to foster thematic integration but as fuel for exploring aesthetic territory which, as contemporary listeners often complained, produced results too artful for easy consumption. The mechanics of Mozart's premises and systems, and the abstract dimensions their pursuit fostered in his style, bring me to my next section.

Composing System: Chamber Music as Laboratory

Many of Mozart's compositions exhibit structures connecting a wide range of parts to a generative premise. Beginning in the mid-1770s, his pursuit of this strategy becomes both consistent and overt. For instance, each of the first six piano sonatas (K. 279–284, composed in 1775) elaborates on an idea presented near the outset. In K. 279, a lower neighbor tone in the left hand in measure 1 echoes prominently in many accompaniments and virtually every melody in all three movements. In K. 280, a descending chromatic scale in measure 3 is woven into subsequent passages throughout. Elsewhere, concrete allusions link disparate gestures, as when a written-out *Eingang* in the third movement of K. 281 recalls the first movement's retransition. And in the Piano Concerto in E-flat Major K. 271 (1776), Mozart's most elaborate system to date, themes in all three movements derive from the soloist's surprise entry at the outset of the piece.[23]

Such cross-referencing speaks to the centrality of variation to Mozart's craft. But a musical system's premises need not be limited to themes and motives, even though this is the context in which contemporaries like Koch and modern-day readers who draw upon his writings generally apply the term. Rather, premises can encompass any feature so omnipresent as to seem generative of the musical narrative. A classic analysis by Howard Boatwright describes the unfinished Minuet K. 355 as a vehicle for Mozart's harmony-bending exploration of the sonority of the augmented triad, and this, as much as any theme, might be considered the premise from which the piece flows.[24] Similarly, in the Piano Concerto in A Major K. 414 (1782–83), melodies across all three movements are accompanied by prominent pedal points.[25] In these pieces, Mozart demonstrates the thematic potential of abstract ideas, and although both works also use familiar variation techniques, the self-referential conversation they sustain among their parts derives primarily from these conceptual premises.[26]

These examples show traces of systematic thought. But system's more comprehensive intellectual ambition—its capacity to serve as a safety-line for exploring remote aesthetic possibilities—would not fully emerge in Mozart's output until 1783, coinciding with his renewed interest in chamber music. The previous decade had seen a hiatus in Mozart's chamber writing: although he composed sets of string quartets in Milan and Vienna in 1770–73 and a handful of violin sonatas and flute quartets in 1777–79, he spent his formative years through the early 1780s honing his technique in the arenas of opera, sacred music, concertos, and symphonies. When he did turn back to chamber music, it was with a newfound inquisitiveness. As Koch observed, chamber genres could support "more development and finer nuance" than public genres.[27] The economic logic was clear. Large-scale compositions such as symphonies or serenades were costly to perform yet would be heard only once by most listeners. Such works therefore had to be immediately accessible to the widest possible audience-base.[28] Chamber music, by contrast, written for publication, was a low-budget but high-stakes medium. Those who purchased printed editions of chamber works could play or listen to them repeatedly, and the music therefore had to be stimulating and challenging enough to reward continued engagement. Considering that the primary audiences for chamber works would include the players themselves, it is hardly surprising that these intimate genres become what Wye Allanbrook has called a "composer's laboratory" for stylistic experimentation.[29] Newly ensconced in this laboratory in the early 1780s, Mozart would use systematic methods both to organize material and to probe the consequences of rigorously pursued premises, pushing into aesthetic regions more abstract and counterintuitive than his public works could risk.

Mozart's return to chamber music also brought a newfound interest in the slow introduction, a formal area he had previously neglected. Slow introductions were rare in chamber music of the time: they were associated most closely with symphonies and opera overtures. Mozart's decision to import this formal area into the intimate chamber medium may signal a heightened compositional ambition, as if claiming for these works an elevated status typically reserved for grand public showings. Given how rarely he used the formal area at all, theorists have tended to dismiss its importance, some even claiming that slow introductions are entirely superfluous since Mozart's expositions efficiently combine the functions of rhetorical *exordium* and *narratio*.[30] Yet it is precisely in light of their rarity that the sudden proliferation of slow introductions in his chamber works is striking. Slow introductions carry a basic expressive potency, building anticipation through a trademark merging of a stately tempo with unstable harmonic or rhythmic elements. To the systematic composer, however, the formal area also offers a suspended temporal space where premises can be established and foregrounded before their consequences unfold, drawing attention to themselves rather like the opening position of a chess problem or the axioms of a mathematical proof.

Mozart's first mature slow introduction begins the Duo for Violin and Viola in B-flat Major, K. 424, composed in 1783 (along with the Duo in G Major, K. 423) as a favor to Michael Haydn, who, unable to complete a commission for six such duos, solicited Mozart's aid.[31] K. 423 and K. 424 are the most intimately scored of Mozart's string works, and it may be as a counterbalance to the small forces that he elected to include a slow introduction in K. 424, lending the movement a grandeur it might otherwise lack. Equally significant is a compositional question the introduction seems to pose: What contrapuntal and expressive relationships are available to two string players? Despite its brevity, the ten-measure introduction undertakes a systematic inventory of the possibilities (Example 1). After the initial unison (m. 1), Mozart methodically explores a series of permutations. The two instruments alternate in playing individual lines as melodies and accompaniments (mm. 2–6); the viola provides a Romanesca bass in 32nd notes beneath contrapuntal double-stops in the violin (mm. 6–8); the players again switch roles, the violin now carrying the 32nd notes while the viola plays double stops (mm. 8–9); and finally,

Example 1. Duo for Violin and Viola in B-flat Major, K. 424, first movement, mm. 1–10.

both instruments play double stops, yielding the four-part texture of a quartet (mm. 9–10). Even within this self-contained formal unit, then, Mozart draws attention to the comprehensiveness with which he will treat the instruments as the rest of the duo unfolds. He also uses familiar means of motivic integration, particularly by developing the lower neighbor tone prominently presented in the opening unison in measure 1 in a wide range of subsequent gestures. Along these axes, the introduction establishes a combinatorial space within which the duo will operate.

The introduction is systematic in that weak sense, but it also takes a generative role in the Allegro that follows, and in this way, the formal area lays the groundwork for more protracted systematizing as well. Virtually everything that occurs in the exposition derives in some way from the introduction—not in the methodical fashion of a variation suite, but as if the introduction has provided a set of raw materials now available for continuous transformation. The opening unison, memorable for its triadic ascent not to the prosaic $\hat{5}$ but to the more searching $\hat{6}$, returns during the exposition's imitative subordinate theme (Example 2a) and later forms the basis for extensive invertible counterpoint in the development. The trills initially presented by the violin in the introduction become propulsive viola flourishes in the exposition (mm. 36–39), in a passage that also recalls a distinctively voiced violin chord initially presented in measure 8 (Example 2b). The viola's Romanesca bass from the introduction, meanwhile, returns in the closing theme, the Adagio's 32nd notes now recast as 8th notes (Example 2c). That such references are thoroughly intermixed is crucial for understanding the duo as a system. Motivic economy serves here not as a hidden expedient but as an aesthetic feature Mozart boldly advertises. Thus, references are not limited to allusions to the introduction. Even within the Allegro, thematic cells regularly infiltrate other formal areas, as, for instance, when the Romanesca that first appeared as viola accompaniment is later used as the protracted harmonic basis for a transitional passage during the recapitulation (Example 2d) and then again to signal the onset of coda-like material in the final eighteen measures (Example 2e). Allanbrook has observed that Mozart often ends movements by drawing attention to a piece of material that was present all along, generative but understated, as if urging us not to miss it—a point that certainly applies in K. 424, as a capstone to this elaborate system without words.[32]

If such development turns K. 424 into a musical investigation of its premises' elaborative potential, the intimate scoring is of particular consequence. Composed partway through Mozart's work on the "Haydn" Quartets, the duo appears to have served as a laboratory in many senses.

Example 2a. Duo for Violin and Viola in B-flat Major, K. 424, first movement, mm. 177–80.

Example 2b. Duo for Violin and Viola in B-flat Major, K. 424, first movement, mm. 34–37.

Example 2c. Duo for Violin and Viola in B-flat Major, K. 424, first movement, mm. 190–96.

Example 2d. Duo for Violin and Viola in B-flat Major, K. 424, first movement, mm. 149–54.

Example 2e. Duo for Violin and Viola in B-flat Major, K. 424, first movement, mm. 197–200.

On one level, it allowed Mozart to isolate the textural and thus contrapuntal possibilities afforded by string instruments at a moment in his career that proved essential for his quartet writing. Indeed, the systematic rigor he pursued here yielded a striking and immediate expansion of the technical vocabulary he brought to his subsequent chamber compositions—an expansion that elevated the instrumental handling in his quartets above anything he had previously achieved. Even Mozart's violin concertos are, from the perspective of string technique, remarkably constrained in comparison with K. 424 and the Quartet in E-flat Major K. 428, composed shortly after. But beyond such technical matters, there is something about K. 424—indeed, about chamber genres more broadly—that seems to turn the musical system into a dramatization of intellectual exploration. The systematic tendencies and sociable spirit animating this duo suggest a narrative of thematic discovery redolent of scientific and philosophical dialogues by the likes of Diderot, Voltaire, Hume, Berkeley, Herder, and countless other contemporaries. K. 424 may begin with a unison that suggests a shared perspective between the players, but what unfolds never again takes alignment for granted, instead staging a musical conversation in which each player ventures ideas that the other critiques, nuances, transforms, or even rejects. To echo Smith's account of musical systems, K. 424 fills the capacity of the mind even as it affords listeners and players a high degree of sensual pleasure.

Systematic exploration does not require a slow introduction, but Mozart's most ambitious experiments of the next year, 1784, continued to use this formal space as their starting point. This was his densest and most fertile period of engagement with slow introductions, one resulting in a remarkable series of musical systems including the Piano Quintet, K. 452, the Violin Sonata K. 454, and the start of the "Dissonance" Quartet, K. 465 (though not its completion). Although K. 452 and K. 454 reprise many of the strategies heard in the Duo K. 424, K. 454 is particularly distinctive in its merging of systematizing with concrete considerations of performance. Mozart composed this sonata for the Italian virtuoso violinist Regina Strinasacchi and premiered it with her on 29 April 1784: Mozart apparently read blank pages and invented the piano part on the fly. Even the origins of K. 454, then, are rich with performative implications. The resulting system incorporates highly practical matters such as written-out embellishment as well as interpretive issues such as the playfully competitive personae of the two performers. Throughout, violin and piano engage in increasingly elaborate exchanges, each trying to outdo the other in a process escalating from gracious handoffs to an all-out battle of virtuosity that erupts in the finale.[33] The slow introduction plants the seed: every time the violinist presents an expressive theme, the pianist ramps up the florid density of the answer. In one particularly generative exchange, the violinist plays a lyrical figure in broken thirds and the pianist repeats the gesture, embellishing it by accelerating the thirds' frequency (Example 3a).

These thirds feature throughout the rest of the piece.[34] In the first movement's exposition, they recur in an embellished dialogue (Example 3b) and later become a standalone figure the pianist uses to undermine the lyricism of the violin's phrases. But the competitiveness cuts both ways, and in the second movement the violinist exacts revenge. Here it is the pianist who attempts to introduce a singing melody that incorporates repeated thirds echoing the previous movement's slow introduction, and

Example 3a. Violin Sonata in B-flat Major, K. 454, first movement, mm. 9–10.

Example 3b. Violin Sonata in B-flat Major, K. 454, first movement, mm. 58–65.

Example 3c. Violin Sonata in B-flat Major, K. 454, second movement, mm. 31–33.

the violinist's turn to thumb her nose by responding with the same boisterous embellishment the pianist had been using throughout (Example 3c).[35] Nor do these foregrounded gestures constitute the sonata's only systematic embellishments. Another figure stated by the pianist in the first movement's slow introduction (m. 7), a sweeping ascending arpeggio, is reprised as thematic material in the second movement as a cadential flourish (m. 109).

Siskin's exploration describes three core features of systems: comprehensiveness, a high ratio of parts to principles, and scalability. My discussion of K. 424 focused on the first two, and the K. 454 embellishments now point toward the third. Intellectual systems were scalable in the sense that the connections they fostered among their parts encompassed small and large phenomena alike. It was the discovery that Jupiter's moons obey the same laws of motion as do the Earth, moon, and sun, that turned the solar system into a unified network across which a single explanation could apply both to individual celestial bodies and to collections of them.[36] Mozart's musical systems, too, are scalable. In K. 454, such scalability brings a single, conceptual premise—here, playful competitiveness between two peers—into various levels of musical discourse. Some implications are structural: melodies generally need to repeat so as to allow for handoffs of material. Those repetitions create frequent rhyming echoes within phrases and across movements, just as they resound through the written-out embellishments in the extreme musical foreground as well as in the highly abstract realm of persona and showmanship when the sparkling drama plays out in performance.

Whereas K. 454 showcases its organizational premise by incorporating system into matters of virtuosity and display, the "Dissonance" Quartet, K. 465, does precisely the opposite. This work's slow introduction conceals its systematic logic so thoroughly that its connection to the sunny Allegro has often eluded listeners. Any internal comprehensiveness the slow introduction of K. 465 advertises through its motivic economy and contrapuntal sophistication might easily seem self-contained. There is the obvious matter of the canon in the three upper parts in mm. 1–8, and the way the imitation unfurls, with the three descending pitches of the opening motto becoming an *idée fixe* as the piece follows its tortured harmonic path (Example 4a). Yet, on first glance, the introduction bears no affective relation to the ensuing Allegro. Even Simon Keefe, who has argued that contemporaries would have expected at least some degree of integration between a slow introduction and the rest of the work, states plainly that "the contrast between the chromatic, harmonically lavish Adagio and the diatonic, harmonically straightforward first theme section in the Allegro is stark, [and] unprecedented."[37] The movement seems to inhabit two distinct universes.

In reality, however, the divergent outlooks belie a tightly controlled integration. If it is easy to miss, this is because the premise upon which this system is based is more abstract than those featured in others from the same era—not a motivic cell at all but the overarching polyphonic network that connects all four voices from the start.[38] The three-note motive developed in the introduction recurs constantly in the exposition, as early as the first theme (Example 4b); but it is only one among many figures that Mozart treats in an almost obsessively imitative manner. Accompaniments introduced in the cello are echoed immediately by the viola (mm. 32–35); later, written-out embellishments are imitated across the parts (mm. 49–50).[39] Moreover, the imitative system carried over from Adagio into Allegro does not simply involve the layering of contrapuntal echoes. More precisely, the echoes emphasize chromatically altered pitches. Despite its ostensible frothiness, then, and *pace* interpreters who detect carefree diatonicism throughout, the Allegro frequently appropriates sonorities from the Adagio. In the introduction, the viola begins by venturing an A♭, which the first violin "corrects" to A♮; soon after, the D and B of a dominant chord in measure 4 are revised downward to D♭ and B♭. This chromatic play extends through the Allegro, where the very dissonances that threatened tonal collapse in the introduction continue to surface. In measure 32, for instance, the cello's neighbor tone F♯ sounds just as the first violin arrives

Example 4a. String Quartet in C Major, K. 465, "Dissonance," first movement, mm. 1–9.

Example 4b. String Quartet in C Major, K. 465, "Dissonance," first movement, mm. 23–26.

on the F♮ of a dominant seventh chord; and when the viola imitates the cello in measure 33, its F♯ likewise sounds against a G in the bass (Example 4c). The extraordinarily detailed contrapuntal writing continues to emphasize uneasy juxtapositions and draws on identical voice-leading principles—but

Example 4c. String Quartet in C Major, K. 465, "Dissonance," first movement, mm. 31–34.

the stresses and strains that attended them in the introduction are now rationalized in the sunlit *buffa* world.

As with K. 454, then, system's notion of "premise" operates in K. 465 on many levels at once. Its concrete manifestations come in the form of straightforward motivic imitation connecting the Adagio to the Allegro. Yet it also encompasses conceptual elements that regulate the general sound-world of the piece. Just as the two duos discussed above are in a sense about the interpersonal dynamics available to two players, so this quartet focuses on the possibilities afforded by four active parts whose interplay—not that of the players but the musical logic of counterpoint itself—becomes the subject of development. How far can tonal coherence stretch before breaking? What harmonic results will emerge, what strange sonorities will become feasible, if a handful of contrapuntal procedures are pursued to their logical limits? That, centuries after Mozart's death, theorists have continued to view this movement with awe and confusion suggests the extent to which its system occasioned a genuine act of musical discovery as Mozart rigorously probed the possibility space following from the principles of voice leading.[40] The "Haydn" Quartets' troubled reception history is, in this light, unsurprising. Dittersdorf's famous complaint to Artaria of their "unrelenting, extreme artfulness" is just one representative example of many showing the extent to which these works were deemed elusive and contrived.[41] Even favorably inclined later listeners such as Alfred Einstein have described them as "music made out of music, filtered art," which is to say that they are maddeningly self-referential, at times so contrapuntally dense as to seem arcane, elsewhere cryptically inaccessible.[42] Understood as experiments in systematic composition, however, the very qualities that have troubled critics emerge as hallmarks of their conceptual ambition. Mozart pursues each musical premise without compromise, and if the quartets are contrived, it is in the same way that any highly interconnected, intellectual system is contrived. As wordless analogues of the literary systems that were central to eighteenth-century knowledge work, they present significant intellectual challenges but yield enduring rewards.

Integrating System: Coherence Across Movements and Works

Many of the examples I discuss above show Mozart constructing systems across multiple movements, as in the Piano Concertos K. 271 and K. 414 and the Violin Sonata K. 454. Yet his efforts at multi-movement systematizing extended beyond even the sophisticated integration already seen in such compositions. Here, as before, it is the "Haydn" Quartets where his systematic experiments are particularly ambitious, at times probing the meta-critical affordances of musical materials themselves.

Considering the range of musical premises available to Mozart, it is unsurprising that he binds these quartets together along multiple axes at once. Some premises give rise to topical or expressive systems, including the D-minor Quartet K. 421, where recurring signifiers such as the lament bass (sometimes a diatonic tetrachord, elsewhere a chromatic descent) bring all four movements into focused dialogue with the pathos-ridden *stile antico*.[43] The "Dissonance" is another example: although none of the ensuing movements recaptures the darkness of the opening, some elements resound throughout. Chromaticism continues to intrude in the Andante cantabile, and the second violin in mm. 5–6 even smuggles in a sly reference to the slow introduction of the first movement. Later in the Andante cantabile, too, a contrapuntal passage above an eighth-note pulse (mm. 58–67) makes another allusion to the opening Adagio. The constant melding of the learned style with prominent chromatic lines throughout the third and fourth movements sustains the chromatic, polyphonic network introduced in the first movement and continues to produce improbably dissonant sonorities like those heard at the outset of the piece.

Other systems arise using different means, with the A-major Quartet, K. 464, pursuing what may be the most sophisticated investigation of all: a demonstration of the extent to which pitch in all its material specificity can be divorced from harmonic function. In a virtuosic analysis, Stephen Rumph tracks the notes E–D♯–D–C♯ throughout all four movements, from the opening gesture of the first to the motto of the tirelessly contrapuntal finale.[44] (That the most direct presentation of this guiding motive comes in the finale is a case of "thematic actualization" *avant la lettre*: the players and listeners alike must work hard through the first three movements before encountering, at last, the basic atoms that have governed the piece throughout.)[45] But by what right should we consider K. 464 a system built from pitch rather than thematic continuity? Rumph notes that each movement highlights these pitches, even, remarkably, when Mozart modulates away from A major. As the exposition reaches E major, the four pitches retain their prominence, rationalized in the new key; and they subsequently recur in the orbits of B minor, E minor, and F-sharp minor. This organizing scheme may well be among the ways these quartets pay homage to Haydn. Across K. 464, Mozart treats even basic parameters as being separable from their erstwhile functions—here, by translating the pitches out of that virtual, imaginative realm where they function as "tones" whose implied harmonic gravity binds them to particular contexts, and bringing them instead into the material world as inert notes that can be manipulated, combined, and transformed much as physical matter in a laboratory.[46] Haydn may have been the first champion of what Daniel Chua has evocatively described as the "chemical style" in reference to that fertile domain of eighteenth-century scientific effort, but the combinatorial abilities Mozart shows off here are no less virtuosic than those of his elder peer.[47]

The compositions I have discussed so far were born as systems. But we can also consider the centrality of system in Mozart's music through cases where he returned to a completed piece and made alterations that thoroughly integrate disparate elements. The Rondo in F Major, K. 494, offers a rare glimpse of this process. A year and a half after finishing this work, Mozart absorbed it as the finale of his ambitious Piano Sonata in F Major K. 533.[48] The impetus may have been his appointment as *Kammermusicus* to Emperor Joseph II in November 1787, which spurred a series of demanding projects. K. 533 is certainly the most formidable of his sonatas: In Christoph Wolff's words, it is "innovative, ambitious, expansive, complex, technically sophisticated, conceptually erudite though on the surface simple and elegant, and aesthetically compelling throughout," a list that recalls attributes of the systems of Newton, Smith, and other eighteenth-century thinkers, particularly the notion of surface-level simplicity as balancing intellectually sophisticated content.[49]

In revising K. 494 for use in K. 533, Mozart inserted twenty-seven measures of new material toward the end of the movement (mm. 143–69). That this expansion is cadenza-like has been widely remarked. It also incorporates a brief passage of exalted counterpoint to complement the sonata's extensive polyphonic writing.[50] Contrary to claims that little else brings the finale into dialogue with the rest of K. 533, however, the insertion alludes repeatedly to a harmonic procedure found in the first movement, where a number of deceptive cadences resolve not to vi but to the more distinctive vii^6/V (sometimes vii$^6_5$/V), maintaining the usual bass and soprano pitches but reworking the inner voices to yield a secondary dominant. Although this is an acceptable progression for eighteenth-century deceptive cadences, Mozart's persistent use of it throughout the first movement is noteworthy (Example 5a). Not coincidentally, it also features prominently in the expanded version of the finale. The insertion begins at a cadence that, in the original version of K. 494, resolves uneventfully to F. In the expanded version, however, Mozart opens the insertion with the deceptive progression from the first movement (Example 5b). As if to underline the effect, he repeats the progression immediately (mm. 146–47), this time preparing it with a C♯ in the bass that builds expectations for a move to vi, drawing further attention to the unexpected reappearance of vii$^6_5$/V. One final attempt at closure leads again to the tenacious secondary dominant (m. 164), now fleshed out as a diminished seventh chord. The insertion ends five measures later, having flamboyantly delayed the expected authentic cadence for the entire length of its twenty-seven measures. It accomplishes this by reviving and irresistibly drawing attention to a harmonic move that has been part of the sonata's vocabulary since the start of the first movement.

Example 5a. Piano Sonata in F Major, K. 533, first movement, mm. 21–22, 81–82, 218–19.

Example 5b. Piano Sonata in F Major, K. 533, third movement (adapted from K. 494), mm. 142–47.

All of the works I have discussed are products of Mozart's musical laboratory, that Enlightenment workshop in which he treated composition as an intellectual enterprise with which he could challenge both himself as an artist and thinker as well as those who consumed the more daring works that his laboratory produced. Up to this point, however, I have focused on comparatively early systematic efforts, all of which date from 1783–85. My final example in this section, the audacious String Quintet in C Major, K. 515, composed in 1787, represents the culmination of these experiments. Here, Mozart deploys systematic methods with a confidence and wit that surpasses even that of the "Haydn" Quartets, investigating many similar expressive and conceptual premises but doing so with a new degree of self-critical precision.

The first movement begins with an ascending arpeggio in the cello, an assertive Mannheim rocket. The first violin responds with a gracious *Seufzer* (mm. 4–5), and it soon becomes clear that the cello's gesture is a foil to the sensitive material that will dominate this and the subsequent movements (Example 6a). The *Seufzer* traces the pitches G–C–B, which, like the pitch class of K. 464, features prominently throughout the quintet including, most recognizably, the closing theme in the first movement and the primary theme in the finale. Although the pitches G–C–B are not themselves remarkable in the context of C major, they too will be treated as raw materials that can be detached from their harmonic or expressive functions and reused in new contexts.[51] Mozart's efforts are clearest in the closing theme (mm. 131–51), whose rustic merging of a musette drone with a bourrée is emblematic of the movement's trajectory from the elevated style of the opening to the terrestrial idiom with which the exposition culminates (Example 6b).[52] This tune begins with the same pitches used at the outset, their harmonic functions reinterpreted within G major. In the recapitulation, convention dictates that Mozart should bring the closing theme into C major by transposing it either up a fourth or down a fifth. Instead, however, he reworks the phrase so as to preserve the pitches even as the harmonies are given in C (Example 6c). At the same time, the bourrée becomes the basis for a spectacular fugal apotheosis that merges this human dance with learned counterpoint of the highest order. This process synthesizes not only the movement's disparate harmonic and motivic materials but the various expressive states it passes through as well (and recalls, in addition, the extraordinary double fugue in the development section that led Charles Rosen to deem this the most daring of Mozart's compositions).[53] Like a mathematical system where simple axioms can give rise to enormously complex theorems, the systematic exploration undertaken here treats these pitches with an exceptional range of combinatorial transformations both as tones within the expressive world of the quintet and as raw, acoustic materials that can be abstracted out and used in new harmonic contexts. It is essential that this integration takes place—that the polarities encountered throughout are resolved—under the aegis of the *Seufzer* cell that was strongly emphasized all along, and whose emergence here caps this most comprehensively ambitious of Mozart's chamber movements.

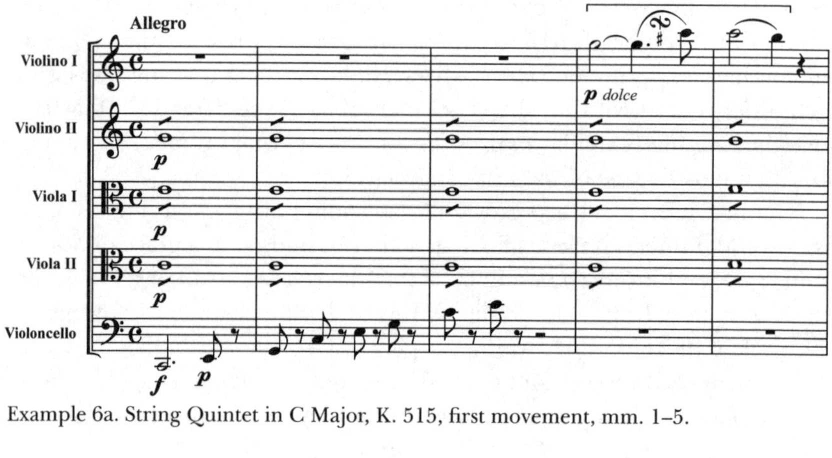

Example 6a. String Quintet in C Major, K. 515, first movement, mm. 1–5.

Example 6b. String Quintet in C Major, K. 515, first movement, mm. 131–37.

But there is still more to admire in the passage, including the compositional presence it suggests. K. 515 is not only a brazen display of technique but also a sophisticated show of wit—specifically, a pun. Puns were subjects of significant theorizing in literary circles in the eighteenth century, as in the critique of unimaginative puns and rhymes in Alexander Pope's 1711 *Essay on Criticism*. Mozart, whose penchant for verbal play is well documented, offers a highly intellectualized musical pun that relies on the same mechanism as verbal puns, the pulling-apart of sound from sense that enables humorous or surprising juxtapositions. In K. 515, the pun depends on the fact that the notes B and C can function either as $\hat{3}$ and $\hat{4}$ in G major or as $\hat{7}$ and $\hat{1}$ in C major—a point that

Example 6c. String Quintet in C Major, K. 515, first movement, mm. 322–29.

would not have been lost on eighteenth-century musicians, whose familiarity with solmization would have sensitized them to the importance of these particular scale degrees in establishing tonality. The harmonic recasting between the closing themes of the exposition and recapitulation may be seen as punning play on music-theoretical analysis itself. Far from impishly joking, this pun points us toward yet another axis along which musical systems can perform conceptual theorizing. If we entertain the possibility that the system of K. 515 is about this very pun, it becomes clear that it is not just the pitches G–C–B that resound throughout the work but countless additional plays on $\hat{3}$ and $\hat{4}$ in other keys as well. As early as the opening phrase, the first violin's Do-Re-Mi schema (mm. 4–15) peaks on $\hat{3}$, a high E that sears against the low F ($\hat{4}$) in the cello (m. 15)—a conflict of range and affect, and the first sign of looming contrapuntal crisis in the work (Example 7a).[54] Just as Mozart's duos systematically demonstrate the affordances of two instruments and K. 465 the contrapuntal potential of four parts, this first dissonance in K. 515 is built from five pitches and thus epitomizes what Edmund Goehring has recently referred to as the work's irreducible "quintet-ness"—yet another dimension of systemic integration embodied in the passage.[55] Soon after, an oscillation between C major and F major chords prominently juxtaposes the pitches E and F in a passage whose hypermeter is so ambiguous that it is unclear whether we are actually in C or F, which is to say, it is unclear whether those pitches are functioning as $\hat{3}$ and $\hat{4}$ or rather as $\hat{7}$ and $\hat{1}$ (Example 7b). These are but a handful of examples, yet they show how thoroughly abstract—theoretical in every sense—Mozart's systematizing has become by this stage. Even more than in the quartets, in K. 515 Mozart uses the medium of wordless music to play out a process of conceptual discovery.

Assembling System: Cycles, Genre, and the "Master System"

Once system took hold during the late seventeenth and early eighteenth centuries, the growing number of systems available in print spawned a new phenomenon, what Siskin refers to as the "master system." As systems proliferated, it became increasingly difficult for individual thinkers to keep track of the collective enterprise of creating knowledge. The solution was to take advantage of scalability to organize systems within systems, yielding more digestible explanatory structures. Larger-scale explanations could engulf smaller ones and bring them into dialogue with one another as components of highly interconnected wholes. "The remediation of system by System was . . . a central activity of the Enlightenment project to know the world," one that made earlier writers' efforts as useful as accessible to later thinkers.[56] The most influential author to champion this genre was Smith. If his *Theory of Moral Sentiments* was a system, his next major work, *The Wealth of Nations*, framed itself as a master system. A glance through its table of contents shows that individual parts are themselves labeled as systems, each integrated into a whole that explains a mind-bogglingly vast amount of human behavior.[57] But as a master system, *The Wealth of Nations* also absorbed Smith's earlier work, building explicitly on the premise that governed the *Theory of Moral Sentiments* by extending its examination of psychology into economics, where "moral sentiments" become the basis for what are now called incentives. Other authors, too, wrote master systems;

Example 7a. String Quintet in C Major, K. 515, first movement, mm. 1–16.

Example 7b. String Quintet in C Major, K. 515, first movement, mm. 38–42.

and although their successes would vary, such efforts all depended on the discovery of new ways to combine parts and wholes. The concept of *discovery* is crucial here. Master systems could rarely be designed in a single burst of creative effort; instead, they would evolve over years or decades as existing systems became sufficiently understood to be brought into productive dialogue. Smith, ever self-aware, described the process explicitly: "The first systems . . . are always the most complex . . . but it often happens that one great connecting principle is afterwards found to be sufficient to bind together all the discordant phaenomena that occur in a whole species of things."[58] To fashion master systems, writers had to discover latent potential for interweaving that may not have been apparent even to those who created the original sub-systems.

Mozart, too, was a master assembler of master systems. One such master system has already featured in my discussions: Each of the quartets dedicated to Haydn constitutes an individual system, but together the group forms a higher-order system of pieces in dialogue with one another. This formulation recalls Sisman's discussion of the eighteenth-century "opus concept." Yet Sisman's "opus concept" is distinct from the systematic integration I have been examining, since not all opuses are systems. Many of the collections Sisman discusses exhibit only rudimentary modes of integration: For instance, she detects a coherent tonal trajectory in Mozart's earlier collections of keyboard sonatas (K. 279–284) and violin sonatas (K. 301–306), but does not investigate internal elements that bind the works together and thus does not frame these collections as master systems in the sense that I mean.[59]

Even when she turns to the "Haydn" Quartets, Sisman understates the set's coherence, noting that adjacent quartets may occasionally echo each other (she cites the first measure of K. 421 and K. 428, both featuring slurred octave leaps) without discussing more thorough modes of integration.[60] Keefe has taken this investigation further, showing that the quartets do hang together and indeed that the slow introduction of the "Dissonance" Quartet serves as a peroration to the entire set.[61] He traces a number of phrases throughout the set that seem to prefigure the unusual sonorities in the introduction of the "Dissonance," particularly those found in the first and second movements of the Quartet in E-flat Major, K. 428. If we widen our view beyond the slow introduction and seek instances of inter-opus dialogue more broadly in the "Haydn" Quartets, other examples also emerge. Some involve unusual stylistic moves that give the set a flavor unlike Mozart's other music: For instance, recapitulated first themes in these works often pinpoint a gesture that functioned in the exposition as a brief, thematic "riposte" but develop it for an extra measure of its own (K. 387/i/116, K. 421/i/87, K. 428/i/109, etc.). But the most striking thread may be the presence of marked chromaticism, even in foregrounded melodic lines. An ascending chromatic tune in the Minuet of the first quartet, K. 387, draws attention to itself with unusual accents that destabilize the meter and later returns in the Andante con moto of K. 428 (m. 90). There is also the descending chromatic line underpinning the entirety of K. 464, with which the cello then begins the slow introduction of K. 465. Indeed, K. 464 ends with the emblematic chromatic descent from E through C♯, such that K. 465, which begins on C♮, seems not only to recall the previous quartet but to continue it, picking up from the precise pitch where the earlier one left off. The source history shows that although this master system originated in two bursts of activity, Mozart conceived the set as a whole and expended significant effort on revisions that would ensure its cohesion.[62]

Like their intellectual analogues, Mozart's master systems rarely originated in a premeditated effort but emerged in hindsight as later compositions could be made to recall and respond to earlier ones. Genre provides an entry point for considering such meta-cyclic efforts, since genres would have served as intellectual niches within which shared systematic impulses could be methodically developed. The three consecutive late violin sonatas K. 454, K. 481, and K. 526, though composed over a three-year period and published separately as if to draw attention to their scope as standalone works,[63] pursue a shared systematic investigation of extreme tonal disruption within the discourse of a chamber dialogue. All three slow movements feature enharmonic crises that traverse the circle of fifths, moving from B-flat minor to B minor in K. 454, from A-flat major to A major in K. 481, and from G major to F minor and ultimately to D major in K. 526. These modulations are striking even when viewed in isolation; but their import is clearer when they are placed in dialogue to reveal a progression in Mozart's efforts. The K. 454 experiment is modest, a modulatory flash within a single, dialogic pair of phrases. The modulation in K. 481 is more discursive: A major provides a brightly tinted haven from the darkness of A-flat major, one attained through significant effort by both players. An entire thematic reprise inhabits this far-away key before the movement returns to A-flat major. Such techniques culminate in the extraordinary second movement of K. 526, whose enharmonic struggles occupy the retransition and first phrase of the recapitulation, exploring both flat- and sharp-side tonal vectors at the precise point in the form where instability is most jarring. Similar methodical explorations occur in other genres as well. For instance, structurally marked cadences in the String Quintets K. 515 and K. 516 are pushed to maximum chromatic saturation while retaining their formal function; and, in the final three symphonies, Mozart constructs a wide range of themes from foregrounded pairs of ascending half-steps. In all of these cases, genre provides a haven for systematic exploration even outside unified opuses.

Mozart's systematic ambitions extended beyond the chamber compositions I have discussed so far. His most ambitious master system is certainly the operatic trilogy he composed in collaboration with Lorenzo da Ponte. These works follow a trajectory of increasing self-awareness of their musical materials. *Le nozze di Figaro* (1786) is the least systematic of the three, employing thematic echoes sparingly and pragmatically. The melody with which Cherubino opens "Non so più" is quoted by Basilio in the trio "Cosa sento" (mm. 16–21) not to further a self-critical agenda but to convey the dramaturgic fact that Basilio was eavesdropping on the aria. Even the most thoroughly integrated echo, the "hat" motive that threads through Susanna's music, serves primarily as a narrative expedient signaling Figaro's insensitivity to his fiancée's musical profile and fueling the mistaken-identity subplot of Act 4.[64] The two subsequent operas, however, enter into dialogue with *Figaro* and elevate the trilogy into a master system with deeply forged connections among its parts. *Don Giovanni* (1787) begins the process. It is, for one thing, an opera that "talks to itself" through numerous internal references, not least of which is the Commendatore's entrance during the Act 2 Finale and its recollection of the slow introduction from the Overture. But, as Thomas Bauman has evocatively put it, "Mozart's operas . . . speak to each other in uncanny ways, each reacting to and building on its predecessors," and in this vein *Don Giovanni* also talks to *Figaro*.[65] The quotation of "Non più andrai" during Giovanni's dinner is a famous and humorous example, and other allusions abound as well. In one telling case, Elvira's aria "Ah chi me dice mai" restates a passage from Figaro's "Aprite un po' quegl'occhi" (Example 8). The two share a distinctive melodic shape as well as a harmonic structure and even orchestral texture. In each passage, a character is bemoaning spousal infidelity—but, as we discover, the accusations Figaro hurls at Susanna are false. Perhaps Elvira's allusion represents yet another way in which Mozart undermines her credibility early in *Don Giovanni*, by suggesting through musical parity that her fury is no more legitimate than Figaro's.[66] Even more, the reference draws attention to a shared philosophical concern that will prove central to the trilogy: the inadequacy of empirical observation for knowing another person's motives and intentions.

Così fan tutte (1790) completes the master system by emphasizing, through what Mary Hunter has referred to as its "pervasively and virtuosically" intertextual tendencies,[67] that same premise latent in *Figaro* and *Don Giovanni*: the impossibility of knowing another person through empirical observation alone, and the centrality of the sympathetic imagination to love. Internally, it is Mozart's most obsessively self-referential opera. Virtually every theme introduced early in the piece is echoed later, a gambit that turns the second act into a running commentary on the first.[68] Unlike the references within *Figaro* and *Don Giovanni*, those in *Così* go far beyond straightforward dramaturgic matters to become fully-fledged philosophical tools. The potency of such references in *Così* derives from the fact that they are, within the fictional world, inadvertent. The material with which Fiordiligi opens "Fra gli amplessi," for instance, alludes to Ferrando's "Un aura amorosa" even though she was not present during the earlier scene. In this and other cases, Mozart underlines the central paradox of the trilogy: Fiordiligi intuits Ferrando's music even without having empirical knowledge of it. Inadvertent quotations saturate the opera, and they are largely responsible both for the painful irony that permeates the piece and for the intellectual agenda it furthers as it reveals a network of musical sympathies between the lovers that arise without observation. To the extent that the piece philosophizes about love, much of its theorizing occurs wordlessly in the musical system that runs alongside the plot.

The internal systematizing that takes place in *Così* is amplified by the cyclical systematizing it undertakes as part of the trilogy, where it integrates and comments on elements of both previous operas. It is

Example 8a. *Le nozze di Figaro*, "Aprite un po' quegl'occhi," mm. 18–21.

Example 8b. *Don Giovanni*, "Ah chi mi dice mai," mm. 31–34.

well known that the Overture and title of *Così* reference material sung by Basilio in the Act 1 trio from *Figaro*. It is also clear that *Così* builds on expressive elements of *Figaro* including through its emphasis on the pastoral style as a frame separating the search for true love from the pursuits of sex, politics, and even philosophy.[69] If *Figaro* begins to establish the pastoral as a rarified realm where social convention matters less than "knowing love" (to quote Cherubino's Act 2 address to his idealized *donne*), *Così* more thoroughly examines the struggles all three women experience as they attempt to inhabit the pastoral. *Don Giovanni* too participates in the inter-opus systematizing. Alfonso's Act 1 arioso "Vorrei dir" borrows a long stretch of music from the Commendatore's death in Act 1 of *Don Giovanni* while also nodding to contemporary operas such as Paisiello's *Il barbiere di Siviglia*.[70]

"The effect of remediating system by System was to change the object to be known," Siskin writes, and interpreting these operas as a master system indeed reveals that *Così* retrospectively illuminates premises operating in all three operas.[71] There are, of course, continuities across the characters of these works. Susanna's blend of wit and worldliness, and her ease in the pastoral style, echo in Zerlina, Dorabella, and Despina, while Figaro's volatility and jealousy recur in Masetto and Guglielmo, and the Countess's paralyzed ambivalence in Elvira and Fiordiligi. The three operas also meditate jointly on disguise and identity and grapple with the relationship between intellect and love. Daniel Heartz has proposed that the trilogy be considered "three schools for lovers" (a nod to the original title of *Così*), and his suggestion is apt.[72] Susanna subjects Figaro to a test of faith in Act 4, and the master system never lets go of the questions her test raises. The characters in all three operas learn that observation is unreliable: a lover's actions may be visible, but it takes imaginative effort to understand what those actions signify. Smith writes in *The Theory of Moral Sentiments* that "our senses . . . never did, and never can, carry us beyond our own person, and it is by imagination only that we can form any conception of [other people's] sensations."[73] This intellectual agenda is implied in *Figaro*, when we feel relief at the recognition of Susanna's voice in the Act 4 Finale; and it develops further in *Don Giovanni*, when Elvira's reference to Figaro's aria underlines the extent to which both characters struggle with evidence of betrayal. But only in *Così* does Mozart systematize the investigation. When Fiordiligi quotes Ferrando's music without having heard him sing it, when the lovers unconsciously echo each other's private thoughts, Mozart draws attention to a moral that was veiled in the earlier operas—that love requires a sustained, imaginative process of mutual- and self-recognition. Figaro learns his lesson easily; the Countess, Elvira, Zerlina, Masetto, and the *Così* couples suffer more deeply. The trilogy as a whole becomes, in this view, a wordless system whose intellectual scope complements that of this flagship Enlightenment genre for understanding the world.

Conclusion: Mozart Among the Systematizers

The outlook I have presented here focuses on a highly intellectual dimension of Mozart's compositional persona, one that complements biographical and interpretive accounts of his activities as a virtuoso pianist and musical showman. Systematic Mozart, like his performing counterpart, also shows off—but he does so by crafting unrelentingly sophisticated music that, in its formal strategies and aesthetic ends, draws on the most successful philosophical and scientific genre of his time. Beginning with that series of experiments in his instrumental chamber works of the 1780s, Mozart engaged increasingly with organizational principles that defined Enlightenment knowledge work, investing his compositions with a conceptual rigor like that pursued by writers of verbal systems. Along the way, he converted musical devices such as counterpoint, embellishment, and even the basic materials of harmony and pitch, into premises from which his argument-like works could unfold.

Such works challenged listeners, as Dittersdorf's complaint to Artaria about the "Haydn" Quartets attests. But in this very respect, Mozart's music is emblematic of its moment. The eighteenth century was, on the one hand, an age in which empiricism presented thinkers with an attractive alternative to arguments from authority that had dominated earlier philosophical traditions; yet systems also enabled their users to move beyond immediate sensory experience into increasingly abstract, theoretical terrain. Mozart's lifetime saw expanded interest in imaginary numbers and Leonhard Euler's pioneering analytic mathematics, where complex logical processes rather than practical geometry drove research. Even Smith, often grouped among empiricists, emphasized the centrality of imagination in his *Theory of Moral Sentiments* and worked in the *Wealth of Nations* with conceptual inventions that transcended observation. As Peter de Bolla argues, the "division of labor" was itself an imaginative discovery on Smith's part, for although one can see divided manufacture, "labor" is invisible: the very concept rests on a significant theoretical synthesis.[74] Smith acknowledges as much, explaining at the outset that he begins with the concrete example of a pin factory precisely so as to forestall skeptics who might doubt conclusions about activities too vast to be observed.[75] Mozart's systematic compositions constitute a musical analogue. The works I have discussed here embody their century's appetite for coherent principles and increasingly comprehensive explanations. Mozart demonstrates that music too could participate meaningfully in the era's broader project of knowledge work and discursive, conceptual exploration.

That many of my observations align with later analytic approaches, particularly those valorizing unity, is hardly accidental. The conviction that every element in a "masterwork" contributes to its final effect traces its lineage to the late eighteenth-century intellectual world that Mozart inhabited. Yet whereas later theorists hailed these procedures as revealing timeless aesthetic truths, such mystique can be stripped away, leaving in its place an outlook sensitive to the same ingenious musical details but sited in the intellectual climate of the time. The Mozart that emerges here is neither an inspired naif nor a proto-Romantic, but one systematizer among many, writing in an age of systems, whose medium was music rather than language. If this outlook provides a fruitful basis for interpreting Mozart, and invests his compositional persona with additional elements of intellectual ambition, it does so not by imposing anachronistic aesthetic ideals but by forging closer connections between Mozart and his intellectual world.

NOTES

For Clifford Siskin.

1. Robert Miles, "Romanticism, Enlightenment, and Mediation: The Case of the Inner Stranger," in *This Is Enlightenment*, ed. Clifford Siskin and William Warner (Chicago: University of Chicago Press, 2010), 173.

2. On the splintering of Enlightenment, see Clifford Siskin and William Warner, "This Is Enlightenment: An Invitation in the Form of an Argument," in *This Is Enlightenment*, 21–22.

3. On concerns surrounding one such portrayal, see Adeline Mueller, "Blackness and Whiteness in *The Magic Flute*: Reflections from Shakespeare Studies," in *The Cambridge Companion to "The Magic Flute*," ed. Jessica Waldoff (Cambridge: Cambridge University Press, 2023), 252–71. On issues of gender and gender conservatism in *opera buffa*, see Mary Hunter, *The Culture of Opera Buffa in Mozart's Vienna: A Poetics of Entertainment* (Princeton: Princeton University Press, 1999), chap. 2 and passim.

4. David Deutsch, *The Beginning of Infinity* (London: Allen Lane, 2011), 12–13, 22–23, and 65–66.

5. Siskin and Warner, "This Is Enlightenment," 1.

6. Clifford Siskin, *System: The Shaping of Modern Knowledge* (Cambridge, MA: MIT Press, 2016), 2.

7. On the "Newtonian System," see Siskin, *System*, 101; quote at 2.

8. Ibid., 105–6.

9. Siskin, "Mediated Enlightenment," in *This Is Enlightenment*, 166.

10. Elaine Sisman, "Six of One: The Opus Concept in the Eighteenth Century," in *The Century of Bach and Mozart: Perspectives on Historiography, Composition, Theory, and Performance*, ed. Sean Gallagher and Thomas Forrest Kelly (Cambridge, MA: Harvard Publications in Music, 2008), 98.

11. On Leopold Mozart's knowledge of Mizler, see Anja Morgenstern, "Der 'gelehrte Musicus': Leopold Mozarts Korrespondenz mit Schriftstellern und Musikgelehrten," in *Leopold Mozart: Chronist und Wegbereiter*, ed. Thomas Hochradner and Michaela Schwarzbauer (Vienna: Hollitzer Wissenschaftsverlag, 2022), 28–41.

12. Cited and discussed in Siskin, *System*, 141–42.

13. Quoted in ibid., 118.

14. Adam Smith, "The Principles Which Lead and Direct Philosophical Enquiries, Illustrated by The History of Astronomy," sec. 4, para. 19, in *Essays on Philosophical Subjects*, in *The Glasgow Edition of the Works and Correspondence of Adam Smith*, vol. 3, ed. W. P. D. Wightman (Oxford: Oxford University Press, 1980).

15. Quoted and translated in Edward Klorman, *Bach: The Cello Suites* (Cambridge: Cambridge University Press, 2025), 43.

16. On variation as wordless, self-referential criticism, see Kofi Agawu, *Music as Discourse: Semiotic Adventures in Romantic Music* (Oxford: Oxford University Press, 2009), 28–29.

17. Grétry and Vogler are quoted in Mark Evan Bonds, *Wordless Rhetoric: Musical Form and the Metaphor of the Oration* (Cambridge, MA: Harvard University Press, 1991), 97–98. On "synecdoche," see John Irving, *Mozart's Piano Sonatas: Contexts, Sources, Style* (Cambridge: Cambridge University Press, 1997), 147. On variation and *De copia*, see Elaine R. Sisman, *Haydn and the Classical Variation* (Cambridge, MA: Harvard University Press, 1993), 27–28 and passim.

18. Adam Smith, "On the Nature of that Imitation which takes place in what are called the Imitative Arts," Part 2, para, 30, in *Essays on Philosophical Subjects*. For a discussion of Smith and variation techniques, see my "Variation at the Intersection of Composition and Performance in the Seventeenth and Eighteenth Centuries," in *The Oxford Handbook of Musical Variation*, ed. Jeffrey Swinkin (New York: Oxford University Press, 2025), 194.

19. Immanuel Kant, *Critique of the Power of Judgment*, sec. 48, trans. Paul Guyer and Eric Matthews (Cambridge: Cambridge University Press, 2000), 190.

20. David Montgomery, "The Myth of Organicism: From Bad Science to Great Art," *The Musical Quarterly* 76/1 (1992): 20.

21. Quoted in Carl Dahlhaus, *Esthetics of Music*, trans. William Austin (Cambridge: Cambridge University Press 1982), 27.

22. On the fantasia's anti-systematic tendencies, see Annette Richards, *The Free Fantasia and the Musical Picturesque* (Cambridge: Cambridge University Press, 2001), 15–20 and 34–40. On the fantasia as revealing the personal essence of its creator, see Richard Kramer, "Diderot's *Paradoxe* and C. P. E. Bach's *Empfindung*," in *C. P. E. Bach Studies*, ed. Annette Richards (Cambridge: Cambridge University Press, 2006), 6–24.

23. K. 279, K. 281, and K. 271 are discussed in Dorian Bandy, *Mozart the Performer: Variations on the Showman's Art* (Chicago and London: University of Chicago Press, 2023), 92–95. See also Charles Rosen, *The Classical Style: Haydn, Mozart, Beethoven*, expanded ed. (New York: W. W. Norton, 1997), 59–60.

24. Howard Boatwright, "Analysis Symposium," *Journal of Music Theory* 10/1 (1966): 29.

25. David Epstein, *Beyond Orpheus: Studies in Musical Structure* (Cambridge, MA: MIT Press, 1979), 179–88. Interestingly, Epstein uses "premise" to describe this and other examples.

26. This is not to say that thematic echoes are absent; for instance, mm. 9–12 of the second movement of K. 414 reprises the melody heard at the outset of the first movement.

27. Quoted in Wye J. Allanbrook, "'To Serve the Private Pleasure': Expression and Form in the String Quartets," in *Wolfgang Amadè Mozart: Essays on His Life and His Music*, ed. Stanley Sadie (Oxford: Oxford University Press, 1996), 132.

28. On the accessible humor in the "Paris" Symphony, "Haffner" Serenade, and other public works, see my *Mozart the Performer*, 179–86.

29. Allanbrook, "Expression and Form in the String Quartets," 135. See also Melanie Lowe's illuminating discussion of the topical and expressive experimentation Mozart undertakes in his "Haydn" Quartets, in "Amateur Topical Competencies," in *The Oxford Handbook of Topic Theory*, ed. Danuta Mirka (New York: Oxford University Press, 2014), 601–28. The self-consciously intellectualized element of Mozart's chamber writing, and its resonances with contemporary thinkers such as Kant, is the subject of Edmund J. Goehring's recent and highly interdisciplinary study *Mozart, Genius, and the Possibilities of Art* (Rochester, NY: University of Rochester Press, 2024).

30. Irving, *Mozart's Piano Sonatas*, 119. William Caplin, too, claims that classical-era slow introductions are primarily atmospheric and bear little relation to the expositions that follow. See his *Classical Form: A Theory of Formal Functions for the Instrumental Music of Haydn, Mozart, and Beethoven* (New York: Oxford University Press, 1998), 205–6.

31. Simon P. Keefe, *Mozart in Vienna: The Final Decade* (Cambridge: Cambridge University Press, 2017), 149.

32. Allanbrook makes this observation in the course of her analysis of the slow movement of K. 421, in "Expression and Form in the String Quartets," 149–50.

33. On K. 454 and musical gameplay, see Roger Moseley, *Keys to Play: Music as a Ludic Medium from Apollo to Nintendo* (Stanford: University of California Press, 2016), 191–96. See also Adeline Mueller's discussion of K. 454 in this volume.

34. This is an instance of the "autonomy of embellishment" discussed in my *Mozart the Performer*, 154–60. Embellishment serves a similar role in the Quartet in B-flat Major K. 458. As early as measure 5 of the first movement, the violins embellish the primary theme with an upper neighbor tone, and this gesture becomes the basis for subsequent embellishments as well as for virtually every subsequent theme in all four movements. It even accounts for the emphasis on extended trills in K. 458, an accelerated version of the same gesture.

35. Keefe discusses these embellishments in *Mozart in Vienna*, 263, but does not connect them to the figure introduced at the start.

36. Siskin, *System*, 22.

37. Simon P. Keefe, *Mozart's Viennese Instrumental Music: A Study of Stylistic Re-Invention* (Woodbridge, UK: Boydell Press, 2007), 104.

38. Bonds, *Wordless Rhetoric*, 102. See also Keefe, *Mozart's Viennese Instrumental Music*, 92.

39. Bandy, *Mozart the Performer*, 158.

40. For instance, Arnold Schoenberg writes of the "thrill of novelty" afforded "over and over again" by engagement with this movement. Quoted and discussed in Keefe, *Mozart's Viennese Instrumental Music*, 90–91.

41. Dittersdorf is quoted and translated in Keefe, *Mozart's Viennese Instrumental Music*, 89. Keefe gives a comprehensive account of these works' reception history. On the charge of contrivance, see also W. Dean Sutcliffe, "Haydn, Mozart and Their Contemporaries," in *The Cambridge Companion to the String Quartet*, ed. Robin Stowell (Cambridge: Cambridge University Press, 2003), 197.

42. Alfred Einstein, *Mozart: His Character, His Work* (London: Oxford University Press, 1947), 183. Quoted in Allanbrook, "Expression and Form in the String Quartets," 134.

43. Allanbrook, "Expression and Form in the String Quartets," 150–51.

44. Stephen Rumph, "What Beethoven Learned from K464," *Eighteenth-Century Music* 11/1 (2014): 55–77.

45. The phrase comes from Jeffrey Swinkin, "Variation as Thematic Actualisation: The Case of Brahms's Op. 9," *Music Analysis* 31/1 (2012): 37–89.

46. On virtual musical "tones" as distinct from physical sounds, see Roger Scruton, *The Aesthetics of Music* (Oxford: Oxford University Press, 1999), chapters 2–3.

47. Daniel K. L. Chua, "Haydn as Romantic: A Chemical Experiment with Instrumental Music," in *Haydn Studies*, ed. W. Dean Sutcliffe (Cambridge: Cambridge University Press, 1998), 120–51.

48. On the genesis of K. 494 and K. 533, see Irving, *Mozart's Piano Sonatas*, 84–85.

49. Christoph Wolff, *Mozart at the Gateway to His Fortune: Serving the Emperor, 1788–1791* (New York: W. W. Norton, 2012), 92.

50. For a reading of the pseudo-improvisatory content, see Keefe, *Mozart in Vienna*, 489–90.

51. This is discussed in Michael Spitzer, "A Metaphorical Model of Sonata Form: Two Expositions by Mozart," in *Communication in Eighteenth-Century Music*, ed. Danuta Mirka and Kofi Agawu (Cambridge: Cambridge University Press, 2008), 213–14.

52. Kofi Agawu, *Playing with Signs: A Semiotic Interpretation of Classic Music* (Princeton: Princeton University Press, 1991), 87–90.

53. Rosen, *The Classical Style*, 268. For a recent assessment of the counterpoint in this movement and Rosen's claim, see Richard Kramer, *Cherubino's Leap: In Search of the Enlightenment Moment* (Chicago: University of Chicago Press, 2016), chap. 2.

54. Spitzer, "Two Expositions by Mozart," 202–5.

55. Goehring, *Mozart, Genius, and the Possibilities of Art*, 279.

56. Siskin, *System*, 116.

57. Ibid., 118.

58. Smith, "The History of Astronomy," Part 4, para. 19.

59. Sisman, "Six of One," 95–98. An opus that does function as a master system is the three Piano Concertos K. 413, K. 414, and K. 415. For an analysis that takes this approach, see Ellwood Derr, "Some Thoughts on the Design of Mozart's Opus 4, the 'Subscription Concertos' (K. 413, 414, and 415)," in *Mozart's Piano Concertos: Text, Context, Interpretation*, ed. Neal Zaslaw (Ann Arbor: University of Michigan Press, 1996), 187–210.

60. Sisman, "Six of One," 99.

61. Keefe, *Mozart's Viennese Instrumental Music*, 89–104 (chap. 4).

62. That he devised these works as a set is suggested by the fact that he offered them collectively to a publisher even when only the first had been completed. See Keefe, *Mozart*

in Vienna, 223. On Mozart's various revisions, see Allanbrook, "Expression and Form in the String Quartets," 133; Keefe, *Mozart in Vienna*, 222–51.

63. Keefe, *Mozart in Vienna*, 450.

64. Daniel Heartz, "Susanna's Hat," *Early Music* 19/1 (1991): 585–89.

65. Bauman's statement comes during his discussion of echoes from *Idomeneo* that recur in *Die Entführung aus dem Serail*, in Daniel Heartz, *Mozart's Operas* (Berkeley and Los Angeles: University of California Press, 1990), 84.

66. For an overview of these readings, see my "Donna Elvira and the Dark Places of the Heart," *Journal of the Royal Musical Association* 149/2 (2024): 484.

67. Hunter, *The Culture of Opera Buffa in Mozart's Vienna*, 247. See also Bruce Alan Brown's account of the "promiscuous miscegenation" of sources from which Mozart and Da Ponte created *Così*, in his *W. A. Mozart: "Così fan tutte"* (Cambridge: Cambridge University Press, 1995), 14 and passim.

68. These cross-references are catalogued in Brown, *W. A. Mozart: "Così fan tutte,"* 95–156.

69. On the wind writing in both operas, see Keefe, *Mozart in Vienna*, chap. 9, esp. 425–41. The pastoral frame for *Figaro* is discussed throughout Allanbrook, *Rhythmic Gesture in Mozart* (Chicago: University of Chicago Press, 1983), and the role of the pastoral in *Così* is discussed extensively in Edmund J. Goehring, *Three Modes of Perception in Mozart: The Philosophical, Pastoral, and Comic in "Così fan tutte"* (Cambridge: Cambridge University Press, 2004).

70. Keefe, *Mozart in Vienna*, 417–18. On "Vorrei dir" and *Don Giovanni*, see Brown, *"Così fan tutte"*, 137–39.

71. Siskin, *System*, 116.

72. Heartz, *Mozart's Operas*, 217–27 (chap. 13).

73. Adam Smith, *Theory of Moral Sentiments*, Part 1, sec. 1, chap. 1, para. 2, in *The Glasgow Edition of the Works and Correspondence of Adam Smith*, vol. 1, ed. D. D. Raphael and A. L. Macfie (Oxford: Oxford University Press, 1976).

74. Peter de Bolla, "Mediation and the Division of Labor," in *This Is Enlightenment*, 90–97.

75. Adam Smith, *An Enquiry into the Nature and Causes of the Wealth of Nations*, Book 1, chap. 1, para. 2, in *The Glasgow Edition of the Works and Correspondence of Adam Smith*, vol. 2, ed. R. H. Campbell and A. S. Skinner (Oxford: Oxford University Press, 1976).

Mozart's Early Viennese Quartets, K. 168–173, and the Question of Stylistic Continuity

EDWARD KLORMAN

[With Haydn's Opus 33 quartets] the principle of motivic work had taken hold of the string quartet, [and thus] *the modern string quartet was invented.*

—Adolf Sandberger[1]

But among the modern four-part sonatas, the six quartets for two violins, viola, and cello by the late *Mozard* [*sic*], published in Vienna with a dedication to *Haydn*, best embody the idea of a true quartet. They are unique in their special mixture of strict and free style and in their treatment of harmony.

—Heinrich Christoph Koch[2]

The string quartets of Joseph Haydn and W. A. Mozart have received parallel reception histories; critics, publishers, and musicians have recognized a precise dividing line that sharply segregates their early efforts from their "mature" ones. For Mozart, this perspective has tended to relegate his early quartets to the status of juvenilia. They are virtually never performed or recorded, except in the context of "complete quartets" compilations.[3] When Haydn's and Mozart's early quartets do receive attention from scholars, they are usually construed as mere preparation for a more masterful style achieved only in the 1780s with Haydn's Opus 33 (composed in summer/autumn 1781) and with Mozart's six quartets dedicated to Haydn (composed 1782–85).[4]

These notable quartets of the early 1780s were conceived after life events led each composer to return to writing string quartets after a decade's hiatus. Haydn, having renegotiated his contract with the Esterházy family in

1779, was newly permitted to sell his music to publishers, an arrangement that enabled him to pursue new opportunities afforded by the recent establishment of the Artaria publishing house in Vienna and that made the composition of quartets more lucrative for him.[5] In December 1781, just after completing his Opus 33 quartets, he wrote to prospective subscribers to announce their imminent publication by Artaria, proclaiming that the collection comprised quartets of "a new and entirely special kind, for I haven't written any for ten years."[6]

Whether this pronouncement of their stylistic novelty—a claim that has launched at least a dozen musicological studies—reflected the composer's newfound entrepreneurial spirit or his more earnest assessment of his evolving approach to quartets is difficult to ascertain. Either way, Haydn's remarks have inspired many influential critics to recognize Opus 33 as marking a turning point in his quartet oeuvre. Scholars have variously pointed to the collection's embrace of the principle of motivic work, a new and more flexible handling of melodic and accompanimental roles, the incorporation of the scherzo genre (rather than the traditional minuet), and a broader range of characters to argue that Opus 33 signified the birth of the "modern string quartet" or even the so-called Classical style itself.[7] Others, dismissing Haydn's remarks as a form of salesmanship, have downplayed claims of Opus 33 as a stylistic revolution, arguing that "no general stylistic change can reasonably be postulated from Haydn's casual remark"[8] and that "Opus 33 was merely one prominent event in the rapidly increasing production of quartets in the 1780s."[9] From this alternative perspective, Opus 33 would be viewed as an extension and development of stylistic elements already present at least nascently in Haydn's Opus 20 quartets (composed in 1772), rather than a radical break or reinvention of the genre.[10]

The influential received view of Haydn's Opus 33 as the birth of the "true" Viennese string quartet has had a spillover effect in the reception of Mozart's quartets (see Table 1).[11] For two centuries, editions with titles such as *Zehn berühmte Quartette* (Ten Celebrated Quartets) have been used to refer to Mozart's ten last quartets (from K. 387 to K. 590); the earliest such publication of which I am aware appeared around 1824 under the title *Partitions des dix principaux Quatuors* (Scores of the Ten Principal Quartets).[12] The view of K. 387 as a turning point in Mozart's quartet output is very much related to Haydn. The publication of the latter's Opus 33 quartets in 1782 has been widely assumed to have inspired Mozart's return to composing in that genre later that same year, and his subsequent publication of a set of six quartets—comprising K. 387, 421, 428, 458, 464, and 465—with an elaborate dedication to Haydn has led musicologists to emphasize the elder composer's influence on the entire collection.[13]

Table 1. Mozart's String Quartets

	Köchel No.	Nickname	Key	Composition Date	First Edition
	Mozart's "Early Quartets"				
	Köchel No.	Nickname	Key	Composition Date	First Edition
	80	Lodi	G	1770	Alte Mozart-Ausgabe
	155	Milanese	D	1772	Peters, 1852–53
	156	Milanese	G	1772	Peters, 1852–53
	157	Milanese	C	1772–73	Oeuvres de Mozart, 1806
	158	Milanese	F	1772–73	Peters, 1852–53
	159	Milanese	B-flat	1773	Peters, 1852–53
	160	Milanese	E-flat	1773	Peters, 1852–53
	168	Viennese	F	1773	André, ca. 1800
	169	Viennese	A	1773	André, ca. 1800
	170	Viennese	C	1773	André, ca. 1800
	171	Viennese	E-flat	1773	André, ca. 1800
	172	Viennese	B-flat	1773	André, ca. 1800
	173	Viennese	D minor	1773	André, ca. 1800
	Mozart's "10 Celebrated Quartets"				
	Köchel No.	Nickname	Key	Composition Date	First Edition
Quartets dedicated to Haydn	387	Spring	G	1782	Artaria, 1785
Quartets dedicated to Haydn	421		D minor	1783	Artaria, 1785
Quartets dedicated to Haydn	428		E-flat	1783	Artaria, 1785
Quartets dedicated to Haydn	458	Hunt	B-flat	1784	Artaria, 1785
Quartets dedicated to Haydn	464		A	1785	Artaria, 1785
Quartets dedicated to Haydn	465	Dissonance	C	1785	Artaria, 1785
	499	Hoffmeister	D	1786	Hoffmeister, 1786
	575	Prussian	D	1789	Artaria, 1791
	589	Prussian	B-flat	1790	Artaria, 1791
	590	Prussian	F	1790	Artaria, 1791

Pushing back against this narrative, Mark Evan Bonds has suggested that Mozart's return to composing quartets may have been motivated partly by a professional rivalry with Haydn's onetime student Ignaz Pleyel, who published his Opus 1 quartets in 1783 and the following year published his Opus 2 quartets with a dedication to his former teacher.[14] According to this theory, Mozart may have decided to dedicate his own quartets to the same composer only after learning of Pleyel's dedication in late 1784, after most of Mozart's "Haydn" quartets had already been composed and only shortly before he submitted them to Artaria.[15] Yet, as Stephanie Klauk and Rainer Kleinertz argue, although "no document exists that would confirm Haydn's role in the conception of this series" of quartets,[16] the timing is unlikely to be a total coincidence. Mozart's move in 1781 to Vienna—a city increasingly associated with the cultivation and publication of quartets—may have put this genre back on his radar, but the publication of Haydn's Opus 33 was likely an important catalyst.

Certain features in Mozart's "Haydn" quartets—such as the enigmatic, fantasia-like opening to the "Dissonance" Quartet, K. 465, or the *stile antico* elements in the fugal finale of Quartet in G Major, K. 387, and in canonic passages in several quartets—may well have been contrived to impress connoisseurs, such as members of Baron Gottfried van Swieten's circle or perhaps Haydn himself with their compositional technique and ingenuity, rather than appealing to the tastes of amateur players and their listeners.[17] The gulf between music appealing to *Kenner* and *Liebhaber* is illustrated in a number of contemporary assessments, including a 1787 report in Karl Friedrich Cramer's *Magazin der Musik* that found that Mozart "aims too high in his artful and truly beautiful compositions" and that his "Haydn" quartets were "too highly seasoned."[18] The composer Carl Ditters von Dittersdorf expressed a similar view in a 1788 letter offering his own quartets to the publisher Artaria: "I am sure that you will do better with mine than Mozart's (which according to my, as well as the great theorists', judgment are worthy of the highest praise but which, however, because of their unrelenting extreme artfulness are not everyone's purchase)."[19] Dittersdorf's faint praise has not aged well, but he was correct as to the judgment of "the great theorists." Whereas he regarded Mozart's incorporation of obscure chromatic harmony and contrapuntal techniques as an excess of artfulness, in 1793 the theorist Heinrich Christoph Koch would highlight these very features as evincing why Mozart's "Haydn" quartets "best embody the idea of a true quartet" (see epigraph).[20]

This essay is devoted to a stylistic analysis of Mozart's earlier set of Viennese quartets, K. 168–173, composed in the summer of 1773 while the teenaged Mozart and his father were in Vienna seeking appointments. I have bracketed Mozart's earlier quartets composed in Lodi (1770) and Milan (1772–73) because a study of those quartets in relation to the Italianate models that might have influenced their conception is beyond the scope of this article. That the quartets K. 168–173 were conceived specifically for Viennese tastes is corroborated by their inclusion in the *Quartbuch*, a thematic catalog that, according to A. Peter Brown, was probably used to facilitate distribution through a Viennese copy shop.[21] These quartets' Viennese origin thus makes them good candidates for comparison with Mozart's later quartets.

If the conventional wisdom holds that the "Haydn" quartets represent a sharp break from all of Mozart's earlier work in this genre, I reexamine these quartets with an eye toward identifying points of continuity with the later ones, despite the decade gap between their respective dates of composition. My aim is not to deny any development of Mozart's style from the 1770s to the 1780s but rather to nuance the notion that an insurmountable gulf separates the earlier Viennese quartets (allegedly juvenilia) from the later ones starting with K. 387.

Quartet in F Major, K. 168, Allegro

The Allegro of K. 168 (Example 1) opens with a main theme presented primarily by the first violin, with an inner-voice parallel-sixths duet taking over for the cadential idea that completes the theme (second violin and viola, mm. 8–9). The ensuing transition, starting in measure 10, takes the form of an incipient repetition of the main theme that veers off into transitional material. An interesting detail is that the first violin's lead-in to the transition (upbeat to measure 10) leads not to thematic material but to a new inner-voice parallel-sixths duet with the viola. The first violin and viola in mm. 10–11 thus adopt roles similar to the second violin and viola at the outset, and it is the *second* violin that takes over the melody at the transition, crossing above the first violin to repeat the opening of the main theme in its original soprano register. This textural exchange may look backward to the trio-sonata-like features in some of Mozart's earlier, Italianate quartets, in which the two violin parts are sometimes treated equally as rival co-*Hauptstimmen*.

Not only does the second violin convey the melody as the transition gets underway, but it also initiates the breakdown of the main-theme material by shifting the focus to a transitional idea in measure 13. Based on the dotted-rhythm figure from measure 3, this transitional motive is imitated across the quartet's upper parts: second violin in measure 13, viola in measure 14, and first violin in mm. 15–16. Ellen Bakulina has demonstrated that such imitative polyphony is a common strategy for formal "loosening" in transition sections and subordinate themes of Mozart's "Haydn" quartets.[22] An instructive comparison might be drawn between the opening movements of K. 168 and K. 387. In the latter, the transition also begins with the second violin briefly restating the first violin's main theme (mm. 11–12), and the transition function first becomes evident through imitative polyphony between the second violin in measure 11 and the first violin in measure 12, and then among all four parts in mm. 16–18. I have described a specific imitative technique as a "cycle of imitation," whereby a motive is stated four times, once by each instrument within a quartet.[23] In K. 168, the imitative treatment of the second violin's motive in mm. 13–16 nearly exemplifies this technique, except that the cello does not participate, and hence the first violin makes two statements in mm. 15–16.[24]

A finely wrought string quartet, according to Koch's discussion in his 1793 treatise, involves masterful handling of textural renewal. The four parts, all considered *Hauptstimmen*, constantly exchange the roles of primary melody, accessory melodies, and galant-style bass such that no instrument dominates or obscures the others.[25] In the present movement, whereas the violins had figured prominently in the melodic action of the first half of the exposition (mm. 1–18), the texture of the subordinate theme (mm. 20ff) is organized around a duet in the lower pair, with the viola's melody supported in counterpoint by the cello's countermelody *qua* bass line. Above it all, the violins play a descant emphasizing the (local) dominant note, G. However, although the lower pair dominates the opening of this sentential theme, the "presentation" phrase, mm. 20–23, by the cadential figure in mm. 26–27, it is the violins (especially the first violin) that convey the melody.[26] Precisely where the melodic viola and duetting cello pass the torch to the violins is difficult to pinpoint. In mm. 24–25, it is not at all obvious whether the violins or the viola (supported by the cello) should be construed as "the" melody. Should the lower pair be preferred, since they are developing their melodic motive from measure 20 using fragmentation and sequential treatment? Or perhaps the violins—when after four bars of static descant in mm. 20–23 they switch in measure 24 to scalar motion—should be heard as newly melodic, with a figure that leads to unequivocably melodic material at the cadential idea (mm. 26–27)? Although the status of the melody in mm. 24–25 cannot be resolved with certainty, I emphasize the subtlety of the exchange because it closely recalls Charles Rosen's remarks about Haydn's Opus 33, No. 1, No. 1, which exhibits a similarly flexible transition of textural roles, one that Rosen praises as "the true invention of classical counterpoint."[27] What Rosen hails as a revolution of the 1780s, Mozart had arguably achieved already a decade earlier.

About the development section (shown in Example 2), it suffices to observe that it opens with cycles of imitation (mm. 42–45 and 46–49) that recall the earlier instance in mm. 13–16: once again, the motive is stated four times, first by each inner part and then with two statements by the first violin, without the cello's participation. This rather four-square,

Example 1. String Quartet in F Major, K. 168, first movement (exposition), mm. 1–31.

Example 1. Continued

Example 1. Continued

stable imitation gives way to overlapping, stretto-like imitation, intensified with *fortepiano* dynamics and syncopated slurs, in mm. 53–55 and again in mm. 57–59. The latter instance is organized with points of imitation in order from first violin to cello, recalling examples found in later quartets by Mozart, Beethoven, and their successors.[28]

Example 2. String Quartet in F Major, K. 168, first movement, mm. 42–61.

Example 2. Continued

Quartet in F Major, K. 168, Minuet and Trio

A similar spirit of role exchange makes for a dynamic texture throughout the minuet (see Example 3). Although the first violin conveys the melody throughout, the texture rarely suggests a simple 1+3 division of melody and accompaniment. Consider the shifting alliances of the opening bars: the second violin's duet in parallel tenths with the cello (m. 1) evolves into a duet shadowing the first violin in parallel sixths (m. 2). Then, in measure 3, the second violin is the only instrument with a unique rhythm, while the other three parts are in homorhythm. The cycle repeats beginning in measure 5, only this time all four instruments join the homorhythm (mm. 7–8).

When the opening material returns for the recapitulation, it is rescored in *piano* dynamic and in miniature, with the viola assuming the bass role, while the second violin and cello rest (mm. 17–20). This intimate anticlimax prepares for the exuberance of the minuet's final bars, where the violins are doubled in octaves, leaving the lower pair to play their first duet (m. 21) before joining the final homorhythm (mm. 23–24).

The segue from minuet to trio—and the modulation from F major to B-flat major—is achieved elegantly by expanding the minuet's initial upbeat gesture (F–C–C), a perfect fourth, into a perfect fifth (F–B♭–B♭). This motive's eighth-eighth-quarter rhythm becomes a point of fascination throughout the trio, passing from the solo first violin (upbeat to measure 1) to the inner-voice duet (upbeat to measure 3) and finally to the cello (upbeat to measure 5), before the ensemble quits the figure for the cadential idea (mm. 5–8).

In the trio's second reprise, that same rhythmic figure is developed through canonic imitation among all four parts in order from top to bottom (mm. 9–11). That the points of imitation occur at intervals of two quarter notes suggests a quasi-2/4 meter that tussles against the underlying, established 3/4 minuet meter. Eighteenth-century theorists including Koch described this type of "false meter" using the Italian terms *la confusione* (confusion) and *imbroglio* (entanglement), which they translated into German as *Verwirrung* (confusion).[29]

This example's combination of strict-style contrapuntal devices and *imbroglio*—of learnedness and artful bungling—exemplifies a characteristic Mozartian witticism found in many familiar examples from his later chamber music.[30] Consider, for instance, the passage of 2/4 vs. 3/4 *imbroglio* in the first movement of the Quartet in A Major, K. 464 (mm. 54–57; see Example 4). Beginning in measure 54, a chain of 2–3 suspensions between the second violin and viola suggest a 2/4 meter, since the pattern of suspension-resolution on alternating quarter notes tends to be heard

Example 3. String Quartet in F Major, K. 168, Menuetto and Trio.

Example 3. Continued

Example 3. Continued

metrically as strong–weak. That strong–weak patterning aligns with sequential repetitions of motivic groups in the first violin part. Only the first violin's slurring supports the notated 3/4 meter. Since the absence of the cello's regulating influence affords several bars of *imbroglio* confusion, it stands to reason that its reentrance in measure 58 assists in reestablishing the proper meter and vanquishing the false one.

Example 4. String Quartet in A Major, K. 464, first movement, mm. 52–58.

Quartet in A Major, K. 169, Molto allegro

In her pathbreaking book on metric manipulations in chamber music by Haydn and Mozart, Danuta Mirka examines several movements, especially by Haydn, in which the sense of meter is attenuated at the outset since musical signals initially lead listeners astray until subsequent cues establish the movement's true meter.[31] Where Mirka's study focuses on the period 1787–91, the opening of K. 169 (composed 1773; see Example 5a) exemplifies a much earlier instance of just the sort of manipulation she studies. Despite the 3/4 time signature, the triple meter is by no means evident from listening to the movement's opening. On the contrary, many signals in the violins' parts point to a meter of 4/4 (see Example 5b). That is, for listeners who provisionally organize their hearing around a quadruple meter, the violins' two appoggiatura figures would fall on beats 3 and 4, and their dotted quarter notes (which receive emphasis as a relatively long

Example 5a. String Quartet in A Major, K. 169, first movement, mm. 1–11 (Mozart's notation).

note and due to the leap to a relatively high pitch) would fall on the second downbeat.[32] Against the undifferentiated, repeated-note accompaniment and the static tonic harmony, these metrical signals in the violins are free of any countervailing cues that emphasize the notated meter.

However, the triple meter soon begins to assert itself. The lower pair's switch from repeated eighth notes to a quarter note on the downbeat of measure 3 subtly emphasizes that note's status as a metrical accent, and the effect is bolstered when another quarter note falls on the following

Example 5b. String Quartet in A Major, K. 169, first movement (a "mis-hearing" of the opening in 4/4 meter).

downbeat. By this juncture, the 4/4 meter initially presumed has receded below a threshold of plausibility, and the music increasingly projects the notated meter. If the viola and cello's quarter note on the downbeat of measure 3 hinted that it probably marked a downbeat, the quarter note on the downbeat of measure 4—introduced with its own anacrustic, "lead-in" gesture—is an even stronger signal. Moreover, beginning in measure 4 and continuing until the cadence in measure 11, each bar line is reinforced with a new rhythmic figure: the first violin's sixteenth notes in measure 4, the second violin's sixteenths and the lower pair's eighths in measure 5, the violins' eighths in measure 6, and their quarters in measure 7. These bar-by-bar rhythmic shifts align with changes of harmony that further reinforce the sense of triple meter.

In sum, this movement begins with a kind of metrical sleight of hand, with music conceived so as to faintly, fleetingly project the "wrong" meter, only for the true meter to emerge just moments later and in a highly stable way, with changes of harmony and surface rhythm coordinated to reinforce every downbeat. The aesthetic effect is not unlike other, later

Mozart quartets—such as the Quartet in E-flat Major, K. 428—that open with ambiguous or misleading material that is subsequently clarified. In the case of K. 428, the unison opening (mm. 1–4) is harmonically vague and difficult to interpret, notably because the first melodic interval (from E♭ to A♮) is a tritone. What follows immediately afterward (mm. 5–12) clarifies the harmony and affirms the key of E-flat major with a cadence, after which comes a restatement of the opening music, now fully realized in four-part harmony (mm. 12–15). In K. 169, the confusion is more short-lived and is limited to the domain of meter (rather than harmony or tonality). But both examples play on the conventional expectation of a stable opening by introducing intentionally misleading material, only to belatedly provide stability in such a way that is paradoxically both orienting and disorienting.

Quartet in E-flat Major, K. 171, Adagio

A similarly disorienting beginning opens the slow introduction to K. 171 (see Example 6). As in the opening measures of K. 428, the E-flat major tonality is obscured by a unison passage comprising unusual, "awkward" intervals that do not outline obvious harmonic progressions. Upon first hearing, one might interpret the first three notes—E♭–B♮–C—as tentatively hinting at the key of C minor rather than E-flat major. This particular sequence of pitches, E♭–B♮–C, E♭–A♮–B♭, exemplifies a Mozartian schema found in the melodies near the opening of several later compositions in the key of E-flat major; familiar examples include the Andante from Symphony No. 40 (mm. 5–6) and Tamino's aria "Dies Bildnis ist bezaubernd schön" from *Die Zauberflöte* (mm. 7–8, on the text "ich fühl' es, ich fühl' es").[33] However, whereas those examples state the schema only *after* the tonality is firmly established, in K. 171 it appears at the very outset and without harmonization, so as to merely adumbrate the sense of key. Even the texture remains murky: should the two unison measures be heard as a melody (as in the aforementioned symphony and aria examples) or as a *tasto solo* bass line?

In the wake of these puzzling opening bars, the first violin tentatively outlines an arpeggio that, once supported by the full ensemble's harmonization (starting measure 3, beat 4) gently affirms the key of E-flat major. When the unison returns in measure 5, a listener might expect to hear a repetition of the opening two measures, only this time heard in the context of an established key. What a surprise, then, when measure 6 is recomposed as E♭–B♭–A♮, compared to E♭–A♮–B♭ in measure 2! Once again, the first violin's cautious arpeggio (m. 7) invites a clarifying harmonization from the complete quartet, this time pointing the way to the dominant, which remains the harmonic center for the remainder of the introduction. The expressive affect for the second half of the introduction is notably lighter, owing to the harmonic clarity and the flowing sixteenths in the second violin. Such counterpoise between a grave, unison opening and the subsequent mellifluous music later on might be comparable to the introduction to the Duo in B-flat Major for Violin and Viola, K. 424.[34]

The Allegro assai that follows begins with just barely enough *stile antico* fugato to get credit (mm. 15–22) before the movement summarily breaks off into galant-style music that would resemble a minuet if not for the extreme tempo. Owing to the fugato's slow note values, it is possible the dotted half notes could be mistaken for quarter notes still belonging to the preceding Adagio. Such a hearing may seem plausible since the fugato style belongs to the same baroque-inspired topical world as the fantasia-like opening of the Adagio. For listeners who do not recognize the double bar and change of tempo at measure 15, the entrance of the galant-style music in measure 23 would signal that the main part of the movement had already begun.[35] This galant music begins in miniature as a violin-viola duet (mm. 23–27) before expanding into a trio (mm. 28–35) and finally a full quartet with the cello belatedly providing a bass line (beginning in measure 36). The opening of this Allegro assai thus resembles that of the Molto allegro finale from K. 387, which likewise begins with a fugato—introducing each instrument in turn with a "white note" subject—that abruptly gives way to contradanse-like music (beginning in measure 17).[36] Koch's praise of the "special mixture of strict and free style" (see epigraph) in Mozart's "Haydn" Quartets might well be applied equally to the innovative, stylistically eclectic opening movement of K. 171.

The Allegro assai is cast as a sonata form without development. Lacking an expositional repeat, the return of the (brief) fugato material (m. 75) marks the recapitulation. A clever detail in the recapitulation (shown in Example 7) involves the second violin "mistakenly" beginning the transition with a wrongheaded modulation to the dominant (mm. 88–89), only to be corrected by the first violin leading back to the tonic one measure later (mm. 89–90).[37] This moment of an abortive second-violin melody interrupted a bar later by the first violin resembles a similar juncture in the first movement of K. 387 (mm. 11–12).[38] Unusually, once the essential sonata form is complete, the fugato material returns again to mark the coda (m. 127), and still more unusually, the Adagio introduction material returns as a "coda to the coda." This strategy of treating introduction material as a frame—heard at the outset and returning at the end—anticipates the first movement of the Quintet in D Major, K. 593. Slow introductions

Example 6. String Quartet in E-flat Major, K. 171, first movement, mm. 1–37.

Example 6. Continued

Example 7. String Quartet in E-flat Major, K. 171, first movement (recapitulation's transition), mm. 83–90.

to chamber compositions of the 1770s are, to the best of my knowledge, rare. This early example suggests a movement of elevated artistic ambition, aspiring toward that of the symphony.[39]

Conclusion

Certain Mozart symphonies, piano sonatas, and violin concertos from the 1770s are widely studied and performed. For other genres, such as the string quartet or opera, traditional views hold that his important contributions date only from the 1780s onward. The central argument here is that the Viennese quartets of 1773 deserve renewed consideration. Without wanting to revive myths of Mozart as a child genius, possessing a fully formed compositional sensibility from an early age, one would nevertheless not want to dismiss earlier compositions merely because of detectable stylistic differences from the more familiar late work.

Of course, one could very well write an article highlighting the undeniable stylistic differences between the quartets examined here and the "celebrated" quartets. For instance, the later quartets do not include any movement in which the lower three parts are as exclusively accompanimental as they are in the Andante from K. 169. Whereas Koch praised Mozart's "Haydn" quartets for their compelling mixture of strict and free styles, the Viennese quartets of 1773 contain more movements with unalloyed baroque inspiration, as in the fugal finales of K. 168 and 173 (resembling those of Haydn's Opus 20) or slow movement of K. 171.[40] In the latter movement, the cello serves as basso continuo, while the violins trade contrapuntal exchanges on fugue-like material, with the viola contributing countersubjects and other "filler" to complete the texture. If, for Koch, a true quartet ought to have four *Hauptstimmen* aspiring toward an exchange on equal terms, this movement adopts a different model with roots in the baroque trio sonata.[41]

Yet for chamber musicians such as myself, steeped in Mozart's "celebrated" quartets and quintets from his last decade, the earlier Viennese quartets contain several movements that are recognizably by the same composer. My analyses have emphasized the flexible exchanges among the instruments, certain ways of integrating free and strict styles, and the witty treatment of meter, form, and musical topic as elements that suggest affinities between these quartets and Mozart's later compositions. By divesting from problematic framings—such as teleological development toward "maturity" or dividing Mozart's quartet oeuvre into categories of celebrated masterworks and forgettable others—and by taking the time to listen to, play, and study them, we will find that these quartets reward our time and attention.

NOTES

1. Adolf Sandberger, "Zur Geschichte des Haydnschen Streichquartetts," in *Ausgewählte Aufsätze zur Musikgeschichte*, vol. 1 (Munich: Drei Masken Verlag, 1921–24), 262, emphasis original. All translations are by the author unless otherwise indicated.

2. Heinrich Christoph Koch, *Versuch einer Anleitung zur Composition*, vol. 3 (Leipzig: Böhme, 1782–93), 325–27. See also the partial English translation published as *Introductory Essay on Composition*, trans. Nancy Kovaleff Baker (New Haven: Yale University Press, 1983), 207.

3. A rare exception is a recent release by the VenEthos ensemble, an Italian period-instrument quartet, comprising Mozart's earliest quartets: the "Lodi" Quartet in G, K. 80, and the "Milanese" Quartets, K. 155–160 (Arcana A497, 2022).

4. Haydn's Opus 20 ("Sun") quartets occupy a middle position, being viewed by many musicologists as predating his mature style but nevertheless performed and recorded not infrequently. His earlier quartets (Opp. 1, 2, 9, and 17), like all of Mozart's quartets composed before the 1780s, are virtually never played. For a sympathetic study of Haydn's early quartets up through Opus 20, see William Drabkin, *A Reader's Guide to Haydn's Early Quartets* (Westport, CT: Greenwood Press, 2000). See also Floyd Grave and Margaret Grave, *The String Quartets of Joseph Haydn* (New York: Oxford University Press, 2006).

5. David Wyn Jones, *The Life of Haydn* (New York: Cambridge University Press, 2009), 101–10.

6. Joseph Haydn, *Gesammelte Briefe und Aufzeichnungen*, ed. Dénes Bartha (Kassel: Bärenreiter, 1965), 106–8. Bartha gives the entire quoted passage in emphatic *Sperrdruck* (spaced text). English translation from James Webster and Georg Feder, *The New Grove Haydn* (New York: Oxford University Press, 2003), 23.

7. For a brief overview of critical responses to Haydn's Opus 33, see Stephanie Klauk and Rainer Kleinertz, "Mozart's Italianate Response to Haydn's Opus 33," *Music and Letters* 97/4 (November 2016): 575–77. On Haydn's Opus 33 ushering in the "classical style," see Charles Rosen, *The Classical Style: Haydn, Mozart, Beethoven* (New York: W. W. Norton, 1997), 116. See also Ludwig Finscher, *Studien zur Geschichte des Streighquartetts*, vol. 1: *Die Entstehung des klassischen Streichquartett: Von den Vorformen zur Grundlegung durch Joseph Haydn*, Saarbrücker Studien zur Musikwissenschaft, vol. 3 (Kassel: Bärenreiter, 1974), 266–67.

8. Jens Peter Larsen and Georg Feder, *The New Grove Haydn* (New York: W. W. Norton, 1982), 102.

9. James Webster, review of *Studien zur Geschichte des Streichquartetts* by Ludwig Finscher, *Journal of the American Musicological Society* 28/3 (1975): 546. See also Webster, *Haydn's "Farewell" Symphony and the Idea of Classical Style: Through-Composition and Cyclic Integration in His Instrumental Music* (New York: Cambridge University Press, 1991), 345.

10. Larsen and Feder, *The New Grove Haydn*, 102. For an illuminating guide to Haydn's early quartets up through Opus 20, see Drabkin, *A Reader's Guide to Haydn's Early Quartets*.

11. For a broader study of the influence of Haydn's reception history on Mozart's, see Simon P. Keefe, *Haydn and Mozart in the Long Nineteenth Century: Parallel and Intersecting Patterns of Reception* (New York and Cambridge: Cambridge University Press, 2023).

12. W. A. Mozart, *Partitions des dix principaux Quatuors pour deux violons, alto et violoncelle* (Offenbach am Main: Jean André, n. d.).

13. Mark Evan Bonds, "The Sincerest Form of Flattery?: Mozart's 'Haydn' Quartets and the Question of Influence," *Studi musicali* 22 (1993): 365–409.

14. Mark Evan Bonds, "Replacing Haydn: Mozart's 'Pleyel' Quartets," *Music & Letters* 88/2 (2007): 201–25.

15. Keefe, *Haydn and Mozart in the Long Nineteenth Century*, 26–27. See also Keefe, *Mozart in Vienna: The Final Decade* (New York: Cambridge University Press, 2017), 220–80.

16. Klauk and Kleinertz, "Mozart's Italianate Response to Haydn's Opus 33," 578.

17. On canonic technique and polyphonic textures in Mozart's "Haydn" quartets, see Olga Ellen Bakulina, "The Loosening Role of Polyphony: Texture and Formal Functions in Mozart's 'Haydn' Quartets," *Intersections: Canadian Journal of Music* 32/1–2 (2012): 7–42. On the conception of Mozart's "Haydn" quartets to appeal both to *Kenner* and *Liebhaber*, see Elaine Sisman, "Observations on the First Phase of Mozart's 'Haydn' Quartets," in *Words About Mozart: Essays in Honor of Stanley Sadie*, ed. Dorothea Link and Judith Nagley (Woodbridge, UK: Boydell Press, 2005), 41–43.

18. Quoted in Otto Erich Deutsch, *Mozart: A Documentary Biography* (Stanford: Stanford University Press, 1965), 290. For a brief overview of early reception of Mozart's "Haydn" quartets among theorists and critics, see Keefe, *Mozart's Viennese Instrumental Music: A Study of Stylistic Re-Invention* (Woodbridge, UK: Boydell Press, 2007), 89–91.

19. Carl Ditters von Dittersdorf to Artaria, 18 August 1788. Translated by Leo F. Balk and quoted in Robert O. Gjerdingen, *Music in the Galant Style* (New York: Oxford University Press, 2007), 437. See also Edward Klorman, *Mozart's Music of Friends: Social Interplay in the Chamber Works* (New York: Cambridge University Press, 2016), 77n14. A similar view was expressed by Johann Baptist Schaul, who compared Mozart's chamber music to "rugged rocks [leading] into a thorny forest strewn only sparsely with flowers" and Boccherini's to "smiling regions with flowery meadows of clear, trickling water, the streams covered in dense groves in which the spirit surrenders itself with pleasure to the sweet melancholy that still grants it sweet refreshment even far from those charming regions." Schaul, *Briefe über den Geschmack in der Musik* (Carlsruhe: Macklots Hofbuchhandlung, 1809), 12. For an analysis and further context, see W. Dean Sutcliffe, *Instrumental Music in an Age of Sociability: Haydn, Mozart, and Friends* (New York: Cambridge University Press, 2019), 515–16.

20. Theorists' responses to Mozart's "Haydn" quartets, and especially to the opening of K. 465, were not uniformly positive. See Julie Anne Vertrees, "Mozart's String Quartet K. 465: The History of a Controversy," *Current Musicology* 17 (1974): 96–114.

21. A. Peter Brown, "Haydn and Mozart's 1773 Stay in Vienna: Weeding a Musicological Garden," *Journal of Musicology* 10/2 (1992): 221–22.

22. Bakulina, "The Loosening Role of Polyphony." On Arnold Schoenberg's metaphors of "tight" vs. "loose" constructions, see William E. Caplin, *Classical Form: A Theory of Formal Functions for the Instrumental Music of Haydn, Mozart, and Beethoven* (New York: Oxford University Press, 1998), 17–21.

23. Klorman, *Mozart's Music of Friends*, 230–33.

24. Mozart's Flute Quartet in D Major, K. 285 (composed 1777) likewise features a motive passed among the upper parts—but excluding the cello—in the finale, mm. 57–65. Mozart's flute quartets K. 285 and K. 285a closely resemble his writing for string quartet. Composed 1777–78, they bridge the stylistic gap between the early Viennese quartets (1773) and the "Haydn" quartets (1782–85).

25. For an overview of Koch's theory of textural roles in string quartets, see Klorman, *Mozart's Music of Friends*, 30–40.

26. On the terms "sentence" and "presentation," see Caplin, *Classical Form*, 35–48.

27. Rosen, *The Classical Style*, 117. Rosen's discussion of the passage begins on page 115.

28. Klorman, *Mozart's Music of Friends*, 230–33.

29. Danuta Mirka, *Metric Manipulations in Haydn and Mozart: Chamber Music for Strings, 1787–1791* (New York: Oxford University Press, 2009), 133–59. As Mirka notes (159–64), eighteenth-century authors carefully distinguished *imbroglio* from *hemiola*; the latter was an older technique associated with church music and is nearly absent in Mozart's quartets and quintets. For examples of imbroglio in Haydn's instrumental music, including in his early quartets, see Floyd Grave, "Metrical Dissonance in Haydn," *Journal of Musicology* 12/3 (1995): 168–202.

30. Mirka observes that "Mozart's metric manipulations are frequently combined with his contrapuntal complexities." Mirka, *Metric Manipulations in Haydn and Mozart*, 303. As a paradigmatic example, she cites the finale of the Quartet in D Major, K. 575 (mm. 140–45 in her Example 5.18), 191. See also my analysis of the minuet and trio from Mozart's "Kegelstatt" Trio, K. 498, in Klorman, *Mozart's Music of Friends*, 255–66 and 280–85.

31. Mirka, *Metric Manipulations in Haydn and Mozart*, 39–92. See also Mirka, "Metre, Phrase Structure and Manipulations of Musical Beginnings," in *Communication in Eighteenth-Century Music*, ed. Danuta Mirka and Kofi Agawu (New York: Cambridge University Press, 2008), 83–111.

32. A detailed explanation of the methodology for my metrical analysis is beyond the scope of this chapter. For a brief introduction, see Klorman, "Notes on Metrical Theory," on the website *Mozart's Music of Friends*, mozartsmusicoffriends.com/wp-content/uploads/2025/07/Notes-on-Metrical-Theory.pdf. A list of "metrical preference rules" is provided in Figure 4 on page 15.

33. I thank Dorian Bandy for drawing my attention to this "Tamino" schema.

34. On the tendency of slow introductions to unify two affective states—the uncertain or unstable and the stately or heraldic—see Caplin, *Classical Form*, 205.

35. For a perhaps comparable instance of Mozart effacing a formal boundary in the Duo in B-flat Major for Violin and Viola, K. 424, see Klorman, *Mozart's Music of Friends*, 136–38.

36. On the finale of K. 387, see Sisman, *Mozart: The "Jupiter" Symphony* (New York and Cambridge: Cambridge University Press, 1993), 71–75. See also Klorman, *Mozart's Music of Friends*, 118–22; and Bandy, "When Is the Brilliant Style Not the Brilliant Style?: Topical Mention, Ambivalence, and Negation in Mozart and Beethoven," *Journal of Musicology* 42/4 (2025): 389–91.

37. On Mozart's staging of "caricatures of incompetence," see Bandy, *Mozart the Performer: Variations on the Showman's Art* (Chicago: University of Chicago Press, 2023), 104–14.

38. For an analysis of the violin rivalry in K. 387, see Klorman, *Mozart's Music of Friends*, 222–27.

39. James Hepokoski and Warren Darcy write that the Adagio introduction to K. 171 "strikes an initial tone of unanticipated earnestness in its 1773 context." Hepokoski and Darcy, *Elements of Sonata Theory: Norms, Types, and Deformations in the Late-Eighteenth-Century Sonata* (New York: Oxford University Press, 2006), 296.

40. A recent study of the fugal finales of K. 168, 173, and 387 is James S. MacKay, "A Lesson from Fux: Species Counterpoint and Fugal Technique in Three String Quartet Finales of Wolfgang Amadeus Mozart (K. 168, 173, 387)," in *Mozart in Salzburg and Beyond: New Perspectives*, ed. Simon P. Keefe (Ann Arbor, MI: Steglein, 2024), 51–67.

41. The trio-sonata-like model of quartet appears to have influenced some of Mozart's earlier Italianate quartets. See the openings of the Quartet in G Major, K. 80, composed 1770 in Lodi, and of the Quartet in B-flat Major, K. 159, composed early 1773 in Milan.

Transcribing the Popular: *Harmonie* Arrangements and Opera Reception, ca. 1800

AUSTIN GLATTHORN

Long before recordings offered listeners access to their favorite music on demand, there were transcriptions, arrangements, and reductions. Such adaptations were the media through which most people experienced repertoire intended for larger ensembles, including opera and symphonies. For this reason, they offer a means to gauge which larger, more expansive pieces captured the popular imagination in the decades around 1800. Considering arrangements and transcriptions as musical reception is not new, of course.[1] Especially helpful are adaptations of music by musicians of that period, for they are not imbued with the same baggage of other "sites of reception," like biography and the press, where ideology, politics, and similar priorities change according to author, audience, and time.[2] Traditionally, scholars have privileged adaptations of operas for keyboard and string quartet. By comparison, far less is understood about the voluminous contemporary settings for *Harmonien*—that is, small wind ensembles—that courts commissioned from the musicians they employed and publishers advertised alongside those for strings and keyboard.

There are reasons for this state of affairs. *Harmonien* were a ubiquitous and integral part of Central European musical life during the late eighteenth and early nineteenth centuries: wind ensembles played just about everything, everywhere, and for everyone. The music that winds performed comprised original compositions and adaptions of instrumental and vocal works by professional composers intended for elite audiences. At the same time, they played popular tunes and dances that were consumed by other parts of society. Music for winds was heard on the field of battle and in the church to celebrate peace. Listeners further encountered wind music at royal courts and in lavish gardens, as well as in boisterous taverns and grimy streets, rendering popular and elite genres accessible to diverse audiences in the process. While emperors supported professional wind groups, commoners in civic centers organized their own amateur ensembles. It is precisely this diversity and omnipresence in early modern Central Europe that render *Harmonien* difficult to engage with in scholarship, as they blur the boundaries between the martial and civic, popular and elite, and public and private. Furthermore, a decision needs to be made about whether to focus on the "serious" original compositions they performed, to be examined in their own right, or the potentially "less serious" arrangements, and whether attention should be paid to renowned composers and celebrated works or to more obscure figures and "ephemera." Even the term traditionally used to refer to music for wind bands of this place and time, "*Harmoniemusik*" (first appearing with regularity only in the early nineteenth century), is not helpful: this word has denoted wind ensembles, the repertoire they performed, and even the social function that they fulfilled. The scholarly response to this diversity has been to focus on standardized ensembles—the so-called Viennese octet of pairs of oboes, clarinets, horns, and bassoons—as supported by courts, and on repertoire related to canonic composers.

Here I will first outline the range of music played by *Harmonien* and the performance spaces they inhabited by drawing on archival examples. I explore the capacity of *Harmonien* as vehicles of popular entertainment at both court and among the wider public in the period around the year 1800. Although there are fewer details regarding the exact instrumentation of groups beyond the court, there is ample documentary evidence to indicate their repertoire and place in popular society. Fashioning these ensembles and the works they played as important sources of contemporary operatic reception, I argue that *Harmonien* were better suited to reach audiences in more places and in greater numbers than other ensembles, paying particular attention to the role of *Harmonien* in disseminating opera in Central Europe in the decades surrounding the French Revolutionary and Napoleonic Wars. *Harmonien* helped popular music reach far more listeners than could have ever attended the theater, and their repertoire could be directly shaped, not only by the tastes of a wealthy patron, but also by the democratic will and expectations of the theater-going public. By exploring the relationship between staged productions in the theater and arrangements of that theater music for winds, I demonstrate that such adaptations offer a vista on the contemporary reception of opera that otherwise may be missed.

Repertoire, Function, and Period Reception

Readers thumbing through the *Magazin der Musik*, edited by Carl Friedrich Cramer, will have encountered the following report from Vienna in a footnote:

> Among all kinds of musical news that has been related to me, one piece that was especially remarkable concerned a group of musicians organized by the emperor, the sound of whose wind instruments has achieved a new high level of perfection. It is known in Vienna as the Imperial–Royal Harmonie. This group consists of eight persons, and it performs by itself as a complete and full ensemble. They even perform pieces that are in fact intended only for voices such as choruses, duos, trios, and even arias from the best operas; the places of the vocal parts are taken by the oboe and clarinet. A member of this Harmonie, the virtuoso and composer Went, has arranged them.[3]

Harmonien and the music they performed, now known as *Harmoniemusik*, had become so popular in Vienna that Emperor Joseph II decided to establish his own in April 1782. The formation of this ensemble has long been interpreted as the beginning of a fad, inspiring (or compelling) other aristocrats to establish their own wind groups modeled on the emperor's *Harmonie,* which comprised paired oboes, clarinets, horns, and bassoons.[4]

But his was not the first in the Holy Roman Empire, let alone in Vienna. The princely families of Schwarzenberg (Vienna, Třeboň, and Český Krumlov), Oettingen-Wallerstein (Wallerstein), Thurn und Taxis (Regensburg and Dischingen), and Fürstenberg (Donaueschingen), for example, had all established *Harmonien* prior to Joseph II.[5] What is more, although the emperor's octet has come to represent the "standard" *Harmonie*, there was no common instrumentation within Vienna or across the Empire. With two horns at their core, almost every *Harmonie* contained pairs of (primarily) wind instruments and frequently a sixteen-foot instrument—most commonly a double bass when indoors or a contrabassoon when outdoors—to either double the lowest voice or otherwise perform an independent part. The remaining instrumentation was driven by local resources and traditions. The Oettingen-Wallerstein *Harmonie*, for instance, contained pairs of flutes, oboes, clarinets, horns, and bassoons;[6] the Fürstenbergs preferred a sextet of clarinets, horns, and bassoons;[7] the Thurn und Taxis had a penchant for oboes, clarinets, horns, bassoons, and often violas in their wind ensemble;[8] and the Schwarzenberg ensemble comprised oboes, English horns, horns, and bassoons.[9] Although the versions of *Harmonien* I mention here are the most common to be found today in their respective court archives, instrumentation was frequently altered—adding individual or pairs of strings, winds, percussion, and even vocal forces—depending on the availability of musicians and performance context. At the Thurn und Taxis court in Regensburg, for instance, there are works that would otherwise be classified as "*Harmoniemusik*" ranging from two clarinets and a pair of horns to four-part choir, pairs of flutes, oboes, clarinets, violas, bassoons, horns, and trumpets, as well as timpani.[10] There is even a work in the collection—composed for the inauguration of the court's new riding school in 1831—calling for two violins and twenty-seven winds.[11] These are only three examples of several hundred from one court collection.

The repertoire of *Harmonien* was as varied as the ensembles themselves. *Harmoniemusik* falls within two principal categories: original compositions and arrangements. Among the former, musicians identified works for small wind ensembles under a plethora of generic indicators including serenade, partita, divertimento, and *Nachtmusik,* to name but a few. Some of these multi-movement pieces were intended as the primary works performed in concert, such as those partitas by Antonio Rosetti for the Oettingen-Wallerstein court, while others were composed to accompany other events, as with the opening of the Thurn und Taxis riding school.[12] Some could be quite expansive, including Mozart's Serenade No. 10 in B-flat Major "Gran Partita," K. 361, which is longer than any of his symphonies. Although such multi-movement works represent the largest proportion of original *Harmoniemusik*, musicians also composed vocal pieces and masses with wind accompaniment. Scored for soprano, alto, tenor, and bass voices, four oboes, two bassoons, three trombones, organ, and basses, *Missa Sancti Hieronymi* (1777; MH254) by Michael Haydn is a relatively well-known example of a mass for *Harmonie*. There are even dramatic works with *Harmonie* accompaniment, and the collection in Regensburg again offers a good, albeit little-known, example. *Vulkans Musik* by music intendant Baron Theodor von Schacht was a short dramatic piece—featuring recitative, aria, chorus, and spoken melodrama—for the bass singer Ludwig Fischer (Mozart's first Osmin), two tenors, and speaker accompanied by pairs of oboes (doubling on English horns), clarinets, horns, trumpets, bassoons, and timpani staged outdoors as part of a court wedding celebration in 1789.[13]

Many of the remaining extant pieces for *Harmonien* are arrangements of genres originally intended for ensembles of greater size, such as symphonies, oratorios, melodramas, ballets, and (especially) operas. The Schwarzenberg collection offers a particularly helpful example. A decade before Emperor Joseph II founded his own *Harmonie*, Prince Joseph Adam founded such a group in the summer of 1771. The ensemble comprised two oboists, two English hornists, two hornists, and two bassoonists. Among its most important members were first oboist Georg Triebensee—who concurrently served in the same role in the Vienna Nationaltheater and later left Schwarzenberg service to join the emperor's *Harmonie* in 1782—and Johann Went, who was mentioned in Cramer's *Magazin der Musik*. Went likewise eventually joined the emperor's ensemble, as second oboist in 1782, but continued to receive an annual stipend to provide six original compositions and arrangements of operas for the Schwarzenberg *Harmonie* every year.[14] He transcribed over fifty operas for both ensembles; sometimes the same pieces include substantial changes to accommodate the ensembles' differing instrumentation.

Arrangements found in princely collections provide a glimpse into those operas that the these families most enjoyed hearing, or at least wanted heard, outside of the theater. A catalogue dated 1799 found in the Schwarzenberg Archive, for example, preserves the works for *Harmonie* then in their collection.[15] It lists thirty-five arrangements of opera excerpts, twenty-eight arias, and nineteen ballets among transcriptions of miscellany and original works (not all arrangements were by Went). Table 1 presents the operas by composer using the title in the language in which it first appeared. The collection preserves the music of seventeen composers premiering across a roughly twenty-year period, from 1774 to 1795. Operas by Paisiello top the list with works premiered in six different locations, reflecting his wide appeal at that time. That so many works originating from Vienna appear on the list is hardly surprising because the Schwarzenbergs maintained a residence in Vienna and had close ties to the Habsburg court. These arrangements of opera excerpts would have allowed the princely family, and their guests, to experience highlights from their favorite operas beyond Vienna and the confines of a theater.

Rather than transcribing the entire opera, arrangements most commonly included a few of the work's more memorable parts. In the case of Dittersdorf's *Der Doktor und Apotheker*, for example, Went's reduction for the Schwarzenberg *Harmonie* comprised six numbers for two oboes, two English horns, two horns, and two bassoons (Figure 1 and Table 2).[16] Unlike original compositions for winds, arrangements like these very often do not have scores, but are preserved as partbooks. Usually one part, commonly the first oboe or second bassoon, would include a text

Table 1: Arrangements of Operas for the Schwarzenbergs in *Beschreibung der nachstehenden Musikalien für die fürstl. Harmonie*, 1799

Title	Composer	Place and Year of Premiere
Il matrimonio segreto	Domenico Cimarosa (1749–1801)	Vienna, 1792
Der Doktor und Apotheker	Carl Ditters von Dittersdorf (1739–1799)	Vienna, 1786
L'amant jaloux	André-Ernest-Modeste Grétry (1741–1813)	Versailles, 1778
La bella pescatrice	Pietro Alessandro Guglielmi (1728–1804)	Naples, 1789
La pastorella nobile	Guglielmi	Naples, 1788
Die beiden Anton	Johann Baptist Henneberg (1768–1822), Benedikt Schack (1758–1826), and Franz Xaver Gerl (1764–1827)	Vienna, 1789
Così fan tutte	Wolfgang Amadeus Mozart (1756–1791)	Vienna, 1790
Don Giovanni	Mozart	Prague, 1787
Die Entführung aus dem Serail	Mozart	Vienna, 1782
Die Zauberflöte	Mozart	Vienna, 1791
Cora och Alonzo	Johann Gottlieb Naumann (1741–1801)	Stockholm, 1782 (finished 1778)
Il barbiere di Siviglia	Giovanni Paisiello (1740–1816)	St. Petersburg, 1782
La contadina di spirito	Paisiello	Vienna, 1785
I filosofi immaginari	Paisiello	St. Petersburg, 1779
La finta amante	Paisiello	Moghilev, 1780
La frascatana	Paisiello	Venice, 1774
La molinara	Paisiello	Naples, 1788
Nina	Paisiello	Caserta, 1789
Il re Teodoro di Venezia	Paisiello	Vienna, 1784
L'incontro inaspettato	Vincenzo Righini (1756–1812)	Vienna, 1785
Axur, re d'Ormus	Antonio Salieri (1750–1825)	Vienna, 1788
La cifra	Salieri	Vienna, 1789
La grotta di Trofonio	Salieri	Vienna, 1785
Palmira regina di Persia	Salieri	Vienna, 1795

Table 1. Continued

Title	Composer	Place and Year of Premiere
Il ricco d'un giorno	Salieri	Vienna, 1784
Il talismano	Salieri	Milan, 1779
I contra tempi	Giuseppe Sarti (1729–1820)	Venice, 1778
Fra i due litiganti il terzo gode	Sarti	Milan, 1782
Giulio Sabino	Sarti	Venice, 1781
L'arbore di Diana	Vicente Martín y Soler (1754–1806)	Vienna, 1787
Una cosa rara	Martín y Soler	Vienna, 1786
Gli sposi malcontenti	Stephen Storace (1762–1796)	Vienna, 1785
Giulietta e Pierotto	Joseph Weigl (1766–1846)	Vienna, 1794
Il pazzo per forza	Weigl	Vienna, 1788
La principessa d'Amalfi	Weigl	Vienna, 1794

incipit to identify the music; often there are no indications, suggesting that none were needed because the music was familiar or recognizable (see Figure 2). Went's transcription of the Dittersdorf includes text incipits for numbers 1 through 4, leaving 5 and 6 blank. The transcription amounts to about twenty minutes from a work for the stage that takes about two hours and thirty minutes to perform in its entirety. Why exactly Went chose those numbers is uncertain. All but "Nur nicht lange sich besonnen" occur quite early on in the opera, and not at particularly dramatic moments. Likewise, it is unclear why Went decided to abandon chronology, placing "Wenn man will zu Mädchen gehen" (No. 5) ahead of "Wann hörst du auf, geliebte Qual" (No. 4). It is likely that order just did not matter: transcriptions like these were usually performed alongside similar arrangements of other operas and as accompaniment to other activities, owing to the flexibility of *Harmonien*.

Performance context frequently determined both the instrumentation of a *Harmonie* and its repertoire. *Harmonien* comprising well-trained musicians performed before elite audiences at court, as was the case with the Schwarzenbergs. This could be to celebrate Mass in the church—like the *Missa Sancti Hieronymi*—or to entertain courtiers in concerts featuring original compositions in the palace's music room, as with Rosetti's

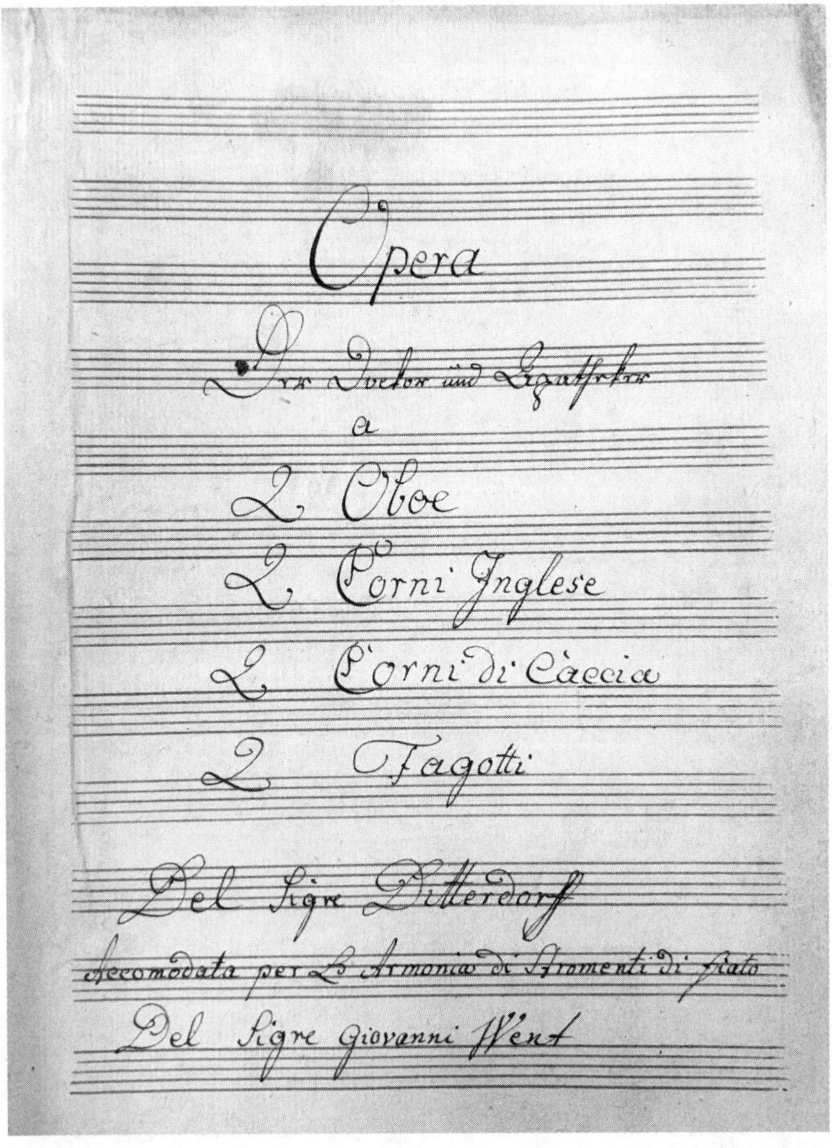

Figure 1. Cover page of Johann Went's Arrangement of Dittersdorf's *Der Doctor* [*sic*] *und Apotheker* for the Schwarzenberg *Harmonie*.

partitas for Oettingen-Wallerstein.[17] A banquet at court would often involve *Tafelmusik* (table music), such as a divertimento or excerpts from "the best operas," as Cramer's correspondent put it. A pleasant summer evening in the Schlossgarten would often be accompanied by the varied

Figure 2. Excerpt from the First Oboe Partbook, "O wie herlich o wie labend" [*sic*].

Table 2. Went's Arrangement of Dittersdorf's *Der Doctor [sic] und Apotheker* for the Schwarzenberg *Harmonie*

Arrangement Number	Title	Location in the Opera
1	"O wie herrlich, o wie labend"	Act 1, scene 1, number 1. Quintet (Stoßel, Sturmwald, Claudia, Rosalie, Leonore)
2	"Wenn man will zu Mädchen gehen"	Act 1, scene 5, number 5. Duet (Gotthold, Sichel)
3	"Wann hörst du auf, geliebte Qual"	Act 1, scene 4, number 4. Aria (Gotthold)
4	"Der Wein ist ein Specifikum"	Act 1, scene 8, number 8. Aria (Sturmwald)
5	["Zwei Mädchen saßen manche Nacht"]	Act 1, scene 9, number 9. Duet (Leonore, Rosalie)
6	["Nur nicht lange sich besonnen"]	Act 2, scene 16, number 20. Aria (Sichel)

timbres of a *Harmonie*.[18] That was at least in part because the projection of wind instruments made them ideal for outdoor performance, as Carl Ditters von Dittersdorf recalled long after attending a festival held for the imperial family at the summer palace of Prince Joseph Friedrich of Saxe-Hildburghausen.[19] Wind ensembles performed at even more prestigious events. At the Pressburg (today Bratislava) coronation of Leopold II as King of Hungary on 15 November 1790, for instance, the *Harmonien* of the princes Esterházy and Grassalkowitz joined forces to perform a new work for twenty-one winds composed by Georg Druschetzky.[20] Yet despite what Cramer's report and the examples thus far might suggest, *Harmoniemusik* was not the exclusive sonic domain of Central Europe's elite.

To be sure, *Harmonien* occupied a place in the musical lives of people from a wide range of backgrounds. While wind music was often heard at public and state celebrations, such as Leopold II's coronations in Frankfurt and Pressburg, it was also commonly featured at concerts open to anyone willing to purchase a ticket or subscription. In fact, on 17 April 1791, Druschetzky's coronation piece for twenty-one winds was given in concert by the Vienna Tonkünstler Societät, the same organization that earlier performed Mozart's "Gran Partita" on 23 March 1784.[21] Wind bands were also heard in more modest locations. While sojourning in Vienna, the English musician and music historian Charles Burney heard music every evening while dining at the tavern in which he stayed. He was not particularly impressed by the intonation of the *Harmonie* that provided his *Tafelmusik*, but other listeners were not so bothered and other ensembles not so iffy.[22] The enthusiastic reception of Vienna's late-night wind serenades during the summer months is recorded in an article that appeared in the *Wiener Theater Almanach* edited by Joseph Sonnleithner. Identifying *Harmonien* as one of the leading serenading ensembles and operatic music as its primary repertoire, the correspondent explains:

> Even if [serenades] might be given very late at night, and at hours during which everyone normally rushes home, one soon notices people in the windows—the musicians are quickly surrounded by a houseful of listeners who applaud, request an encore more often than in the theater, and seldom leave until the serenade is over, though they even more frequently follow them to other parts of the city in droves.[23]

This excerpt shows the appreciation the Viennese had for wind ensembles at a time when very few had access to music on demand. Rather than simply going home or going about their domestic chores, listeners would eagerly consume the evening serenades and even follow the *Harmonien* as they made their way from one place to the next. What is more, by claiming that audiences requested "an encore more often than in the theater," the report draws a direct connection to the city's thriving theatrical scene. And it is no coincidence. The most popular music *Harmonien* played was closely entangled with the theater.

Wind bands made music for the stage (more) accessible. During Advent and Lent, when Vienna's theaters were closed, arrangements of operas performed by *Harmonien* helped extend the theatrical season throughout the entire year.[24] But for those who could not afford to attend the theater regularly (or at all), wind bands played a more fundamental role. Although some could experience music for the stage on their own terms by simply performing it themselves in arrangements for keyboard and voice(s), those who lacked the musical training, instrument, and funds to purchase and perform an arrangement—likely a substantial number of Vienna's ca. 250,000 residents—relied on street musicians as their primary means of consuming popular tunes from the theater. The eyewitness goes on to explain the process behind music theater escaping the confines of the opera house and permeating the city:

> When an opera appears here . . . one finds in only weeks the pieces that have pleased the most announced in the

> newspapers as keyboard arrangements. The most melodic pieces are very quickly in everyone's mouths . . . the musicians, who let their parts be heard on the most unfavorable instruments in the wine and beer houses and on the promenades, produce the loveliest pieces from Mozart's *Zauberflöte*, [Martín y Soler's] *Cosa rara*, and so on. . . . These opera pieces spread through all classes, and even find their way to places where they should not be expected.[25]

Thus, arrangements and musicians who performed them on "the most unfavorable instruments"—likely to include winds of all types—were integral to bringing beloved music to "all classes" and "places where they should not be expected." This included Vienna's two principal gardens, the Prater and Augarten, which Joseph II opened to the public in 1766 and 1775 respectively.[26] While exploring a possible performance context of Mozart's Serenade No. 12 in C Minor, K. 388, Ian Woodfied has demonstrated how *Harmonien* accompanied opera-themed firework displays in the gardens, performing airs from the featured work before crowds reported to be as large as 70,000.[27]

Through *Harmonien*, opera was made widely accessible. To this end, Mark Everist tells us that "most large-scale concerted pieces circulated in versions for reduced forces that had immense levels of exposure; in short, the circulation and consumption of the symphony was more frequently in the form of some sort of arrangement."[28] The same can be said for opera. By means of arrangement, opera and *Harmoniemusik* were inextricably linked. Arrangements of opera for *Harmonien* were a significant and, according to the account in the *Magazin der Musik*, defining part of *Harmoniemusik*. But the operas *Harmonien* performed were not just any works, they were those that contemporary audiences wanted to hear most, as they "requested an encore more often than in the theater" and were willing to follow ensembles "to other parts of the city in droves," as the *Wiener Theater Almanach* would have it. By performing before very large groups in public spaces, *Harmonien* were in part responsible for offering opera tunes not just to those who could afford the theater, but also to all members of society across Vienna.

Yet most scholarly investigation of opera arrangements has focused on those for keyboard instruments. For Everist, even though they represent a "key means of repeatedly hearing works, both new and old" for period audiences, arrangements are "misunderstood and mostly reviled" by scholars today.[29] If keyboard arrangements are "reviled," then those for *Harmonie* can be considered, at best, neglected. This is despite the ability of *Harmonien* to reach elite and general audiences in ways that other ensembles could not, as well as the close contemporary association between their repertoire and that for the musical stage. Even scholars of wind music seem to prefer exploring original compositions rather than arrangements.[30] And when attempting to document the significance of *Harmonien* and opera arrangements for them in Viennese society in the waning years of the eighteenth century, many stop at the *Tafelmusik* scene in the second-act finale of *Don Giovanni* (1787) in which the eponymous character's *Harmonie* performs then-recognizable tunes from Vicente Martín y Soler's *Una cosa rara* (1786), Giuseppe Sarti's *Fra i due litiganti il terzo gode* (1782), and Mozart's own *Le nozze di Figaro* (1786), three pieces also present in the Schwarzenberg *Harmonie* collection, indicating their contemporary appeal.

The meta-theatricality of this finale's *Harmonie* is equally familiar to opera scholars, especially as a site of reception.[31] But this is not all *Harmoniemusik* has to offer. While keyboard arrangements are essential in gauging the popularity of an opera at the turn of the nineteenth century, the medium has its limitations. Because of the cost of purchasing and maintaining keyboard instruments, not to mention the expense, time, and skills associated with learning to play one, these arrangements came mostly into the hands of the middle and upper classes. A keyboard's relative immobility relegated it to the drawing room and concert hall, reaching at most a few hundred listeners.[32] Such limitations did not apply to transcriptions for *Harmonie*. Advertised alongside piano arrangements, adaptations for wind band could be heard not only at court or in domestic settings, but also in the theater, garden, tavern, coffeehouse, and on the street.[33] Their mobility, projection, and versatility allowed wind ensembles to reach a wide and general audience, flooding Vienna with music and in the process transcended the confines of the theater to bring operatic music to the populace, regardless of status or income. Transcriptions for *Harmonie* thus offer a non-textual glimpse into one of the most common Viennese operatic encounters around the year 1800.

Harmonie Arrangements of French Opera in Vienna, ca. 1800

French opera was all the rage in Vienna at the dawn of the new century. The Austrian territories had been in a near-constant state of conflict with Revolutionary France ever since war broke out in April 1792. According to performance records, Viennese audiences then preferred Italian opera and German *Singspiel*, owing to the large Italian community in Vienna and the Habsburg reluctance to allow French operatic imports on the stages of their *Residenzstadt*.[34] But following two crucial defeats in 1797 and 1801, regulations were relaxed, and theaters were free to stage operas that were popular in France. In March of the following year, the Theater an der Wien, under the direction of Emanuel Schikaneder, staged *Lodoïska* (1791), a revolutionary opera composed by Luigi Cherubini, in German adaptation.[35] Competition between Vienna's theaters was strong, and houses like Schikaneder's had for some time been attracting larger audiences than the two court-affiliated national theaters.[36] *Lodoïska*'s enthusiastic reception by Vienna's theatergoers forced the intendant of the court theaters, Baron Peter von Braun, to respond by producing Cherubini's more recent *Les deux journées* (1800) as *Die Tage der Gefahr* in the Kärtnerthortheater that August.[37] Although Vienna was at peace—indeed, precisely because it was at peace—the French invasion of the city had nevertheless begun. Theaters were now being overrun by French operas of fashionable composers such as Cherubini, Henri-Montan Berton, Etienne-Nicolas Méhul, and Jean-François Le Sueur.

Just as the *Wiener Almanach* described in 1794, the press quickly responded to the success of these composers and their works for the stage. Vienna's publishing houses rushed to make available selected numbers for keyboard as well as string quartet soon after their premieres to capitalize on the popularity of these operas.[38] But the *Wiener Zeitung* also advertised arrangements of these operas for *Harmonien*, as it had done since at least the 1780s.[39] Of the ninety or so individual operas by twenty French composers staged in Vienna between 1790 and 1810, fifty-five (or about 60 percent) were arranged as *Harmoniemusik*.[40] Most were transcribed on multiple occasions and were available to purchase in publishing houses across Europe. Such was the case for Vienna's most performed French opera in this period, Cherubini's *Les deux journées*. This work was staged at the Theater an der Wien (as *Graf Armand, oder Die zwey unvergeßlichen Tage*) and in the court theaters (as *Die Tage der Gefahr*) in competing translations on about 160 occasions between their premieres on 13 and 14 August 1802, respectively, and early 1810.[41] There are twenty known single- and multi-movement transcriptions for *Harmonie* of this Cherubini opera in circulation throughout Europe around that time.[42]

A number of Viennese composers and arrangers were active in this scene, and one of the most prolific was Josef Triebensee. Son of Georg Triebensee and Johann Went's son-in-law, Josef Triebensee was a virtuoso oboist who studied with his father as well as with Johann Georg Albrechtsberger. The younger Triebensee was well acquainted with the theater, serving as second oboist at the Theater auf der Wieden. In 1793, he accepted a position at the Kärtnerthortheater and a year later was appointed Kapellmeister and first oboist in the *Harmonie* of Prince Alois I Joseph Liechtenstein.[43] Later in life, he composed for the theater and became the director of the Prague opera until his retirement in 1836. Triebensee's familiarity with both operatic and instrumental genres placed him in an ideal position to provide Vienna's public with *Harmonie* transcriptions of theater music.

In January 1804, Triebensee advertised a subscription series of *Harmoniemusik* in the *Allgemeine musikalische Zeitung* (*AmZ*).[44] These works were likely intended for the Viennese public, for at this time Emperor Franz II and Triebensee's employer, Prince Liechtenstein, were the only aristocrats in the city known to still fund *Harmonien*, with the continued hostilities compelling other aristocrats to disband their ensembles.[45] Triebensee's announcement began by acknowledging that for years the works of the most celebrated composers had appeared in wind band transcriptions for connoisseurs.[46] But for Triebensee, the spirit of the composers had been "completely mutilated" ("*ganz verstümmelt*"), in part because other arrangers for *Harmonie* had failed to set the works idiomatically, to the point where they were no longer recognizable.[47] What made his transcriptions superior, so the notice claimed, was his experience writing for wind instruments. Triebensee thus guaranteed an idiomatic "collection of the newest and best operas and ballets as well as original partitas for eight-part Harmonie."[48]

Triebensee announced that arrangements of six operas or ballets would appear every year alongside six original works for wind band. In addition to three partitas of his own composition, the first subscription would contain excerpts from *Das Labyrinth* (1798) by Peter von Winter, Cherubini's *Elise, oder Der Bernhardsberg* (*Eliza, ou Le voyage aux glaciers du Mont St. Bernard*; 1794), and *Kastor und Pollux* (*Castore e Polluce*; 1787) by Georg Joseph Vogler, music that premiered on Viennese stages in 1798, 1802, and 1803 respectively. However, his decision to adapt these works came with the following caveat:

> The entrepreneur reserves the right, if, during this time, a great new opera or ballet is received with unanimous praise on some stage or other in Vienna, to make changes [to the operas he selected to arrange] in order to provide the gentlemen subscribers with similarly excellent works that are even newer[.] Also, the gentlemen subscribers are requested to indicate with their subscription which operas or ballets from the repertoire of older works they might like to have transcribed for *Harmonie* in the future.[49]

His disclaimer is revealing, demonstrating as it does not only that Triebensee set out to adapt what he considered to be the latest and greatest the theater had to offer, but that he also actively sought the opinion of his subscribers. And in so doing, he fostered both novelty culture and canon formation.

The public did indeed influence which pieces he adapted. Triebensee had already made alterations to future arrangements when the first issue was ready for collection just over a month later on 25 February 1804.[50] Although he prepared Winter's *Das Labyrinth* as announced in the initial advertisement, Triebensee made use of his caveat and changing public opinion. Cherubini's *Eliza* was no longer going to be prepared for a future issue. Instead, he would now arrange selections from the ballet *Bacchus und Ariadne* by Thäddeus Weigl, for it was "generally admired and . . . received with such definitive acclaim."[51] Indeed, Weigl's ballet was far better received than *Eliza*, which according to one critic "fell flat at the Theater an der Wien because multiple roles were very badly filled."[52] Cherubini's opera had been performed only seven times in the Theater an der Wien between its premiere (18 December 1802) and what would be its final performance on 11 January 1803.[53] *Bacchus und Ariadne*, on the other hand, had already been staged on at least twelve occasions between its much later premiere on 13 December 1803 and Triebensee's announcement in early 1804.[54] A correspondent for the *AmZ* wrote a glowing review of the "excellent, new, [and] grand" ballet, which "was really enchanting and also charmed everyone" in Vienna as no ballet had since Jean-Georges Noverre sojourned in the city during the mid-1770s.[55] *Bacchus und Ariadne* would go on to be staged on no fewer than thirty occasions in the court theaters before it fell out of the repertoire on 5 September 1804.[56]

By the time Triebensee announced Weigl's ballet ready for collection in May 1804, plans had changed yet again. Vogler's *Kastor und Pollux* was no longer going to be transcribed as originally intended.[57] This is understandable, given that the Burgtheater had performed the opera only twice, on 22 and 23 December 1803.[58] Thus, the opera was being prepared for its premiere and had only just been performed when Triebensee—who was well connected with the theater—selected it for his original January 1804 advertisement. He must have thought that the work showed potential or was banking on the promise attached to the composer's name. But the public thought otherwise. Triebensee's notice in the *Wiener Zeitung* explained that the subscribers' wishes for the third issue were divided: half had requested that he arrange *Zwei Posten* (*D'auberge en auberge*; 1800) by Angelo Tarchi, while the other half wanted Berton's *Aline, Königin von Golkonda* (*Reine de Golconde*; 1803).[59] Apparently, Vogler's *Kastor und Pollux* did not even factor into the equation, as the opera had already likely been forgotten. The two French operas, on the other hand, had premiered in Vienna (18 January and 6 March 1804 respectively) around the same time Triebensee invited suggestions for which operas he should arrange in the future.[60] The Tarchi work would be staged on thirty-seven occasions over the next two years until 9 October 1806; by comparison, Berton's opera saw twenty performances until it was dropped from the court theaters' repertories on 5 February 1805.[61] In an indication of how crucial arrangements were to the success of his subscription series (not to mention keeping his subscribers happy), Triebensee arranged both operas, forgoing the issue's original partita.[62]

The experienced musician did not transcribe the entire opera for his subscribers. Rather, he chose approximately twelve numbers from each work, one of which was usually the overture.[63] While the opera selected for adaptation was based in part on popularity and dramatic grounds, individual numbers were not. Triebensee informed his subscribers that he would select operatic excerpts that he found especially suitable for *Harmonien*.[64] The arrangements discussed above have not yet been found, so it is currently impossible to evaluate more closely which numbers were chosen from each opera and on what grounds. In fact, there appear to be no further advertisements for this subscription series. It is possible that by the end of 1804 Triebensee was unable to continue offering his arrangements because of obligations to his patron, Prince Liechtenstein, or because of the continually deteriorating relations and eventual resumed hostilities with France, whose forces entered Vienna in 1805.

When the French next occupied the city, in 1809, Triebensee began advertising a new collection of works. In a departure from his previous series, and as a gesture toward the city's new political circumstances, he titled this issue the *Miscellanées de musique*, which consisted of thirty-two monthly installments of *Harmoniemusik* until 1812.[65] It is uncertain whether Emperor Franz I commissioned this collection, even if he was at this point the only patron who could afford to finance a *Harmonie* in Vienna. In any event, the transcriptions were available to the city's public, as the oboist again advertised the subscription in the press.[66] Each installment included twelve movements. Of the 308 total movements in the collection, thirty-six were original works, while the overwhelming majority—some 272—were transcriptions of ballets, symphonies, keyboard works, and operas.[67] Indeed, the pieces that made up each individual issue of this new subscription series comprised an eclectic mix of genres and works, both new and old. In two instances, Triebensee even included pieces that had not yet been performed in Vienna's theaters.[68] The contents of the second issue from 1809, shown in Table 3,

Table 3. Contents of Triebensee's *Miscellanées de musique*, year 1, issue 2 (1809)

No.	Piece (Date of Premiere)	Composer
1	Overture from the opera *Sofonisba* (1805)	Ferdinando Paer (1771–1839)
2	Andante cantabile from the Quintet for Piano and Winds, Op. 16 (1796)	Ludwig van Beethoven (1770–1827)
3	A movement from the ballet *Amphion* (1806)	Franz Weiss (1778–1830)
4	March from a Divertimento for Keyboard	Johann Baptist Cramer (1771–1858)
5	Duet from the opera *Mitternacht* (1807)	Ignaz von Seyfried (1776–1849)
6	Pas de deux and Pantomime Arlequin from the ballet *Amphion* (1806)	Franz Weiss
7	Aria "Wo [find] ich ihn" from the opera *Die Temperamente* (1803)	Etienne Nicolas Méhul (1763–1817)
8	Andante from Symphony in C Major, K. 425 (1783)	Wolfgang Amadeus Mozart (1756–1791)
9	"Der Kaledonier" march from the opera *Der Barden* (*Ossian, ou Les bardes*; 1804)	Jean-François Le Sueur (1760–1837)
10	Presto from Symphony No. 102 in B-flat Major (Hob.I: 102, 1794)	Joseph Haydn (1732–1809)

demonstrate this especially well.[69] Most of the composers represented were active in Vienna, although others such as Cramer and Méhul were based in London and Paris. There is a similarly fair representation of genres (operas, ballets, symphonies, keyboard works) and dates of premieres (ranging from 1783 to 1807). Considering that subsequent issues of the publication were equally diverse, Triebensee provided his subscribers with pieces composed by the leading musicians of the day and those developing canonic status thanks in no small part to collections like his.[70]

An extant, yet undated, issue of the *Miscellanées de musique* contains selections from "*Aline*, *Die Tage der Gefahr*, *Das unterbrochene Opferfest*, [and] *Zaira*" and provides a glimpse into how Triebensee chose which specific numbers to adapt, as well as how he went about adapting them.[71] His decision to score this music for pairs of oboes, clarinets, horns, and bassoons with ad libitum contrabassoon and trumpet was probably because it was an accessible orchestration. While there was nothing standard about a *Harmonie*'s instrumentation, his choice was a safe bet, allowing other instruments to be added and substituted as appropriate. Of the four operas in this issue, Triebensee had also arranged two of these works for his earlier series. Berton's *Aline* was among the operas that the public requested he arrange for the third *Lieferung* of the 1804 subscription series.[72] Of all the possible selections to arrange from this opera, Triebensee decided to transcribe the last two scenes (12 and 13) from the first act, which includes the chorus of soldiers "Rühmt und preist mit frohem Mund," an instrumental march, and Graf Carlo's "Vom weit entlegnen schönem Lande."[73] Working from a German version of the score, Triebensee transcribed the chorus measure by measure, but inserted a measure at the end of the march so as to avoid the original *attacca* transition into the recitative.

The subsequent arrangement in this same issue comprised selections from Cherubini's *Die Tage der Gefahr*, which was not only the most frequently performed French opera in Viennese theaters before 1810 (including *Graf Armand*) but also the Cherubini opera most frequently adapted for wind band.[74] The first of these two selections is the trio "O edelmüth'ger Mann!" (Act 1, scene 4), involving Constance, Armand, and Mikeli.[75] Triebensee sets Constance (soprano) as an oboe and Mikeli (baritone) as a bassoon as one might expect given their voice parts. But instead of setting Armand (tenor) in the upper register of a second bassoon or in the chalumeau register of one of the clarinets, as might best match the voice part, he presents Armand's voice in the second oboe. His decision to do so was likely because the second bassoon was needed to provide the bass. But it is unclear why Triebensee did not place Armand's tenor part in the clarinet's lower register or in any other instrument that would have preserved the original tessitura. Perhaps it was because the orchestration of the other parts took priority in preserving the essence of the original music. The final selection from *Die Tage der Gefahr* in this issue is, like that of *Aline*, taken from a finale: the chorus of soldiers "Ja, wagt er Widerstand" (Act 2, scene 8).

That the selections from *Aline* and *Die Tage der Gefahr* include marches and martial choruses is understandable, as Triebensee had made known that he would choose music that he found especially suited for *Harmonien*.[76] Not only was such music idiomatic, as wind bands were long associated with the military, but he may have also been choosing movements on dramatic grounds, given that both selections here are taken from finales that constitute memorable and crucial moments in the drama. The martial themes presented in these transcriptions were hardly surprising in a society that had been at war for decades.

Winds of Change: *Harmonien* and the Effects of War

Harmonien and arrangements like those explored here took on new importance as the wars with France dragged on. By 1803, Austrian debt was 600 million florins; prices had risen to three times what they were twenty years earlier.[77] Within four years, hastily printed banknotes raised the debt by an additional 100 million florins.[78] Even during the occupations, when many people with means fled ahead of advancing French troops, the court theaters managed to persist, although only with substantial government intervention.[79] But the costly and drawn-out conflict had taken its toll on the princely *Hofkapellen* (princely ensembles) that had once entertained Vienna's elite residents. Only four years into the war, Johann Ferdinand von Schönfeld seemed to reminisce in his *Jahrbuch der Tonkunst von Wien und Prag* that while it was once "very much normal for our great princely houses to maintain Kapellen," they were now being "dissolved one after another to the point where almost no more exist apart from that of the Prince of Schwarzenberg."[80] Rather than abandon their enthusiasm for music altogether, these princely houses and Vienna's populace turned to more economical *Harmonien*:

> Prince Grassalkowitz has reduced his Kapelle to a *Harmonie*. Baron von Braun maintains his own *Harmonie* for *Tafelmusik*. There is yet another *Harmonie*, which is mostly funded by the Court Innkeeper Herr Jahn. They play *Tafelmusik* in the Augarten during the summer. The local artillery band is composed of very skilled people; Herr Gromann plays the oboe admirably. This society performs every summer evening by the lemonade hut on the bastion and is also very good to employ in private concerts.[81]

War and occupation put people's priorities in order. Many had to forgo the entertainment provided by a private orchestra and the public theater to ensure that more fundamental needs were met. Those who could no longer afford such luxuries could nevertheless still rely on *Harmonien* to perform the works in private and public spaces. The *Journal militairischer Musik* promised its subscribers that its contents contained not only marches, maneuvers, and dances, but also "works by Beethoven, Clementi, Cherubini, Dussek, Haydn, Hummel, Méhul, Mozart, Naumann, Paisiello, Reichardt, Righini, Weber, Zumsteeg, and others," all for wind band.[82] Such arrangements were performed by professional ensembles as well as those by dilettantes in the Augarten.[83] Even during difficult periods of war, the public could still hear regular performances of *Harmonien*.[84]

Harmonien were just as important in the private theaters that popped up around Vienna as they were in outdoor spaces, as Johann Friedrich Reichardt discovered in December 1808. On his sojourn in Vienna, the former Prussian Kapellmeister attended a performance at a noble *Liebhabertheater*, in which amateur actors staged as a spoken play the opera *Schloss Limberg* (*Adolphe et Clara*; 1799) by Nicolas Dalayrac.[85] But there were always enough resources to ensure music was heard between acts when theatergoers enjoyed refreshments. Reichardt explained:

> The music consisted of a rather pleasant *Harmonie* of eight wind players, the best music for such small plays especially when the musicians are wise enough to select more cheerful and entertaining little tunes rather than performing larger movements . . . since one can pay attention at such moments in between the acts.[86]

As hostilities with France continued into the next decade, the same ensembles accompanying military maneuvers to display strength by day were performing stage works by night to help take the conflict off the minds of war-weary audiences. *Harmonien* continued to provide musical respite to those affected by a seemingly endless war.

Even after the war ceased, *Harmonien* maintained an important function especially for the elite whose situations were altered by it. Take, for instance, the princely family of Thurn und Taxis. As erstwhile directors of the imperial postal system, the Thurn und Taxis generated vast wealth. And, as the emperor's representative to the Reichstag in Regensburg, they had a duty, or at least an opportunity, to present the emperor and themselves to ambassadors from around the Empire in lavish displays of culture.[87] To do so the Thurn und Taxis invested significantly in court music as well as opera theaters between 1760 and 1806. By way of comparison, Vienna spent an average 38,000 florins per year between 1784 and 1786 on Italian opera, but the Taxis were not far behind the emperor's court, peaking at over 40,000 florins in 1786 and averaging 33,000 florins on their Italian opera in the same period.[88]

Prolonged war, the Empire's restructuring in light of the *Reichsdeputationshauptschluss* (1803), and the eventual dissolution of the Empire in August 1806 were catalysts of change. No longer possessing a monopoly of the Empire's postal system and without an imperial office, Karl Alexander of Thurn und Taxis ordered his court music dissolved one month later, a decree that went into effect on 31 October 1806.[89] Following a period of uncertainty, the Taxis were able to establish a new ensemble at their palace in Dischingen with the permission of the King of Württemberg.[90] The ensemble was formed in summer 1820 and named the Gardemusik, for it was intended to accompany a small honor guard (*Ehrenwache*) at the Taxis palace in Württemberg. The honor guard never materialized, but the Gardemusik was indeed established with twelve wind musicians and two violists (the instrumentation was somewhat flexible). Although the musicians were meant to appear in military uniform, they only did in Dischingen until 1822 and never did when accompanying the prince in Regensburg, which by this point had been incorporated into the newly created Kingdom of Bavaria.

Music of the former princely *Hofkapelle* formed the foundation of the Gardemusik's repertoire. As usual, the music for their new wind band comprised original compositions as well as many transcriptions of works once intended for performance by the Thurn und Taxis *Hofkapelle* and court opera. These included symphonies, oratorios, and operas. Many of the transcriptions of operas were overtures and extracts, of course. The arrangements were written specifically for the Gardemusik by Kapellmeister Anton Schneider and compiled in large collections of partbooks bound for each of the ensemble's instruments, which are preserved today in the Thurn und Taxis Hofbibliothek und Zentralarchiv in Regensburg.

What is striking about this collection, however, is that it includes arrangements of complete operas. Take, for instance, the Gardemusik's setting of Mozart's *Don Giovanni* (1787): "Del Opera Don Juan v. Mozart."[91] Arranged by Schneider around 1822, it has parts for flute, two oboes, four clarinets, two bassoons, two horns, trumpet, bass trombone, and serpent.[92] It is clear that the Taxis enjoyed *Don Giovanni*, as Schneider's is one of quite a few arrangements of the opera's music extant in their collection, most of which are excerpts for various performing forces, including earlier settings for *Harmonie*. Yet what sets this arrangement apart from the other transcriptions is that it is of the entire opera. What is more, there is no full score for *Don Giovanni* extant in the collection. This arrangement for winds, therefore, was perhaps the most complete version the Thurn und Taxis possessed.

I say "perhaps" because Schneider evidently used the first printed full score of *Don Giovanni*—published by Breitkopf & Härtel in 1801—as the source for this arrangement. Just as this score included an appendix of Mozart's additions for the 1788 Vienna version, so too did they appear appended in the Taxis partbooks in the same place and order. Appearing with dual Italian and German text, the incipits of the Breitkopf & Härtel score match, on the whole, the text incipits in the flute part of Schneider's arrangement with occasional orthographic variation; for example, "Wen du fein from̄ bist, will ich dir helfen" and "Wenn du fein fromm bist, will ich dir helfen."[93] The arranger and performers of this transcription, as well as audiences for it, were certainly more familiar with the opera as *Don Juan* than as *Don Giovanni*, as was the case for most of Central Europe at this time. The title *Don Juan* reflected one of any number of German-language adaptations common across the region that dropped simple recitative in favor of spoken dialogue and, in some cases, even interpolated characters and scenes.[94] The Breitkopf & Härtel score acknowledges this practice by including German text under accompanied recitatives, whereas simple recitative contains only Italian text, as it was expected to be substituted with spoken dialogue. Likewise, Schneider's arrangement for the Taxis Gardemusik does include accompanied recitative, which might also contain substantial portions of what would otherwise be considered simple recitative, such as "Don Ottavio, son morta!" But Schneider did decide to include at least some simple recitative, even where the Breitkopf version thought it unnecessary, as indicated by the use of Italian text only. The index of the full score notes, for example, that "O statua gentilissima" ("Herr Gouverneur zu Pferde")—in which Don Giovanni, through his servant Leporello, mockingly invites the graveyard statue of the Commendatore, whom he has murdered, to dine with him—begins on page 416. This is one of the few times Schneider's text incipits vary from the Breitkopf index. The reason for this is because Schneider decided instead to begin earlier in the scene at the Adagio "Di rider finirai pria dell'aurora" ("Verwegner gönne Ruhe den Entschlafnen"), when the statue warns Don Giovanni that he will have had his last laugh before dawn. There are two significant strands of dialogue between Don Giovanni and Leporello, rendered in simple recitative, from that point until the beginning of "O statua gentilissima." Conforming to expectations, the editor of the Breitkopf & Härtel edition clearly thought German translation unnecessary, providing as he did only the Italian text underlay. Yet Schneider subverted expectations. He realized this scene's simple recitative in the four clarinets, second bassoon, and serpent, placing Leporello's and Don Giovanni's dialogue both in the first bassoon. Why he did so, rather than in two separate range-appropriate instruments, as he usually did throughout, is unclear. Yet what is certain is that Schneider did not pick selections from the opera (those that may have been particularly suited for winds), as Triebensee did, or by slavishly using the index to flip to the next number. Instead, he went through the full score page by page, creating a complete transcription for fourteen winds that included music that, although important for developing the plot—such as the recitative of the graveyard scene—was not required by local performance tradition and subverts its intended dramatic function when performed by winds alone.

The question remains why Schneider transcribed the entire opera for an ensemble that for so long had been expected to play excerpts from music theater. The completeness of the Gardemusik's *Don Juan*, not to mention the time it would have taken to make the transcription, suggests that it was performed in its entirety. It may even be that it was performed to wind accompaniment by the princely family and members of the court. To be clear, there is no evidence that this was the case, although there are precedents. Records indicate that members of the Taxis family and their wider court participated in opera performances accompanied by the former *Hofkapelle*, but the frequency of such productions cannot be determined.[95] In the summer of 1791, for example, members of the Taxis court staged at their palace in Dischingen a production of *Die Entführung aus dem Serail* that included "Duchess Charlotte von Hildburghausen as Konstanze; her sister Princess Therese von Thurn und Taxis as Blonde; Magdalena Willmann as Belmonte; Leopold Mozart's former student Heinrich Marchand as Pedrillo; Baron Theodor von Schacht, music intendant of the Thurn und Taxis court, as Osmin; and Count Ignaz von Klenau as Bassa Selim."[96] It is possible that, without an orchestra, the Taxis tasked Schneider with adapting the opera for the only ensemble they now possessed so that they could perform it. The Taxis had, after all, in *Vulkans Musik* at least one earlier experience with their court performing dramatic music accompanied by wind ensemble at Dischingen. That Schneider's version of *Don Giovanni* replicates the tessitura of the original vocal parts in an appropriately corresponding instrument—unlike Triebensee's transcriptions—suggests that the instruments may have been intended to support amateur voices in the learning of parts, or weak ones in actual performance. This may also explain why Schneider included some simple recitative at dramatic highpoints, yet placed Don Giovanni's and Leporello's parts in the first bassoon, which he distinguishes between two bassoons elsewhere, for example, in the Act 2 finale. Even if he knew parts would be sung at the outset of making the arrangement, it is understandable why Schneider would nevertheless adapt the vocal parts for instrumental ones: it meant that his transcription could later be performed as a full *Harmonie* adaptation, or in the first instance if a planned staged performance fell through. Had one actually taken place, the instruments doubling the voices could simply remain tacet. If *Don Juan* and the other complete opera transcriptions extant in the Gardemusik collection really were intended only as instrumental transcriptions, then the Thurn und Taxis must have been so familiar with, or desperate to hear, opera that moments of (simple) recitative performed by wind instruments alone meant as much to them as the more common arias, duets, and ensemble numbers that were long the standard fare of *Harmonien*.

Whether the Gardemusik's *Don Juan* was staged or (partly) sung is a matter of speculation. What is beyond doubt is the simple fact that this music, and any for large ensemble that the Thurn und Taxis wanted to hear (on demand) in the 1820s, had to come from the Gardemusik: it was the only ensemble they employed after they dissolved their *Hofkapelle* in 1806. For them, it was a means to experience once again the music of those earlier, more prosperous times—when they held an imperial position and controlled the Imperial Post—and to stay in tune with the latest music across Europe.

Music for *Harmonien*, particularly opera transcriptions, played a pivotal role in shaping the reception and circulation of theatrical music in the decades around 1800. Investigating this repertory offers a way to supplement or circumvent the limitations of textual criticism alone when evaluating the reception of opera in these decades. More than arrangements of opera for string quartets and keyboards, transcriptions for winds offer fresh insight into popular music not only because of who performed them, but also because of how many could hear them.

Once the domain of Central Europe's elite families, arrangements of popular music for winds began to appear with increasing frequency in a gradually musically literate and hungry public. Those who encountered the music of *Harmonien* in Vienna did so in its court, private homes, gardens, and streets, as well as in its twenty-one coffeehouses, forty-five guesthouses, and 111 beer gardens, to name but a few possible locations.[97] The original works and transcriptions Vienna's residents heard were not merely chosen by an arranger because they were the newest or most performed operas; in Triebensee's case, his decisions were informed by popular vote. What is more, he was not alone: when Sigmund Anton Steiner began publishing the rival Viennese *Journal für die Harmonie*, he likewise promised that transcriptions of cherished operas would be published every two months according to the preferences of its subscribers.[98] In so doing, their transcriptions, and others like them, translated the most beloved music for the stage into instrumental works that could be heard by all classes across different parts of Vienna.

As the unrest caused by the French Revolutionary and Napoleonic Wars began to challenge and weaken the social norms of the Old Regime, arrangements for winds assumed new meanings. For the elite, *Harmonien* became the sound of nostalgia, for they continued to perform the music that their former—and exclusive—*Hofkapellen* and *Hoftheater* once had. Such was the case with Vienna's aristocracy that once maintained orchestras that were disbanded in favor of smaller *Harmonien* during the 1790s. Yet this was not only the case in Vienna, but also in other key regions of Central Europe. After dissolving their *Hofkapelle* in 1806, the Thurn und Taxis employed a *Harmonie* between 1820 and 1828 to provide all of their music, which included the operas that had decades earlier been performed in their court theater.[99] For other strata of society, *Harmonien* comprised a sound of changing circumstances, performing in public, for the public, and (sometimes) music chosen by the public, works for larger ensembles that certain parts of society may otherwise have not been able to encounter only a generation earlier. At the end of the eighteenth and beginning of the nineteenth centuries, *Harmonien* played an important role in helping to bring music from the theater to all parts of society and to all the spaces in which they might expect to encounter it, sometimes for thousands of listeners at a time.

NOTES

1. See for instance, Mark Everist, "Reception Theories, Canonic Discourses, and Musical Value," in *Rethinking Music*, ed. Nicholas Cook and Mark Everist (New York: Oxford University Press, 1999), 378–402; Wiebke Thormählen, "Playing with Art: Musical Arrangements as Educational Tools in van Sweiten's Vienna," *Journal of Musicology* 27/3 (2010): 342–76; Nancy November, *The Age of Musical Arrangements in Europe, 1780–1830*, Cambridge Elements: Music and Musicians, 1750–1850 (Cambridge: Cambridge University Press, 2023); and November, *Opera in the Viennese Home from Mozart to Rossini* (Cambridge: Cambridge University Press, 2024).

2. On "sites of reception," see Mark Everist, *Mozart's Ghosts: Haunting the Halls of Musical Culture* (New York: Oxford University Press, 2012), 4–18.

3. All translations are mine unless stated otherwise. Carl Friedrich Cramer "Den 21ten Dec. 1783, Auszüge aus Briefen, Nachrichten, Todesfälle u.," *Magazin der Musik* 1/2 (1783): 1400–401.

4. Sterling E. Murray, *The Career of an Eighteenth-Century Kapellmeister: The Life and Music of Antonio Rosetti* (Rochester, NY: University of Rochester Press, 2014), 94.

5. See Ian Woodfield, "Fireworks and Wind Bands in 1780s Vienna: A Context for Mozart's 'Nacht Musique'?," *Music & Letters* 98/4 (2018): 527; Murray, *The Career of an Eighteenth-Century Kapellmeister*, 94–95; Christoph Meixner, "Harmoniemusik am Hof der Fürsten von Thurn und Taxis in Regensburg: Musikpflege im Zeichen politischen und gesellschaftlichen Wandels," in *Zur Geschichte und Aufführungspraxis der Harmoniemusik*, ed. Boje E. Hans Schmuhl and Ute Omonsky (Augsburg: Wißner, 2006), 239–40; and Felix Loy, "Harmoniemusik in der Fürstenbergischen Hofkapelle zu Donaueschingen" (PhD diss., University of Tübingen, 2011), 55.

6. Murray, *The Career of an Eighteenth-Century Kapellmeister*, 95.

7. Bastiaan Blomhert, "Zur Harmoniemusik am Donaueschinger Hof," in *Zur Geschichte und Aufführungspraxis der Harmoniemusik*, ed. Schmuhl and Omonsky, 214.

8. Meixner, "Harmoniemusik am Hof der Fürsten von Thurn und Taxis," 244.

9. Roger Hellyer, "The Transcriptions for 'Harmonie' of 'Die Entführung aus dem Serail,'" *Proceedings of the Royal Musical Association* 102 (1975–76): 54.

10. Johann Baptist Kolb, "65 Sätze für 2 Klarinetten und 2 Hörner" (Fürst Thurn und Taxis Hofbibliothek und Zentralarchiv, Regensburg, hereafter D-Rtt), Kolb 7; and Johann Michael Haydn, [arr. anonymous], "Tantum ergo" (D-Rtt, M. Haydn 14).

11. Anonymous, "Musicalien. welche diejenigen Musik stuck enthalten, die im Jahre 1831 bei dem zur Einweihung der neuen Stallungen, und des Reitschul-gebäudes gehaltenen Carosels durchgeführt wurden" (D-Rtt, Inc.Iva/29).

12. Rosetti composed twenty works for winds in multiple combinations of instruments. On Rosetti's wind music, see Murray, *The Career of an Eighteenth-Century Capellmeister*, 269–86.

13. Theodor von Schacht, "Vulkan und die Cyklopen. Divertimento Campestre per le feste de Dischinga 1789" (D-Rtt, Schacht 116); and Austin Glatthorn, "In the Name of the Emperor: Representational Theater and the Princes of Thurn und Taxis," *Journal of Musicology* 35/1 (2018): 22–26 and 31–36.

14. Jiří Záloha, "Das Repertoire der schwarzenbergishchen Bläserharmonie zu Ende des 18. Jahrhunderts," *Studien zur Musikwissenschaft* 44 (1995): 175–90, at 178.

15. "Beschreibung der nachstehenden musikalien für die fürstl. Harmonie," Stántí oblastní archiv v Třeboni, pobočka Český Krumlov, Český Krumlov (hereafter CZ-K), Schwarzenbergisches Familienarchiv, F. P. h/1, box 1.

16. "Opera / Der Doctor und Apotheker / a / 2 oboe / 2 Corni Inglese / 2 Corni da Càccia / 2 Fagotti / Del Sigre Ditterdorff / Accomodata per L'Armonia di Stromenti di fiato / Del Sigre Giovani Went [sic]" (CZ-K, 17-1-284).

17. On *Harmonien* in liturgical settings, see David Gasche, *Die Unterhaltungsmusik für Harmoniemusik in Wien (1760–1820)* (Weikersheim: Margraf, 2015), 139–45.

18. See, for instance, John A. Rice, *The Temple of Night at Schönau: Architecture, Music, and Theater in a Late Eighteenth-Century Viennese Garden* (Philadelphia: American Philosophical Society, 2006).

19. Carl Ditters, *Karl von Dittersdorfs Lebensbeschreibung: Seinem Sohne in die Feder diktirt* (Leipzig: Breitkopf und Härtel, 1801), 68. On outdoor performances in Vienna, see Gasche, *Die Unterhaltungsmusik für Harmoniemusik*, 169–76.

20. See Roger Hellyer, "The Wind Ensembles of the Esterházy Princes, 1761–1813," *The Haydn Yearbook* 15 (1974): 16–17.

21. "Musikalische Akademie von Stadler Virtuos auf dem Klarinet," *Litterarische Fragmente*, vol. 2 (Graz: Widmanstätten, 1785), 286; and "Anhang zur Wiener-Zeitung," *Wiener Zeitung*, 24 March 1784, 617. This is the only known reference to the Gran Partita during Mozart's lifetime.

22. Charles Burney, *The Present State of Music in Germany, the Netherlands, and United Provinces*, 2 vols. (London: Becket, 1773), 1:330–31.

23. Joseph Sonnleither, *Wiener Theater Almanach für das Jahr 1794* (Vienna: Kurzbeck, 1794), 173–74.

24. Gasche, *Die Unterhaltungsmusik für Harmoniemusik*, 64.

25. Sonnleither, *Wiener Theater Almanach*, 174–75.

26. Woodfied, "Fireworks and Wind Bands," 519.

27. Ibid., 519–43.

28. Everist, *Mozart's Ghosts*, 6.

29. Ibid., 75.

30. Although most composers of the period were in some way involved with *Harmonien*, Mozart's three Viennese wind serenades—those in E-flat Major (K. 375), C Minor (K. 388), and B-flat Major (K. 361)—remain the best known (for many, the only known) and researched examples that are considered the pinnacle of Viennese *Harmoniemusik*. By way of indicating the contemporary importance placed on wind music, those studying the repertoire often reference a letter Mozart sent to his father in which he describes how he must hastily arrange his opera *Die Entführung aus dem Serail* for *Harmonie* before someone else beats him to it—indeed that someone was to be Johann Went. Hellyer, "The Transcriptions for 'Harmonie,'" 53–56.

31. See, for instance, Nicholas J. Chong, "Music for the Last Supper: The Dramatic Significance of Mozart's Musical Quotations in the *Tafelmusik* of *Don Giovanni*," *Current Musicology* 92 (2011): 7–52; Daniel Herwitz, "Kierkegaard Writes His Opera," in *The "Don Giovanni" Moment: Essays on the Legacy of an Opera*, ed. Lydia Goehr and Herwitz (New York: Columbia University Press, 2006), 131–32; and Everist, *Mozart's Ghosts*, 75–125.

32. Everist, *Mozart's Ghosts*, 92–93.

33. On the performance spaces of *Harmoniemusik*, see Gasche, *Die Unterhaltungsmusik für Harmoniemusik*, 289–322.

34. See Dorothea Link, *The National Court Theatre in Mozart's Vienna: Sources and Documents 1783–1792* (Oxford: Clarendon Press, 1998).

35. David Wyn Jones, *Music in Vienna: 1700, 1800, 1900* (Woodbridge: Boydell & Brewer, 2016), 130–31.

36. According to one report dated 5 October 1791, "At the moment the two suburban theaters are more frequently attended. . . . The national theater is almost completely forgotten [and] is less frequently attended." *Bayreuther Zeitung* 121, 11 October 1791, 947.

37. Jones, *Music in Vienna*, 131.

38. Ibid., 131.

39. For instance, Lorenz Lausch advertised alongside keyboard arrangements, operas by Christoph Willibald Gluck, André-Ernest-Modeste Grétry, Mozart, Giovanni Paisiello, Antonio Salieri, Giuseppe Sarti, and Ignaz Umlauf adapted for *Harmonie*. See *Wiener Zeitung* 87, 30 October 1784, 2470.

40. My analysis is based on the performances listed in Link, *The National Court Theatre*; Anke Sonnek, *Emanuel Schikaneder: Theaterprinzipal, Schauspieler und Stückeschreiber* (Kassel:

Bärenreiter, 1999); Anton Bauer, *150 Jahre Theater an der Wien* (Vienna: Amalthea-Verlag, 1952); Michael Jahn, *Die Wiener Hofoper von 1794 bis 1810: Musik und Tanz im Burg- und Kärtnerthortheater* (Vienna: Apfel, 2011); and Jon A. Gillaspie et al., *The Wind Ensemble Catalog* (Westport, CT: Greenwood Press, 1998).

41. Sonnek, *Emanuel Schikaneder*, 326–38; and Jahn, *Die Wiener Hofoper*, 97–127.

42. Gillaspie, *The Wind Ensemble Catalog*, 367. The twentieth arrangement not mentioned here is from Josef Triebensee's *Miscellanées des musique*, from the operas: *Aline, Die Tage der Gefahr, Das unterbrochene Opferfest, Zaira.* Österreichische Nationalbibliothek (hereafter A-Wn), Mus.Hs.3794.

43. Roger Hellyer, "Triebensee [Trübensee], Josef," *Grove Music Online*, accessed 16 June 2025.

44. Joseph Triebensee, "Subscriptions-Anzeige der besten und neuesten Opern und Ballete wie auch Originalparthieen für achtstimmige Harmonie gesetzt von Joseph Trübensee," *Intelligenz-Blatt zur AmZ* 6 (January 1804), cols. 25–27.

45. See Gasche, *Die Unterhaltungsmusik für Harmoniemusik*, 203–303, esp. 256.

46. Triebensee, "Subscriptions-Anzeige der besten und neuesten Opern," col. 25.

47. Ibid.

48. Ibid.

49. Ibid., col. 27.

50. "An die (P. T.) Herren Subscribenten der Sammlung von den beßten und neuesten Opern und Balleten," *Wiener Zeitung*, 25 February 1804, 694.

51. Ibid.

52. Friedrich Theodor Mann, ed, *Musicalisches Taschen-Buch auf das Jahr 1805* (Penig: Dienemann, 1805), 209–10.

53. See Sonnek, *Emanuel Schikaneder*, 327–28.

54. Jahn, *Die Wiener Hofoper*, 110–12.

55. "Wien, den 20sten [1803]," *AmZ* 6 (4 January 1804), col. 226.

56. See Jahn, *Die Wiener Hofoper*, 110–17.

57. "An die (P. T.) Herren Subscribenten auf die Sammlung der besten und neuesten Opern und Ballete," *Wiener Zeitung*, 2 May 1804, 1727–28.

58. Jahn, *Die Wiener Hofoper*, 110.

59. "An die (P. T.) Herren Subscribenten auf die Sammlung der besten und neuesten Opern und Ballete," *Wiener Zeitung*, 2 May 1804, 1728.

60. Jahn, *Die Wiener Hofoper*, 111–12.

61. Ibid., 111–38.

62. "An die (P. T.) Herren Subscribenten auf die Sammlung der besten und neuesten Opern und Ballete," 1728.

63. "Subscriptions-Anzeige der besten und neuesten Opern," 27.

64. Ibid., 27.

65. Roger Hellyer, "'Harmoniemusik': Music for Small Wind Band in the Late Eighteenth and Early Nineteenth Centuries" (PhD diss., University of Oxford, 1973), 157.

66. Gasche, *Die Unterhaltungsmusik für Harmoniemusik*, 248; and Hellyer, "Harmoniemusik," 158–59.

67. Gasche, *Die Unterhaltungsmusik für Harmoniemusik*, 69.

68. These were *Federica ed Adolfo* by Adalbert Gyrowetz and *Jean de Paris* by François-Adrien Boieldieu (both 1812). Gasche, *Die Unterhaltungsmusik für Harmoniemusik*, 249.

69. Hellyer, "Harmoniemusik," 164.

70. Ibid., 164–65.

71. A-Wn, Mus.Hs.3794.

72. Ibid.

73. These numbers are the chorus "Honneur! Honneur aux Français" and St-Phar's recitative "Magnanime et Puissante Reine." For the French text, see *Aline, reine de Golconde: Opéra*

en trois actes (Paris: Masson, 1803). For the German text, see *Aline, Königin von Golkonda: Oper in drey Aufzügen*, n.p., n.d.; Washington D.C., Library of Congress, ML48 [S885].

74. Sonnek, *Emanuel Schikaneder*, 326–38; Jahn, *Die Wiener Hofoper*, 97–127; Gillaspie, *The Wind Ensemble Catalog*, 367; and A-Wn, Mus.Hs.3794.

75. "O mon libérateur!" in the original French version. *Les deux journées: Comédie lyrique en trois actes* (Paris: Barba, 1802).

76. "Subscriptions-Anzeige der besten und neuesten Opern," 27.

77. Joachim Whaley, *Germany and the Holy Roman Empire*, vol. 2 (Oxford: Oxford University Press, 2012), 581.

78. Carolyn Kirk, "The Viennese Vogue for Opéra-comique, 1790–1819" (PhD diss., University of St. Andrews, 1983), 113.

79. Ibid., 114–26.

80. Johann Ferdinand von Schönfeld, *Jahrbuch der Tonkunst von Wien und Prag* (Vienna: Schönfeld, 1796), 77.

81. Ibid., 77–78.

82. "Anzeige für militairische Orchester und für alle Freunde der Harmonie-Musik," *Intelligenz-Blatt zur AmZ* 7 (4 December 1804), col. 197.

83. Gasche, *Die Unterhaltungsmusik für Harmoniemusik in Wien*, 173.

84. Ibid., 174.

85. Johann Friedrich Reichardt, *Vertraute Briefe geschrieben auf einer Reise nach Wien und den Oesterreichischen Staaten zu Ende des Jahres 1808 und zu Anfang 1809*, 2 vols., (Amsterdam: Kunst- und Industrie-Comtoir, 1810), 1:236.

86. Ibid., 237–38.

87. See Glatthorn, "In the Name of the Emperor," 1–41.

88. Christoph Meixner, *Musiktheater in Regensburg im Zeitalter des Immerwährenden Reichstages* (Sinzig: Studio Verlag, 2008), 298 and 564.

89. Christoph Meixner, "Die Thurn und Taxis'sche Hofmusik in Regensburg: Höfische Musikkultur unter reichspolitischen Vorzeichen," in *Süddeutsche Hofkapellen im 18. Jahrhundert*, ed. Silke Leopold and Bärbel Pelker (Heidelberg: Heidelberger Akademie der Wissenschaften, 2014), 466.

90. Hugo Angerer, "Die Gardemusik des Fürsten von Thurn und Taxis 1820–1828," in *Im Dienst der Quellen zur Musik: Festschrift Gertraut Haberkamp zum 65. Geburtstag*, ed. Paul Mai (Tutzing: Schneider, 2002), 538.

91. Wolfgang Amadeus Mozart, "Del Opera Don Juan v. Mozart," transcribed for winds by Anton Schneider, D-Rtt, Sammelband 16.

92. Ibid.

93. Compare ibid. and *Il dissoluto punito / osia / Il Don Giovanni / Dramma giocoso in due Atti poste in musica da Wolfgang Amadeus Mozart /Don Juan / oder / Der Steinerne Gast / komische Oper in zwey Aufzügen / in Musik gesezt von / W. A. Mozart / Mit unterlegtem deutschen Texte nebst sämmtlichen von dem Komponisten später eingelegten Stücken* (Leipzig: Breitkopf & Härtel, [1801]), [5].

94. Martin Nedbal, *Mozart's Operas and National Politics: Canon Formation in Prague from 1791 to the Present* (Cambridge: Cambridge University Press, 2023), 185–86.

95. Meixner, "Die Thurn und Taxis'sche Hofmusik in Regensburg," 459.

96. Dexter Edge and David Black, "*Die Entführung aus dem Serail* at the Thurn und Taxis Court in Dischingen (Summer 1791)," in *Mozart: New Documents*, ed. Dexter Edge and David Black. First published 30 September 2019; updated 18 January 2023: https://www.mozart-documents.org/documents/summer-1791/, accessed 24 July 2025. The performance material is preserved in D-Rtt, W.A. Mozart 22/I and II, the latter of which notes the names of the performers on the voice parts.

97. Gasche, *Die Unterhaltungsmusik für Harmoniemusik*, 305.

98. [Sigmund Anton Steiner], Journal für Neunstimmige Harmonie 2 (1810), 1v.

99. Angerer, "Die Gardemusik des Fürsten von Thurn und Taxis 1820–1828," 537–49.

A Reading of *The Magic Flute*

EDMUND J. GOEHRING

My God, where is that ancient heat towards thee,
Wherewith whole showls of *Martyrs* once did burn,
Besides their other flames? Doth Poetry
Wear *Venus* Livery? only serve her turn?
Why are not *Sonnets* made of thee? and layes
Upon thine Altar burnt? Cannot thy love
Heighten a spirit to sound out thy praise
As well as any she? Cannot thy *Dove*
Out-strip their *Cupid* easily in flight?

—George Herbert, First Sonnet (1610)[1]

"This disappearance of forms and of individuality itself would reduce the *Paradiso* to just one note, . . . if the earth did not come into it, and with the earth other forms and other passions."[2] Thus wrote one of Italy's premier literary critics, Francesco de Sanctis, on Dante's last *cantica*. Umberto Eco finds a larger question stirring de Sanctis's hesitations about the *Paradiso*, one leading to other worlds and their art: whether the spiritual realm, as de Sanctis says, "*possa avere una rappresentazione*" (can be represented as art).[3] Eco takes de Sanctis to mean that genuine poetry can exist "only in representations of the carnal passions and those of the heart." Whether composers and their critics also face this problem is less clear. Eco does not think so, inasmuch as a "poetry of pure understanding" is nothing other than music itself.[4] Yet important commentary on *The Magic Flute* likewise wonders whether music in its speculative modes can be convincing and urgent. For Richard Kramer, one of today's most distinctive and penetrating interpreters of music of the Classical era, Mozart's *große Oper* also fails to ward off the threat that overcame Dante—that winking out of individuality in form and color:

> The essence of Enlightenment . . . is to be sought and found less in the staging of [the] rituals and ceremonies that inspire so much of the music in the opera than in the play of its all-too-human personae—Pamina and Tamino, chiefly—over against these inert, monolithic structures in which they dwell.[5]

Stylistically, the ceremonial music of Sarastro's temple and the poetry of Dante's empyrean strike only "*una corda sola*"; ethically, they flatten out individuality; psychologically, they mute human passion.

Kramer is not the only critic to propose that some music from this era no longer bends its knee before representations of the heavens, nor is *The Magic Flute* the only work to prompt this question. Theodor Adorno, for example, called the *Missa Solemnis* a failure for "not at all break[ing] out of the pre-planned objectivity of the model through a subjective dynamic."[6] Even poets and not just critics will take this view of art. Perhaps most famously was William Blake, who offered this diagnosis of *Paradise Lost*: "The reason Milton wrote in fetters when he wrote of Angels and God, and at liberty when of Devils and Hell, is because he was a *true poet*, and of the Devil's party without knowing it."[7] Of course, *The Magic Flute* is, strictly speaking, musical theater rather than poetry, and here Kramer adds another layer to an anti-metaphysical poetics. Just as the Roman Rite is the rigid form that enfetters the *Missa Solemnis*, so, too, is the chain in *The Magic Flute* forged of an alloy of theater and ritual:

> Yet, if this ordeal [the Trial of Fire and Water] were to have any real meaning as a test of character, as evidence of a maturation of thought, if the true experience of *Aufklärung* is in the recognition of a process of mind no longer dependent upon mythic superstition, upon unquestioned authority, then it would appear that . . . an opportunity to embody the genuine experience of a truly enlightened coming of age has been sacrificed in favor of theatrical display. . . . Here again, the opera traffics in the devices of ritual and ceremony, its principal players manipulated more as puppets than as independent, thinking beings.[8]

Enlightenment as self-direction, "mythic superstition" as a crutch for the immature mind, authenticity partitioned from theatrical display—each of these positions has a history and its own adherents and detractors. Noteworthy about the last item, theatricality, is Kramer's linking of wariness about a sensuous stage to skepticism about the speculative potential of the arts. Generally speaking, the two have not run in tandem: no cleric, not from Mozart's culture and not from an earlier Patristic one, thundered against the stage for shortchanging carnality. Rather, what Jonas Barish calls the "anti-theatrical prejudice" issues from different and deeper sources. Distrust of the stage is seated in the collective psyche, as our basic vocabulary shows. The word *theatrical*, for example, bears a taint that is not inherent in descriptors taken from the other arts. To disparage someone's manner of speech as "poetic," I would have to supply ironic quotation marks, whereas terms like *theatrical* and *stagy*, also *operatic*, speak for themselves.[9]

The psychic dimension of theater as a form of disobedience lends the prejudice against it the capacity to generate art, and not just commentary on it. The archetype of the actor as grand, cosmos-defying villain is Iago, whose monosyllabic "I am not what I am" (*Othello*, Act 1, scene 1) blasphemes holy writ, all while providing a textbook definition of *actor*. The opposite of Being is Acting—being what one is not. So, too, with Don Giovanni. When, in the Act 1 quartet, his adversaries get a chance to gaze at him for more than a moment, what hits them is a "*cangiarsi di colore*," a changing of color. His chromatic flickering is obviously not like the light of Dante's heavens. Instead, the light that refracts off Don Giovanni fills his onlookers with a vague horror, and it is this opacity, this acting, that elevates the libertine's disobedience from civil crime to theological sin.

An opposition between authenticity and theatricality also takes one far into *The Magic Flute*. Just not all the way. Were the anti-theatrical prejudice to be allegorized as a character in the opera, only the door of Reason (or better, Rationalism) would open before it, and not the portal leading to *Weisheit*. *The Magic Flute* beckons its viewers with a contrasting vision of spectacle: a view, darkly luminous, of theater and music as suprarational sources of social harmony *and* self-realization, the one not possible without the other. To see how, one has to look beyond the years immediately preceding *The Magic Flute* back to the Counter-Reformation—or rather, to recognize in this opera, from the twilight of the Enlightenment, the persistence and reconception of an older Baroque culture of ceremonial piety.[10]

The Magic Flute and the Counter-Reformation Legacy of a Sacramental Universe

A guide to this worldview comes from R. J. W. Evans, in his magisterial study of the intellectual foundations of Counter-Reformation Europe. His thesis runs that the dynastic power of these Catholic territories rested on a sacramental cosmology, what he calls "white magic." But where there is white magic, there must be black magic, or superstition. Just as Habsburg authorities gave considerable license among elites to explore the former, so too did they counterbalance that liberality with considerable suppression in the populace of the latter. As Evans continues, reaching a definition of the two kinds of magic "was, in the nature of things, impossible."[11] Thus stood the entire Habsburg project on an unstable foundation. In one area only did this *Weltanschauung*, however fraught politically, backwards economically, and obscurantist intellectually, achieve an "outstanding and distinctive memorial," and that was in art:

> Only there could the synthesis of classical and Christian traditions still be successfully sustained. Only there could the gulf between high and low cultures be bridged: esoteric visual and literary programmes joining with popular creativity and a mass response. Only there could genuinely native idioms be evolved, which nevertheless show an unmistakable family likeness. Only there could the religious and the secular truly complement one another.[12]

Evans's summary reads like a précis of *The Magic Flute,* starting with the acceptance of the world as enchanted, a position that the opera never seriously questions. It does, however, take a different perspective on its Baroque heritage. Earlier Habsburg art, says Evans, conceals in its grandeur an anxiety, a substrate of "nervous power which derives precisely from the essential fragility of its socio-political base in Central Europe."[13] *The Magic Flute*, in contrast, is less fretful, yet not for ignoring the obvious follies and dangers hedged about such a world, but for finding moral value and creative opportunity in it. Indeed, it can be productive to imagine Tamino's (and, to a lesser extent, Pamina's) journey toward Enlightenment as an adventure through which they learn to distinguish beneficent from baleful magic.

This view stands in stark contrast to one like Kramer's. His interpretation leaves little ambiguity about *The Magic Flute*'s theatrical magic. Ritual and spectacle impede Enlightenment, full stop. They are forms of superstition, instruments by which the knowing Few enslave the gullible Many. That thought has so many eighteenth-century advocates that it can safely be called a tenet of the official rationalist Enlightenment. Kant, for example, inveighed against the hypocrisy and moral laziness that religious ritual abetted. In the same treatise in which he advances a theory of radical evil, he also writes: "To this end [of appealing to God for grace] the human being busies himself with every formality he can think of, to give sign of how much he *respects* the divine commands, in order that it will not be necessary for him to *observe* them."[14]

At the same time, Kramer isolates another, more vital current in the opera that runs against such rationalism. He calls it an "aesthetic" Enlightenment[15] and finds representatives in the novels of Pierre de Marivaux, the operas of Mozart and Da Ponte, and the philosophies of Kant's friend Johann Georg Hamann and Kant's student Johann Gottfried Herder. This art and literature avers and demonstrates that thought is rooted in language and culture rather than in system and abstraction. It does not deny value in a work like the First Critique but finds it most credible when taken as a form of poetry instead of philosophy. Oswald Bayer summarizes Hamann's revised Kantianism as follows: "It is not 'the' pure reason that comes to an understanding of itself in the *Critique of Pure Reason*, but Immanuel Kant from Königsberg who writes and evaluates. Analyzing and synthesizing is individual hearing and reading, individual responding and writing."[16] Although figures like Hamann and Herder are sometimes described as "anti-Enlighteners," Kramer thinks that such anti-Kantians come closest to a true Enlightenment. In what he calls an "Enlightenment moment," the "aesthetic" branch represents "genuine human impulse" in contrast to "the grain of conventional morality" espoused by the rationalists.[17] One might say that it took Hamann and Mozart to realize some of the power that Kant did not recognize in his rallying cry "*sapere aude*."

If, however, Kramer's sympathies run with the aesthetic Enlightenment, his premises derive from the rationalist faction. That is, the construct "Enlightenment moment" relies on the very separation of "understanding and sensuousness, . . . contingent truths of history and necessary truths of reason" that the Other Enlightenment disavows.[18] Although there are logical and historical reasons for questioning this polarization, the opera itself points to a different configuration. For example, the temple scene alluded to above presents Wisdom as something other and more encompassing than Reason (and Nature). The *manner* in which Schikaneder presents these words also bears on their meaning and authority. When engraved on temples, words become hieroglyphic; they acquire an energy that they cannot draw from the dais or the pulpit, not to mention the thesaurus. Nor can even the opera's plainer forms of speech be separated from its speakers and visualization. The opera's most vociferous opponent of "*Blendwerk und Aberglauben*"—machinations and superstition—and "*die Heuchler*"—hypocrites—is Sarastro, even though he heads a clerical order.[19]

Perhaps these forms of spectacle provide more evidence of a fundamental incoherence in Schikaneder's text. Or, perhaps they trace out cultural tensions in Josephinism like the ones that Evans saw imprinting Counter-Reformation art. Just as it was impossible to erect a stable dynasty on a sacramental cosmology, so too was the imaginative realm of art the only place where it was not impossible to be, all at once, Austrian, Enlightened, Masonic, and Catholic. Still more problematically, these visual examples might misread the more direct evidence of music and drama. Again, the Trial of Fire and Water in *The Magic Flute* is keenly illustrative for Kramer, because here he finds the music of an oppressive Enlightenment in closest proximity to that of a liberating one. In contrast to the warm, living lyricism of Tamino and Pamina's duet (Example 1)

Example 1. *The Magic Flute*, Act 2 finale, m. 372.

stands the cool, imperturbable music that Tamino uses to harrow the underworld (Example 2):

Example 2. *The Magic Flute*, Act 2 finale, mm. 362–64.

Charles Rosen ascribes a "symbolic" function to this gentle march. In it, musical light vanquishes chthonic gloom. "The majestic dwelling on the tonic," he says, "is the musical equivalent for the steadfastness of the

Masonic initiate," and the march's "strange sonority . . . of flute, brass, and timpani reflects and enhances the absolute simplicity here."[20] Kramer instead finds the march "drab." Unlike Blake with Dante, however, he speculates that Mozart knew what he was doing. "Perhaps that was precisely his intent: to display the aridity of a music deprived of true imagination."[21]

The very fact that Tamino's march needs an apology like Rosen's might point out Mozart's failure to draw compelling art out of the starry sky above or the moral law within. But there are other contexts to consider. With respect to staging, the simplicity of the march provides *chiaroscuro* for the spectacle of Tamino and Pamina's descent into the underworld. With respect to musical design, the march, when heard against the duet, gives a different kind of contrast. Here, Mozart used a scoring that may not have been part of Schikaneder's conception, as the published libretto calls for a solo:

PAMINA [solo]

Wir wandelten durch Feuergluthen,	We walked through the burning fires,
Bekämpften muthig die Gefahr.	Bravely fought the danger.
(Zu Tamino)	*(To Tamino)*
Dein Ton sey Schutz in Wasserfluthen,	May your music be protection from the flood,
So wie er es im Feuer war.	Just as it was from the fire.[22]

There are many ways of defending Schikaneder's conception (if that is whose it was). From the standpoint of plot, giving Pamina a solo puts a musical point on her place in the history of the Magic Flute. It was she who told Tamino of its making; it was she who urged Tamino to play it; and now it is she who, along with the Flute, guides Tamino through the underworld. By this interpretation, when Pamina says "*dein Ton*"—"your music"—the *your* must mean Tamino and not the Flute. In contrast, Mozart, in changing the texture to a duet, also changes its object. Now, "*dein*" refers to the Flute and its music.

Mozart has thus dramatized a paradox like the one that Eco saw in the *Paradiso*. Depersonalized art can intensify rapture and just therein deepen intimacy between humans. Such a metaphysics governs the duet even on its own, apart from its placement against the march. Although its parallel thirds and sixths are hallmarks of love duets, this is no "Andiam, andiam, mio bene" (from the conclusion of Don Giovanni and Zerlina's duet, "Là ci darem la mano"). Its character is not coyly pastoral but unguardedly reverent, in the way that Gustave Doré (Figure 1) renders Dante and

Figure 1. Gustave Doré, engraving representing *Paradiso* 31:1–4.

St. Bernard standing before the heavenly multitude, arrayed as a rose. The couple's love does not close in upon itself. Nor is it a form of servility or immaturity. It arises from and is intensified in a mutual contemplation of a superabundant cosmos.

Heroism and Sensibility in *The Magic Flute*

Ritual, light, knowledge: in art, the argument running across Blake, de Sanctis, Kramer, and even a few theatrophiles is that their hues appear cool, remote, and abstract. In *The Magic Flute*, they appear warm, immanent, and passionate. To what extent does this use touch the opera's heroic pair in their private and not just ceremonial moments? Even before the curtain goes up, the opera does not hold out much hope, as its playbill advertises a world of types instead of all-too-human individuals. Names like Tamino, Pamina, and Sarastro have allegorical resonances that Figaro, Susanna, and Bartolo do not. Yet it would be ruinous to the opera's mythic dignity to give these characters "depth" or to make them "three-dimensional"—to be told, say, that the Queen of the Night has a first and last name, along with a street address and a Bluesky account.

For Tamino and Pamina, who are the main embodiments of Kramer's "aesthetic" Enlightenment, intimacy obviously comes through other means, and in the attainment of other ends. Guiding even their most spontaneous perceptions and reactions is a self-possession without which their emotion would lose force and credibility. That synthesis of reason and sentiment has fewer operatic precedents than is often thought.

The first solo number to show this musical reconception of heroism and sensibility is the Portrait aria. On the face of it, the setting of a prince falling in love with a picture is unpromising material for such an ambition, more the stuff of parody or easy sentimentality. One of Mozart's most musically astute early biographers, Ignaz Arnold, wrote in 1803 that a more typical composer would have set the number as an allegro and, further, would have larded its text "with numerous melismas: clumsy, nonsensical passages." In Mozart's hands, in contrast, we get "pure feeling, without excess, just correctly laid out and therefore correctly expressed."[23] Mozart's talent for representation is so great as to make "Dies Bildnis" an *exemplum*, "a classical model from which young composers can study the step-wise progression of emotions."[24]

Like Arnold, Kramer also speaks of the distinctiveness of Mozart's musical achievement (although without adopting Arnold's neoclassical aesthetic). Against the frequent objection that *The Magic Flute*'s success came in spite of Schikaneder's text, Kramer finds a much greater concourse between word and tone, nowhere more so than in the passage in Example 3.

It is as if Mozart made patent the music latent in the sound and syntax of Schikaneder's text, especially "the inflection of '*würde*' in the conditional mood, and the sonorous depth of the word as it is sung." These four measures of sound and one of silence weave tone and discursive thought so finely together as to render their synthesis untranslatable: Mozart's music "makes sense only as an expression of *these* words, in *this* language."[25]

Example 3. *The Magic Flute*, "Dies Bildnis," mm. 40–44.

Kramer buttresses his defense of Schikaneder through comparison with some of his English translators, especially W. H. Auden and Chester Kallman (from 1956): "O tell me image, grant a sign — / Am I her choice?" This wording, along with sanitizing Tamino's encounter, diminishes his agency. It makes Pamina's image into an oracle that commands him instead of a living presence that speaks through him. In any case, a more precise test of inimitability would require looking at German versions. Here, Kramer's position also holds up. Two of the earliest and most influential adaptations, Christian August Vulpius's libretto, of 1794, and the 1814 edition of the score, change much of Schikaneder's original, including the text surrounding the two lines at hand—"*Ich würde . . . / Was würde ich*?"—but not those lines.

Kramer's insights about sound and meaning have broader ramifications for Tamino's character. At least since Goethe, Tamino's passivity has made him seem a very odd sort of hero.[26] True heroes slay dragons instead of faint before them. Although for sure no Odysseus, Tamino does have precedents in theater and opera. Prime inspiration comes in the eponymous heroine of Samuel Richardson's *Pamela*, who, especially through Carlo Goldoni's plays and librettos, provided the archetype for the subgenre of sentimental, bourgeois drama.[27] Heroism among these characters has a distinctive quality and manner of expression. They do not meet assaults to their virtue so much as react to them, and with a distress in which passion overwhelms the ordinary functions of speech and reasoning. Here, authenticity means absence of display and even of forethought. In its more intense forms, psychic distress causes these heroines to fall asleep, a vulnerability that encourages onlookers to admire their beauty, which is the outer manifestation of their inner virtue. The spectacle of the sleeping beauty occurs in the prototype of sentimental opera, Niccolò Piccinni and Carlo Goldoni's *La buona figliuola* (1760; Act 2, sc. 12–13), as well as in Tamino (Act 1, scene 1) and Pamina, the latter of whom, furthermore, is found slumbering in "an agreeable garden . . . with an arbor of roses and flowers" (Act 2, scene 7). (By this point, we are far from Richardson's Pamela, for whom the defense of virtue requires unceasing wakefulness instead of pastoral languor.)

What *music* do composers find in this character type? Don Alfonso's cavatina "Vorrei dir," from *Così fan tutte* (Example 4), shows that musical depictions of virtue in distress have become formalized enough by this time to attract parodies, as Mozart all but copies the number from Martín y Soler's enormously popular *Una cosa rara* (1786):

Example 4. Mozart, *Così fan tutte*, "Vorrei dir," mm. 3–5.

Così's philosopher-*cum*-actor announces that his lips are stuttering, that he would like to speak, if only he could get the words out. But about all he can manage are syllables—sounds, not language.[28]

Yet if the sense and rhetoric of Tamino's music really do belong to the category of "ardent aria of sensibility,"[29] then it must be on different terms than those of heroines of sensibility. It is not even clear that

Pamina, much less Tamino, follows type.[30] True, like other sentimental heroines, she (and Tamino) counts among the rescued rather than the rescuers. Other similarities with distress cavatinas extend to the music, especially her aria's rhythmic monotony (Example 5):

Example 5. *The Magic Flute*, "Ach, ich fühl's," mm. 1–2.

But elements must be viewed against their contexts and even in isolation can have more than one use. The obsessive orchestral backdrop typical of the sentimental distress aria tends to work in tandem with regular melodic and verbal stresses to produce a sensation that is less spontaneous than motoric.[31] Taken by itself, the orchestral pattern in "Ach, ich fühl's" seems, if anything, still more autonomic and hence a token of sentimentalism through and through. As used, however, the pattern acts more as a neutral scaffolding that allows spontaneity and formal eloquence to intertwine. William R. Braun goes so far as to call the aria *sui generis,* in part because Mozart does not use the 6/8 meter to lock Pamina's phrases into a ♪. ♬ ♪ pattern. Her melodic thought, "almost unbelievably," takes on "a new rhythm in just about every bar."[32]

Indeed, separating form from spontaneity in the aria is meaningful only hypothetically, for purposes of illustration. In reality, Mozart treats form in her aria as generated rather than ready-made. This dynamic sense of form is most perceivable in the closing areas of Pamina's two paragraphs. Although both use the same material, the two passages do not align (Example 6).

It is common for Mozart to alter closing areas of recapitulations, and almost always to increase tension just before the sections reach a cadence (as in the finale of the "Jupiter" Symphony). In "Ach, ich fühl's," however, Pamina's florid statement on "Freude" contracts when thoughts of death intrude. Her immediate continuation also draws pathos from brevity, first by turning to the plangent Neapolitan A♭ in measure 32, and then to a closing melisma that is even more restrained than the one on "Tod" (Example 7).

Example 6. *The Magic Flute*, "Ach, ich fühl's," mm. 12–16, mm. 30–33.

Example 7. *The Magic Flute*, "Ach, ich fühl's," mm. 37–38.

Unlike her predecessors in sentimental opera, Pamina is a character in whom there is more than a modicum of art and composure, all to make the sentiment more vivid and compelling.

The miscasting—if that is what to call it—of "Ach, ich fühl's" as an aria of sensibility has a long history. In 1815, the composer and theorist Jacob Gottfried Weber wondered why the public "almost always" found the aria "pretty boring."[33] The main culprit, he concluded, was tempo. Although Mozart called for an andante, most of Weber's contemporaries imposed an adagio on it. The result, says Weber, is that a passionate aria from a woman who is "outraged" and who "heaps reproaches upon Tamino for his coldness" becomes sentimentalized into a "lamentation."[34]

If Pamina's musical character does not comport well with that of the sentimental heroine, still less does Tamino's. Certainly, there is little sense that he is being engulfed by feeling, either spontaneously, as in *La finta giardiniera*'s "Crudeli, fermate," or ironically, as in *Così*. Instead, Mozart shows Tamino thinking through his emotions. Revisiting the latter part of "Dies Bildnis," one sees that, following each wave of passion, Tamino reflects on it: first, on what the feeling is, then, having discovered it to be "*die Liebe*," on how to act on it. The music is more than a representation or embellishment of Tamino's perceptions and reactions. It is their form and voice.

Tamino's movement from "*die Regung*"—impulse—to understanding begins with a provisional answer to the question "*Was würde ich*?" (Example 8):

Example 8. *The Magic Flute*, "Dies Bildnis," mm. 45–49.

Formally, only a harmonic return accompanies Tamino's resolve to "press Pamina to his hot breast." His melody, in contrast, probably has no overt analogue in the first section of the aria—"probably," because both melody and harmony (along with accompaniment) are too non-descript to point to a discrete referent. The moment is genuinely lyrical, but on account of grammar, in a three-fold repetition whose last iteration extends itself and then climaxes with another weighty rest (Example 9):

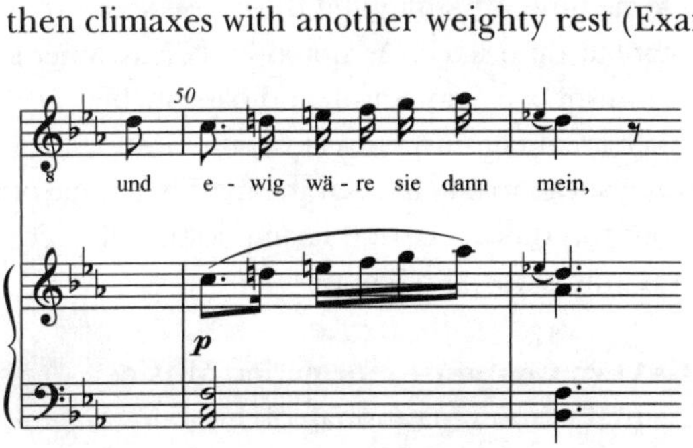

Example 9. *The Magic Flute*, "Dies Bildnis," mm. 50–51.

As a matter of psychology, this return, at once surprising and deeply satisfying, clarifies and refines Tamino's potent but initially shapeless passion. As a matter of text-setting, this melody does not require thinking that Schikaneder's words demanded this, and only this, music from Mozart. Instead, Mozart makes an independent creation out of Schikaneder's text. Mozart's use of the clause "*und ewig wäre sie dann mein*" (and then will she be mine forever) tells all, because he sets it on *both* sides of his formal divide. Tamino's first utterance, a question, becomes, with the return of the melody, an affirmation. In highlighting the presence and use of the *musical* returns of these arias, returns that are not prescribed in the text, I am not suggesting that Pamina or Tamino is thinking Sonata Form (although Mozart is).[35] But the two are *thinking*, and not just feeling (as if it were easy to separate the two). Further, their thinking-through-senses does not appear as the application of a preexisting form, as the way an oration can go, but as the invention of a new form, in Tamino's case one inspired by being seized by an image.

To sum up: the preceding has offered several preliminary responses to Kramer's probing analysis of the heroic pair's music and what kind of Enlightenment it represents. Most differences are minor, more matters of coloration than substance. For example, they accord Mozart slightly more agency: yes, the initiates' text and music form a genuine harmony, but as something that *Mozart* achieved, through *his* singular musical inventiveness. Likewise, noting the rational, form-generating qualities of Tamino's and Pamina's arias helps to explain their structural and emotive distance from standard operatic representations of sensibility. That position, too, arguably goes hand in hand with Kramer's interpretation of the two as embodiments of the humane, intimate rather than mechanistic, remote Enlightenment. As Kramer states, "It is precisely [Tamino's and Pamina's] fluent play with syntax that, to my mind, is at the core of Enlightenment thought. *There is reason behind it*, of course, but language and music give the impression of spontaneous wit, of a mind in motion."[36] At the same time, I highlighted the clause about reason to bring out a more substantial difference. As noted earlier, Kramer's interpretation turns on an antagonism between reason and passion, between theatricality and authenticity. Such an antagonism forecloses the possibility of seeing in *The Magic Flute* "an implicit rationality in even the most irrational of human imaginings." Working out this difference and its implications for *The Magic Flute* as metaphysical art requires a separate exposition.

Mozart Invents His Own Counter-Reformation Music

"An implicit rationality in even the most irrational of human imaginings": this insight comes from the historian Hayden White, in his learned and influential *Metahistory*.[37] White's authorship matters here because Kramer builds his interpretation of *The Magic Flute* on a nearby passage in *Metahistory*: "Kant," says Kramer, quoting White, "apprehended the historical process less as a development from one stage to another in the life of humanity than as merely a conflict, an *unresolvable* conflict, between *eternally opposed* principles of human nature: rational on the one hand, irrational on the other."[38] A common thought, but different stances toward it. Kramer takes this conflict as axiomatic for *The Magic Flute* and its unfolding, the two sides, rationality and irrationality, grappling with each other. White, in contrast, thinks that only a rationalist would frame the matter thus and that so strong a separation of rationality from irrationality is inadequate for understanding history as well as the work of reason and of the imagination.

It is not that Kramer's position lacks standing in the eighteenth century. On the contrary, it drove Habsburg cultural reform from around 1750 onward, including that regarding the stage. Against nearly two millennia of clerical and then Rousseauian animus toward theater, an assembly of nobles, playwrights, actors, critics, impresarios, and clerics started to promote the stage as a school of morals for a nation. Still, that unprecedented patriotic enthusiasm came with an important check: that the stage be "*regelmäßig*." The term, usually translated as "regular," designates written-out plays as opposed to the "*Stegreifspiel*," or improvised comedy, that had sustained Vienna's Kärntnerthortheater since its founding in 1709. But *regular* gets only to the technical side of the change. The higher ambition, an ethical, cultural one, was to develop a repertoire that took the law (*die Regel*) as its measure (*das Maß*, hence, *regelmäßig*).

The weight that eighteenth-century politics on the arts placed on law as an ordinance of reason is felt across region and confession, whether to the South, in Goldoni, the Protestant North, in Kant, or the anti-clerical West, in Voltaire.[39] Catholic, Enlightened Vienna also thought that a nascent national theater had no chance of attaining its didactic and social potential without supervision. It needed the law, whose custodian was the State (rather than the Church). In 1780, the playwright and pro-Enlightenment, pro-Catholic polemicist Anton Cremeri published a treatise that used Joseph's ascension to sole regency as an occasion to honor his role as theater reformer. He entitled it *Eine Bille an Joseph II.*, that is, a legislative proposal.[40] Another advocate of a rule-bound stage, the journalist and dramatist Christian Gottlob Klemm (1736–1810), spells out this position in a review of some plays of Tobias Gebler (ca. 1720–86):

> [Gebler] is convinced that the theater be regarded and used as a supplement to the law, that the state must pay

> considerable attention to this obligation, and that the state is permitted to correct anything therein that falls outside the secular arm. Only his patriotic zeal has kept the German stage from lapsing swiftly back to its old wasteland, to its previous turpitudinous barbarism.[41]

That the theater can reach into regions of the human heart that the law cannot seems to have been a thought that this school of theatrical reformers did not or would not entertain.[42]

The reductiveness in viewing theater as a supplement to the law marks a theoretical reason for skepticism about the categories that Kramer and the rationalist Enlightenment use. When it comes to interpreting *The Magic Flute*'s plot, imagery, and music, more practical ones arise, too. Recall the setting of the Act 1 finale: a grove, at the center of which stands a temple inscribed with the word *Wisdom* and flanked by two other temples, one dedicated to Reason, the other to Nature. Tamino, of course, is rebuffed before the temples to Reason and Nature, with only the one consecrated to Wisdom opening before him. Whatever the allegory, it is unlikely that the scene was intended to set Wisdom in opposition to Reason. More likely, this setting points up Wisdom as a quality that aspires to, facilitates, or springs from a union of our rational and material natures. Indeed, the opera's staging indicates that Wisdom and Reason, as well as Nature, are related, for the temple to Wisdom has columns running to the other two ("*führt mit Säulen*," Act 1, scene 15).

However that may be, this scene marks an extraordinary moment in light of other things, including the sensibility/rationality dualism that governs Kramer's interpretation. For one, the person who steps out from the Temple of Wisdom to greet Tamino is not Kant, much less Voltaire, but one of Sarastro's priests. For another, it is this scene that first brings into focus the genuine impediment to the noble pair's quest for Enlightenment. It is the Queen of the Night and her siren-like voice. If any character in *The Magic Flute* incarnates the corrosiveness of the culture of Habsburg ceremonial piety and the need for Enlightenment to steer it toward wholesome ends, it is she. Although Mozart makes art out of this view, the opera also conveys it with almost no art whatsoever, namely, in the spoken dialogue that opens Act 2. This is the occasion for Sarastro's warning, cited earlier, that the Queen "hopes to beguile the populace through machinations and superstition."[43] That slogan could have come from Joseph II or, before him, the historian Johann Christian Lünig, who in his *Theatrum Ceremoniale* (1719) opined that "most people, especially the lower orders, are so constituted that sensual impressions and imagination accomplish more with them than wit and understanding. . . . This wonderment yields respect and reverence, whence come subordination and obedience."[44] That Sarastro, the head of a priestly order with its own rituals and ceremonies, propounds this view indicates that the question before the opera and its wider culture is not *whether* the two aspire to Enlightenment, but what they mean by Enlightenment. Put more finely, what does it mean, and how does it look artistically, that *The Magic Flute* takes the task of attaining Enlightenment as the Josephine one of reform rather than the French anti-clerical one of renunciation?[45]

In brief, Mozart creates for *The Magic Flute* his own Counter-Reformation art. Like the official Habsburg one that it amends, Mozart's accepts and draws inspiration from its white magic/black magic opposition. Unlike it, the opera finds it too easy to think of reason as a manifestation only of the former and superstition only of the latter. Like the Baroque cultural world he inherited, Mozart does not abjure ceremony. Unlike it, he also shows how it sometimes intertwines with interiority. Like the Josephine reformers, he accepts the premise of a moral stage. Unlike them, he does not accept the status of music and the arts as mere adjuncts to reason: it is not as if Mozart acceded to the entire program of a virtuous stage and just added some extra-ravishing music to sell it. The arts are objects upon which reason must reflect. They are innate and not just derivative sources of happiness, harmony, and well-being.

The opera's reinterpretation of spectacle along the dimensions of character, situation, and musical style is most vivid in the Queen of the Night, both as an independent character and also in contrast to Sarastro and his Order. To be sure, there is no getting around the inconsistencies in Schikaneder's portrayal of her, including at what point in the first act her mask comes off (or whether it comes off at all). Even so, there is at least some method in Schikaneder's ambiguity. It is essential to the tale's unfolding and its moral vision that the Queen's intentions in the first act be opaque—that her status as wronged, grieving mother or as fomenter of parricide remain, for a while, indecipherable. The search for truth, for Enlightenment, is just that: a *search*, a quest, as opposed to a thing attained once and for all. Attempts to isolate musical "tells" can wipe out that ambiguity, as in speculation that her plaint's irregular, three-measure phrasing (Example 10) "may allow us to question her sincerity."[46] Ingmar Bergman tacitly admits that the music and text do not adequately spell out her motivations, but should have, in directing Birgit Nordin to give this side-long glance during her first-act scena (Figure 2), or when he veils the Three Women upon the introduction of the Three Boys.

These and similar attempts to unriddle the mystery of the Queen minimize the potency and hence danger of magic. Skilled magicians, good

Example 10. *The Magic Flute*, "O zittre nicht," mm. 22–24.

and evil, know how to hide their tricks. More than that—they know that their spectators often *want* to be deceived, or find themselves inveigled even when they know better. Odysseus *has* to hear the Sirens' song; in Dante's weird dream in *Purgatorio* 19, it is *he* (or his dreaming self) who transforms a "*femmina balba*" (stuttering woman; l.7) into a "*dolce sirena*" (sweet siren; l.19). Mozart and Schikaneder trade out Dante's psychological complexity for greater ambiguity, as they do not show the Queen undergoing a similar transformation from true, repugnant core to false,

Figure 2. Ingmar Bergman, *The Magic Flute*.

alluring surface. The problem facing Tamino, then, is not one of a weak will (that is obviously Papageno's problem) but of insufficient knowledge. Simply rejecting the Queen's commission is not an option for him, inasmuch as what he desires is nearly identical to what she offers: the closing hope of his aria, that Pamina "would then be [his] forever" ("*ewig wäre . . . dann mein*"), mirrors the Queen's closing promise in her aria, that "thus will she be ever yours" ("*so sey sie dann auf ewig dein*"). Nor does rationalization offer much help, including the use of irony to keep magic at arm's length. This world is enchanted, either to its inhabitants' bliss or ruin, and Tamino's path to Enlightenment must run *through* that enchantment.

But Tamino is not wholly witless or resourceless before the Queen's splendor. Her visitation leaves him perplexed: "Is what I saw real, or did my senses leave me dazed?" ("*Ists denn auch Wirklichkeit, was ich sah? oder betäubten mich meine Sinnen?*"; Act 1, scene 7).[47] Some of Tamino's other confrontations with miracle, mystery, and authority also point to a conflict that turns on a critique of spectacle instead of on its interdiction. Sonically, there is the music accompanying the Queen's entrance. The libretto calls it "a violently shocking chord" ("*ein heftig erschütternder Akkord*"; Act 1, scene 5), and Mozart did not orchestrate the cacophony (as far as we know). The fanfares that usher in the entire opera, contrariwise, renounce such a coercive, sense-deafening noise for a persuasive, noble austerity. Visually, there is the manner of the Queen's appearance. It uses the arch-Baroque contrivance of the deus ex machina. When that descent is combined with her very first words, "do not tremble, my dear son" ("*O zittre nicht, mein lieber Sohn*"), it probably does not go far enough to call her bearing and this moment regal. They form an Annunciation. Sarastro's realm is also obviously imposing and mysterious—in a word, sacred—but it mounts no assault on the senses. Sarastro's emissary, an old priest, meets Tamino on the same plane and, in the venerable tradition of prophets and philosophers, on foot. Nor does the peripatetic overwhelm the wanderer in Melos but instead engage him in Dialogue.

For an opera to develop a style that is austere and to promote an ethic that trusts words more than images—and sometimes more even than sounds—is to invite a host of troubles. A word-dominated opera aesthetic is more at home in the prior generation of Metastasio and Handel. As Rosen observes, that earlier world of court opera excelled at using music to "transfigure . . . sentiment . . . and situation." But for *Mozart* to have adopted this view amounts to turning his back on arguably his most profound technical contribution to opera, which was that of incorporating "action [and] movement," thereby making opera dramatic and not just expressive.[48]

A moment's reflection brings out other shortcomings. An operatic Calvinism threatens the core of the genre, if there is merit to Jacques

Barzun's view of opera as "spectacle—not drama, not even theater."[49] It is suspect on the common philosophical and historical grounds that knowledge involves more than the mobilization of information; the senses also must have their say, as anyone from a Jesuit of Mozart's day to John Dewey knew. It is especially dubious in light of the argument advanced here, which is that *The Magic Flute* dramatizes the reality of a concourse between radiant, abstract splendor and soul-shaking, worldly Eros. The lover beholding the beloved sees, all at once, a person *and* an ideal.

But Mozart found creative opportunity in these obstacles, inventing a style where restraint acquires its own magic, so to speak. Tamino's long dialogue with Sarastro's priest in the Act 1 finale is striking evidence of this achievement. Of course, Mozart had musical precedents. Rosen notes general stylistic ones in Gluck and some of Haydn's symphonic slow movements, and Mozart obviously did not invent the accompanied recitative, the vocal style that presides here.[50] Its routine use in opera, however, was to convey emotions too intense for the more decorous aria, as in the recitative preceding Donna Anna's "Or sai chi l'onore." Nor does the cantata furnish a sufficient model. The accompanied recitatives in the Masonic Cantata, K. 623, for example, also forswear the emotional excess of more conventional operatic scenas, but in service of a festive tone. *The Magic Flute*, in contrast, uses the operatic and oratorical commonplace to trace out a spiritual/intellectual journey.

The Magic Flute's elevation of musical theater to *große Oper* in virtually every way—visually, morally, thematically, musically—extends to other operatic conventions, including that of portrait arias. The singularity of Mozart's inventiveness shows itself not just with its text/music relations, discussed above, but even with the device of the orchestral incipit. Here is the music that Tamino hears upon beholding this "*bezaubernd schön*" image (Example 11):

Example 11. *The Magic Flute*, "Dies Bildnis," mm. 1–2.

The fanfare of string triads with wind punctuation seems too inconspicuous to merit critical reflection. Indeed, it sometimes gets overlooked altogether. Even as attentive a listener as Ignaz Arnold says that the aria appears "without a [proper] ritornello—just a few generic triads simply to give the singer his pitch."[51]

But Mozart can give character to even the most trivial elements, whether a timbre, a device, or an incipit. To stay only with operatic introductions and, of those, only the most laconic, there is the opening flourish from *Don Giovanni*'s graveyard scene (Example 12):

Example 12. *Don Giovanni*, "O statua gentilissima," mm. 1–2.

Measured by topic and duration, the two introductions appear identical. Both are marches, and both occupy two measures. But within these general parameters, Leporello's introduction differs in its stiff formality, with a string pattern that is rhythmically, melodically, and formally detached from his salutation to the Stone Guest. The overall idea is of a terrified buffoon struggling to keep it together.

In contrast, the opening of the Portrait aria strikes a harmony between orchestral incipit and ensuing song. To stop with that observation, however, would be to stop too soon. As a number like "Dove sono" shows (Example 13), Mozart has more than one way of weaving orchestra and voice into a single line:

Example 13. *Le nozze di Figaro*, "Dove sono," mm. 1–4.

Whereas voice and orchestra start out as a unity in "Dove sono," the unity of the Portrait aria is emergent, with Tamino's melody growing out of and completing the string melody in the fanfare (Example 14):

Example 14. *The Magic Flute*, "Dies Bildnis," mm. 1–4.

Mozart here has created the operatic equivalent of free indirect style, in which the narrator's voice and the character's voice intertwine.

Tamino's melody is not the only element that links love as an ideal with love as a passion. Gesture as well as the complex of key and timbre have a place, too. Even listeners who cannot identify the pitch E♭ can still perceive that Tamino understands the world through and with the sights, sounds, and ethos of Sarastro's realm. The Queen may have given Tamino the portrait, but the portrait itself speaks to him in the priestly, ritualistic language that constitutes the opera's *tinta*.

The above interpretation expands Rosen's argument about the stylistic distinctiveness of *The Magic Flute*. Roughly, he maintains that the opera creates a new kind of elevated manner by blending the musical syntax of the Classical style he inherited and helped to create with some of the textures and all of the ethos of Palestrina. This achievement has two sides: one regarding the materials of Mozart's inspiration, the other regarding the conception of music that shapes those materials. As a rule, when Mozart turned to the musical past to project dignity and monumentality, he went no further than Bach and Handel. The main elements of what Laurence Dreyfus calls his "neo-Baroque high style" include "extreme chromaticism, strict part writing and imitation, contrapuntal artifice and, above all, an appeal to nearly extinct gestures" (in the case of the Adagio and Allegro for mechanical clock, K. 594, the *lamento* bass).[52] In *The Magic Flute*, however, only one number, the chorale cantus firmus, meets these criteria. This is why the style of *The Magic Flute* requires different terms and names—Counter-Reformation and Palestrina rather than neo-Baroque and Bach.

What is the reach of this Counter-Reformation style in an opera known for its eclecticism? The passages that Rosen cites as evidence come from the opera's ceremonial ensembles, not solo numbers like the Portrait aria. The Priests' march, in particular, is at once "Classical" and a "hymn" because, unlike its Baroque predecessors, it has periodic phrasing, simplified inner voices, and little "harmonic dissonance" (Example 15).[53]

Mozart's hymnology does not abandon all dissonance, of course. Some of it is exceedingly pre-Tridentine, as in the first violin's leap of a seventh into the downbeat of measure 6. The March, however, confines such pan-diatonic heresies of voice leading to the closing half of phrases, only after the first half has established a more straight-and-narrow Tridentine character.

Invention, then, and not imitation. This is the second side of Mozart's achievement, one concerning the creative mind and its interaction with its musical world. Here, too, Dreyfus shows how two distinctive styles can spring from one musical mind. Whether the "old master" was Palestrina or Bach, Mozart's engagement with their music was not "a matter of

Example 15. *The Magic Flute*, March of the Priests, mm. 1–8.

copying [them] but of reinventing a musical metaphysic." Creating an art that aspired to "other-worldly necessity and enduring validity"[54] required a supreme command of musical craft, of course, yet technical mastery could not by itself generate a compelling speculative music. In this context, musical materials cannot be thought of as givens, and a composition cannot be regarded as a collage, whether of musical topics like the sublime or of prefabricated tiles tastefully pressed together, all to produce agreeable works that were easy to copy. Creating a genuine metaphysical music entailed something more: a thinking through of the materials of the musical universe. Although writing some two hundred years before Rosen and Dreyfus, Ignaz Arnold also felt this quality in *The Magic Flute* and went on to call it neo-Renaissance in everything but name. Presiding over the Act 2 March, he says, is "the most beautiful, *purified* [gereinigte] church music, and Gluck's and Handel's choruses remain far behind it in noble simplicity, grace, and distinctiveness of [musical] character."[55]

In light of these qualities and criteria, the Portrait aria, an emblem of the "aesthetic Enlightenment," also has a place in this metaphysic, its pure, sensuous triads replacing arcane counterpoint as the touchstone of the otherworldly. Further, Tamino's aria is not the only place where Mozart elevates solo song. Some later episodes are more transparently hymn-like. Although no single element can bear all of the expressive weight of this reconception, a lot of it falls on the bass part. In songs, bass parts tend to remain static and take on a supportive role. In hymns, bass lines tend to move with the rest of the voices. By this criterion, the Portrait aria is not a hymn, but the setting of Tamino and Pamina's reunion, despite its nearly identical melodic contour, certainly is (Example 16):

Example 16. *The Magic Flute*, Act 2 finale, mm. 278–85.

Although it would mean overlooking the melismas, Ignaz Arnold might have judged Tamino's consequent phrase especially "*kirchlich*" for its versification and part-writing. Scanned independently of Mozart's music, the meter of Schikaneder's text is iambic:

Tămī/nŏ mēin/, Ŏ wēlch/ ĕin Glṻck.

As Example 16 shows, however, Mozart follows Schikaneder's iambs only in the opening of Pamina's and Tamino's statements, not in their continuations (mm. 280 and 284). A composer demanding a tighter alignment of poetic with musical meter might have set the lines as in Example 17 (or with eighth-note instead of quarter-note upbeats):

Example 17. Metrically "proper" text-underlay of *The Magic Flute*, Act 2 finale, mm. 278–81.

By placing a weak poetic accent on a musical downbeat, Mozart produces a more spondaic rhythm, thus avoiding the sing-song lilt of the hypothetical version. By giving an extra rest at mm. 279 and 283, Mozart also turns breath and punctuation into ravishing silence.

As for the part-writing, the moving bass and pervasive suspensions are the main elements that imbue the solo song with a hymn-like aspect. In so concentrated a style, even the slightest gesture can be meaningful, as is the case with the viola part in measure 284. By having quarter notes sound on each beat for the first time in this passage, that line does the following: 1) introduce more metrical flexibility to vocal parts that hover between spontaneous speech and more formal song; 2) create a little more momentum to close off the period (a Classical priority); and 3) move the setting still closer to a hymn, thanks to the inner voices' step-wise motion. In sum, this measure solemnizes the pair's reunion, transforming it from an operatic gesture to the first stage of a ritual purification.

Mozart, Dante, and the Metaphysics of the Everyday

To recall Francesco de Sanctis: the *Paradiso* could not match the *Inferno* in conviction without bringing in earthly "forms and . . . passions." Throughout, I have been trying to show that Mozart's musical equivalent of radiance fills and elevates the opera's more terrestrial forms, the latter losing no authority whatsoever from that association. Even the Trial of Fire and Water may brim with human passion much more than its characterization as "inert [and] monolithic" might allow. At least Ignaz Arnold found it hard to separate a description of its musical features from the human passions that he thought they represented:

> The Trial by Fire with its chorale is indisputably the *non plus ultra* of dramatic representation. The first shattering tones between the eerie pauses express the prince's shuddering at the first glimpse of the raging elements, and the discrete, plaintive interludes with the flutes and oboes accompanied by the bassoon express, with an inimitable beauty, the feeling of helplessness, the overwhelming weakness that are Terror's immediate companions. The rugged armored men sing their chorale . . . in

> long notes quite independently of the accompaniment, while the movement of the violins and the sustained notes in the woodwinds express, in an excellent manner, the restlessness of the elements and the prince's surging fear. During their song, the men of terror seem to take no notice of their novice's fear and continue their chorale calmly but resolutely.[56]

But the music of the trial scene also shows terrestrial forms influencing sacred ritual. Even the neo-Baroque in *The Magic Flute* qualifies as a distinctive reconception instead of as an excellent forgery of Handel and Bach because some of its most involved polyphonic forms will take their basic material from the voice instead of from instruments.

The fullest realization of this lyrical sublime occurs in the polyphonic madrigal to music that the pair sings along with the two armed men (Example 18):

Example 18. *The Magic Flute*, Act 2 finale, mm. 331–35.

(This is an instance where it is difficult to tell whether the opera's characters are conscious of singing. "Tamino mein" is obviously not a staged song in the manner of Cherubino's "Voi che sapete," but it does not seem quite right to say that music is absent from Pamina's or Tamino's consciousness. Song can often feel like their mother tongue.) On the one hand, there is the high artifice of invertible counterpoint, with each pair (Tamino/Pamina, and the two armed men) switching its lines in the repetition of the phrase (mm. 339

to 348). On the other hand, underlying its intricate writing are the baldest of harmonic progressions, a simplicity that Mozart dignifies by using V-I cadences to help check the passage of time. The phrasing, too, is a marvel of inventiveness, *a* music created for *this* opera. It is arch-galant in its periodicity and, with the sixteenth-note passages at measures 338 and 347, its ornamented close. At the same time, it is archaic in its use of the hemiola to impose two-beat units upon its triple meter (mm. 337–39 and 345–47).

But the most arrestingly lyrical feature of this polyphonic ensemble are its themes. Its melody draws on two components from Pamina's earlier solo. The first is a simple turning figure (Example 19):

Example 19. *The Magic Flute*, Act 2 finale, mm. 294–95.

The second begins with the leap of a sixth (Example 20):

Example 20. *The Magic Flute*, Act 2 finale, mm. 303–4.

The common use of the sixth in her solo and in the madrigal shows how closely even the most intricate forms of counterpoint—the quintessence of music as a speculative art—can sit to an exclamation of joy, one of the most spontaneous of human utterances.

This essay has in effect offered an anatomy of a miracle: how, out of the "intellectual provincialism" that Evans sees in the legacy of Josephinism, a provincialism that "stunted creativity on the whole," *The Magic Flute* could spring forth.[57] It is not that the law, an interest in which was at the center of the official Enlightenment project of moving theater from a courtly diversion to a site of national Bildung, has no bearing on the stage. Think only of the Oedipus trilogy, *Figaro*'s "*droit du seigneur*," or *Così*'s "*legge di natura*." Still, it is difficult to sustain a vibrant stage on an aesthetics that makes theater a vassal of the law. At the same time, no theory is perfectly consistent, and all theories need interpreters. Within a Josephine dramaturgy, facing off against its legalism was a vision, audacious for its time, of the stage as preeminent among the sciences, including philosophy, precisely because of its sensuality. A medium that instructs by radiant example is more likely to win over hearts than one that relies on cool precept. Cremeri, who, like many members of this avant-garde, was a cleric, further refined this hierarchy. At the summit of works of the imagination stood, of all things, opera, because in it alone were "all of the fine arts superbly united, especially on account of its music."[58]

But then we get to the model that official reformers prescribed in order to seduce their charges into a love of virtue. It was a bourgeois genre, middling between comedy and tragedy, in which the non-pretentious idioms and just-like-us characters of the former were imbued with the moral dignity and social refinement of the latter. That is, not myth, not ritual, not *The Magic Flute*. If Mozart's opera took the lead from Josephinism at all, it was to the distinctive end of joining the sensuality that Josephinism embraced to a metaphysics of art that it rejected.

The other side of this configuration, in which sensibility marched in lockstep with the official, rationalizing Enlightenment, was, however, pretty common. Indeed, a sentimentalist like Goldoni despised that arch-myth, the Don Juan legend, and Richardson uses the bulk of *Pamela* to work out the social complexities of a marriage between a commoner and a nobleman. The last thing Richardson wanted was for his story to follow the romance and its "irresponsible fantasy."[59] Mozart's opera is obviously far more a fairy tale than Richardson's letters from a life, but even here myth is no prop for the immature mind. Myth is a creative surge of the mind, without which reason becomes aimless and passion turns mechanical, manipulative, or farcical.[60]

The topics of metaphysics and abstraction obviously recall Eco and his objections to Dante's Romantic interpreters, and revisiting them can help clarify this larger theme of the quality and authority of metaphysical art. In his own journey for illumination, Dante needs help, and on every plane: from Virgil, to get him through Hell and to the threshold of Purgatory; from Beatrice, to guide him through parts of the Empyrean; and even at the end, now from the increate Light itself:

se non che la mia mente fu percossa	but then my mind was struck by light that flashed
da un fulgore in che sua voglia venne.	and, with this light, received what it had asked. (*Paradiso*, 33:140–41)

Dante does not spell this out, but implicit in his portrayal of light is a conception of abstraction in the arts as an extension of their life-expanding and meaning-making energies.

Someone who does spell this out is a representative of the "aesthetic Enlightenment," Hamann. In the following, he abandons his promiscuously allusive manner for a tighter form of reinvention. Pulling out threads from the First Critique, he weaves a counter-epistemology that takes "sounds and letters," rather than space and time, as

> pure forms *a priori*, in which nothing belonging to the sensation or concept of an object is found; they are the true, aesthetic elements of all human knowledge and reason. The oldest language was music, and along with the palpable rhythm of the pulse and of the breath in the nostrils, it was the original bodily image of all temporal measures and intervals.[61]

The move is away from sensuality as understanding's accessory to sensuality as understanding's wellspring.

But for whom aside from Dante and Hamann is this true? Eco reminds us that, even though we may strain, as a medieval populace did not, to think of light and color as passions, our everyday lives are filled with different forms of sensuous abstractions, as "when we dream about the sinuous gracefulness of a movie star, the elegant lines of a car," and so on.[62] In *The Magic Flute*, the passionate nature of form, color, and sound is felt on several planes, one of them being the eerie orchestration. (In this respect, it makes more sense to call the opera "The Magic Bassoon.") It is there, too, in the most elemental of melodic gestures, the $\hat{3}$–$\hat{2}$–$\hat{1}$ descent. The noble pair's journey through the underworld begins with a dusky version of this primal figure, the one that Ignaz Arnold found so terrifying (Example 21):

Example 21. *The Magic Flute*, Act 2 finale, mm. 191–92.

When the Pamina and Tamino reemerge, that pattern becomes refulgent (Example 22)

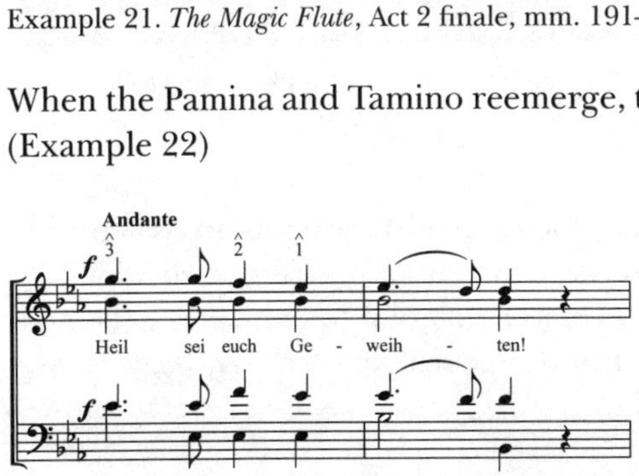

Example 22. *The Magic Flute*, Act 2 finale, mm. 830–31.

Mozart's cosmology, then, is not so remote from that of Dante, who needed the human instruments of geometry and poetic simile to see and describe his own mind, which appeared to him "*sì come rota ch'igualmente è mossa*"—"like a wheel revolving uniformly." Naturally, light is present at the end of the *commedia*, too, as an emanation of "*l'amor che move il sole e l'altre stelle*"—"the Love that moves the sun and the other stars." For Mozart, geometry and light appear thanks to a stage instruction from Schikaneder that calls for "the entire theater [to] transform itself into a sun" ("*verwandelt sich das ganze Theater in eine Sonne*"). David Hockney, among others, captured the moment by turning to color, line, and arcs (Act 2, scene 30; see Figure 3):

Figure 3. Mozart, *The Magic Flute*, director John Cox, production design by David Hockney, San Francisco Opera, 1987.

Schikaneder is directing the stagehands to turn the lights up. When projected through Mozart's music, however, that simple instruction could just as well have been giving wings to a promise: that of a Josephine Enlightened dramaturgy and its spectacularly improbable realization in *The Magic Flute*.

NOTES

I am grateful to Paul Bruno for comments on a draft of this essay.

1. Cited in Joan Bennett, *Four Metaphysical Poets: Donne, Herbert, Vaughan, Crashaw* (New York: Vintage Books, 1960), 60–61.

2. Francesco de Sanctis, *Storia della letteratura italiana* (Florence: Salani, 1965), 246; Umberto Eco, "La profezia del software," *La Repubblica*, 6 September 2000. Translation adapted from Umberto Eco, "A Reading of the *Paradiso*," in *On Literature*, trans. Martin McLaughlin (Orlando, FL: Vintage, 2006), 17.

3. De Sanctis, *Storia*, 237. Only Eco's original cites this passage, not the translation.

4. Eco, "A Reading of the *Paradiso*," 18.

5. Richard Kramer, "Seeking Enlightenment in Mozart's *Magic Flute*," in *The Cambridge Companion to "The Magic Flute,"* ed. Jessica Waldoff (New York: Cambridge University Press, 2023), 188–89. Hereafter *CCMF*.

6. Theodor W. Adorno, "Verfremdetes Hauptwerk: Zur Missa Solemnis," in *Gesammelte Schriften*, vol. 17 (Berlin: Suhrkamp, 2003), 151; Theodor W. Adorno, "Alienated Masterpiece: *Missa Solemnis*," in *Essays on Music*, trans. Susan H. Gillespie (Berkeley: University of California Press, 2002), 574.

7. William Blake, *The Marriage of Heaven and Hell* (Boston: J. W. Luce, 1906), 10. Emphasis added.

8. Kramer, "Seeking Enlightenment," 190.

9. Jonas Barish, *The Antitheatrical Prejudice* (Berkeley: University of California Press, 1981), 1–2.

10. For a contrasting approach to the opera "as the product of a specific historical moment," that is, the year 1791, see, for example, Austin Glatthorn, "*The Magic Flute* in 1791," in *CCMF*, 61. Yet this moment has a history, and Mozart's interaction with it necessarily remains open to interpretation. Activity from that year could set into relief the distinctiveness of *The Magic Flute*, as when Martin Nedbal notes how out of place the opera is in a suburban operatic culture that served up more farcical, ribald entertainments. Nedbal, *Morality and Viennese Opera in the Age of Mozart and Beethoven* (London: Routledge, 2017), 125.

11. R. J. W. Evans, *The Making of the Habsburg Monarchy, 1550–1700: An Interpretation* (New York: Oxford University Press, 1979), 345.

12. Ibid., 442, 443. Charles Rosen identifies another model for the opera in Carlo Gozzi's *Fiabe teatrali*. See *The Classical Style: Haydn, Mozart, Beethoven*, expanded ed. (New York: W. W. Norton, 1997), 318.

13. Evans, *The Making of the Habsburg Monarchy*, 443.

14. Immanuel Kant, *Religion Within the Boundaries of Mere Reason and Other Writings*, trans. and ed. George di Giovanni and Allen Wood (New York and Cambridge: Cambridge University Press, 1998), 190. Emphasis in original. Kant introduces his theory of radical evil in Part 1.

15. Kramer, "Seeking Enlightenment," 188.

16. Oswald Bayer, *A Contemporary in Dissent: Johann Georg Hamann as Radical Enlightener* (New York: Eerdmans, 2012), 86.

17. Kramer, "Seeking Enlightenment," 192.

18. Bayer, *A Contemporary in Dissent*, xii.

19. Emmanuel Schikaneder, *Die Zauberflöte: Eine große Oper in zwey Aufzügen* (Vienna: Alberti, 1791), Act 2, scene 1; Act 2, scene 30. All subsequent references to the libretto are from this edition.

20. Rosen, *The Classical Style*, 320.

21. Kramer, "Seeking Enlightenment," 190.

22. Mozart's autograph also shows some indecision at this point, although it does not seem related to vocal texture. He considered setting repeat signs around the March instead of writing it out the second time. I am grateful to Miguel Arango Calle for sharing this information about the autograph.

23. [Ignaz Ferdinand Arnold], *Mozarts Geist: Seine kurze Biographie und ästhetische Darstellung seiner Werke. Ein Bildungsbuch für junge Tonkünstler. Mit dessen Portrait* (Erfurt: Hennings, 1803), 271–72. All translations are my own unless otherwise indicated.

24. Ibid., 272.

25. Kramer, "Seeking Enlightenment," 195 (his emphasis).

26. Jane K. Brown, "'The Monstrous Rights of the Present': Goethe and the Humanity of *Die Zauberflöte*," *Opera Quarterly* 28/1–2 (2012): 8.

27. Edmund J. Goehring, "The Sentimental Muse of *Opera Buffa*," in *Opera Buffa in Mozart's Vienna*, ed. Mary Kathleen Hunter and James Webster (New York and Cambridge: Cambridge University Press, 1997), 115–45.

28. In musicological circles, it is common to view sensibility as an irrational cult that overwhelmed eighteenth-century culture, including in Austria. It is striking, then, to read in Evans's essay that Austria *isolated* itself "from *Sturm und Drang*, the cult of sensibility, and their derivatives," an isolation, further, that "yielded bitter [political] fruit" by the early nineteenth century. See R. J. W. Evans, "Culture and Authority in Central Europe, 1683–1806," in *Austria, Hungary, and the Habsburgs: Essays on Central Europe, c. 1683–1867* (New York and Oxford: Oxford University Press, 2006), 74. How Mozart's responses to sensibility as an ethic and musical style relate to sensibility as a cultural and political phenomenon awaits explication.

29. Matthew Head, "Birdsong and Hieroglyphs: Exoticism and Enlightened Orientalism in *The Magic Flute*," in *CCMF*, 204. Head adds that Tamino "reports *forensically* on the sensations of love and imagines an ecstatic union with his beloved" (emphasis added). "Forensically" is at once too Gothic and too chaste, as if an abstract, idealized response would be purer, more authentic.

30. For example, Mark Ferraguto states that "Ach, ich fühl's" "exemplifies an aria type associated with sentimental heroines in distress." Ferraguto, "Musical Topics, Quotations, and References," in *CCMF*, 134.

31. Yuval Sharon's 2025 production of *Così fan tutte* at the Detroit Opera House brought out this mechanistic quality in his staging of "Vorrei dir."

32. William R. Braun, "Measures of Greatness," *Opera News*, December 2013, 20. For a rich defense of "Ach, ich fühl's" as a *siciliana* lamentation, see Mítia D'Acol, "Constructing Pamina's 'Ach, ich fühl's' as a siciliana Lament," in *Mozart in Salzburg and Beyond: New Perspectives*, ed. Simon P. Keefe (Ann Arbor, MI: Steglein Publishing, 2025), 269–98.

33. Gottfried Weber, "Ein Zweifel," *Allgemeine musikalische Zeitung* 17 (12 April 1815): col. 248. I am grateful to Margaret Cormier for pointing out Weber's commentary.

34. Ibid., col. 248. Braun discusses some modern-day variations in tempo and their implication for character and affect in "Measures of Greatness," 21 (right-side column).

35. Nicholas Till has argued that "Mozart virtually dispensed with sonata form in *Die Zauberflöte*," and it is easy to concede his point. Some of the ensembles, not to mention the opera as a whole, are patently episodic, a quality that runs contrary to sonata form's more integrated, goal-oriented, event-driven character. Concomitantly, a distinguishing feature of full-blown sonatas—that transitional material is made thematic—is often absent from many of the opera's ensembles. Mozart is generally content to use simple formulas to move from one section to the next, as in mm. 33–34 and 77–80 of the first-act quintet. Even so, *The Magic Flute* does not forsake sonata form. If the overture is the most obvious exception, both Tamino's and especially Pamina's arias count as subtler and imaginative engagements with sonata principles. Nicholas Till, *Mozart and the Enlightenment: Truth, Virtue, and Beauty in Mozart's Operas* (New York: W. W. Norton,

1993), 270. On the limitations of sonata form as a means of organizing the music of *The Magic Flute*, see Nicholas Marston, "'All Together, Now'?: Ensembles and Choruses in *The Magic Flute*," in *CCMF*, 119–31. Especially trenchant is his critique of the first-act quintet as a sonata form, 122–24.

36. Kramer, "Seeking Enlightenment," 195.

37. Hayden White, *Metahistory: The Historical Imagination in Nineteenth-Century Europe* (Baltimore: Johns Hopkins University Press, 1973), 52.

38. Ibid., 58; Kramer, "Seeking Enlightenment," 188. Emphasis in both original.

39. Kant's main pronouncement on tragedy comes in "On the Common Saying: 'That May Be True in Theory but It Does not Apply in Practice,'" in *Political Writings*, ed. Hans Reiss (New York and Cambridge: Cambridge University Press, 1991), 88. Voltaire gives an example of how rationalism looks as theater criticism in his "Dissertation sur la tragédie Ancienne et Moderne," in *La tragédie de Sémiramis, et quelques autres piéces de littérature* (Paris: Mercier, 1749), 1–34. For example, he judges his own five-act tragedy *Sémiramis* (1748) against *Oedipus Rex* almost entirely according to their respective maxims.

40. Frankfurt and Leipzig, 1780. In 1785, Cremeri had it republished in Linz under the title *Fromme Wünsche eine ächte Schaubühne und würdige Schauspieler für dieselbe zu bekommen*.

41. Christian Gottlob Klemm, *Dramaturgie, Litteratur und Sitten* (Vienna: Kurzbeck, 1769), 590.

42. Schiller, however, made just this case in his remarkable speech, given before the Deutsche Gesellschaft in 1784, titled "The Theatre Considered as a Moral Institution" ("Die Schaubühne als eine moralische Anstalt betrachtet").

43. "Das Weib . . . hofft durch Blendwerk und Aberglauben das Volk zu berücken" (Act 2, scene 1).

44. Johann Christian Lünig, *Theatrum Ceremoniale Historico=Politicum, oder Historisch=und Politischer Schau=Platz Aller Ceremonien*, vol. 1 (Leipzig: Widmann, 1719), 12. Translated in Evans, "Culture and Authority," 57.

45. Here is Kramer's version of that question: "What view of Enlightenment is conveyed in Mozart's music and Schikaneder's libretto, and how does this view accord with those strains of thought and expression, of wit and sensibility, that we take to constitute the defining aura of the Enlightenment?" "Seeking Enlightenment," 187.

46. Julian Rushton, "Music as Stagecraft," in *CCMF*, 90.

47. The entryway into Sarastro's realm makes quite a different impression on Tamino, as he says that its gates show "*dass Klugheit und Arbeit und Künste hier weilen*"—"that intelligence, labor, and craft dwell here" (Act 1, scene 15). Sarastro's realm is verbal, practical, geometric, tactile.

48. Rosen, *The Classical Style*, 289.

49. Jacques Barzun, "Why Opera?," *Opera News*, 28 January 1967, 10.

50. Rosen, *The Classical Style*, 319.

51. [Arnold], *Mozarts Geist*, 270. See also Waldoff, who goes further than Arnold by linking musical economy to intimacy of character: "Mozart creates a sense of affective immediacy by having Tamino begin without any preamble from the orchestra." Jessica Waldoff, "Pamina, the Queen, and the Representation of Women," in *CCMF*, 238.

52. Laurence Dreyfus, "The Hermeneutics of Lament: A Neglected Paradigm in a Mozartian 'Trauermusik,'" *Music Analysis* 10/3 (October 1991): 330–31.

53. See Rosen, *The Classical Style*, 319.

54. Dreyfus, "The Hermeneutics of Lament," 330.

55. [Arnold], *Mozarts Geist*, 281–82. His emphasis. In personal correspondence, Bruce Alan Brown suggested that Arnold's "*Bestimmheit des Karakters*" (distinctiveness of character) was related to his criticism of Gluck and Handel for their overreliance on recycled music, hence my insertion of the modifier "musical" into the translation. I assume that

Arnold's use of "*edle Einfalt*" (noble simplicity) is deliberate and polemical, meant to crown Mozart instead of Gluck as Winckelmann's true musical inheritor.

56. Ibid., 282–83.

57. Evans, "Culture and Authority," 74.

58. Cremeri, *Eine Bille*, 76.

59. Goldoni inveighs against the Don Juan legend in his preface to *Don Giovanni Tenorio* (1736), in volume 9 of *Tutte le opere di Carlo Goldoni*, ed. Giuseppe Ortolani (Verona: Mondadori, 1950), 215–18. On Richardson and the romance, see John Mullan, *Sentiment and Sociability: The Language of Feeling in the Eighteenth Century* (New York and Oxford: Oxford University Press, 1988), 58.

60. On the creative aspect of myth, see especially Hans Joas, *The Creativity of Action*, trans. Jeremy Gaines and Paul Keast (Cambridge: Polity Press, 1996), 73.

61. Johann Georg Hamann, "Metacritique on the Purism of Reason," in *Hamann: Writings on Philosophy and Language*, ed. Kenneth Haynes (Cambridge: Cambridge University Press, 2007), 211. Hamann is quoting, among other places, from Kant's *Critique of Pure Reason*, A20, B34.

62. Eco, "A Reading of the *Paradiso*," 20.

Seduction and the (Mis)Representation of Love in Mozart's Da Ponte Operas

JESSICA WALDOFF

In Mozart's Da Ponte operas, seduction is both a subversive element and a prominent feature of the opera's imbroglio. The seducer—whether a practiced libertine like Don Giovanni or a student at Don Alfonso's "scuola degli amanti"—attempts to present himself as a lover, drawing on an established language of love and its conventions of courting. The ruse is likely to succeed if the seducer's "inamorata" is impressionable and relatively unfamiliar with the world. The seduction scene, then, transforms a moment of amorous declaration and newly formed intimacy into a locus of deception and danger. In a genre—opera buffa—that celebrates the social benefits of love and marriage, seduction is a disruptive and potentially destructive force. It develops episodes involving "wrong" couples that will have to be worked out later and raises questions about the possibility of fidelity and the nature of love.

The prominence of seduction in Mozart and Da Ponte's collaborations perhaps explains why *Le nozze di Figaro*, *Don Giovanni*, and *Così fan tutte* have sometimes been considered a trilogy, even though they were certainly not conceived as such. Each of these operas is centered on the threat seduction poses. In *Figaro*, the Count's desire to seduce Susanna underlies much of the action, thereby creating both the central problem Figaro and Susanna must overcome in order to marry and the principal reason the Countess must conspire with her servants to win back her husband's affection. In *Don Giovanni*, seduction is, famously, the protagonist's principal occupation; and, whatever his other crimes, it is his attempt to seduce—or force—Donna Anna that sets the main plot in motion. (His subsequent attempts to seduce Zerlina and Donna Elvira drive much of Acts 1 and 2, respectively.) In *Così*, seduction may even be regarded as the opera's *raison d'être*—it is the method Don Alfonso employs to prove his case that there is no fidelity in women.

The best known of all Mozart's seduction moments is surely the duet "Là ci darem la mano" (No. 7) in which Don Giovanni proposes "marriage" to the peasant girl Zerlina. Having chanced upon the wedding of Masetto and Zerlina (Act 1, scene 5), Don Giovanni sets his sights on the bride. With Leporello's help, he is soon alone with her making his case to take the bridegroom's place with obvious double entendre: "Orsù non perdiam tempo; in questo istante io vi voglio sposar" (Come, let's not waste time; I want to marry you right now).[1] As Don Giovanni and everyone in the audience knows, he has no intention of leading her to the altar, only as far as the "*casinetto*" he mentions as a place where they can be together. At the beginning of the duet, Don Giovanni requests Zerlina's hand in an eloquent declaration set to a beautiful melody in A major, a key often associated with love in the operas of Mozart and his contemporaries. Don Giovanni's text develops the double meaning of the recitative's marriage proposal—"Là ci darem la mano, / Là mi dirai di sì" (There we will join hands, / There you will tell me yes)—but the music (Andante in 2/4) implies a new level of emotional intimacy. The characters move from independent statements through dialogue until the moment of Zerlina's acquiescence (on "Andiam") ushers in a second tempo (Allegro in 6/8) in which the "lovers," now in agreement, sing the same text and tune *a due* in celebration of their anticipated union.

It has become commonplace over the last century to call this duet and others in Mozart's Da Ponte operas—"Crudel! perchè finora" (No. 17) in *Figaro* and "Il core vi dono" (No. 23) and "Fra gli amplessi" (No. 29) in *Così*—"seduction duets." The exact origin of this label is unknown, but Alfred Einstein uses it to describe "Là ci darem la mano" as early as 1941, and its repetition in a significant number of commentaries and studies suggests that the seduction duet was already considered a recognizable type before Richard Stiefel codified this point of view in his 1983 essay "Mozart's Seductions."[2] The seduction-duet typology invites us to think of these duets as a group, to look for ways they resemble each other, to imagine that one may be modeled on another, and so on.[3] The fact that these duets share dramatic and musical features has led many to ask whether Mozart and Da Ponte are doing something special here. At the same time, when we consider the so-called seduction duets as a separate group (as the label invites us to), we unwittingly separate them from the duet type on which they were modeled and which we need to have in mind in order to understand them, namely the love duet.

A type well known to Mozart's first audiences, the love duet provided the formal framework and much of the poetic and musical language Da Ponte and Mozart drew on to create six seduction scenes in four operas:

La villanella rapita, *Figaro*, *Don Giovanni*, and *Così*. These seduction ensembles are indeed unusual, even when viewed in the context of the larger repertoire with which they shared the stage. To understand why that is, I believe they need to be considered in the broader context of the conventions of love duets and lovemaking in the operas of Mozart and his contemporaries. This is the subject of my essay. After all, seduction depends on the ability of the seducer to play the role of the lover persuasively. For Mozart and Da Ponte, this means the ability to adapt the love duet to a new purpose. The counterfeit version might approximate, adapt, or distort the expected form, but its deception creates a disturbing dramatic irony. The love duet was a recognizable convention that engendered trust: a familiar form that dignified and validated the professions of feeling it inspired and with its private celebration of love pointed toward the public confirmation of human affection in society that the ending of the opera would eventually bring. In contrast, the "pretend" love duet exploits this convention to achieve a false union of hearts, creating plot complications that will have to be resolved before the opera can reach its happy ending. The introduction of a "pretend" love duet raises questions about the fate of the real lovers, about the possibility of genuine feeling, and about whether the moral and social order upheld elsewhere in the opera (and in opera of this period more generally) will be affirmed or controverted in the end.

The Love Duet in Mozart's Operas and Mozart's Vienna

By the time Mozart and Da Ponte met in 1783, the love duet was a familiar convention with a long history. In opera seria of earlier decades (reaching back to the first half of the century), this duet for noble lovers was frequently the only ensemble in a three-act work and often served as the conclusion to the first or second act. Mozart's A-major duet "Vanne a regnar ben mio" (No. 7) for Elisa and Aminta, which concludes the first act of *Il re pastore* (Salzburg, 1775), provides one example. It is the only duet included in this two-act Metastasian "serenade" in the seria style. In Goldoni's paradigmatic structure for Italian comic opera, the love duet is given pride of place in Act 3 as the penultimate number before the final chorus. The recitative and duet "Dove mai son! . . . Tu mi lasci?" (No. 27) for Count Belfiore and Sandrina in Mozart's *La finta giardiniera* (Munich, 1775) is a case in point. This extended love duet, which forms the center of musical interest in the short third act, serves as a dramatic climax and follows the usual Goldonian design. In *Singspiele*, love duets were also included and followed similar conventions. The recitative and duet "Welch ein Geschick! . . . Meinetwegen sollst du sterben!" (No. 20) for Constanze and Belmonte in *Die Entführung aus dem Serail* (Vienna, 1782) appears in the usual position in Act 3 just before the denouement and final vaudeville.

The love duet provided a private moment for an opera's central pair of lovers that was essential to the plot and—just as important—essential to the pleasure of opera. The effectiveness of this scene depended on its dramatic and musical trajectory, which moved inevitably from independent statements and dialogue toward a celebratory moment in which the lovers sing the same text (marked "a2" in the libretto) in an *a due* texture (homophonic thirds and sixths). This intimate moment where two voices become one served as a musical representation of the lovers' union of hearts and was often marked by a new tempo and meter as well as by other signs of operatic elation. Mozart's expansive second tempo in "Vanne a regnar ben mio" offers a perfect illustration. The move from the first tempo (Andante) to the second (Allegro) at measure 37 marks the initial shift from dialogue to a joyous *a due* as the lovers come together for the first time (mm. 38–69). Following a re-composition of earlier material, Mozart heightens the pleasure of the final *a due* section by preceding it with a sudden and disturbing arrival on ♭VI (F in the key of A major) at measure 95, *forte*, on the dark thought "Ah che crudel timor!" (Ah, what cruel fear!), before quickly restoring the tonic. The second *a due* (mm. 98–163) is twice as long as the first and even more exultant. As Daniel Heartz points out, Mozart captures the exuberance of the lovers in a procedure he also employs in other love duets: "Having one voice hold a pedal while the other embroiders, then reversing roles."[4]

Love duets did not follow a single formula, of course, and in operas of different genres—seria, buffa, and *Singspiel*—they were created to suit different characters, singers, and situations. Like the operas for which they were written, they vary in length, musical style, complexity, placement, and so on.[5] Nonetheless, audiences were sure to recognize the love duet and its role. A list of Mozart's love duets in the years leading up to *Figaro*, included in Table 1, illustrates this point. He composed them for every genre. Mozart chose the key of A major, whose association with love is well known, more frequently than any other.[6] With two exceptions, "Meine Seele hüpft vor Freuden" (No. 5) for the incomplete *Zaide* (1779–80) and "Spiegarti non poss'io" for the Vienna version of *Idomeneo* (1786), he marked the arrival of the *a due* section with a change of tempo and/or meter. What is distinct and special to the love duet is a combination of dramatic, musical, and formal characteristics. But the dramatic situation is the essential feature that makes it a recognizable type.

Convention dictated that love duets were composed for a pair of socially appropriate and well-matched lovers, a couple whose desired

Table 1. Love Duets in Mozart's Operas before Figaro (1786)

Opera	Librettist	Genre	Premiere	Love duet(s)	Key
Bastien und Bastienne	Weiskern/Schachtner	Singspiel	?Vienna, 1768	"Geh! Herz von Flandern!"	B-flat major
Mitridate, re di Ponto	V. A. Cigna-Santi	Opera seria	Milan, 1770	"Se viver non degg'io"	A major
Lucio Silla	G. De Gamerra	Opera seria	Milan, 1772	"D'elisio in sen m'attendi"	A major
La finta giardiniera	?Petrosellini	Opera buffa	Munich, 1775	"Tu mi lasci?"	B-flat major
Il re pastore	Metastasio	Opera seria	Salzburg, 1775	"Vanne a regnar ben mio"	A major
Zaide (incomplete)	Sebastiani/Schachtner	Singspiel	[none, 1779–80]	"Meine Seele hüpft vor Freuden"	E-flat major
Idomeneo, re di Creta	Metastasio/Varesco	Opera seria	Munich, 1781	"S'io non moro a questi accenti"	A major
Idomeneo (revised)	?G. B. Casti	Opera seria	Vienna, 1786	"Spiegarti non poss'io"	A major
Die Entführung	Bretzner/Stephanie	Singspiel	Vienna, 1782	"Meinetwegen sollst du sterben"	B-flat major
L'oca del Cairo (incomplete)	Varesco	Opera buffa	[none, 1783–84]	"Così si fa" (spoof)	A major

union is destined to be rewarded by the events of the plot. Occurring at a moment before the outcome for these lovers is certain (however inevitable it may seem), the love duet achieves a union of hearts that anticipates and helps to bring about the reconciliation(s) still to come at the end of the opera. In this way, the love duet may be understood to advance the plot in the direction of its ultimate goal, the happy ending, with its attendant pairings common to almost all late eighteenth-century operatic genres, including opera buffa.

Opera buffa was enormously popular in Vienna, as it was elsewhere, but the repertoire that influenced Mozart and Da Ponte's collaborations more than any other was the *opere buffe* brought to the stage by the Italian troupe Joseph II established in Vienna in 1783. In her magisterial study of this repertoire, *The Culture of Opera Buffa in Mozart's Vienna: A Poetics of Entertainment*, Mary Hunter identifies duets as the most frequent form of ensemble in this repertoire, with duets between lovers accounting for about a third of that number (approximately one per opera).[7] She also considers the form and habits of other duets and small ensembles, which share with the love duet a tendency often referred to as the "ensemble principle": characters make individual statements, engage in dialogue in the middle (often a modulatory section), and finally join in a tutti (which can occur whether characters are in a state of agreement, disagreement, or confusion).[8] At the same time, ensembles were becoming increasingly prevalent—*Così* includes more ensembles than arias and *Figaro* almost as many, six of them being duets. Since the love duet now shared the stage with other duets and small ensembles (especially trios) built on the same principles, it was the love duet's dramatic situation more than its musical trajectory that made it distinct and special.

Consideration of the love duet "Pianin pianino" (C major) from Da Ponte and Martín y Soler's *L'arbore di Diana* (1787) leads Hunter to highlight familiar features.[9] In it, Diana surprises the sleeping Endimione, a shepherd for whom she, as goddess of chastity, should not have feelings. Reluctant to reveal herself, Diana initiates the duet with a game of hide-and-seek (the lovers make statements); Diana covers his eyes to continue the game in an exchange (dialogue) that fires their passions (they declaim their different texts homophonically) and leads to the moment of discovery. A "striking modulation" to E-flat major (♭III) on "Apri quei lumi, / Mio bel tesor" marks the moment when she uncovers his eyes and he recognizes her.[10]

DIANA:

Ah che resistere	Ah, I can no longer
Non posso ancor!	Resist.
Apri quei lumi,	Open those eyes,

Mio bel tesor.	My beautiful treasure.
(Qui cava le mani)	*(Here removes her hands)*
ENDIMIONE:	
Cintia!	Cynthia!
DIANA:	
Sì, caro!	Yes, dear!
ENDIMIONE:	
Sogno, o son desto?	Am I dreaming, or awake?
DIANA and ENDIMIONE:	
Deh, fate o Numi,	Oh Gods, grant that
Se un sogno è questo,	If this is a dream,
Che ambi possiamo	We will be able to stay asleep like this
Dormire ognor.	Forever.

In the final *a due* section the pair rejoice, restoring the tonic to sing the same text together in thirds for the first time. The placement of this scene, late in the second act, exemplifies the customary double function of the love duet. The duet's happy ending serves as the culmination of the lovers' story; at the same time, as Mary Hunter points out, the resolution of this plot strand, confirming Diana's transformation from goddess into a woman in love, makes possible the opera's denouement and conclusion.[11]

This situation in which the reconciliation achieved in the love duet aligns with and makes possible the larger reconciliation to come at the end of the opera is typical. But what happens when a duet for lovers does not conform to expectations? "Occhietto furbetto" (A major), the first love duet in *L'arbore di Diana*, is a case in point. The "lovers" here are Amore (Cupid, a trouser role) and Doristo (a shepherd). Amore is a disrupter in this opera, whose desire to make the chaste Diana and her nymphs fall in love is the central driver of the plot; he considers their chastity an affront. Doristo was chosen to guard the titular Tree of Diana, but he is far too interested in Diana and her nymphs to keep to his task. In the scene leading up to this duet, Amore, dressed as a shepherdess, flirts with Doristo, who steals a kiss. Amore opens the duet by chastising Doristo, but the banter that ensues is highly suggestive:

AMORE:	
Occhietto furbetto,	Roguish little eye,
Che cosa m'hai detto	what do you mean by
Baciandomi qui?	kissing me thus?
DORISTO:	
Se furba tu sei,	If you are clever,
Capire lo dei.	You will understand.
AMORE:	
Capisco, sì, sì.	I do understand, yes.
DORISTO:	
Ebben, che diss'io?	Well, then, what did I say?
AMORE:	
Che sei l'idol mio.	That you are my idol.
DORISTO:	
E poi?	And then?
AMORE:	
Che vorresti . . .	That you would like . . .
DORISTO:	
E poi?	And then?
AMORE:	
Che faresti . . .	That you wanted . . .
AMORE and DORISTO:	
Ah, taci, mio bene,	Ah, stop, my love,
Ah, basta così.	Ah, that's quite enough.

The music is given in Example 1. A second exchange, even more risqué than the first, leads to a reprise of the *a due* section. The entire duet takes only two and a half minutes to perform. In his *Memoirs*, Da Ponte described *L'arbore di Diana* as "voluptuous without overstepping into the lascivious."[12] The presence of the love-duet type here seems to raise the question: When is a love duet not a love duet? Amore and Doristo are not an appropriate match, and their union is not even in question. This intimate scene for two

Example 1. Vicente Martín y Soler, *L'arbore di Diana*, "Occhietto furbetto," Act 1, scene 10, mm. 1–35. Vocal arrangement by Christian Gottlob Neefe, published by Simrock, Bonn, n.d. (ca. 1788).

Example 1. Continued

"lovers" who are clearly taking advantage of each other makes a kind of sport with the love duet that fits this opera's erotic vision of the pastoral.

The presence of "Pianin pianino" and "Occhietto furbetto" in the same opera suggests that the love duet model could be adapted in a broad and unexpected way. While the former is clearly the love duet for the principal couple, the latter appears to take the place of a second love duet for a second couple, something often included in *opere buffe*. The significant deviation with "Occhietto furbetto," of course, is that Amore and Doristo are not a "real" couple. Still, as a standalone number, this A-major duet works perfectly as a love duet. In fact, it was inserted into a 1790 London production of *La villanella rapita* as a duet for the lovers Mandina and Pippo in the usual spot before the conclusion.[13] It was also published separately as the "favorite duet" from this work. Nancy Storace (star of the Viennese stage and the first Susanna in *Figaro*), who created the role of Mandina in this production at the King's Theatre, was probably the source of the insertion though she did not sing the role in Vienna.

Like "Occhietto furbetto," "Là ci darem la mano" is a love duet that also raises the question: When is a love duet not a love duet? It seems that by October of 1787, the month in which both *L'arbore di Diana* and *Don Giovanni* premiered (in Vienna and Prague, respectively), it was possible to adapt the love duet for characters who were not "real" lovers. The connection here is Da Ponte, who wrote both libretti. Just how much license might librettists and composers have felt free to take in composing love duets in opera buffa? To get a sense of the state of affairs at this moment, we can turn to the list of operas that author Johann Pezzl highlighted in the 1787 installment of his guidebook *Skizze von Wien* as the "pieces which have so far received the most general acclaim":[14]

Il barbiere di Seviglia [*sic*] [Paisiello/Petrosellini, 1782; Vienna, 1783]
Fra i due litiganti il terzo gode [Sarti/anon. after Goldoni, 1782; Vienna, 1783]
La grotta di Trofonio [Salieri/Casti, 1785]
Il re Teodoro in Venezia [Paisiello/Casti, 1784]
Una cosa rara, ossia Bellezza ed onestà [Martín y Soler/Da Ponte, 1786]

All five of these operas include duets for lovers, meeting the dramatic expectations of the love-duet convention, and none for "wrong" couples. But several exhibit a flexible approach to the love duet. *Il barbiere di Siviglia*, which features eight ensembles, does not include a free-standing love duet. Instead, the Count and Rosina come together, in the briefest of love duets, at the beginning of the Act 4 finale. *Fra i due litiganti il terzo gode* does not have the expected love duet (a departure from Goldoni's *Le nozze di Dorina*, on which this opera is based). Instead, in Act 3 where the love duet should be, we find a comic trio in A major modeled on the love duet. The lovers Masotto and Dorina come together—quite literally behind the back of Dorina's suitor Titta—in an ensemble brimming with double meaning.[15] *La grotta di Trofonio* includes two love duets for correctly matched couples (one in each act), but allows the magic of the cave, which transforms the personalities of those who enter it, to introduce comic imbroglio into the second of these love duets (in A major) for Artemidoro and Ofelia. In addition, two more duets for the lovers (also colored by the confusion of the cave) are included in the Act 1 finale. In *Il re Teodoro*, Lisetta and Sandrino (who are betrothed) sing a kind of duet with chorus (Act 1, scene 4) that merges the parts of the love duet into a larger form. Curiously, the short duet here, which is entirely *a due*, is in the parallel minor (G minor).

Finally, *Una cosa rara* includes one of the most celebrated love duets of the decade: "Pace, caro io sposo" (Act 2, scene 25) for Lilla and Lubino, the central pair. Lilla is the "rare thing" described by the title of this opera—a woman whose virtue cannot be compromised. The role was created for Nancy Storace, as was the role of Susanna in *Figaro*, which had premiered only months earlier. This brief duet (in C major) reduces each of the customary parts of the love duet to the shortest imaginable unit. The lovers exchange brief statements of affection (mm. 1–8); engage in a dialogue where they complete each other's thoughts (mm. 9–16); and arrive quickly at the *a due* (mm. 17–24). A brief second dialogue leads to a reprise of the *a due* as they (and the audience) imagine the sweet consummation of their love. The *a due* text is strikingly intimate, and the two sing as one (see Example 2):

LUBINO and LILLA:

Vieni, tra i bracci miei,	Come, into my arms,
Stringi, o mio caro ben,	Embrace me, my dearest love,
L'anima mia tu sei,	You are my soul,
Ti vo' morir nel sen.	I want to die on your breast.

Vienna's oft-quoted diarist, Count Zinzendorf, who was not always enthusiastic about what he heard at the opera, seems to have been overwhelmed by this duet. He writes, on 4 December 1786: "The pretty duo between Mandini and Storace was repeated; it is very voluptuous. I left disturbed." On 17 January 1787 he returns to the subject: "I find the duo . . . so tender and expressive that it poses a danger to the young members of the audience. One needs to have had some experience in order to see it with a cool head."[16] Da Ponte reported in his *Memoirs* that this duet "electrified" the audience, and also that Joseph II called for an encore, thus controverting his

Example 2. Vicente Martín y Soler, *Una cosa rara*, "Pace, caro io sposo," Act 2, scene 25, mm. 17–24. Vocal arrangement by C. D. Stegmann, published by Simrock, Bonn, n.d. From John Platoff, "A New History for Martín's *Una cosa rara*."

own decree (made in response to encores for ensembles in *Figaro* earlier in the same season) that numbers for more than one vocalist would not receive encores.[17] Pezzl reports that the opera "took the town by storm" and also that at every performance three to four hundred people had to be turned away.

The variety of approaches here is perhaps surprising. The love duet was ubiquitous, and it was expected; at the same time, it was continually being adapted to a new purpose. The love duet might be included in the finale (as in *Il barbiere* and *Trofonio*); it might be given to the "right" couple at the wrong moment (as in *La grotta*); it might even be turned into a comic trio (as in *Fra i due litiganti*). Other operas provide additional examples: *La scuola degli amanti*, by Salieri and Mazzolà, the inaugural production of Vienna's new Italian company in 1783, includes two duets for "lovers" (married couples), but they are talking past each other; *Il burbero di buon cuore* (1786), by Martín y Soler and Da Ponte, opens with a love duet for Angelica and Valerio that includes a third character (Angelica's maid). At least one earlier opera shows that the love duet could be spoofed: *La fiera di Venezia* (1772), by Salieri and Boccherini, includes a love duet for two mismatched lovers, Duke Ostrogoto and Falsirena (in the traditional spot in Act 3), in which they agree their flirtation is over.[18] In my survey of about twenty operas from this repertoire I naturally found conventional love duets by Salieri, Paisiello, Haydn, and others, but also much variety. I hope this brief discussion is sufficient to offer a glimpse of an expanding and shifting role for the love duet in opera buffa.

Mozart's "seduction" ensembles in the Da Ponte operas were clearly conceived as a part of this continuum. But Mozart and Da Ponte subverted the convention in a way not witnessed in the operas of their contemporaries. They appropriated the love duet to serve the needs of seducers and deceivers, and in so doing imbued its musical and dramatic trajectory with a painful dramatic irony. In the moment, these counterfeit love duets enact a very real musical drama, giving them emotional weight and prominence. Mozart thus transformed the love duet into a locus of danger. This contradiction lies at the heart of Mozart's seduction scenes. We need to understand how the "seduction" duet is modeled on the love-duet type to fully understand its subversive power.

Adaptations of the Love Duet in *La villanella rapita* and *Le nozze di Figaro*

In November 1785, Mozart and Da Ponte created their first counterfeit love duet for a mismatched or "wrong" couple. The scenes leading up to this moment on stage might seem familiar. A nobleman and his companion arrive in a country village just in time for a wedding. Infatuated with the bride, the nobleman insults the bridegroom, and soon manages to be alone with the country girl to plead his case: "I cannot live without you."[19] This may sound like *Don Giovanni*, but it describes the early scenes of *La villanella rapita* by Francesco Bianchi and Giovanni Bertati (Venice, 1783), which premiered at the Burgtheater on 25 November 1785. Mozart composed two insertion ensembles for the Viennese production: a trio (K. 480) for Act 1, a number clearly modeled on the love duet, and a quartet (K. 479) for Act 2. Both ensembles were included in the original Viennese libretto (the trio, completed just four days before the premiere, appears at the end as a late addition) and Mozart is named as the author of the music.[20] The author of the text is not named, but is generally assumed to be Da Ponte since additions and adaptations for the Italian company were part of his remit as the official theater poet.

The trio "Mandina amabile" for *La villanella rapita* clearly borrows the form and emotional intensity of the love duet to develop the relationship between the Count and Mandina in its first half (Andante); Mandina's fiancé Pippo then shows up for the second half (Allegro), which is a trio for the opera's love triangle.[21] The Count (sung by Vincenzo Calvesi, for whom Mozart would later create the role of Ferrando in *Così*) is in love with Mandina, who is engaged to Pippo (an appropriate match). As the Count explains to his friend Paolino, he loves Mandina and cannot allow her to marry another. He speaks words of love to Mandina, asking her to live with him, while carefully dissembling what the terms of that arrangement might be. He offers her a purse (of money), which Mandina naïvely understands as a gift. Later in Act 1, when it becomes clear she does not understand his intention, the Count plies the wedding guests with doctored wine and abducts her. Over the course of Act 2, Mandina is recovered unharmed, and the original lovers are reunited. It is impossible to defend the Count's behavior, which fits the model of the rakish seducer; still, despite his deception, he is portrayed as a man in love. The opera characterizes him as overwhelmed by passion and confident in his privilege. This type of plot in which a young nobleman pursues a woman beneath his station whom he does not intend to marry did not always end well for her in sentimental novels of this period, but all is resolved happily at the end of *La villanella rapita*. The opera received eight performances in Vienna (from November through February) and Mozart's ensembles found a wider audience.[22]

"Mandina amabile" (in A major) opens as a love duet in which both text and music are carefully composed to preserve the double nature of the scene. The Count and Mandina grow closer even as they willfully misunderstand each other. Here is the text:

IL CONTE:

(Il Conte cava di tasca una borsa e la da a Mandina)	*(The Count takes a purse from his pocket and gives it to Mandina)*
Mandina amabile,	Charming Mandina,
Questo denaro,	This money,
Prendilo, tientilo,	Take it, keep it,
Tutto per te.	All for yourself.

MANDINA:

Oh come siete (Mandina prende la borsa)	Oh, how dear *(Mandina takes the purse)*
Grazioso e caro,	And kind you are,
Quante monete,	So much money,
Tutto per me?	All for me?

IL CONTE:

La mano porgimi	Give me your hand
D'amore in pegno.	As a pledge of love.

MANDINA:

Ecco, servitevi,	Here it is, help yourself,
(gli da la mano)	*(gives him her hand)*
Ve la consegno.	I give it to you.

IL CONTE and MANDINA:

Oh che contento,	Oh what happiness
In cor mi sento!	I feel in my heart!
Più dolce giubilo	There is no sweeter joy
Per me non v'è.	For me.

In opening musical statements of equal length, the Count presents his gift, which Mandina gratefully accepts (mm. 1–30). In the dialogue section, Mandina questions whether this money can really be all for her (in the dominant) and receives repeated assurances from the Count. Once this point is settled, the Count makes his real request: "La mano porgimi / D'amore in pegno," at measure 47 (see Example 3). Mandina acquiesces immediately, although a slight tinge of chromaticism on "*servitevi*" seems to betray momentary discomfort. The *a due* section now begins in the tonic (at measure 60) and continues for sixty measures. As the "lovers" celebrate their happiness in homophonic thirds, Mozart's music suggests an affinity between these characters that goes far beyond what is socially appropriate and certainly beyond what Mandina acknowledges in words.[23] A brief recapitulation of the earlier "Quante monete" exchange provides a reason for the reprise of the initial *a due* at measure 93.

This intimacy is not lost on Pippo, who now steps forward:

PIPPO:

Eccellenza, seguitate,	Your excellency, please continue,
Io già so, che voi lo fate	I know well that you are acting
Per bontà, per amicizia.	Out of kindness, out of friendship.
Qui non c'entra la malizia,	Malice has nothing to do with it,
Oh non c'entra, Signor, nò.	Oh no, nothing to do with it, Sir, no.

Pippo turns the duet into a trio, moving from Andante (3/8) to Allegro (C), prompted by a shift in poetic meter, and turning A major to A minor. The ensemble shifts to one of accusations and confusion. Pippo, whose

Example 3. Mozart, "Mandina amabile," K. 480, insertion ensemble composed for the Viennese production of Francesco Bianchi's *La villanella rapita*, mm. 47–68. Vocal arrangement from *Mozartschen Arien* (Leipzig: Breitkopf und Härtel, 1804).

Example 3. Continued

musical lines are blustering and repetitive, has every right to be angry, and Mozart allows him to make an impact by accompanying his initial statement with the sudden forte arrival of the full orchestra, including all the winds—flutes, oboes, clarinets, bassoons, and horns. (See Example 4.) Accents on offbeats emphasize the C♮ that marks the key of A minor, and even after the others restore the key of A major (at their entrance), Pippo returns to this C♮ repeatedly (with orchestral emphasis) as Mozart makes something of a game of reharmonizing it without restoring the minor key. In the final tutti of this trio, the characters cannot sing the same text since they are not in agreement. The harmonious expression of joy sung *a due* by the Count and Mandina earlier and this simultaneous stalemate at the end of the trio in which all three characters declaim their different texts to different musical lines *sotto voce* make for a striking contrast.

With its internal love duet, "Mandina amabile" strongly implies the possibility of romance between the Count and Mandina, developing this affinity well beyond the recitative (Act 1, scenes 12–13) that this trio replaced. While it is true that Mandina never expresses any unequivocal words of affection for the Count, nor any inclination to leave Pippo, the music makes it difficult to resist the impression that the Count and Mandina share a special understanding in this moment, even if it is not destined to be rewarded by the plot. The fantasy that a country girl might marry "up" was a favorite theme in literature, although on the opera buffa stage the girl in question was usually revealed in the end to be a long lost

Example 4. Mozart, "Mandina amabile," K. 480, insertion ensemble composed for the Viennese production of Francesco Bianchi's *La villanella rapita*, mm. 114–19. From *NMA* II/7/3.

Example 4. Continued

(or disguised) member of a noble family.[24] In *La villanella rapita*, Mozart breathed life into this fantasy by harnessing the power of the love duet.

"Crudel! perchè finora," the duet Mozart composed for the Count and Susanna in Act 3 of *Figaro*, which premiered 1 May 1786, adapts the form of the love duet in a completely different way. Whatever the Count's feelings, as a married man he can hardly play the honorable lover. Susanna is fully aware of his intentions and has agreed to deceive him at the request of his wife. She plays her part with obvious discomfort. The situation here, therefore, dramatizes a shared experience from two points of view. The Count opens the duet in a state of disbelief: "Crudel! perchè finora / Farmi languir così?" (Cruel one! Why have you let me languish like this until now?). He is not quite able to accept her assertion in the recitative immediately preceding that, after refusing for so long, she is now willing to acquiesce to his wishes. It is surely for this reason that the duet opens in A minor, not the parallel key of A major so often associated with love duets. Susanna responds in the relative major (C major), attempting an explanation: "Signor, la donna ognora / Tempo ha dir di sì" (Signor, a woman always needs time before she says yes). In the question-and-answer passage that follows, however, the Count restores A minor until his doubts are allayed by Susanna's repeated insistence that she will keep their rendezvous.[25] His effusion of joy at the moment he is persuaded she is in earnest is represented in the music by a striking shift to A major and a soaring new melody at the words "Mi sento dal contento." (See Example 5.) Da Ponte's verse clearly indicates "a2" in the libretto.

COUNT:	
Mi sento dal contento	I feel such happiness,
Pieno di gioia il cor.	My heart is filled with joy.
SUSANNA:	
Scusatemi se mento,	Forgive my deception,
Voi che intendete amor.	You who understand love.

The expected *a due* confirmation of apparent affection is problematized here by the fact that Susanna sings her own text (an aside) to a different musical line. In a reprise of the question-and-answer section from the first part of the duet, the Count returns to his questions, and, in her anxiety, Susanna slips up twice, giving him "wrong" answers (at mm. 45 and 51) and then quickly corrects herself. In the second *a due* at measure 54, Susanna dissembles a little better while still indicating her reluctance. She maintains her text, but she takes the Count's "Mi sento" tune, delaying the *a due* texture for as long as she can (until measure 61).

As Daniel Heartz suggests, "Crudel! perché finora" is the "closest thing to a love duet in the opera."[26] The ways in which this duet approximates the form of—but ultimately fails to work as—a love duet are crucial to its dramatic efficacy. The framework of the love duet is familiar enough to assuage the Count's disbelief but sufficiently flawed to indicate Susanna's discomfort. Indeed, the manipulation of the form almost invites us to

Example 5. Mozart, *Le nozze di Figaro*, "Crudel! perchè finora" (No. 17), mm. 29–36. From Bärenreiter vocal score based on *NMA*.

believe that the singing characters are as much aware of the love-duet convention as members of the audience. The Count wants to share this illicit, intimate moment with Susanna—a foretaste of the imagined moment to come in the garden; Susanna does not want to share the intimacy of a love duet with anyone but Figaro. This duet's complex dramatic irony depends on its problematic approximation of the love-duet type.

In a fascinating but little-known turn of events, Susanna was able to sing this duet with Figaro a few years later when it was inserted into a 1789 pasticcio adaptation of Giuseppe Gazzaniga's *La vendemmia* at the King's Theatre in London. The production featured Nancy Storace (the first Susanna) and Francesco Benucci (the first Figaro), one of whom must have suggested how well the duet would fit into Act 2, scene 4.[27] Benucci played an adventurer named Count Zefiro and Storace an apparent country girl named Agatina. The duet was encored and received praise in the press. This was apparently the first excerpt from a Mozart opera performed on the London stage. The duet was published a year later as "A Favorite Duett . . . sung in the Comic Opera of La Vendemmia . . . by Sig^{r} Benucci & Sig^{ra} Storace."[28]

The Seducer's Command of the Love Duet: *Don Giovanni*

Don Giovanni is described in the *dramatis personae* of the original libretto as "an extremely licentious young nobleman," but that hardly seems an adequate description of Da Ponte and Mozart's elusive, inscrutable version of the legendary Don Juan figure. He is an enigma. As Bernard Williams writes in a now classic essay, "We have no sense of what he is like when he is by himself. He is presented always in action—the action, notoriously of a seducer."[29] Don Giovanni reads people and situations with remarkable acuity and seems to possess the ability to reinvent himself at a moment's notice, adapting his behavior to achieve his goal. In the opera's Introduzione, he is masked, attempting to escape from Donna Anna. She speaks first: "Do not hope, unless you kill me, that I will ever let you escape." Taking her melody, he replies: "Foolish woman! You scream in vain! You shall not know who I am." In the exchange that follows, he fashions almost all of his music—and some of his text—from Donna Anna's lines. In the duel with the Commendatore, in his banter with Leporello, and in many other scenes he readily assumes the musical language and form appropriate to the situation. In two scenes where he plays the lover, he adapts the love duet with unparalleled dexterity and precision. And we are tempted here to ask with Edward T. Cone, "Does a vocal persona know that he is singing?"[30] In other words, who is the agent of operatic song? Of course, this complex relationship between the character and the singer is always present in opera, but Don Giovanni often gives the impression of an awareness of musical style and form, as if he is responsible for creating his own music.

Wye Jamison Allanbrook describes "Là ci darem la mano" as "the sweetest imaginable of love duets."[31] Nothing in its musical form or materials spoils its representation of mutual affection. In the recitative immediately before, Don Giovanni tells Zerlina she was not meant to be a peasant, a fiction perfectly designed to support his "marriage" proposal. The duet opens, as we have already seen, with two statements of four lines each. (For an overview of this duet including text and translation, see Table 2.) Don Giovanni requests Zerlina's hand with a melody of exceptional eloquence and beauty; Zerlina responds with a statement of similar length though it betrays her ambivalence: "Vorrei, e non vorrei, / Mi trema un poco il cor." Still, the music reveals all; she is singing his tune. She decorates it with sighs and adapts it in ways that show her hesitation, especially in her repetition of the key phrase, "Ma può burlarmi ancor." He now moves to the dominant at the line "Vieni, mio bel diletto," attempting to overcome her resistance with new entreaties. Her admission "Presto non son più forte," with its slurred sixteenth notes emphasizing half-steps, all within the compass of a minor third, illustrates her indecision. Poised over the dominant, Zerlina's hesitation is already pointing in the direction of Don Giovanni's desire. Don Giovanni takes up her dominant with one last "Vieni" and then restores the tonic. He repeats the lines of his initial statement, now engaging her in dialogue. When he repeats, "Io cangierò tua sorte," she exclaims again that she will not be able to resist much longer ("Presto non son più forte") in another closely written sixteenth-note passage. At last, she relents, responding in the affirmative to his entreaty, "Andiam." She has been won over. In this final section of the duet (Allegro in 6/8), which is marked by a change in tempo, meter, texture, and tune, the pair celebrate their anticipated union by singing *a due* in thirds, sounding like "lovers" for the first time. (See Example 6.) The action is kinetic, unfolding over the course of the duet so that the arrival of the *a due* passage at the second tempo—precisely the moment of greatest dramatic satisfaction—signals the change in situation that was the goal of the number. As Kristi Brown-Montesano suggests, the music's "unpretentious, lilting melody and static harmony serve to reinforce the fantasy of arcadian simplicity"; Don Giovanni's command of a language appropriate for this situation is par for the course.[32] Confirmation of the "lovers'" mutual understanding, if further confirmation is needed, is offered during the duet's postlude by the stage direction indicating they move arm in arm toward the "*casinetto*" Don Giovanni had mentioned earlier ("Vanno verso il casino di Don Giovanni, abbracciati, etc.").[33]

As the opera's reception history shows, this duet quickly became a favorite, and it has inspired the contemplation of larger questions: Zerlina's sensuality (a topic with a rich literature), Don Giovanni's mastery of the conventions of lovemaking, the role of the hand clasp and its later

Table 2. "Là ci darem la mano" (No. 7) from *Don Giovanni*

Mm.	Key	Tempo/Meter	Text	Translation	Main Action
			DON GIOVANNI:		**Statements:**
1	A	**Andante (2/4)**	Là ci darem la mano, Là mi dirai di sì, Vedi, non è lontano, Partiam, ben mio, da qui.	There we will join hands, There you will tell me yes; See, it's not far, Let's go, my dear, from here.	Giovanni makes his overture.
			ZERLINA:		
9			Vorrei, e non vorrei, Mi trema un poco il cor; Felice, è ver, sarei, Ma può burlarmi ancor.	I would like to, and I would not, My heart trembles a little; I would be happy, it's true, But he may yet be tricking me.	Zerlina hesitates, but to his tune.
			DON GIOVANNI:		**Dialogue:**
19	E (V)		Vieni, mio bel diletto;	Come, my beautiful darling!	Giovanni and Zerlina alternate phrases.
			ZERLINA: Mi fa pietà Masetto;	I have pity for Masetto.	
			DON GIOVANNI: Io cangierò tua sorte.	I will change your fate.	
			ZERLINA: Presto non son più forte.	Soon I will no longer be strong.	
30	A (I)		[Repetition of lines]		Dialogue on first theme. Giovanni repeats his initial overture; Zerlina responds, one line at a time, still clinging to the dominant.
47	V7		[Mozart's addition: exchange on "Andiam"]		Fermata.
			DON GIOVANNI and ZERLINA:		
50	A (I)	**Allegro (6/8)**	Andiam, andiam, mio bene, A ristorar le pene D'un innocente amor.	Let's go, let's go, my dearest, To ease the pains Of an innocent love.	***A due*:** Change of tempo, meter, texture; tune suggests a "union" of hearts. Theme here preserves the rising fourth of Giovanni's initial overture.
			(*Vanno verso il casino di Don Giovanni, abbracciati etc.*)	(*They go toward Don Giovanni's house, arm in arm, etc.*)	

Example 6. Mozart, *Don Giovanni*, "Là ci darem la mano" (No. 7), mm. 47–56. From Bärenreiter vocal score based on *NMA*.

significance in the opera, to name just three.[34] It also inspired a host of variations by Beethoven, Chopin, Liszt, and others. These developments may be understood in many ways, but I believe the abiding fascination with this duet stems at least in part from the seductive appeal of its romance in miniature. The duet's union of hearts—the exquisite *a due*—is a moment of unparalleled vicarious emotional pleasure for the audience, even though it is compromised by a disturbing dramatic irony. Unlike Zerlina, we already know that Don Giovanni is a serial seducer—the scoundrel who attacked Donna Anna and abandoned Donna Elvira. And yet, in the moment, Don Giovanni's appropriation of the love-duet form—so perfect in every way—makes it difficult to remember that the union of hearts achieved in this duet is false. Indeed, it is the moment when the danger of the counterfeit love duet is exploited to the fullest. The immediacy of this music overwhelms us, just as it overwhelms Zerlina. This is the mechanism at the heart of its illusion. Here, more than anywhere else in the opera, Mozart allows us to glimpse Don Giovanni's dark virtuosity. The counterfeit love duet is virtually indistinguishable from the genuine. Nothing could better demonstrate how very dangerous he is.

The extraordinary afterlife of "Là ci darem la mano" is too varied and complex a topic to cover here, but it is important to mention its inclusion in a production of *Fra i due litiganti* staged in Udine in 1793.[35] The situation is similar to the insertion of "Crudel! perchè finora" into *La vendemmia* in London. "Là ci darem la mano" was inserted unchanged into a scene in Act 2 for a pair of mismatched lovers, Titta and Dorina (although Titta is a comic character and hardly the suave lover). John Platoff suggests that this insertion was likely proposed by the singer who played Titta, Felice Ponziani. He was the first Leporello in *Don Giovanni* in 1787 in Prague; he also played the title role in *Figaro* (Prague, 1786) and Titta in *Fra i due litiganti*, again with the Prague company.[36] As far as we know, this is the first time any music from *Don Giovanni* was staged in Italy.

Turning now to the Act 2 trio from *Don Giovanni*, "Ah taci, ingiusto core" (No. 15), the special complications attending on the adaptation of the love-duet model are considerable. For starters, this number is a trio; but it opens as a soliloquy, and on Don Giovanni's arrival it appears to Donna Elvira to be a duet. Unlike Zerlina, who narrowly escapes danger, Donna Elvira is a woman already ruined and abandoned by Don Giovanni.[37] But she is also a woman desperately in love. From her perspective, "Ah taci, ingiusto core" unfolds as a love duet with its declarations of affection and attempts to achieve a reconciliation. (For an overview of this ensemble, see Table 3.) Wishing to get Donna Elvira out of the way so that he can approach her maid, Don Giovanni has asked Leporello to woo Donna Elvira in his place. Master and servant have switched cloaks, and both stand under her window, though Don Giovanni remains unseen by Donna Elvira. The Don

Table 3. "Ah taci, ingiusto core" (No. 15) from *Don Giovanni*

Mm.	Key	Tempo/Meter	Text	Main Action
1	A	**Andantino (6/8)**	*Ah taci, ingiusto core*	**Aria?:** Elvira, alone on stage, begins what appears to be an aria. Giovanni and Leporello formulate their plan.
21	E (V)		*Elvira, idolo mio . . .*	**Duet:** Leporello steps forward in Giovanni's cloak and hat. Unseen by Elvira, Giovanni sings her tune back to her as Leporello pantomimes.
36	C (♭III)		*Discendi, o gioia bella*	Moving unexpectedly to C major (♭III), Giovanni sings a courtly plea to a melody he borrows from his serenade, "Deh vieni" (No. 16).
46	modulating		*No, non ti credo*	Elvira exclaims she does not believe him. Giovanni counters that she must or he will kill himself. Elvira falls silent, overcome.
54	A (I)	[*a due*]	*Dei, che cimento è questo!*	Three characters sing their different private thoughts simultaneously to slightly different versions of Elvira's original tune, a problematic approximation of the expected *a due*.

Giovanni who interrupts her private thoughts, then, is a composite of the "Don" she can see (really Leporello in Don Giovanni's cloak), and the familiar voice with its passionate entreaties she can hear. The dialogue of this impromptu love duet is interrupted by the hushed interactions of Don Giovanni and Leporello, which Donna Elvira, at a remove from them on her balcony, apparently cannot hear. (Conveniently, verisimilitude is often a law unto itself in opera buffa.) Mozart distinguishes the two conversations clearly. Don Giovanni responds to Donna Elvira with her own tune, "Elvira, idolo mio," at measure 21, while master and servant address each other before this (and later) with shared musical lines. As she begins to weaken, Don Giovanni introduces a new approach, melody, and key area. The melody is "borrowed" from his upcoming serenade "Deh vieni alla finestra" (No. 16), set to a very similar text, beginning "Discendi, o gioia bella" (at measure 36).[38] (See Examples 7a and 7b.)

In the ensuing dialogue, Donna Elvira exclaims, modulating, that she does not believe him. Don Giovanni counters by threatening to kill himself ("Ah credimi, o m'uccido!"), a stratagem well calculated to affect a woman of her sensibilities. She falls silent for several measures and Mozart includes a stage direction that she is overwrought and almost in tears. Don Giovanni then begs her to join him, restoring the tonic for the final section of this "duet," in which all three participants sing different texts (all asides) in a highly problematic approximation of a concluding *a due*. Donna Elvira does not actually agree to Don Giovanni's request to come down from the balcony during the course of this ensemble, but the vacillation of her concluding lines suggests that she is likely to succumb. Shortly afterwards, she goes off with the "Don," the disguised Leporello.

The role of the "serenade" melody deserves a special word. This imported melody is set apart from the immediate context by its unexpected new key area, C major (♭III), although this key area remains unconfirmed by the key signature throughout this section, perhaps suggesting Don Giovanni's intention to return to A major (and Donna Elvira's tune) as soon as he has achieved his purpose. In the moment, Mozart makes it appear that Don Giovanni is the agent of this borrowing. The serenade "Deh vieni," after all, is an example of stage song (an operatic utterance that the plot requires to be actually sung), so it seems reasonable to understand this serenade tune as part of the seducer's arsenal. It is a prop, like the mandolin with which he later accompanies himself, that Don Giovanni keeps in reserve for such occasions. It will be remembered that Don Giovanni has already tried singing Donna Elvira's melody back to her, without achieving the desired effect. It is perhaps for this reason that he introduces the serenade melody and its new key

a) [Andantino]

b) [Allegretto]

Example 7. Mozart, *Don Giovanni.* a) "Ah taci, ingiusto core" (No. 15), mm. 35–39; b) "Deh vieni alla finestra" (No. 16), mm. 4–8. Both from Bärenreiter vocal score based on *NMA*.

area. This imported melody, then, appears as a musical anticipation; that is, it occurs before the primary exposition of the "borrowed" melody. The presence of this single melody in two contiguous scenes, set to very similar texts and used for exactly the same purpose, tells us something about the character of this music and its role in the drama. Not only does the trio's attempted seduction approximate the form of a love duet, the climactic avowal of feeling at its center is a prefabricated declaration we can safely assume Don Giovanni has used before. The dissonance with the dramatic situation could hardly be stronger: Donna Elvira is deceived again by someone who has already cruelly wronged her. It is no wonder Leporello concludes his portion of the *a due* section with a plea to the gods to protect Donna Elvira from her own credulity: "Deh proteggete, o Dei, / La sua credulità!"

Pretend Love Duets in *Così fan tutte*

The love duet is central to *Così fan tutte* in a way unlike any of Mozart and Da Ponte's previous collaborations. This opera, which premiered on 26 January 1790, develops a familiar theme in comedy whereby fidelity may be tested through playacting and disguise.[39] And this is how we find stalwart lovers Guglielmo and Ferrando, in a significant breach of gentlemanly conduct, each making love to the other's fiancée for the sake of a wager. The mastermind here is Don Alfonso, who sets out not as his counterpart had done in the earlier *La scuola de' gelosi* to restore partners with a wandering eye to each other,[40] but to prove that fidelity in women (which he compares to the mythical Phoenix) does not exist. Guglielmo and Ferrando vehemently disagree. They are not libertines; they are devotees of sentimental culture. It was their ardent protestations of love in the opera's first scene that set Don Alfonso on this path. In the little experiment he sets in motion, Don Alfonso upends the tenets of sentimental culture by setting the immediacy of feeling *against* the vows of constancy it was supposed to engender.[41] Dressed in their absurd disguises, Guglielmo and Ferrando seem like the most contrived and affected of suitors, but the ruse takes on a life of its own when, in intimate scenes for each pair of "lovers," Dorabella succumbs to her relentless Albanian suitor (Guglielmo in disguise) and Fiordiligi to hers (Ferrando in disguise).

"Il core vi dono," the first of these intimate scenes, follows the love-duet model closely. In its opening statements, a slightly reluctant Guglielmo presents Dorabella with a small heart (as a token), asking for hers in return. She replies that while she accepts his gift, her heart is already taken. The ensuing exchange leads to the first *a due* section (at measure 29), which already represents their two hearts beating as one. During a second dialogue section, Dorabella allows Guglielmo to replace Ferrando's miniature with his heart. This is followed by a second, extended *a due* section (at measure 81). Neither shift to the *a due* texture is marked by a change in meter or tempo. Instead, Mozart adapts the love-duet principle to represent stages of the action: following their initial statements in the tonic, the "lovers" engage in dialogue and a first *a due* section in the dominant; the restoration of the tonic is then delayed to the moment at which Dorabella accepts Guglielmo's heart (at measure 60). The second, celebratory, *a due* (at measure 81) confirms the union of the "lovers": "Oh cambio felice / Di cori e d'affetti!" (Oh happy exchange of hearts and affections!). Both before and after this duet, the playacting Guglielmo acknowledges the deception in brief asides: "Infelice Ferrando!" (Unhappy Ferrando!) in the recitative before the duet opens, and "Ferrando meschino! / Possibil non par" (Poor Ferrando, it doesn't seem possible), when, in the course of the duet he remembers his friend again at mm. 63–68. On the second occasion, Mozart emphasizes the moment by giving the return of the opening melody (at measure 69) to a pair of horns that suggest the cuckold's horns Ferrando must now be wearing.

Così's "Fra gli amplessi" is the most complex and difficult of Mozart's adaptations of the love duet. At about six minutes in performance, it is longer, more exceptional in design, and better prepared by the opera's preceding events than any of the other counterfeit love duets we have considered. Ferrando has reached this moment as a result of the wager that set the plot in motion; he is spurred on to make a final attempt to win Fiordiligi because Guglielmo has just succeeded with Dorabella (in "Il core vi dono").[42] We were assured of Ferrando's affection for Dorabella as recently as his cavatina, "Tradito, schernito" (No. 27), in which he insists, despite his rage, that he still loves her. Ferrando may at first have assumed the role of seducer reluctantly, but the events of Act 2 strengthen his resolve and in "Fra gli amplessi" he proves himself to be an able and persuasive suitor. Fiordiligi, for her part, has no idea Ferrando's attentions are a ruse. She has developed feelings for her new admirer but is determined to hide them from him and to remain faithful to Guglielmo, as we know from her rondò "Per pietà" (No. 25). In the recitative immediately preceding "Fra gli amplessi," Fiordiligi imagines the sisters can escape temptation by leaving for the front to join their fiancés.

Even by the standards of the Mozart-Da Ponte operas, this is a rather convoluted situation. Mozart creates a unique version of the love duet to dramatize "Fra gli amplessi," distinguishing the positions of the two characters with special care. (For an overview, see Table 4.) At the center of its extended and complex design is the expected dramatic trajectory of the

Table 4. “Fra gli amplessi” (No. 29) from *Così fan tutte*

Mm.	Key	Meter	Tempo	Text	Main Action
1	A	**Cut time**	**Adagio**	*Fra gli amplessi*	**Aria?:** Fiordiligi, alone on stage initiates what appears to be an aria.
12	E (V)		**con più moto**	*Oh che gioia*	She introduces a new affect.
16	e (v)			*Ed in tanto*	**Interruption/Duet:** Ferrando makes himself known to her, and turns her dominant to minor.
24	[C] (♭III)		**Allegro**	*(-dita!) Deh partite!*	Fiordiligi asks Ferrando to leave, modulating to C major (♭III). The melody and key are borrowed from Ferrando’s “Una bella serenata” melody in No. 3.
40	C			*(-mè!) Son abbastanza*	The key signature finally confirms C major. A first *a due* marks the moment when Fiordiligi’s constancy begins to falter.
57	modulating			*Sorgi, sorgi*	Fiordiligi in distress. Ferrando says give me love or death.
76	A (I)	**3/4**	**Larghetto**	*Volgi a me pietoso*	Ferrando makes his final plea, knowing Fiordiligi can no longer resist. As she relents, Alfonso has to prevent Guglielmo from interrupting.
101	—	**Cut time**	**Andante**	*(par.) Abbracciami*	The pair sing *a due*, signaling their “union” of hearts.

love duet, moving through several tempos, and culminating in an apparent union of hearts represented by an expansive *a due*. But this duet opens in a very curious manner: as an aria for Fiordiligi, and both this private moment and the entire exchange with Ferrando that follows are witnessed by Guglielmo and Don Alfonso, who, according to the stage directions, observe everything from their vantage point in another room. The intimacy we normally associate with love duets is therefore already compromised. The key of A major with its amorous associations is certainly important, though it functions here as an ambiguous signifier. Is it the key of the "aria" Fiordiligi initiates, thus connoting a genuine affection for Guglielmo, or is it the key of Ferrando's aria "Un'aura amorosa" (No. 17), thus suggesting some sort of musical kinship with him at this moment when she has just acknowledged (in the previous recitative) feelings for her new suitor?

From the moment of Ferrando's interruption, this duet presents a mighty struggle: from aria to duet, from A major to the unexpected key of C major (at measure 24), through Ferrando's insistence while brandishing his sword that Fiordiligi should either kill him or yield, to the moment when A major is restored for the Larghetto (m. 76) and Andante (m. 101) where the "lovers" sing *a due* at last. The early parts of the love duet (statements and dialogue) have been adapted and expanded to dramatize this struggle: Ferrando's entrance with its sudden turn to minor (m. 16), the striking musical return of Ferrando's "Una bella serenata" melody from the trio No. 3 (coinciding with the move to C major at measure 24), which leads to a brief first *a due* moment at measure 52 and the ensuing dialogue that forces Fiordiligi's hand during which Ferrando insists that Fiordiligi give him love or death: "Il tuo cor, o la mia morte" at measure 62. Even the Larghetto is approached by deflection: just before the double bar, Fiordiligi prepares the dominant of A minor as she exclaims, "Dei, consiglio!" (Gods, help me!); Ferrando corrects course to A major. The moment when she yields just before the Andante is visually upended by the stage direction: Don Alfonso has to prevent Guglielmo from entering at this point: "Don Alfonso trattiene Guglielmo che vorrebbe uscire." (See Example 8.) The final Andante offers a compelling musical portrait of a union of hearts, but it depends on a deception that we can hardly forget with Guglielmo on the stage.

Much more might be said about this duet, and I have written about it in greater detail elsewhere, but the most important question that needs to be considered here concerns its dramatic effect.[43] In this moment—and others in the second act—we sense with Bernard Williams "the undeniable presence of passion."[44] Even though the libretto tells us that Ferrando is only playing the lover (he gloats in the next scene), this duet has often been

Example 8. Mozart, *Così fan tutte*, "Fra gli amplessi" (No. 29), mm. 101–11. From Bärenreiter vocal score based on *NMA*.

Example 8. Continued

celebrated as the emotional climax of *Così*, the place where the development of amorous feeling is most fully realized.[45] "Fra gli amplessi," it seems, has been received by many as a love duet. And it is not difficult to see why. After over two hours of confused courting, we long to hear a duet that reinforces the affection the opera's scenes and music have seemed to develop. Other factors may influence us as well. As Daniel Heartz points out, the pairing of the voices leads us to privilege this moment: "Fiordiligi belongs with the tenor Ferrando because by all the laws of opera, if not of Heaven, high voices should be paired together."[46] Fiordiligi and Ferrando share an exquisite moment, hard won after one hundred measures and confirmed by the dramatic intensity and musical intimacy of the love-duet form. As we have seen, however, their union of hearts creates a new dramatic problem: it is based on a deception and will not survive the revelations to come in the denouement. Studies of this opera's compositional history, which confirm some ambiguity about which gentleman was originally meant to be paired with which lady, even suggest that Mozart himself wrestled with this problem.[47] At the end of *Così*, we may find ourselves longing for a pair of devoted lovers who transcend the obstacles of the plot to be together, but the opera tells a different story.

"Fra gli amplessi" and "Ah taci, ingiusto core" are by far the most problematic examples of Mozart's counterfeit love duets. Interestingly, they have a great deal in common. I am not the first to make this observation, but it seems newly important in the present context.[48] Both ensembles dramatize a scene in which the lovemaking is false—that is, the gentleman's feelings are not engaged. This falsehood is complicated in both cases by the fact that the lady's feelings *are* engaged. The appearance of sincerity required to win her is therefore painful for the audience.

Both ensembles are in A major; both open as arias (soliloquies, really) for women who do not know they are being observed (and are about to be interrupted); both center on the seducer's use of an imported melody for the purpose of persuasion; and both share the same tonal plan, moving from the tonic of A major to the dominant (E major) and then to the unexpected key of ♭III (C major). Significantly, C major, a distant key, is introduced in each case as something of a surprise and in company with a new melody imported from elsewhere in the opera. In each case, the imported melody is significantly associated with love, though not with love for the lady currently being addressed in this intimate moment. Both "Fra gli amplessi" and "Ah taci, ingiusto core" depend in crucial ways on the conventions of love duets, conventions they deliberately disrupt and with devastating consequences for their respective plots.

Counterfeit Love Duets and the Conventions of Ending

Over the course of this essay I have attempted to demonstrate that the musico-dramatic foundation of Mozart's seduction scenes is the love duet. In terms of their form and structure, these duets are best understood as examples of the love-duet type, some more complex and convoluted than others. In terms of their dramaturgy, however, these ensembles distort the love-duet model in one or more ways: there is a deliberate attempt to deceive, the two "lovers" are wrongly matched, the male seducer enjoys a position of power, and so on. The question remains—is the "seduction" duet a distinct type? My view is that it is not. It is a subversion of the love-duet convention, and that is the source of its dramatic power. Mozart and Da Ponte put the love duet in the service of duplicitous and dangerous situations, placing vulnerable young women at risk in scenes that carry the plot away from its desired goal.

To better understand how Mozart subverted this convention and bearing in mind the immediate operatic context, I have looked at love duets Mozart composed over his entire operatic career. Table 5 provides an overview: "straight" love duets, adaptations of various types, and counterfeit love duets. As we have seen, he composed love duets for operas in every genre. Like his contemporaries, he seems to have regarded the convention as flexible. He created an opening duet for Figaro and Susanna, providing a duet for lovers rather than a love duet *per se*. His opening duet for Sesto and Vitellia in *La clemenza di Tito* merges elements of love and revenge. He created two exquisite love duets within finales: for Figaro and Susanna (in Act 4 of *Figaro*) and Papageno and Papagena (in Act 2 of *Die Zauberflöte*). He also spoofed the love duet in the incomplete *L'oca del Cairo*, as two comic characters mix clichés about the pain of love ("Alas, from the pain I'm already dying") with absurdities ("I have

Table 5. Mozart's Love Duets and Counterfeit Love Duets

Opera	Love Duet(s)	Key	Initial Tempo	Comments
Bastien und Bastienne	"Geh! Herz von Flandern!" (No. 15)	B-flat major	Allegro moderato (2/4)	More than 2 tempos
Mitridate, re di Ponto	"Se viver non degg'io" (No. 18)	A major	Adagio (2/4)	Allegro (C) for *a due*
Lucio Silla	"D'elisio in sen m'attendi" (No. 7)	A major	Andante (3/4)	Molto allegro (C) for *a due*
La finta giardiniera	"Tu mi lasci?" (No. 27)	B-flat major	Adagio (C)	More than 2 tempos
Il re pastore	"Vanne a regnar ben mio" (No. 7)	A major	Andante (3/4)	Allegretto (C) for *a due*
Zaide	"Meine Seele hüpft vor Freuden" (No. 5)	E-flat major	Allegretto ma moderato (6/8)	No new tempo for *a due*
Idomeneo, re di Creta	"S'io non moro a questi accenti" (No. 20a)	A major	Un poco più Andante (C)	Allegretto (3/8) for *a due*
Idomeneo (rev. Vienna)	"Spiegarti non poss'io" (No. 20b)	A major	Larghetto (C)	No new tempo for *a due*
Die Entführung	"Meinetwegen sollst du sterben" (No. 20)	B-flat major	Andante (3/4)	Allegro (C) for *a due*
L'oca del Cairo	"Così si fa" (No. 1)	A major	[Tempo unmarked] (C)	A spoof; tempo given for *a due*
Le nozze di Figaro	"Cinque, dieci, venti, trenta" (No. 1)	G major	Allegro (C)	A duet for lovers; no new tempo for *a due*
	"Pace, pace, mio dolce tesoro" in Act 4 finale	B-flat major	Andante (6/8)	Duet within finale; no new tempo for *a due*
Die Zauberflöte	"Pa-Pa-Pa" in Act 2 finale	G major	[Allegro] (cut time)	Duet within finale; no new tempo for *a due*
La clemenza di Tito	"Come ti piace imponi" (No. 1)	F major	Andante (cut time)	Love duet + revenge; second tempo for *a due*
	"Ah, perdona" (No. 7)	A major	Andante (2/4)	No new tempo for *a due*

Opera	Counterfeit Love Duet(s)	Key	Initial Tempo	Comments
La villanella rapita	"Mandina amabile," K. 480	A major	Andante (3/8)	Love duet turns into trio at the Allegro (C)
Le nozze di Figaro	"Crudel! perchè finora" (No. 17)	A minor/A major	Andante (cut time)	Begins in minor; no second tempo; *a due* problematic
Don Giovanni	"Là ci darem la mano" (No. 7)	A major	Andante (2/4)	Mozart places "Andiam" before *a due*, Allegro (6/8)
	"Ah taci, ingiusto core" (No. 15)	A major	Andantino (6/8)	Begins as an aria; duet for 3 voices; no second tempo
Così fan tutte	"Il core vi dono" (No. 23)	F major	Andante grazioso (3/8)	No new tempo for *a due*
	"Fra gli amplessi" (No. 29)	A major	Adagio (cut time)	Begins as an aria; more than 2 tempos

Note: Only three of Mozart's completed operas omit the love duet altogether: *La finta semplice*, K. 51, *Ascanio in Alba*, K. 111, which does include a trio for the lovers with Alceste, and *Il sogno di Scipione*, K. 126.

ricotta in my heart"). Mozart's counterfeit love duets, as I have shown, adapt the language and form of real ones. All of these duets follow the same general trajectory, and most coordinate the *a due* texture with the arrival of a new tempo and/or a change in meter. (In instances where there is no new tempo for the *a due*, I have indicated this in my table in the comments column.) The two-tempo design is varied at times by the presence of additional tempos, which can indicate a more extended and/or complicated dramatic situation. As might be expected, given the associations of A major with love, more of Mozart's love duets are in A major than in any other key. Strikingly, five of the six counterfeit love duets are in A major.[49] It is worth noting that Mozart's contemporaries also set adaptations of the love duet in A major, including the spoof in *La fiera di Venezia*, the trio in *Fra i due litiganti*, and "Occhietti furbetto" in *L'arbore di Diana*. It seems that A major was understood by many as an extra inducement to love, even (or perhaps especially) when the situation was being parodied.

In closing, I would like to turn to the pressing question of how seduction and the (mis)representation of love in Mozart's Da Ponte operas contributes to our sense that the endings of these operas are conflicted. Opera buffa as a genre was fundamentally concerned with love and marriage, and plots generally focused on two (or more) pairs of lovers who—after a series of plot complications—are able to marry (or reconcile, if already married). Convention dictated that this happy ending, known as the *lieto fine*, culminated in a final celebratory *tutti*, an extended moment shared by all the characters in which the collective act of singing often broke the fourth wall of the stage. Mozart's Da Ponte operas conclude with scenes of recognition and reconciliation that unfold directly into their celebratory endings and attendant pairings. And yet, in these operas the sense of the happy ending is undermined by scenes of seduction and counterfeit lovemaking. Just as the seducer attempts to pass himself off as a "real" lover, the seduction scene attempts to displace the "real" love scene(s) in these works. Love duets in their expected form are all but absent from these collaborations and it is at the moment of joyous reconciliation in the finale when love and marriage are celebrated that we feel this absence most acutely. Is the Count's reform at the end of *Figaro* to be believed? He has spent the entire opera chasing Susanna but now asks for his wife's forgiveness in one of the opera's most sublime moments ("Contessa, perdono"). All has ended well for today, but what, we might ask, will happen tomorrow? The final scene of *Don Giovanni*—from which the legendary seducer is excluded—confirms the future marriages of Don Ottavio and Donna Anna and Masetto and Zerlina, but it struggles to achieve a celebratory mood. For many, especially the Romantics, thoughts of the anti-hero overshadow the ending with its assertion of moral order. Joseph Kerman neatly identified the problem when he complained, "How drab life is without the Don."[50] For much of its reception history the *scena ultima* was dispensed with altogether—a tradition that may have originated with Mozart himself at the Vienna production in 1788.[51] The celebration at the end of *Così* is perhaps the most disturbing. As the lovers reconcile, it is impossible to forget the scenes of lovemaking in the middle, which engaged real feelings for some. Don Alfonso tells Fiordiligi and Dorabella that he only deceived them in order to undeceive their lovers. How can the lovers return to their original partners as if nothing has happened? As Allanbrook reminds us, the celebratory ending asserts the proper order of things, but it can also feel like "a lid clapped on disorder and despair."[52] Traditions of staging these works tend to highlight our sense of dissatisfaction and disbelief. The emotional entanglements and misdirections of counterfeit love duets leave their mark, casting a shadow on the celebrations at the ends of these operas.

The modeling of seduction on the love-duet type, then, reflects an ironic view of the conventions that govern these operas. It usurps the intimacy and heightened emotion of the love duet while at the same time signaling the danger of such conventions—both in opera and in the world that opera strove to reflect. Seduction is a staging of power, and the appropriation of the love-duet form showed how such a thing might be easily accomplished. The presence of the counterfeit love duet subverts both the theme of love and its modes of operatic discourse, reminding characters and audiences alike of the threat seduction posed to an ordered society. In this way, scenes of deception and seduction contribute to our sense that the Mozart-Da Ponte operas reflect a more emotionally complex, uneasy, and contradictory worldview than one generally finds in Mozart's operas or elsewhere on the late eighteenth-century operatic stage.

NOTES

1. Quotations are given in consultation with original libretti and translations are mine unless otherwise indicated.

2. See Alfred Einstein, "Mozart's Choice of Keys," *The Musical Quarterly* 27/4 (1941): 416. Spike Hughes discussed the "seduction" numbers, making connections between them, in his *Famous Mozart Operas* (London: Robert Hale Limited, 1957; repr. New York, Dover, 1972); they feature prominently in Frits Noske, *The Signifier and the Signified: Studies in the Operas of Mozart and Verdi* (The Hague: Nihoff, 1977; repr. Oxford: Clarendon, 1990). Richard Stiefel attempted a definition of the "type" in his "Mozart's Seductions," in *Current Musicology* 36 (1983): 151–66. This terminology has been so widely adopted that it would be impossible to name all the authors here.

3. Hughes, Noske, and Stiefel all make observations along these lines, as do many others.

4. Daniel Heartz, *Haydn, Mozart and the Viennese School: 1740–1780* (New York: W. W. Norton, 1995), 610.

5. Manfred Hermann Schmid surveys all Mozart duets in his "Das Duett in Mozarts Opern," *Mozart Studien* 26 (2019): 173–231, esp. 173–89 (love duets), and 192–208 (false lovers). See also Michele Calella, "Mozart, das Operndueтt und die Repräsentation der Liebe," *Acta Mozartiana* 51/1–2 (2004): 37–57.

6. See for example, Daniel Heartz, *Mozart's Operas*, ed. Thomas Bauman (Berkeley: University of California Press, 1990), 38–39, and *Mozart, Haydn, and Early Beethoven: 1781–1802* (New York: W. W. Norton, 2009), 80 and 303; on 231 he identifies a "melodic type the composer particularly associated with this key, the fall of a third from the fifth degree." In her "Catalogue of Characteristics Imputed to Keys," Rita Steblin provides contemporaneous evidence: Georg Joseph Vogler associates A major with "the fire of an amorous and tender passion"; Schubart associates it with "innocent love." See Rita Steblin, *A History of Key Characteristics in the Eighteenth and Early Nineteenth Centuries*, 2nd ed. (Rochester, NY: University of Rochester Press, 2002), 182.

7. Mary Hunter, *The Culture of Opera Buffa in Mozart's Vienna: A Poetics of Entertainment* (Princeton, NJ: Princeton University Press, 1999), 162.

8. Ibid., 157–75, esp. 158–60. See also John Platoff, "How Original was Mozart?: Evidence from *Opera Buffa*," *Early Music* 20/1 (1992): 105–17, esp. 109–10; and Ronald Rabin, "Mozart, Da Ponte, and the Dramaturgy of Opera Buffa" (PhD diss., Cornell University, 1996), 284–314, esp. 285 and 287–88.

9. Hunter, *The Culture of Opera Buffa in Mozart's Vienna*, 163–68.

10. Ibid. The translation is Hunter's. Her discussion includes a musical reduction of this passage on page 167.

11. Ibid., 168.

12. See Dorothea Link, "*L'arbore di Diana*: A Model for *Così fan tutte*," in *Wolfgang Amadè Mozart: Essays on His Life and His Music*, ed. Stanley Sadie (Oxford: Clarendon Press, 1996), 366–68. For Da Ponte's comment, given in Link, see *Memoirs of Lorenzo da Ponte*, trans. Elisabeth Abbott (1929; repr. New York: Orion Press, 1957), 85.

13. *La villanella rapita: A comic opera in two acts, as performed at the Theatre-Royal in the Hay-Market* (London: H. Reynell, 1790), 64–66; and [*La villanella rapita,*] *The Favorite Duett, Sung by Sig^ra^ Storace & Sig^r^ Borselli in the Opera Villanella Rapita* (London: Longman and Broderip, 1790). See also Peter Morgan Barnes, *Pasticcio Opera in Britain: History and Context* (Manchester, UK: Manchester University Press, 2024), 176–81; and Curtis Price, Judith Milhous, and Robert D. Hume, *Italian Opera in Late Eighteenth-Century London: The King's Theatre, Haymarket, 1778–1791* (Oxford: Oxford University Press, 1995), 430–32.

14. Johann Pezzl, "Wälsche und deutsche Oper," *Skizze von Wien* 3 (1787): 421–26, esp. 422; see also H. C. Robbins Landon, *Mozart and Vienna* (New York: Schirmer Books, 1991), 137. To Pezzl's list of titles, I have added the names of composer and librettist

along with the year of the Vienna premiere. The first two operas received their Vienna premieres a year after they were first created for theaters in St. Petersburg and Milan, respectively. The remaining three were conceived for the Viennese opera buffa troupe.

15. I want to thank John Platoff for drawing my attention to this scene and for providing access to materials. There were many adaptations of Goldoni's 1755 *Le nozze* libretto and Mozart knew at least one, which was performed by a traveling troupe in Salzburg in 1775. He composed an insertion aria for this production: "Voi avete un cor fedele," K. 217, sung by Dorina (Act 1, scene 4).

16. Zinzendorf is quoted in John Platoff, "A New History for Martín's *Una cosa rara*," *Journal of Musicology* 12/1 (1994): 101. For the originals (in French), see Dorothea Link, *The National Court Theatre in Mozart's Vienna: Sources and Documents 1783–1792* (Oxford: Clarendon Press, 1998), 284 and 286.

17. Da Ponte, *Memoirs*, 81. See also Otto Erich Deutsch, *Mozart: A Documentary Biography*, trans. Eric Blom, Peter Branscombe, and Jeremy Noble, 3rd ed. (London: Simon & Schuster, 1990), 275; Deutsch, *Mozart: Die Dokumente seines Lebens* (Kassel: Bärenreiter, 1961), 241.

18. Hunter, *The Culture of Opera Buffa in Mozart's Vienna*, 160n11.

19. "Non intendi ch'io bramo / Che tu viva con me, / Perch'io non saprei star senza di te?" (1:12). *La villanella rapita* (Vienna, 1785), in *The Librettos of Mozart's Operas*, ed. Ernest Warburton, 7 vols. (New York: Garland, 1992), 5:184.

20. Ibid., 298. See also Dexter Edge, "A Report on the Viennese Premiere of *La villanella rapita* (28 November 1785)," in *Mozart: New Documents*, ed. Dexter Edge and David Black, first published 12 June 2014, updated 20 January 2018, www.mozartdocuments.org.

21. Several authors have observed the "seduction" scenario at the heart of this trio. See Tim Carter, *W. A. Mozart: Le nozze di Figaro* (Cambridge: Cambridge University Press, 1987), 9; Julian Rushton, *Mozart* (Oxford: Oxford University Press, 2006), 189; and esp. Simon P. Keefe, *Mozart in Vienna: The Final Decade* (Cambridge: Cambridge University Press, 2017), 306–10, who focuses on the transition from duet to trio.

22. Rupert Ridgewell, "A Newly Identified Mozart Edition," in *Mozart Studies 2*, ed. Simon P. Keefe (Cambridge: Cambridge University Press, 2015), 106–39, esp. 106–12.

23. In her *Seduction Narrative in Britain, 1747–1800* (Cambridge: Cambridge University Press, 2009), Katherine Binhammer raises important questions about how we might understand what "yes" meant in a context where women were able to assert agency (to know their own hearts) but might not "know" how "yes" would be understood and what might happen next. See esp. 1–19.

24. Mary Hunter, "'Pamela': The Offspring of Richardson's Heroine in Eighteenth-Century Music," *Mosaic* 18 (1985): 61–76; Jessica Waldoff, "Reading Mozart's Operas for the Sentiment," in *Mozart Studies*, ed. Simon P. Keefe (Cambridge: Cambridge University Press, 2006), 74–108.

25. For a reading that focuses on the question-and-answer construction of this duet, see David Lewin, "*Crudel! perchè finora . . .*," in *Studies in Music with Text* (New York and Oxford: Oxford University Press, 2006), 31–46. See also, among others, Carter, *Le nozze di Figaro*, 82–83; Wye Jamison Allanbrook, *Rhythmic Gesture in Mozart: "Le nozze di Figaro" and "Don Giovanni"* (Chicago: University of Chicago Press, 1983), 137–40; and Manfred Hermann Schmid, "Das Duett Almaviva—Susanna in Mozarts 'Figaro' oder: Wer hat Mitleid mit dem Grafen?," *Acta Mozartiana* 43/3–4 (1996): 45–60.

26. Heartz, *Mozart, Haydn, and Early Beethoven*, 141.

27. *La vendemmia: A New Comic Opera, in Two Acts* (London: L. Wayland, Dogwell-Court, White Friars, 1789), 72.

28. See Alfred Loeweberg, "Some Stray Notes on Mozart V. 'Don Giovanni' in London," *Music & Letters* 24/3 (1943): 165; Price, Milhous, and Hume, *Italian Opera in*

Late Eighteenth-Century London, 413–15; and Dorothea Link, "Mozart's 'Batti, batti, o bel Masetto' Performed in London in 1789," *Mozart Society of America Newsletter* 20/2 (2016): 5.

29. Bernard Williams, "Don Giovanni as an Idea," in Julian Rushton, *W. A. Mozart: "Don Giovanni"* (Cambridge: Cambridge University Press, 1981), 32. For an essay inspired by Williams, see Joseph Kerman, "Reading *Don Giovanni*," in *The "Don Giovanni" Book: Myths of Seduction and Betrayal*, ed. Jonathan Miller (London: Faber and Faber, 1990), 108–25. For my view, see Jessica Waldoff, *Recognition in Mozart's Operas* (New York: Oxford University Press, 2006), 165–83.

30. Edward T. Cone, *The Composer's Voice* (Berkeley: University of California Press, 1974), 30, esp. 29–33; and "The World of Opera and Its Inhabitants," in Edward T. Cone, *Music: A View from Delft*, ed. Robert P. Morgan (Chicago: University of Chicago Press, 1989), esp. 130 and 133.

31. Allanbrook, *Rhythmic Gesture in Mozart*, 262.

32. Kristi Brown-Montesano, *Understanding the Women of Mozart's Operas* (Berkeley: University of California Press, 2007), 68.

33. They are prevented from leaving together by the appearance of Elvira. It is very likely that concerns about censorship guided Da Ponte's dramaturgical choices. See Lisa de Alwis, "Censorship and Magical Opera in Early Nineteenth-Century Vienna" (PhD diss., University of Southern California, 2012), esp. 33 and 99. See also Martin Nedbal, "Sex, Politics, and Censorship in Mozart's *Don Giovanni/Don Juan*," in *The Oxford Handbook of Music Censorship*, ed. Patricia Hall (New York: Oxford University Press, 2015), 175–202.

34. Allanbrook, *Rhythmic Gesture in Mozart*, 262–74, 313–15, and 379n49; Wye Jamison Allanbrook, Mary Hunter, and Gretchen Wheelock, "Staging Mozart's Women," in *Siren Songs: Representations of Gender and Sexuality in Opera*, ed. Mary Ann Smart (Princeton, NJ: Princeton University Press, 2000), 47–66; Berthold Hoeckner, "Homage to Adorno's 'Homage to Zerlina,'" in *The Don Giovanni Moment: Essays on the Legacy of an Opera*, ed. Lydia Goehr and Daniel Herwitz (New York: Columbia University Press, 2006), 211–23; Waldoff, *Recognition in Mozart's Operas*, 178; Stephen Rumph, *Mozart and Enlightenment Semiotics* (Berkeley: University of California Press, 2012), 67–71.

35. John Platoff, "A Mozart Duet in a Sarti Opera: 'Là ci darem la mano' in Udine, 1793," *Eighteenth-Century Music* 14/1 (2017): 117–22.

36. Ibid., 121.

37. See Elaine Sisman, "The Marriages of *Don Giovanni*: Persuasion, Impersonation and Personal Responsibility," in *Mozart Studies*, ed. Simon P. Keefe (Cambridge: Cambridge University Press, 2006), 163–92.

38. Many have noticed this repetition of the serenade tune: among them, Charles Gounod, *Mozart's "Don Giovanni": A Commentary*, trans. Windeyer Clark and J. T. Hutchinson (Robert Cocks & Co., 1895), 84; Hughes, *Famous Mozart Operas*, 113; and Stefan Kunze, *Mozarts Opern* (Stuttgart: Philipp Reclam, 1984), 428–30.

39. Bruce Alan Brown, *W. A. Mozart: "Così fan tutte"* (Cambridge: Cambridge University Press, 1995), 57–81; see also Bruce Alan Brown and John A. Rice, "Salieri's *Così fan tutte*," *Cambridge Opera Journal* 8/1 (1996): 17–43.

40. Brown, *Così fan tutte*, 79. *La scuola de' gelosi* was the inaugural production for the Italian troupe in 1783.

41. Waldoff, *Recognition in Mozart's Operas*, 184.

42. Ferrando is outraged on discovering Guglielmo in possession of his portrait: "Il mio ritratto! Ah perfida!" (My portrait! Ah, traitress!) and later in the same exchange he promises to tear out her heart and avenge his betrayal: "A trarle il cor dal scellerato petto / E a vendicar il mio tradito affetto." Guglielmo inflames the situation by taunting his friend with Fiordiligi's fidelity, "Ti pare che una sposa / Mancar possa a un Guglielmo?" (Do you think a woman could resist a Guglielmo?).

43. Waldoff, *Recognition in Mozart's Operas*, 250–64.

44. Bernard Williams, "Passion and Cynicism: Remarks on 'Così fan tutte,'" *Musical Times* 114 (1973): 361.

45. Among others, see E. H. Gombrich, "*Così fan tutte* (Procris Included)," *Journal of the Warburg and Courtauld Institutes* 17 (1954): 373; Roger Warren, "'Smiling at Grief': Some Techniques of Comedy in *Twelfth Night* and *Così fan tutte*," *Shakespeare Survey* 32 (1979): 83; Scott Burnham, "Mozart's *felix culpa*: *Così fan tutte* and the Irony of Beauty," *The Musical Quarterly* 78/1 (1994): 85–89; and Ian Woodfield, *Mozart's "Così fan tutte": A Compositional History* (Woodbridge, UK: The Boydell Press, 2008), 133–41.

46. Heartz, *Mozart's Operas*, 250.

47. See Ian Woodfield, "Lovers Crossed or Uncrossed?," in *Mozart's "Così fan tutte,"* 99–150.

48. Among others, see Brown, *Così fan tutte*, 101; Hans Keller, "Mozart's Wrong Key Signature," *Tempo* 98 (1972): 21–27; and Waldoff, *Recognition in Mozart's Operas*, 258–63.

49. For a discussion of Mozart's music in A major, see Tim Carter, *Mozart: A Tale of Two Keys* (Oxford: Oxford University Press, 2025). Unfortunately, this book (published in September) was not yet available when this essay went into production.

50. Joseph Kerman, *Opera as Drama*, rev. ed. (Berkeley: University of California Press, 1988), 103.

51. For a summary of the situation, based on crossings out in the autograph score of the Act 2 finale, see Keefe, *Mozart in Vienna*, 382.

52. Wye Jamison Allanbrook, "Mozart's Happy Endings: A New Look at the 'Convention' of the 'lieto fine,'" *Mozart-Jahrbuch* (1984–1985), 5.

The Importance of French Mozart Mysteries: Revisiting the Reception of *Les mystères d'Isis* (1801)

SIMON P. KEEFE

On 20 August 1801, a version of *Die Zauberflöte* as French *grand opéra* not German Singspiel titled *Les mystères d'Isis* premiered at the Paris Opéra, to a libretto by Étienne Morel de Chédeville and music arranged and adapted by the Bohemian musician Ludwig Wenzel Lachnith.[1] The new French libretto followed the trajectory of Mozart's plot, but made significant alterations in tone, content, and orientation. The music reordered and adapted numbers from *Die Zauberflöte* (omitting some entirely) as well as incorporating several from *Le nozze di Figaro, Don Giovanni, La clemenza di Tito*, a brief segment from Haydn's Symphony No. 103, and new recitatives by Lachnith. Like *Die Zauberflöte*, which took German-speaking Europe by storm in the 1790s,[2] *Les mystères d'Isis* enjoyed stupendous popular success, in contrast to earlier Parisian adaptations of Mozart's *Figaro* (1793) and *Die Entführung aus dem Serail* (1798).[3] It was performed almost 130 times between 1801 and 1827, and more than any other work at the Opéra in the first decade of the nineteenth century.[4] According to the *Journal du Soir* soon after the premiere, "To undertake to convey into the souls of simple readers the enthusiasm which the opera . . . excited in the spectators . . . would be impossible."[5] Crowds were "prodigious," and the auditorium packed; the success of the work was also said to have accrued with every performance.[6] The Théâtre du Marais in Paris staged a two-act parody (*Les mystères d'Issy*, by Théophile Marion Dumersan and Louis Ponet) in September 1801, only a few weeks after the opera's premiere, both evidencing and exploiting its early popular success. The enthusiasm for *Les mystères* did not diminish, moreover, in the ensuing years: it was "almost as successful in Paris as the *Magic Flute* was here," one Prussian Kapellmeister reported in 1805, after direct experience of performances.[7] Around twenty editions of extracts from *La flûte enchantée* appeared in Paris between 1793 and 1800,[8] but were dwarfed in number by publications under the title *Les mystères d'Isis* in the early decades of the nineteenth century. Arrangements amply document active engagement with the opera in domestic and public musical settings in the 1800s, 1810s, and 1820s. They include arrangements for solo instruments such as piano, guitar, flute, and a wide range of instrumental combinations, including harp and piano, two violins, piano-harp-cello trio, clarinet-bassoon-horn trio, piano-violin-cello trio, four-hand piano, flute quartet, cello duo, string quartet, string trio, and clarinet duo.[9]

Set against the public popularity of *Les mystères* is its dismal critical reception and marginalization in the last two hundred years or so. Few, if any, works by or directly associated with Mozart have suffered the relentless, unremitting critical opprobrium meted out to *Les mystères* by distinguished writers. Sigismund von Neukomm (1816), a Salzburg native, pupil of Mozart and prominent nineteenth-century Mozart promoter in Austria and abroad, could hardly believe what Lachnith had done, "mutilating" (he believed) almost every number from *Die Zauberflöte*.[10] Louis Spohr, in a letter from Paris in 1820, condemned the changes to Mozart's music, the inclusion of non-*Zauberflöte* material, and the substitution of serious texts for the lighthearted and comical ones in the original.[11] Hector Berlioz unleashed a stingingly indignant, sarcastic attack on "the whole lamentable concoction" from "criminals" who "assassinated" Mozart.[12] Alexandre Oulibicheff and Otto Jahn each issued a panoply of objections in their Mozart biographies, including about the changes to the identities of individual characters, distortions and omissions of Mozart's music, and the eradication of comedic elements of text and plot.[13] Other nineteenth-century writers dismissed more bluntly "a monstrous pastiche," a "monstrous compilation," and an "abominable compilation."[14] For J. S. Shedlock, *Les mystères* even constituted "probably the worst crime ever committed."[15]

Reception has not improved since 1900 either. For Jacques-Gabriel Prod'homme it was a "monstrous pasticcio" and for Hermann Abert the "most insane chapter in the work's [*Magic Flute*'s] history. . . . Rarely if ever can a work of art have been treated with such contempt."[16] Alex Hyatt King in 1956 talked of a "hotch-potch . . . [given] to the total exclusion of the real opera" and Paul Nettl of an opera "[stripped] of all its wonderful and amusing elements" where pieces from other works are "smuggled in."[17] Jacques Chailley, identifying a "shameless massacre" and a "scandalous version," dreamt up a scenario of Morel's influence at the Opéra "doubtless [explaining] the obstinacy with which every attempt to make known the original of *Die Zauberflöte* rather than his arrangement of it was rejected."[18] For Winton Dean, this "notorious arrangement" and "travesty" is an example of the impoverished "artistic integrity" ca. 1800 in Paris under Napoleon.[19] Peter Branscombe did not conceal his disdain for *Les mystères*. This "French perversion" was a stylistic disaster coming close "to the world of intentional parody."[20] For James Johnson, it was a "bastardized, bowdlerized" work undeserving of the epithet "Mozartian" and for Hervé Lacombe a "disturbing . . . hodgepodge of arias."[21] In more dispassionate, less explicitly critical secondary sources, the specter of disapproval is still apparent. In *Grove Music Online*, for example, the rhetoric and chosen anecdotes are weighted against *Les mystères*: even if unintended, the mentions of "infamy," Berlioz's retorts, and the supposed contemporary nickname *Les misères d'ici* (The Miseries Here) represent, in effect, an indictment.[22] Various entrenched critical values self-evidently underscore the kinds of criticisms cited above, including disapproval at meddling with the work of a musical master, burgeoning love and admiration for the original *Zauberflöte* and Mozart's music more generally, and the primacy of both historically informed study and the (supposed) intentions of the composer.

While several of *Les mystères d'Isis's* detractors such as Berlioz, Jahn, Dean, and Branscombe acknowledge the great popularity of the opera in the first quarter of the nineteenth century, they attempt neither to explain and contextualize the popularity nor understand it in relation to the subsequent critical mood. Spohr expressed bafflement that the French had "always highly disapproved of this vandalic mutilation of a great masterpiece," but had let it remain in the repertory for almost twenty years—especially when the public "as I see every day, rule so despotically in the theater, and manage to have everything their own way."[23] Deliberately obtusely or not, Spohr misleadingly elided public and critical opinion. Berlioz, in contrast, was exasperated at the public not holding the likes of Lachnith to account: "No one came forward to treat these criminals as they deserved, or at least to expose their crimes. Alas, what if anyone had? The public is little troubled by such things. Not only in France but in Germany, England and elsewhere the greatest works of all kinds are suffered to be adapted, which means smirched and abused, by any nonentity."[24]

It is rare in Mozart's world to encounter a chasm between public and critical opinions of a work, even when this world stretches to include a project like *Les mystères*. In an attempt to understand the dramatically diverging views inspired by *Les mystères*, it is time to dial down the rhetoric on it (much of which ungenerously impugns the moral conduct of Morel and Lachnith, as we have seen, with talk of criminality and so on). After all, *Les mystères* is only one among many late eighteenth- and early nineteenth-century adaptations of *Die Zauberflöte*. Even in 1794, seven years before the premiere of *Les mystères*, the *Journal des Luxus und der Moden* complained that no opera had been "produced, shaped, trimmed, used and abused, edited, modeled, parodied, imitated, and corrupted in such innumerable ways as Mozart's *Zauberflöte* in Germany."[25] We also need to reopen the files on *Les mystères* and revisit understandings of it because of its important position in the history of French reception of Mozart's music, and, therefore, Mozart reception more broadly. In order properly to do so, we need first to contextualize more thoroughly than hitherto the opera's musical, historical, and cultural environments, including Morel's and Lachnith's involvement, the political atmosphere in Napoleonic France ca. 1800, the identity and ontology of the work itself, and the opera's explicitly Egyptian setting.

Les mystères d'Isis in Context

Morel's and Lachnith's interests, experiences, and orientations prior to 1801 help inform discussion of *Les mystères*. As early as 1783, under the *ancien régime*, Morel, a key administrative and artistic figure at the turn-of-the-century Opéra, penned the libretto for an opera set in Egypt by André Ernest Modeste Grétry, *La caravane du Caire* (The Cairo Caravan). This was an important work in the history of the Paris Opéra. As Grétry explained, "I saw the public tired of endless tragedies" and in *La caravane* more than any of his other operas of the time, "determined public opinion on the need to establish lyric comedy at this theatre."[26] The work, credited above all for its novelty of plot, thus initiated a new epoch at France's most prestigious opera venue.[27] Shortly after his death, Morel received historical credit in this area of endeavor: "It was he who introduced on to the lyrical stage, or who at least supported there, the cheerful and graceful genre."[28] *La caravane* was an exceedingly popular work, receiving 506 performances and many revivals, including one in 1800, shortly before the premiere of *Les mystères*.[29] Moreover, not only is it set in Egypt like *Les mystères*, but its plot also bears a striking resemblance to that of Mozart's *Die Entführung aus dem Serail*: the Pascha keeps captive in his harem a slave woman, Zélime, whom he is obsessed with, subsequently giving her up magnanimously for a similar reason to Pascha Selim's granting freedom to Konstanze in Mozart's opera. Here he gives her up when realizing that her lover, Saint-Phar, is the long-lost son of one of the Pascha's loyal and heroic henchmen, Florestan.

While Morel presumably did not know Mozart's *Entführung* (1782) when writing his own libretto for *La caravane*, he would have familiarized himself with it when produced in Paris in 1798, given the closeness of its plot to his own work. In short, location- and plot-related circumstances feeding the success of his earlier opera *La caravane*, connected as it is to *Die Entführung*, may have stimulated Morel to think about how Mozart's music—as yet mostly unfamiliar in France—was well positioned for impact on the stage of the Opéra.[30]

Like Morel, Lachnith was familiar with Mozart's music before working on *Les mystères* for the Opéra. In 1798, he jointly authored with Louis Adam a piano fingering method that included Mozart passages.[31] More important, for around two years in the 1790s he worked on an ultimately unperformed version of *Die Zauberflöte* for the Théâtre Feydeau in Paris, as documented in a letter from November 1801; an almost complete extant manuscript of *La flûte enchantée* in two volumes, with some text missing, apparently contains Lachnith's hand.[32] Lachnith was already an experienced music arranger before *Les mystères*, including of Haydn's and Pleyel's music.[33] He was also, like Morel, well connected at the Opéra, as one of the three shortlisted candidates in 1800—albeit an unsuccessful one—for the position of deputy conductor under Jean-Baptiste Rey.[34]

Thus, Morel and Lachnith were both invested in making *Les mystères* a popular success. On the one hand Morel, a mainstay of the Opéra who would know that a spectacular and lavish production was expected at this most august of venues,[35] had a reputation to uphold and, directly or indirectly, the finances of the institution to consider. Lachnith, on the other hand, had something to prove after failing to obtain the conducting role at the Opéra and had a lengthy period of work on an unperformed *Die Zauberflöte* behind him. Lachnith was certainly possessive of *Les mystères*, asserting a belief about his full authorial rights over it and consequent entitlement to substantial financial compensation for it, especially given the difficulties (he said) of adapting Mozart's *Zauberflöte* to suit the Opéra. In the aforementioned letter of November 1801, he explained to the director of the Théâtre des Arts (the Opéra), Jacques Cellerier, that he deserved the 300 francs per performance mandated to other composers at the Opéra and would have tried his luck with the opera at the Théâtre Feydeau had he thought this amount were not forthcoming.[36]

The path to a successful production of *Les mystères* would have been a narrow and intricate one, though, in the political climate of the French Consulat (1799–1804). Napoleon himself kept a close eye on opera, believing that it "had a special power to inspire subjects with patriotic sentiments in his cause" but also represented a potential "threat as a medium for whipping up hostile feelings towards him."[37] Napoleon was a famous chameleon among his own subjects and others at the turn of the nineteenth century, with an uncanny knack of changing his attitude and behavior to suit—and dominate—specific groups.[38] He met a shrewd political operator in Morel, who was commended in an official diktat from 1802 as a talented and experienced director general of the Opéra with "a very deep knowledge of the administration of opera in all its parts." Moreover, it was believed that the Opéra would continue to "redouble their efforts to merit the benevolence of the government and to fulfill the just hopes of the public."[39] If Napoleon, as James Johnson points out, "had a clear vision of the audience he wanted at the Opéra: orderly, fashionable, and above all in unified adoration of His Majesty," and required pomp and patriotism at a work's core,[40] then Morel would have felt obliged to provide it all in *Les mystères*. (Napoleon attended an early performance of *Les mystères* in autumn 1801.)[41] Like the original *Zauberflöte*, politicized in a pro-Jacobin interpretation in the wake of the French Revolution in the mid 1790s,[42] *Les mystères* was also understood to have expressed specific political sentiments. Writing in 1803 Johann Heinrich Campe, for example, detected references in the first scene to the supposed brotherhood, fraternity, and national solidarity of Napoleonic France, and expressed surprise that audiences seemed to be missing them.[43] The clearest political dimension to *Les mystères*, though, is its Egyptian location and subject matter, coinciding as it did with Napoleon's Egyptian campaign (1798–1801). Although *Les mystères* does not invoke Napoleon specifically, the association between the glories of ancient Egypt and those of Napoleonic France would have been lost on no one. Vivant Denon's dedication to Napoleon, in an 1802 book about the Egyptian campaign, alerts us to the de facto requirements of authors and artists at that time: "To combine the lustre of your name with the splendour of the Monuments of Egypt is to associate the glorious annals of our own time with the history of the heroic age."[44]

French interest in Egypt throughout the eighteenth century is evidenced in Egyptian-themed operas such as *La caravane de Caire*, Voltaire's article from 1756 on the Egyptian mysteries, and an entry on music in ancient Egyptian culture in the *Encyclopédie méthodique: Musique* (1791), focusing on instruments and on musical activities in weddings, funerals, and processions.[45] Interest reached fever pitch in a Napoleonic context, however, at the turn of the century. The quantity and range of books published or made available in France in the run-up to the premiere of *Les mystères* in 1801 documents French "Egyptomania": on voyages to, and memories of Egypt,[46] in journals focused on Egypt and in collections of letters to and from the country,[47] and in politically motivated studies, including descriptions of military activities.[48] Egyptian art and imagery was also a source of great fascination, including obelisks, sphinxes, and pyramids.[49] Considerable attention at the end of the eighteenth and beginning of the nineteenth centuries is also paid to the mysteries of Isis themselves—ancient religious initiation rites in the cult of the Egyptian goddess Isis—sometimes emphasizing links to Freemasonry.[50] Morel used one well-known, frequently reissued source in particular: Etienne-François de Lantier's *Voyages d'Antenor en Grèce et en Asie avec des notions sur L'Egypte* (Antenor's Voyages in Greece and Asia with Ideas about Egypt) first published in 1798.[51] With its extended discussions of initiation rites, celebrations, and processions, the state of the underworld, and emblems of the mysteries of Isis, it provided Morel with useful information about ancient Egyptian myth and legend.[52] At least two reviews of *Les mystères* in *La Décade Philosophique* and the *Gazette nationale* soon after the premiere also made connections between the trials depicted by Lantier and Morel.[53]

To be sure, the original *Zauberflöte* has a prominent Egyptian dimension. Schikaneder's sources included Abbé Jean Terrasson's 1731 French novel *Sethos, histoire ou vie tirée des monumens anecdotes de l'ancienne Egypte* (Sethos, His History Taken from the Monuments and Anecdotes of Ancient Egypt).[54] In addition, prayers are made to Isis and Osiris, the mysteries of Isis are mentioned, the pyramids feature in stage directions, and the original published libretto includes a picture of an obelisk with hieroglyphics.[55] The opera was also referred to around the time of its premiere as *Die ägyptischen Geheimnisse* (The Egyptian Secrets) by, for instance, Johann Jakob Haibel, a singer at Schikaneder's Wiednertheater where *Zauberflöte* was first performed.[56] Yet it is not located in a "culturally specific setting," either in Egypt or anywhere else, and features an eclectic rather than uniform exoticism.[57] Indeed, for musicologist Matthew Head, "the opera unfolds in a place of the imagination. . . . If it can be located at all, it might be thought of as a picturesque parkland—these were fashionable at the time and often adorned with the rocks, temples, grottos, and even pyramids that appear in the opera—or the make-believe, exotic landscape of an oriental fairy tale."[58]

The location of *Les mystères* in Egypt is confirmed unambiguously right at the beginning of the opera in one of the most significant dramatic and structural adjustments to *Die Zauberflöte*. Instead of having Tamino appear in a rocky scene of uncertain location after the Overture, Morel begins straightaway with a scene between Zarastro and his priests in Egypt, explaining in the libretto:

> The theater represents the porticos that surround the enclosure inhabited by the Priests of Isis. We see, on one side, the entrance to the palace of Myrrenne, on the other that of the underground which leads to the residence of the Priests and

> at the Temple of Isis. Farther away, a bridge over a canal of the Nile: we discover in the background various Pyramids and in the distance the view of Memphis [the ancient capital of Egypt]. At sunrise, the Priests and Priestesses are lined up in the theater where they wait for the time assigned for offering a sacrifice to Isis. (It is night.)[59]

In spite of the liberties taken by Morel and Lachnith with Mozart's and Schikaneder's original, this is the only instance in *Les mystères* of music from *Die Zauberflöte* migrating from the second to the first half of the opera or, indeed, the first half to the second. (*Die Zauberflöte* is in two acts and *Les mystères* in four.) With Zarastro announcing in this first scene the trials and initiation of the heroic Isménor (Tamino, from *Die Zauberflöte*), as well as his intended union with Pamina, the plot immediately focuses on Isménor's journey ahead, thereby simplifying the original narrative—downplaying its magical component in particular—as critics have noted.[60] The scene is just as important, though, as the first illustration of the "Egyptianization" of the opera. This includes name changes for several characters (Tamino to Isménor; Papageno to Bochoris; the Queen of the Night to Myrrenne; the three ladies to three women from Myrrenne), the replacement of the magic flute with an Egyptian sistrum, numerous references to Egyptian features of original costumes and clothing, and the appearance of ostentatious Egyptian iconography on stage, including for Act 2:

> The theater changes and represents a vast avenue of sphinxes that lead from the habitation of the profane to the Temple, and to the places reserved for the residence of the Priests. We come across terraces with plantings surrounding these monuments.[61]

Both stage sets for Acts 1 and 2 attracted contemporary praise. According to the *Courrier des spectacles*, 22 August 1801, two days after the premiere: "The first colors that daylight brings into a vast building [in Act 1] have been imitated and graduated with great intelligence. These gradations were produced by the blue glasses placed on the lamps; frames then partially removed, and replaced by white glasses."[62] The critic Ducray-Duminil in *Petites affiches* (1801) also found the decor very beautiful: "The first [scene], lit initially by blue glasses, has the tone of half-light, and its proportions are large and imposing."[63] In the *Journal des débats* (1801), "We see under the porticos of the Temple of Isis the priests and priestesses settled around the theater, and the pontiff in the middle: nothing has been neglected in the elegance, accuracy, and richness of the costumes."[64] The "allée de Sphinx" also receives special commendation in the *Courrier des spectacles*.[65] For the *Petites affiches*, "The Sphinx gallery, in the second [act], is of great effect, and proves that we were right to observe . . . [repeatedly] that oblique points will always succeed for the optics and perspective of the theater."[66] As we shall see below, the decor produced by Ignazio Degotti consistently received high praise in the early reception of *Les mystères*.

Thus, from the start, *Les mystères* represented a juggling act for Morel and Lachnith. They needed simultaneously to demonstrate a political orientation pleasing to the Napoleonic regime, to meet the expectations of the Opéra (including a lavish production), and to introduce their French audiences to Mozart, a composer with whom the majority were not yet familiar. Even the inclusion of numbers from other Mozart operas, strange to modern listeners, has a certain logic to it, when the necessity for an operatic hit in complex circumstances trumped the need for anything resembling fidelity to Mozart. The appearance of numbers from the opera seria *Tito* in both halves of *Les mystères*—with *Don Giovanni* and *Figaro* confined to the first and second halves respectively—also lends an additional air of gravity to a new opera shorn of most of the humor of *Zauberflöte*. The combination of a simplified plot and specific location for events on the one hand, and a complicated score, with numbers altered, added, and excluded on the other, is the product, then, of a unique set of historical, artistic, and cultural conditions and circumstances.

The Early Reception of *Les mystères d'Isis*

French critical opinion of *Les mystères* in the first decade of the nineteenth century was, in most respects, positive. Like the original *Zauberflöte*, the libretto and subject matter of *Les mystères* received a mixed reception.[67] It was said that the weak plot, containing no situations of interest, could have been better planned. And Morel, writing in a serious tone rather than in the original's combination of comedic and serious, made unwelcome and inappropriate textual substitutions, such as the sentimental couplets of Bochoris's "Sous les yeux" as a contrafactum for Papageno's joyous and rustic "Vogelfänger bin ich ja."[68] In *La Décade Philosophique*, too, Morel's "thankless and painful" task of adapting *Die Zauberflöte* saw him criticized for trying to integrate the tales of the cowardly Bochoris and the ancient mysteries.[69] Elsewhere, though, Morel's text was described as a "*tour de force*, which does infinite honor to his musical knowledge."[70] The music had a smoother ride early on, with Lachnith's adaptations apparently not affecting judgments, perhaps because of an unfamiliarity at this stage with Mozart's original *Zauberflöte*. The influential critic Geoffroy (1801) described the music as "truly new . . . what purity of melody! What simplicity! What religious character, somber and melancholic."[71] The *Courrier des spectacles* remarked upon Mozartian qualities of melodiousness, rich expression, delicacy, dignity, and well-distributed accompaniment parts, also commending Lachnith's care at arranging the score.[72] For *La Décade Philosophique*, the music "made people admire . . . the real talent of Mozart," with the "finesse and grace, the melancholy and gaiety, [and] the accompaniments always in agreement with the character of the melody and the song."[73] According to the *Gazette nationale*, the music conveyed lively enthusiasm, vigor, freshness, warmth, beauty, and originality.[74]

The costumes, staging, and dancing in *Les mystères* elicited praise from the outset, with Degotti and Pierre-Gabriel Gardel—responsible for the decor and ballet respectively—receiving enthusiastic commendations.[75] For one critic in 1801, everything was delightful, and for another spectacular and magnificent.[76] In Act 4, the "magic of the spectacle, [and] the beauty of the decorations" attracted the attention of the audience, according to the *Gazette nationale*.[77] The ballet in Act 4 was acknowledged, moreover, as "superb."[78] For the *Magasin Encyclopédique*, "The costumes have all the accuracy one could desire; and the decorations are of the greatest beauty, to which is added a perfect knowledge of Egyptian architecture."[79]

Experiencing the combined music and production of *Les mystères*, and on occasion the text as well, also provoked positive reactions. The charming music and the magnificence and magic of the decor contributed to the huge success of *Les mystères* for the *Courrier des spectacles*. The journal exclaimed, furthermore, "what purity of style, and what imposing severity in the decorations, what richness in the costumes, and what magnificence in the ballets! Everything captures the senses, everything commands attention! The music is one of the most beautiful we know."[80] In the *Petites affiches*, Grimod de la Reynière believed that Morel had adapted the mediocre libretto of *Die Zauberflöte* in an effective, organized way; moreover, *Les mystères* was the most beautiful spectacle witnessed at the Opéra, with charming dancing and Degotti's magical and glorious decor. Ducray-Duminil in the same journal was also a self-professed admirer, pronouncing the opera "magnificent in that it unites the beauty of the music with the charm of the ballets, the decorations, all the prestige that distinguishes the first lyric theater of Europe."[81] For the *Mercure de France*, music, staging and ballets were all remarkable. Numbers such as Zarastro's aria and the Act 3 choruses proved that *Les mystères* had the required nobility to merit inclusion at the Opéra; and the production surpassed anything previously witnessed at this venue. Overall, "it would perhaps be impossible to form elsewhere a spectacle, which, by the perfection of several parts and the majesty of the whole, exercised more influence over the senses and the imagination."[82] At revivals, too, the music and the production were mutually reinforcing. For *La Belle assemblée,* a British journal often focusing on fashionable French activities, "*Les mystères d'Isis* . . . [is] a majestic production. Music, dancing, and scenery all unite in one of the finest operas ever produced."[83] In the *Journal de l'Empire*, "The senses are pleasantly occupied: we see beautiful decorations, magnificent processions, delicious dances; we hear superb music, music by Mozart, taken from a serious opera and an opera-buffa."[84]

Time and again in the first decade of *Les mystères'* life, critics returned admiringly to one moment in Act 2, scene 7, that brings together several aspects of the operatic experience to apparently charming effect—Bochoris's use of his magical instrument to tame and enchant the slaves who are about to capture him and Pamina. (This is the passage "Das klinget so herrlich, das klinget so schön!" from the Act 1 finale of *Die Zauberflöte*, immediately before Pamina and Papageno sing "Könnte jeder brave Mann," in which they express their wish that music could always exercise such power.) For Geoffroy, music and dance together created a "prodigious effect."[85] According to the *Magasin Encyclopédique*, Bochoris "draws from [his magical instrument] the most harmonious sounds, and enchants the guards and slaves, who dance while showing their admiration. This piece is of such great beauty, the dance follows so perfectly the chords of the harmonica and the harp, joined to the voice of Lays [in the role of Bochoris], that this piece was requested again and heard, for the second time, with the greatest enthusiasm."[86] The distinguished critic Johann Friedrich Reichardt, who intensely disliked *Les mystères* (like many Germans), thought it an exquisite moment, "something completely perfect of its kind, such as one only sees in Paris." In short, "It is not possible to imagine anything more piquant and perfect in composition and performance. In such important and pleasant tableaux, Gardel [the dance master] has his real strength, and . . . knows how to draw from the situation and the personnel every time. . . . The repetition of this unique scene was generally requested and given with the same love and perfection as the first time."[87] For the *Journal de l'Empire*, "We do not see every day a scene such as that of the delighted Ethiopians, transported by the charms of harmony, falling at the feet of the musician. This situation, so well placed at the Opéra, produces the most piquant effect."[88]

After such a positive start to its French reception, the critical tide began to turn for *Les mystères* in the second and third decades of the nineteenth century. Two articles capture this change, by "A. de G." in the *Journal de Lyon* (1814) and the famous Castil-Blaze in *De l'Opéra en France* (1820). For A. de G., Mozart's skills as a dramatist required attention rather than

Mozart as just a musician. Expertly attuned to sequences of numbers and progressions of emotions in his operas, we are told, Mozart demonstrated highly refined and distinctive dramatic sensibilities. According to A. de G., this is precisely what was lost in *Les mystères*; the reordering of numbers from *Die Zauberflöte* and material interpolated from other operas compromised dramatic integrity. In effect, the French public were to blame for a work like *Les mystères*, A. de G. felt, as they considered Mozart a musician and were only vaguely interested in his dramatic perspectives, predilections, and achievements.[89] Castil-Blaze also could not stomach the adjustments, additions, and cuts to the original *Zauberflöte* in *Les mystères* and found the reordering of material unconscionable; he admitted special sensitivity to Mozart's music in this respect, since he knew it so well. (Indeed, Castil-Blaze planned a version of *Zauberflöte* as *La flûte enchantée ou La belle au bois dormant*. A single surviving extract of the vocal score exists at the Bibliothèque nationale de France.)[90] He accepted that original versions of operas often needed adjustments before performances in France, arranging and adapting many Italian and German works for the French stage himself, but favored carefully cutting numbers rather than engaging in what he considered more invasive practices. While Castil-Blaze recognized that works in bad taste such as *Les mystères* would continue to be published, he was baffled at this opera being staged at the very best theater in France.[91]

Subsequent French critics either expressed surprise at the popular success of *Les mystères*, or (erroneously) denied it had ever been popular in the first place. An entry on Morel in the *Biographie nouvelle* (1824), presenting him as an untalented parodist and populist, claimed that the triumph of a parody had never been "more surprising and more complete than in *Les mystères d'Isis*, a work conceived and written in spite of common sense."[92] An accusation of populism thereby usurped recognition or discussion of original contexts informing the work. M. A. Delaforest, claiming that no pasticcio could ever be successful in France, talked of the "repugnance which [*Les mystères*] has always inspired in the public; it is a masterpiece in stupidity." He stated: "After all the tests undergone by this insipid work, it is not easy to realize the motives that could have made the administration [at the Opéra] decide to take up *Les mystères*."[93] Put simply, Delaforest harnessed an (imagined) interpretation of the musical public's perpetually negative reactions to *Les mystères* to his own perception of the weaknesses of the work.

Thus, we witness in French writings from the second and third decades of the nineteenth century a wedge driven between popular and critical opinion of *Les mystères*. It is true that the popular appeal of *Les mystères* may not have been as pronounced in the later part of its twenty-six years on the boards at the Opéra than in the earlier part—with fifty performances between 1816 and 1827 after seventy-nine up until 1812[94]—and the spectacle may have diminished a little as well. The 1816 revival, for example, was reduced from four acts to three, omitting several numbers from the earlier *Mystères* and the entire fire and water trials; it was said that Morel, who died in 1814 and had been a great proponent of fine decor at the Opéra, would not have approved.[95] We might expect a reduction in the performance count across such a protracted period, though, and substantial receipts continued to be taken at each rendition from 1816 onward.[96]

The contrast between public enthusiasm and critical negativity surfaced from the outset in the Germanic reception of *Les mystères*, because of consistently low critical opinions of the work no doubt inflected by experiences of *Die Zauberflöte* in German, as well as greater general knowledge of Mozart's music than in France. Yet German critics in at least the first decade of the nineteenth century neither denied nor downplayed French public approbation, and often referenced the high quality of the production. The *Allgemeine musikalische Zeitung* (*AmZ*), for example, issued a damning indictment of the music and text, but admitted the seductive power of individual performers (such as Lays, as Bochoris) and of the enchanting ballets that combined music and dance in remarkable ways.[97] The *Zeitung für die elegante Welt* reported *Les mystères* as shallow and heartless and in possession of a dreadful libretto, but acknowledged that brilliant costumes, picturesque decorations, and Gardel's ballets would ensure large attendances for a long time to come.[98] E. J. L. Meyer strongly disapproved of all the musical and textual adjustments, but acknowledged both the suffocating crowds in attendance and the "truly magical effect" of the decorations, pomp, costumes, dances, ballets, and dramatic scene changes.[99] Carl Julius Weber found Mozart's music mutilated almost beyond recognition, but the production completely enchanting. Waxing lyrical about the decorations and stage machinery, he explained: "In an instant all the metamorphosis in the scenery took place. . . . The clothing was selected and was mainly the most accurate Egyptian costume, which even the strictest antiquarian would not have been able to criticize." He was especially enamored of one sequence of scenes: "A priest opened up the large background of the wide scene and allowed glimpses into the sky. It was indeed a heaven in the taste of Muslims, full of lush, beautiful houris here—the actors grouped amphitheatrically on a green lawn in magical lighting and fantastically ideal decoration! The curtain fell on this one and another one opened. Now one saw hell, all red-hot devils in flames." The trade-off for Weber, then, was explicit: "The pleasure that the eye derives from the splendor and magnificence of decorations, dances, and costumes must compensate for any deprivation or mistreatment of the ear."[100]

At around the time French critics distanced themselves from the public popularity of *Les mystères*, German critics began to do the same. In 1812 *AmZ* was irritated by the latest *Mystères* revival, and in no mood to reference its continued popularity. With outrageous cuts, additions, and other changes, it "drags its way to the end with lame legs" and its characters are "like noble statues, whose limbs have been cut off and reattached, colorful robes painted on, but above all red cheeks and coarse moustaches smeared on."[101] For Ernst Ludwig Gerber, who made no attempt to distinguish between critics and the general music public, the "patchwork" (*Flickwerk*) of *Les mystères* did not please a great deal and became known by the nickname referenced above, *Les misères d'ici*.[102]

The shift in critical emphasis from the second decade of the nineteenth century onward is attributable to two simultaneously occurring temporal factors: the intricate context around the genesis and production of *Les mystères* fading into the distance, and historical circumstances evolving. "What is the importance of investigating whether Mozart's chords contributed less to [the audience's approbation] than the talents of the decorator and the prestige of the stagehand?" *Mercure de France* asked rhetorically in 1802.[103] A little over a decade later, production values had become less significant to critics than identifying misrepresentations of Mozart the musician and dramatist to coincide with ever increasing recognition of his musical achievements and general historical position. For example, Mozart—often alongside Haydn—usurps Beethoven in musical-historical respects in a number of French critical sources from the 1810s and 1820s.[104] In turn, these shifting sands set the scene for frequently vitriolic attacks in the ensuing two hundred years when *Les mystères* was temporally still further removed from an original context that was invariably of very little interest to critics. Mozart's reputation grew exponentially in the first two decades or so of the nineteenth century, in France as elsewhere; he was considered qualitatively supreme in breadth of talent and achievement by Sevelinges and in his status as a demigod by theorist Jérôme-Joseph de Momigny.[105] Any parody at all therefore would have been unpalatable for some.

Extreme musical popularity, however, even when short-lived, can tell important stories. Morel and Lachnith worked within a constrained set of political, cultural, and musical circumstances, from introducing Mozart's music to Paris and meeting expectations of the Opéra audience to pleasing Napoleon and his retinue. Consequently, Morel and Lachnith would have had limited opportunity or need to focus narrowly on music and drama and every reason to consider the holistic impact of their endeavor—including musical, dramatic, extra-musical, and production elements—on their exalted and less exalted audience members alike. Even if it is subsequently acceptable for us to identify and condemn musical and dramatic failings in areas that Morel and Lachnith did not prioritize, we owe it to *Les mystères*, when reexamining the context and reception of the work, to explain its landmark status in the history of Mozart in France.

Les mystères d'Isis and Nineteenth-Century French Reception of Mozart

The year 1801 proved to be a crucial launching pad for Mozart reception in France, with the stratospheric popularity of *Les mystères* at its core. Two influential books by Théophile Winckler and C. F. Cramer, both published in the wake of *Les mystères*' initial success in 1801 and derived from seminal German writings, referenced the opera and in turn stimulated further French biographical interest in Mozart. Winckler's 1801 *Notice biographique sur Mozart* took almost all of its text from Friedrich Schlichtegroll's 6,000-word German obituary of Mozart, which is itself the first authentic biography of Mozart.[106] In Winckler's second paragraph, before presenting Schlichtegroll's material, he acknowledged the attention to Mozart wrought by *Les mystères*, thereby establishing it as the de facto entry point for his biography.[107] In the best traditions of early biography, the message is clear: if we admire Mozart's music (in this case through *Les mystères*), we will also want to know about his life. Cramer, translating Johann Friedrich Rochlitz's famous Mozart anecdotes originally published in the *AmZ* in 1798, includes a lengthy interpolation on *Les mystères*.[108] Acknowledging disquiet about the license Morel and Lachnith took, he also defends *Les mystères* on the grounds that Schikaneder's original libretto is itself problematic. If we are to reproach Morel and Lachnith, Cramer claims, it should be because they "took too much trouble . . . [to] bring this opera closer to the *noble genre* to the detriment of this variety and variegation of tones which reigns in the original."[109] Cramer believes we also need to remember the compromises Morel and Lachnith had to make in order to render Mozart's opera performable in a French theater.[110] Winckler's and Cramer's books circulated widely in the early nineteenth century, in their original forms and re-publications; Winckler also became the primary source for Stendhal's important, much-read 1814 biography of Mozart.[111] With *Les mystères* at the helm, Winckler, Cramer, and Morel and Lachnith together ignited the nineteenth-century French reception of Mozart.

The impact of *Les mystères* in France goes beyond its association with two key French Mozart texts. Accounting for the French premiere of *Don Giovanni* (as *Don Juan*, in 1805), the *Archives littéraires de l'Europe* claimed, surely with justification, that the "success of *Les mystères d'Isis* . . . prompted the Opéra administration to make us enjoy another work by Mozart."[112] When *Die Zauberflöte* finally received its Parisian premiere in German in 1829, it included an aria for Tamino taken from *Die Entführung aus dem Serail*.[113] The cross-fertilization of *Zauberflöte* with other Mozart operas initiated in *Les mystères* thereby continued, albeit in less pronounced fashion. The influence of *Les mystères* also persists in Charles Nuitter and Adolphe Beaumont's French translation *La flûte enchantée* (1865), as determined by dissimilarities with Mozart and Schikaneder's *Zauberflöte* and connections to *Les mystères* instead. The Masonic elements and emphasis on religious mysteries are downplayed, the partnership between Tamino and Pamina is established before the opera has started rather than during it, and the end "marks a closing in on the married couple celebrated by Isis, not an opening up to the harmony of all men and women to the greater good of civic morality."[114] In 1824, Morel's text is a cultural reference point. At the beginning of the second of two volumes devoted to Jeanne Maillotte, a legendary tavern owner in sixteenth-century Lille who helped quell Protestant rebels, author A.-J.-B. Defaunconpret quotes a passage from *Les mystères* about the sweet power of harmony residing with the gods, and subjecting everyone to its persuasive charms. (This text immediately follows the moment popular with French audiences in which Bochoris enchants the ominously aggressive slaves with his magical instrument.) Even in the mid-nineteenth century, French publications continue to refer to *Les mystères* as the primary reference point for music from *Die Zauberflöte*, capturing in microcosm the opera's protracted presence in French musical culture.[115]

In conjunction with both its impact in France and its troubled critical reception, *Les mystères* offers a salutary reminder of the power of publicly popular events and works to influence reception-related activity. The great biographer Otto Jahn, establishing legitimate and illegitimate lines of Mozart work in the sixty or so years between Mozart's death and the publication of his biography, would have assigned *Les mystères* to the illegitimate category; he clarifies his disapproval of it in any case, as we have seen.[116] Yet *Les mystères* unlocks the door to French Mozart reception, achieving a previously unimagined level of popularity for the composer. It also acts as progenitor to an adventurous kind of French Mozart reception that we cannot neatly characterize. Like *Les mystères* with Morel and Lachnith's alterations, omissions, and substitutions, many of the most interesting landmarks of nineteenth-century Mozart reception in France involve the modification or completion of his music, or do not concern Mozart alone. These include Jacques Offenbach's use of an existing German adaptation of *Der Schauspieldirektor* for his adaptation of the opera in 1856, designed to help him promote his new Parisian theater; the plethora of midcentury transcriptions of *Don Giovanni*; and the sanctification of the *Don Giovanni* autograph by virtuoso singer Pauline Viardot.[117] Even the Requiem, featuring a brilliant, high-profile French premiere from Luigi Cherubini in 1804, scarcely conceivable without the popular success of *Les mystères* three years earlier, could never be about Mozart alone. Unfinished at Mozart's death, it was performed in a version completed by his associate Franz Xaver Süssmayr (whether this was known to the audience or not).[118] Moreover, the performance of Mozart's Requiem at Napoleon's reinterment at Les Invalides on 15 December 1840 was probably the single most important act of French nineteenth-century Mozart reception precisely because it transcended association with Mozart alone. The spirit of the revered honoree (Napoleon), the commemorative occasion, Mozart's music, the seductive legend around the work, and the superb performers under the great French conductor François Habeneck came together powerfully to create a remarkable musical experience documented by contemporary critics. Fittingly, the Requiem received a repeat, similarly acclaimed performance the following year at the Opéra, scene of *Les mystères*' landmark triumph forty years earlier.[119]

Thus, with reception history properly factored into the equation, we should not regard Morel and Lachnith as villains, who supposedly mutilated and ultimately assassinated Mozart for their own purposes. Lachnith was castigated once for emotionally claiming to one of his neighbors at a performance of *Les mystères*: "It's over . . . I don't want to do any more opera. . . . I would never compose one superior to this."[120] Irrespective of how we interpret his authorship in *Les mystères*, he would have had cause to reflect on that famous maxim *Vox populi, vox Dei* (The voice of the people [is] the voice of God). Where Mozart reception in France is concerned, Lachnith and Morel can lay claim to be heroes. By virtue of their huge popular success, not remotely experienced before by Mozart in France and perhaps not by any German opera in France at that time,[121] they set the scene for all that was to follow for Mozart in Francophone musical cultures, in popular and serious domains alike.

NOTES

I extend my thanks to Mark Everist for comments on an earlier draft of this essay.

1. The Opéra was then the Théâtre de la République et des Arts, and renamed seventeen times between the onset of the French Revolution in 1789 and 1830. See Nicole Wild, *Dictionnaire des théâtres parisiens au xixe siècle: Les théâtres et la musique* (Paris: Amateurs de livre, 1989), 299–300. I shall refer to the venue as the Opéra throughout.

2. On this topic, see for example, Otto Erich Deutsch, *Mozart: A Documentary Biography*, trans. Eric Blom, Peter Branscombe, and Jeremy Noble, 3rd ed. (London: Simon & Schuster, 1990), and Deutsch, *Mozart: Die Dokumente seines Lebens* (Kassel: Bärenreiter, 1961), passim (forthwith *MDB* and *MDL* respectively); Simon P. Keefe, *Haydn and Mozart in the Long Nineteenth Century: Parallel and Intersecting Patterns of Reception* (Cambridge: Cambridge University Press, 2023), 20; Ian Woodfield, "*Zauberflöte*: A Cultural Phenomenon in an Age of Revolution," in *The Cambridge Companion to "The Magic Flute,"* ed. Jessica Waldoff (Cambridge: Cambridge University Press, 2023), 275.

3. On the less positive reception for *Figaro* and *Die Entführung*, see Jean Gribenski, "De *La Flûte enchantée* aux *Mystères d'Isis*: Les éditeurs de musique parisiens face au dernier opéra de Mozart," in *"Die Zauberflöte": Sources–Contexte–Répresentations*, ed. Henri Vanhulst (Brussels: Peter Lang, 2018), 49–64.

4. For lists and statistics of performances of *Les mystères d'Isis*, see Rudolph Angermüller, "'Les Mystères d'Isis' (1801) und 'Don Juan' (1805, 1834) auf der Bühne der Pariser Oper," in *Mozart-Jahrbuch 1980–1983*, 32–97, at 51–54. On the success of *Les mystères* in the first decade of the nineteenth century, see Belinda Cannone, *La réception des opéras de Mozart dans la presse parisienne* (Paris: Klincksieck, 1991), 68–69.

5. Cannone, *La réception des opéras de Mozart*, 189. All translations are my own unless otherwise indicated.

6. See ibid., 68, 69; *Journal Helvétique* 36 (2 December 1801): 287.

7. See *Correspondance des amateurs musiciens* (1802–1805) (Geneva: Minkoff Reprint, 1972), no. 10 (9 March 1805): 1.

8. See Gribenski, "De *La Flûte enchantée* aux *Mystères d'Isis*."

9. For listings of editions, see for example *Correspondance des amateurs musiciens* (1802–1805), passim; *Tablettes de Polymnie* 1–2 (1811): 223, 512; *Allgemeine musikalische Zeitung* (*AmZ*) 14 (1812), Intelligenz-Blatt: col. 56; *AmZ* 19 (1817), Intelligenz-Blatt: col. 28; *AmZ* 19 (1817): col. 620; Carl Friedrich Whistling, *Handbuch der musikalischen Literatur* (1817) (Hildesheim: Georg Olms, 1975), passim; Whistling, *Handbuch der musikalischen Literatur* (1828) (Hildesheim: Georg Olms, 1975), passim.

10. Angermüller, "'Les Mystères d'Isis' (1801)," 32.

11. *Louis Spohr's Autobiography*, trans. anon (London: Longman, Green, Roberts, 1865), 109–11.

12. David Cairns, trans. and ed., *The Memoirs of Hector Berlioz* (1870) (London: Cardinal, 1990), 53–54 (written in 1836).

13. Alexandre Oulibicheff [Ulybychev], *Mozarts Leben* (1843), vol. 1 (Stuttgart: Becher, 1847), 14–41; Otto Jahn, *Life of Mozart* (1856–59), trans. Pauline Townsend, vol. 3 (London: Novello, 1891), 351–52.

14. Joseph d'Ortigue, *Le balcon de l'opéra* (Paris: Eugene Renduel, 1833), 107; François-Joseph Fétis, *Biographie universelle des musiciens*, vol. 6 (Paris: Fournier, 1840), 9; Henri Blaze de Bury, "La flûte enchantée," *Revue des deux mondes* 56/2 (1865): 439.

15. J. S. Shedlock, "The Maltreatment of Music," *Proceedings of the Musical Association* 10 (1883–84): 95–123, at 99.

16. Jacques-Gabriel Prod'homme, "Two Hundred and Fifty Years of the Opéra (1669–1919)," *The Musical Quarterly* 5 (1919): 527; Hermann Abert, *W. A. Mozart* (1919–21), trans. Stewart Spencer, ed. Cliff Eisen (New Haven: Yale University Press, 2007), 1303.

17. Alex Hyatt King, *Mozart in Retrospect: Studies in Criticism and Bibliography* (London: Oxford University Press, 1956), 13; Paul Nettl, *Mozart and Masonry* (New York: Dorset Press, 1957), 41.

18. Jacques Chailley, *"The Magic Flute" Unveiled: Esoteric Symbolism in Mozart's Masonic Opera. An Interpretation of the Libretto and the Music* (Rochester, VT: Inner Traditions International, 1971), 45, 44.

19. Winton Dean, "French Opera," in *The Age of Beethoven, 1790–1830*, ed. Gerald Abraham (Oxford University Press, 1982), 73, 74.

20. Peter Branscombe, *W. A. Mozart: "Die Zauberflöte"* (Cambridge: Cambridge University Press, 1991), 165.

21. James H. Johnson, *Listening in Paris: A Cultural Critique* (Berkeley: University of California Press, 1995), 175; Hervé Lacombe, *The Keys to French Opera in the Nineteenth Century* (1997), trans. Edward Schneider (Berkeley: University of California Press, 2001), 26.

22. See Ethyl L. Will (revised by Elisabeth Cook), "Lachnith [Lachnitt], Ludwig Wenzel [Louis-Wencelas]," *Grove Music Online*.

23. *Spohr Autobiography*, 111.

24. *Memoirs of Berlioz*, 54.

25. As given, in German, in Anne-Laure Munch, "Aegyptische Geheimniss: Auf der literarischen Spuren der 'Zauberflöte,'" *Neue Zeitschrift für Musik* 152 (1991): 5–11.

26. As given in David Charlton, *Grétry and the Growth of Opéra Comique* (Cambridge: Cambridge University Press, 1986), 201.

27. See Johnson, *Listening in Paris*, 107.

28. M. Lepeintre, *Suite du Répertoire du Théâtre Français: Grands-Opéras*, vol. 5 (Paris: Dabo, 1823), 5.

29. The overall number of performances is documented in Charlton, *Grétry and the Growth of Opéra Comique*, 202, and performance listings for the 1800 revival of *La caravane* in, for example, *Journal général de la littérature de France* 3 (1800): 95, 158, 191.

30. Negotiations between Morel and Lachnith and the administration of the Opéra about the staging of *Les mystères d'Isis* took place in 1798. See Angermüller, "'Les Mystères d'Isis' (1801)," 43.

31. See Louis Adam and Lachnith, *Méthode ou principe général de doigté pour le forté-piano* (Paris: Sieber, 1798).

32. On the manuscript, see Henri Vanhulst, "Une traduction française inachevée de *Die Zauberflöte* (B-Br Fetis 2817)," in *D'un opéra l'autre: Hommage à Jean Mongrédien*, ed. Jean Gribenski, Marie-Claire Mussat, and Herbert Schneider (Paris: Presses de l'Université de Paris-Sorbonne, 1996), 273–86. For Lachnith's letter documenting two years of work on *Die Zauberflöte* for an intended production at the Théâtre Feydeau, see Angermüller, "'Les Mystères d'Isis' (1801)," 50.

33. See Barry Cooper, "An Unrecorded Collection of Early Music Sources in Lampeter: Description and Annotated Inventory," *RMA Research Chronicle* 41 (2008): 93–120, at 113; Malcolm S. Cole, "A Pleyel Collection at UCLA," *Notes* 29 (1972): 215–23, at 222; Wolfgang Matthaeus, "Die Frühdrucke der Londoner Sinfonien Joseph Haydns: Ein Versuch der Darstellung ihrer Zusammenhänge," *Archiv für Musikwissenschaft* 21 (1964): 243–52, at 245; Ian Woodfield, "John Bland: London Retailer of the Music of Haydn and Mozart," *Music & Letters* 81 (2000): 210–44, at 216. Lachnith's activities as an arranger continued after *Les mystères*; for listings of published editions of arrangements carried out by him, see Carl Friedrich Whistling and Friedrich Hoffmeister, *Handbuch der musikalischen Literatur* (1817–27) (New York: Garland, 1975), passim.

34. See David Charlton, "'A maitre d'orchestre . . . Conducts': New and Old Evidence on French Practice," *Early Music* 21 (1993): 340–53, at 349, 352.

35. On the quick return to the kind of pomp and artifice expected during the ancien régime at the Paris Opéra soon after the fall of Robespierre in 1794, see Johnson, *Listening in Paris*, 157–58.

36. Angermüller, "'Les Mystères d'Isis' (1801)," 50.

37. Geoffrey Ellis, "Review of *Napoleon et l'Opera: La politique sur la scene, 1810–1815* by David Chaillou, Paris: Fayard, 2004," *English Historical Review* 122 (2007): 486–90, at 486.

38. Johnson, *Listening in Paris*, 170.

39. *Nouvelles politiques, nationale et étrangères* 11 (1802–1803): 4 (26 December 1802). See also *Journal de politique de Mannheim* (1 January 1803): 3–4.

40. Johnson, *Listening in Paris*, 170, 173–74.

41. *Zeitung für die elegante Welt* 1 (1801): col. 999.

42. Woodfield, "*Zauberflöte*: A Cultural Phenomenon in an Age of Revolution," 280.

43. *Kinder- und Jugendschriften von Joachim Heinrich Campe: Neue Gesamtausgabe der letzten Hand*, vol. 33 (Braunschweig: Schulbuchhandlung, 1830), 115. The editorial note is signed 1803.

44. Vivant Denon, *Travels in Upper and Lower Egypt in company with several divisions of the French Army during the campaigns of General Bonaparte in that country; and published under his immediate patronage . . . embellished with numerous engravings* (1802), trans. Arthur Aikin, vol. 1 (London: T. N. Longman and G. Rees, 1803), iii.

45. Voltaire, *Essai sur les moeurs et l'esprit des nations, et sur les principaux faits de l'histoire depuis Charlemagne jusqu'a Louis XVIII*, vol. 1 (Paris: Pierre Didot, 1805), 103–4 (written in 1756); Nicholas Etienne Framery and Pierre-Louis Ginguené, eds., "Egyptiens," in *Encyclopédie méthodique: Musique*, vol. 1 (Paris: Panckoucke, 1791), 499–504.

46. Such as *Mémoires sur l'Egypte* (Paris: P. Didot, 1800), vols. 2 and 3; James Bruce, *Voyage aux sources du Nil, en Nubie [South Egypt/N. Sudan] et en Abyssinie, pendant les années 1768, 1769, 1770, 1771, & 1772*, trans. J. H. Castera, vol. 1 (Paris: Hotel de Thou, 1790); Eyles Irwin, *Voyage de l'Inde en Europe par l'Egypte* (Paris: Prault, 1793); Pierre-Sylvain Maréchal, *Voyages de Pythagore en Egypte*, vol. 2 (Paris: Deterville, 1798); Constantin-François Volney, *Voyage en Syrie et en Egypte, pendant les années 1783–85*, vol. 1 (Paris: Dugour and Durand, 1798); Fréderic-Louis Norden, *Voyage d'Egypte et de Nubie*, vols. 1 and 2 (Paris: Pierre Didot, 1795); Charles Nicolas Sigisbert Sonnini de Manoncourt, *Voyage dans la haute de basse Egypte*, vol. 1 (Paris: Buisson, 1798); W. G. Browne, *Nouveau voyage dans la haute et basse Egypte, La Syrie, Le Dar-four ou aucun Européen n'avoir pénetère*, trans. J. Castera, vol. 1 (Paris: Dentu, 1800); Guillaume Antoine Olivier, *Voyage dans l'Empire Othoman, l'Egypte, et la Perse*, vols. 1–3 (Paris: H. Agasse, 1801).

47. Including *Courier de l'Egypte* (from 1795); *Lettres de l'Armée en Egypte au Gouvernement François* (London and Turin: L'Académie Royale des Sciences, 1800); Claude Savary, *Lettres sur l'Egypte*, vol. 1 (Paris: Bleuet, 1798); Edouard T. Simon, *Correspondance de l'armée en Egypte* (Paris: Garnery, 1799).

48. For example, P. E. Henin, *Conquêtes des Français en Egypte* (Paris: Pougens, 1799); H. Viviand-Bellerive, *Les Pyramides d'Egypte, Ode au Premier Consul* (Paris: Brasseur, 1801); Louis-Alexandre Berthier, *Relation des campagnes du général Bonaparte en Egypte et en Syrie* (Milan: Rue Neuve, 1800); *Mémoires sur l'Egypte publiés pendant les campagnes du Général Bonaparte, dans les années VI et VII* (Paris: Didot, 1799).

49. Lacombe, *Keys to French Opera in the Nineteenth Century*, 180.

50. See for example, François Noël, *Abrégé de la mythologie universelle, ou Dictionnaire de la Fable* (Paris: Normant, 1805), esp. 425; V.-R. Barbet Du Bertrand, *Loge centrale des véritables francs-maçons* (Paris: Michelet, 1802), esp. 28–29; Jean Baptiste Claude Izouard (called Delisle de Sales), *De la Philosophie de la Nature ou Traité du Morale pour le genre humain*, vol. 9 (Paris: Gide, 1804), esp. 299–300; Antoine Caillot, *Annale mac* [i.e. *maconniques*], vol. 3 (Paris:

Caillot, 1809), 216–19; Étienne-François Bazot, *Manuel du Franc-Maçon*, 3rd ed. (Paris: Moronval, 1817), 30–36; T. P. Boulage, *Des Mystères d'Isis* (Paris: Delestre-Boulage, 1820).

51. Lantier, *Voyages d'Antenor en Grece et en Asie avec des notions sur L'Egypte*, 8th ed. (Paris: Buisson, 1805). Lantier's volume had gone through a fourth edition by 1801 and a tenth by 1809.

52. For identification of Lantier's volume as a source for Morel's *Mystères d'Isis*, see James Smith Allen, *A Civil Society: The Public Space of Freemason Women in France, 1744–1944* (Lincoln: University of Nebraska Press, 2021), 141.

53. See *La Décade Philosophique, Littéraire et Politique* 9 (1801): 438; *Gazette nationale* 28 (1801): 1390.

54. On Terrasson's *Sethos*, see in particular Branscombe, *W. A. Mozart: "Die Zauberflöte,"* 10–18. See also Nicholas Till, *Mozart and the Enlightenment: Truth, Virtue, and Beauty in Mozart's Operas* (London: Faber, 1993), 275–76.

55. For a reproduction of the original libretto frontispiece, see Austin Glatthorn, "The *Magic Flute* in 1791," in *Cambridge Companion to "The Magic Flute,"* ed. Waldoff, 74.

56. See Cliff Eisen, ed., *New Mozart Documents: A Supplement to O. E. Deutsch's "Documentary Biography"* (Stanford, CA: Stanford University Press, 1991), 70, 73.

57. Matthew Head, "Birdsong and Hieroglyphs: Exoticism and Enlightened Orientalism in *The Magic Flute*," in *Cambridge Companion to "The Magic Flute,"* ed. Waldoff, 200–220.

58. Ibid., 201.

59. *Les mystères d'Isis: Opéra en IV actes, représenté sur le Théâtre de la République et des Arts* (Paris: Prault, 1801), 1. For a set model for Act 1, which does not contain all features described in the libretto, see https://www.bnf.fr/fr/mediatheque/les-mysteres-disis.

60. In a similar vein, Bochoris and Mona (Papageno and Papagena) encounter each other early in the opera in contrast to late on in *Die Zauberflöte*, realizing that they are intended to be together.

61. *Les mystères d'Isis: Opéra en IV actes*, 19. On the original costumes, see Angermüller, "'Les Mystéres d'Isis' (1801)," 46–48.

62. Cannone, *La réception des opéras de Mozart*, 66.

63. Ibid., 175.

64. Ibid., 151–52.

65. Ibid., 66.

66. Ibid., 175.

67. For early criticisms of Schikaneder and his libretto, see Simon P. Keefe, "*The Magic Flute* in Biography, Criticism, and Literature," in *Cambridge Companion to "The Magic Flute,"* ed. Waldoff, 291–303, at 292–96.

68. Cannone, *La réception des opéras de Mozart*, 58–61, 156, 167–68.

69. *La Décade Philosophique* 3 (1801): 437–38.

70. *Annales dramatiques* 6 (1810): 384.

71. Cannone, *La réception des opéras de Mozart*, 63.

72. Ibid., 64.

73. *La Décade Philosophique* 3 (1801): 438.

74. *Gazette nationale* 337 (1801): 1390.

75. The lavish splendor of Schikaneder's original production of *Die Zauberflöte* was also praised; see, for example, *MDB*, 433–34. For an extended discussion, see Miguel Arango Calle, "Sets, Staging, and Spectacle in Early Performances of *Die Zauberflöte*," in *Mozart in Salzburg and Beyond: New Perspectives*, ed. Simon P. Keefe (Ann Arbor, MI: Steglein Publishing, 2024), 299–328. See also Glatthorn, "*The Magic Flute* in 1791," 61–82.

76. Cannone, *La réception des opéras de Mozart*, 185, 188–89.

77. *Gazette nationale* 337 (1801): 1390.

78. Cannone, *La réception des opéras de Mozart*, 68.

79. *Magasin Encyclopédique* 7/2 (1801): 540.
80. Cannone, *La réception des opéras de Mozart*, 156, 164.
81. Ibid., 171, 175.
82. *Mercure de France* 5 (1801): 444–47, at 447.
83. *La Belle assemblée, or Bell's Court and Fashionable Magazine* 1, part 1 (1806): 101.
84. *Journal de l'Empire* (7 August 1808): 2.
85. Cannone, *La réception des opéras de Mozart*, 479.
86. *Magasin Encyclopédique* 7/2:537.
87. Reichardt, *Vertraute Briefe aus Paris geschrieben in den Jahren 1802 und 1803*, vol. 1 (Hamburg: Hoffmann, 1804), 438, 439–40.
88. *Journal de l'Empire* (7 August 1808): 19.
89. *Journal de Lyon* 1 (1 January 1814): 3–6.
90. I thank Mark Everist for alerting me to Castil-Blaze's own *Zauberflöte* project.
91. M. Castil-Blaze, *De l'opéra en France*, vol. 2 (Paris: Janet et Cotelle, 1820), 145–91, at 154–76. By 1833, Castil-Blaze had descended into vitriol in his assessment of *Les mystères*. The "wretches" Morel and Lachnith, who shamefully tore up *Die Zauberflöte*, produced a mere "pitiful pastiche" that constituted an outrage not only against Mozart but also against French honor. See *Revue de Paris: Année 1833* (Paris: 1838), 209–36, at 215–16. Castil-Blaze was severely criticized by Berlioz for his own adaptations to Weber's *Freischütz*. See *The Memoirs of Berlioz*, 53–55. For more on Castil-Blaze, see Cormac Newark, "Castil-Blaze [Blaze, François-Henri-Joseph]," *Grove Music Online*.
92. A. V. Arnault, A. Jay, E. Jouy, J. Norvins et al., eds., *Biographie nouvelle des contemporains*, vol. 14 (Paris: Hotel d'Aligre, 1824), 138.
93. M. A. Delaforest, "Académie Royale de Musique: Reprise des *Mystères d'Isis*," in *Cours de littérature dramatique*, vol. 1 (Paris: Allardin, 1836), 224–27, at 226. This review is dated 1823.
94. See Angermüller, "'Les Mystéres d'Isis' (1801)," 51–54, for performance listings between 1801 and 1827.
95. On the 1816 revival, see *Journal des débats politiques et littéraires* (12 January 1816): 1–2.
96. See Angermüller, "'Les Mystéres d'Isis' (1801)," 51–54, on the takings at individual performances between 1801 and 1827.
97. *AmZ* 4 (1801–1802): cols. 69–73.
98. *Zeitung für die elegante Welt* 1 (1801): col. 863.
99. Meyer, *Briefe aus der Hauptstadt und dem Innern Frankreichs*, vol. 2 (Tübingen: Cotta'schen Buchhandlung, 1803), 236–38.
100. *Vermischten Schiften aus dem Nachlasse von C. J. Weber* (Stuttgart: Hallberger, 1843), 37–39. Weber's letter from Paris is dated 27 April 1806.
101. *AmZ* 14 (1812): cols. 261–62.
102. Gerber, *Neues historisch-biographisches Lexikon der Tonkünstler*, vol. 3 (Leipzig: Kühnel, 1813), col. 158.
103. *Mercure de France, littéraire et politique* 6 (1802): 120.
104. See Keefe, *Haydn and Mozart in the Long Nineteenth Century*, 57–66.
105. For the increase in Mozart's reputation in the early nineteenth century, see Keefe, *Haydn and Mozart in the Long Nineteenth Century*, chaps. 1 and 2, 14–85. The quotes from Sevelinges and Momigny are on 44 and 60.
106. Winkler, *Notice biographique sur Mozart* (Paris: Fuchs, 1801). See also the translation of and extended introduction to Schlichtegroll's biography in this volume.
107. Winckler, *Notice biographique sur Mozart* (Paris: Fuchs, 1801), 5.
108. *Anecdotes sur W. G. Mozart*, trans. C. F. Cramer (Paris, 1801), 18–26.
109. Ibid., 22.
110. Ibid., 20–21.

111. See Keefe, *Haydn and Mozart in the Long Nineteenth Century*, 39n136; and Henri Beyle (Stendhal), *Vies de Haydn, de Mozart et de Métastarse* (1814), trans. Richard N. Coe (London: Calder & Boyars, 1972). On Stendhal's relationship to Winckler, and use of other sources too, see Keefe, *Haydn and Mozart in the Long Nineteenth Century*, 69.

112. See *Archives littéraires de l'Europe* 7 (1805): lxxxii. Overall, the first *Don Juan* was considerably less successful than *Les mystères*, receiving twenty-nine performances between 17 September 1805 and the end of its run on 27 January 1807. For performance numbers, see Angermüller, "'Les Mystéres d'Isis' (1801)," 73–74. For reception documents, see Cannone, *La réception des opéras de Mozart*, 211–67.

113. *Journal des comédiens* 1 (1829): 7.

114. See Allen, *A Civil Society*, 143–44, at 144.

115. See for example, *Gazette musicale* 5 (1838): 494, 508; Auguste L. Blondeau, *Histoire de la musique moderne* (Paris: Tantenstein et Cordel, 1847), 216, 318.

116. For discussion of Jahn's legitimate and illegitimate lines, see Keefe, *Haydn and Mozart in the Long Nineteenth Century*, 115.

117. On these important activities in nineteenth-century French Mozart reception, see Mark Everist, *Mozart's Ghosts: Haunting the Halls of Musical Culture* (New York: Oxford University Press, 2013), 54–74, 75–125, 157–88.

118. On the Paris 1804 performance, see Simon P. Keefe, "'Die Ochsen am Berge': Franz Xaver Süssmayr and the Orchestration of Mozart's Requiem, K. 626," *Journal of the American Musicological Society* 61/1 (2008): 1–2.

119. For discussion of the Napoleon performance of the Requiem at Les Invalides and at the Opéra, see Simon P. Keefe, *Mozart's Requiem: Reception, Work, Completion* (Cambridge: Cambridge University Press, 2012), 88–90.

120. Maxime de Villemarest, ed., *Souvenirs de F. Blangini (1797–1834)* (Paris: Charles Allardin, 1834), 370.

121. Kasper von Kooten, *"Was Deutsch und echt…": Richard Wagner and the Articulation of a German Opera, 1798–1876* (Leiden and Boston: Brill, 2019), 141.

Opera Seria and Cultural Politics in Early Nineteenth-Century Vienna: Mozart's *Idomeneo* and *La clemenza di Tito* in the Age of Napoleon

MARTIN NEDBAL

Throughout the nineteenth century, Mozart's late *opere serie—Idomeneo* (Munich, 1781) and *La clemenza di Tito* (Prague, 1791)—were not performed much, especially when compared with his late Italian comedies (*Le nozze di Figaro, Don Giovanni,* and *Così fan tutte*) and his *Singspiele* (*Die Entführung aus dem Serail* and *Die Zauberflöte*). The first two decades of the century, however, present a striking exception at the Vienna court theater, which mounted three productions of *La clemenza di Tito,* in 1804, 1811, and 1817, and two of *Idomeneo,* in 1806 and 1819. Today, Mozart's operas are often framed as timeless, canonic masterpieces, but the very notion of a musical canon was only beginning to emerge in the early nineteenth century. The renewed interest in Mozart's *opere serie* at the Vienna court theater was closely bound up with the shifting social and cultural conditions of the Habsburg capital during the turbulent Napoleonic era.[1] Moreover, unlike modern performances, these productions appeared in adaptations that many present-day audiences and critics would regard as irreverent in relation to Mozart and his librettists' original ideas. Such adaptations were also intertwined with the cultural politics of early nineteenth-century Vienna.

Mozart's Operas in Vienna in the 1790s

After Mozart's death in 1791, his collaborator Emanuel Schikaneder continued performing *Die Zauberflöte* at the suburban Theater auf der Wieden, where it had premiered, and introduced German adaptations of *Don Giovanni* and *Le nozze di Figaro* in 1792, followed by *Così fan tutte* in 1794. At that time the Vienna court theater, operating in two separate buildings, the Burgtheater and the Kärntnertortheater, lacked a German opera ensemble, and its Italian company ignored Mozart's works. The situation changed in the late 1790s, when the court theater came under the directorship of Peter von Braun. Braun leased the theater from the imperial authorities in 1794, and in the spring of 1795 established a new German opera company. By 1798, this opera company added German adaptations of *Le nozze di Figaro* and *Don Giovanni* to its repertoire, with *Così fan tutte* following in 1804 under the title *Mädchentreue*.[2] The reintroduction of the German opera company at the Vienna court theater sparked intense debates, in which court officials and intellectuals criticized Italian opera and celebrated German performances as exemplary of emerging ideas about German cultural identity.[3] The inclusion of three of Mozart's Italian operas in the German company's repertoire suggests that some associates and supporters of the company, similar to German critics elsewhere, were beginning to view Mozart's Italian works as reflective of German culture, and Mozart himself as an iconic German artist.[4]

Mozart's *opere serie* were initially excluded from the national canon of the Vienna court theater. This exclusion may have reflected the negative views of *La clemenza di Tito* as an inferior product of non-Germanic tastes, promoted by German critics in the 1790s. An early explicit expression of such views is an anonymous 1796 review of an early edition of *La clemenza di Tito* (published by Günther & Böhme in Hamburg in 1795) in the first volume of Johann Friedrich's Berlin journal *Deutschland*.[5] The review claims that the opera consists mainly of "literal imitations of the most ordinary Italian compositional style, which is offensive to every noble German artistic heart."[6] In the early nineteenth century, critical views of *La clemenza di Tito* and *Idomeneo* as imitating inferior foreign styles had become widespread and generally accepted, shaping the critical response to the first Viennese productions. Yet, in the context of these productions, the perception of the two works' position within the German operatic canon began to shift.

Prior to the productions of the early 1800s, *La clemenza di Tito* was performed only occasionally in Vienna, primarily in concert form, and these events were closely tied to the posthumous cult of the composer, promoted by his widow, Constanze Mozart. The first of these concerts took place at the Kärntnertortheater on 29 December 1794; the second at the Burgtheater on 31 March 1795. Both were organized by Constanze, with her sister Aloysia Lange appearing as Sesto.[7] A third performance occurred on 27 April 1798.[8] A valuable, previously overlooked record of this latter concert survives in the diary of Joseph Carl Rosenbaum, husband of singer Therese Gassmann and friend of Joseph Haydn (and notoriously involved in the theft of Haydn's head for phrenological research). Rosenbaum explicitly calls the 1798 event "[Constanze] Mozart's concert" ("*Conzert der Mozart*") and provides details of the cast, which included his wife:

> In the evening, I went to [Constanze] Mozart's concert, which was quite full. She gave *La clemenza di Tito*, sang herself, then Therese, [???], Umlauf, Stengel, and Rathmayer; Clementi played a violin concerto and played very beautifully. Therese sang quite nicely despite her catarrh and pleased everyone. I would so much have liked to kiss her and thank her for the pleasure her beautiful singing gave us; I will do it tomorrow. I conversed in the theater with [???], with Agnes, and Klimbke; the latter accompanied me home as far as the St. Johannes chapel.[9]

Further concerts followed in Schikaneder's Theater auf der Wieden, notably on 8 September 1798 and 25 March 1799.[10] Another, previously unnoticed, performance in the court theater, is noted in Rosenbaum's March 1801 diary, again in connection to Constanze and his wife, Therese:

> Sunday the 29th [of March 1801] . . . Therese today received, for the benefit performance of the theatrical poor, the role of Vitellia in *La clemenza di Tito*.
>
> Monday the 30th . . . Therese went early to Paër's about some variations, then to the rehearsal of *Clemenza*. . . . After midday came Madame Mozart, Madame Lefevre, and Agnes, who dressed Pepi's hair. . . .
>
> Tuesday the 31st . . . Early I went to Walther, to Weinmüller, to the rehearsal of *Clemenza di Tito*. . . . Had Therese driven to the Burgtheater for *Clemenza di Tito*, for the benefit of the court theater poor. . . . Afterwards I followed Therese, who was not well, to the theater.[11]

Thus, in Vienna *La clemenza di Tito* was initially regarded less as a stage work than a festive, commemorative, and charitable offering, closely tied to the memory of Mozart and to the activities of his widow. According to John A. Rice, Constanze's concert activities, including the Vienna performances, "encouraged the audiences to think of [*Tito*] as a kind of oratorio, a counterpart to the Requiem amongst Mozart's last works."[12]

La clemenza di Tito and the Competition between Viennese Theaters

Greater appreciation for *La clemenza di Tito* as a fully-fledged opera emerged only in the early 1800s, driven by the competition between Vienna's two main opera theaters: the court theater and the newly constructed Theater an der Wien, which replaced the Theater auf der

Wieden in June 1801. During the 1790s, supporters of German opera at the court theater often criticized productions at the Viennese suburban theaters as generally lowbrow, claiming they endangered the taste and morals of their audiences. By contrast, German operas at the court theater aimed to project high standards of didacticism, patriotism, and good taste.[13] With the 1801 opening of the Theater an der Wien, Schikaneder's German opera company began to embrace a more serious repertoire, comparable to the German operatic offerings at the court theater. This new focus was exemplified in the company's first production at the new theater, which premiered on 13 June 1801: the "heroic, grand" opera *Alexander*, with a libretto by Schikaneder and music by Franz Teyber. In its emphasis on patriotic sentiments and exemplary deeds, *Alexander* resonated with the ethos of many court theater operas from previous years.

It is striking that just over three months after *Alexander*, on 22 September 1801, Schikaneder's company produced Mozart's *La clemenza di Tito*. As Emanuele Senici points out, the work fit seamlessly into the series of grand, heroic operas that Schikaneder had launched at the new theater.[14] Yet, the choice of a Mozart work that had never been staged in Vienna may also have reflected Schikaneder's rivalry with the court theater—allowing him to outdo its 1798 revivals of *Don Giovanni* and *Le nozze di Figaro*.

Although the decision to stage *La clemenza di Tito* at the Theater an der Wien in 1801 was likely motivated, at least in part, by a desire to commemorate and honor Mozart's legacy in Vienna, the opera underwent substantial adaptation that brought it in line with the grand, heroic operatic style of the time.[15] Like Mozart's other Italian operas, *La clemenza di Tito* was presented in a German version, created by Joseph von Seyfried, journalist and brother of Theater an der Wien music director Ignaz von Seyfried. One of Seyfried's most substantial alterations was the removal of the secco recitatives—a common feature of German adaptations of Italian operas during this period. Unlike most of the earlier Viennese German adaptations of Italian operas, including *Don Giovanni* and *Le nozze di Figaro*, Seyfried did not replace the recitatives with spoken dialogue. Instead, his brother Ignaz set new texts as accompanied recitatives. The solution was unusual in Viennese adaptations around 1800, and the motivations behind it may have included a desire to underscore the seriousness and grandeur of Mozart's work and honor the composer's legacy.

La clemenza di Tito at the Court Theater in 1804

The first production of *La clemenza di Tito* at the Theater an der Wien can be seen as an attempt to present the new institution as a worthy rival to the court theater, whereas the 1804 staging at the court theater reflected the changing relationship between the two venues in the years that followed. On 16 February 1804, the court theater impresario Braun purchased the Theater an der Wien and assumed its directorship. Less than two months later, on 12 April, a revised version of Seyfried's adaptation of *La clemenza di Tito* premiered at the court theater. At the same time, however, it incorporated significant changes shaped by the court theater's institutional structure. Most notably, the 1804 *La clemenza di Tito* was performed in Italian to accommodate the theater's Italian company and its leading stars: Antonio Brizzi as Tito, Victoria Sessi as Vitellia, and Marianna Sessi as Sesto.[16]

The accommodation of the Italian singers also influenced the set pieces, a process that had already begun at the Theater an der Wien in 1801, when Seyfried cut all three of Tito's arias, possibly to avoid their archaic style and da capo structure.[17] To compensate for the loss of Tito's solo arias, Seyfried inserted new numbers: an aria, "Mehr als Triumphe beglückt mich die Liebe," that roughly corresponds to "Del più sublime soglio"; a duet for Tito and Sesto placed immediately after Tito sends Annio to fetch Servilia, "Grosser Fürst! Ach wie verdient' ich"; and a scene and aria, "Arie und Szene"—"Freundschaft war ihm nicht heilig," that replaced Mozart's accompanied recitative "Che orror! Che tradimento!"[18]

These insertions, probably set to music by Ignaz von Seyfried (though the music itself is now lost), were most likely replaced in 1804 by new numbers that more clearly reflected the sensibilities of the court theater. Although no printed libretto from the 1804 production survives, and the conducting score was later altered for nineteenth-century revivals, the Italian version of *La clemenza di Tito* from that year can be reconstructed from circumstantial evidence—such as reviews, diary entries, and later productions based on the 1804 Viennese staging.[19] At the point corresponding to Seyfried's first-act replacement aria for Tito, "Mehr als Triumphe beglückt mich die Liebe," which originally replaced "Del più sublime soglio," the 1804 production featured an aria with chorus by the court theater music director Joseph Weigl, "Splende di Roma il fato." Its musical setting reflects the idiom of Italian opera around 1800—closer to early Rossini than to Mozart. An even more significant transformation occurred in Act 2, where the 1804 version likely restored the accompanied recitative "Che orror! Che tradimento!" and replaced Seyfried's scene and aria, "Freundschaft war ihm nicht heilig," with a re-texted grand aria with chorus from Giovanni Simone Mayr's *Misteri eleusini* (1802). A review in the *Allgemeine musikalische Zeitung* (*AmZ*) of the 1804 production suggests that both new arias were introduced to accommodate the court theater's Italian tenor Antonio Brizzi who had "only a middle voice and no true tenor" ("*nur eine Mittelstimme und keinen eigentlichen Tenor*").[20] As Senici points out, Brizzi was under contract at Milan's La Scala in the spring of 1802, shortly after the premiere of Mayr's opera, and likely knew the work.[21] It is therefore plausible that Brizzi himself proposed the insertion of Mayr's aria into the 1804 *La clemenza di Tito*. The *AmZ* does not mention the third new interpolation into the 1804 version: the replacement of Seyfried's first-act duet for Tito and Sesto with a much longer one, set to music by Weigl, "Incolpar tu non dovrai."

It also seems likely that the 1804 production reverted to Mozart's original simple recitatives. Although the surviving manuscript conducting score from the Vienna court theater's archive was used in later nineteenth-century German productions, its oldest layer is that of the Italian version of the opera and therefore probably dates to 1804, the only time when the opera was presented in the original language.[22] During the later German productions, more recent manuscript copies of Seyfried's accompanied recitatives were inserted into the score, but portions of the original Italian recitatives remain. Since there is no Italian text in the German recitative manuscripts, they must have been inserted only when the opera switched to German in 1811.

Cultural Patriotism in the 1806 *Idomeneo*

The 1804 Italian *La clemenza di Tito* ran for less than a year (though it achieved sixteen performances in 1804 alone) and was last given on 22 January 1805. The Italian opera ensemble at the Vienna court theater was disbanded shortly thereafter, giving its final performance on 20 March 1806. As Claudio Vellutini has explained, after Austria ceded control of its Italian territories to France in the Treaty of Pressburg (26 December 1805), Italian culture increasingly came to be regarded as a foreign import.[23] In the following years, Austrian institutions embraced a patriotic agenda that emphasized German opera with renewed intensity—an early nineteenth-century national ideology that combined adoration of local institutions and histories with an awareness of belonging to a larger German community.[24] These patriotic tendencies became particularly evident under the directorship of the Gesellschaft der Kavaliere, a group of Viennese music patrons who assumed management of the court theater from Braun on 1 January 1807. One of the most explicitly patriotic results of the Gesellschaft's new policies was the revival of operas by Christoph Willibald Gluck, which, according to Vellutini, "filled the void left by Italian *opera seria* . . . in the highbrow realm of tragic opera."[25] The first production introduced under the new directorship on 1 January 1807, was a German adaptation of Gluck's *Iphigénie en Tauride*, followed with a German revival of *Les pèlerins de la Mecque*, and in 1808 by *Armide* and *Iphigénie en Aulide*.

Although it preceded the ascension of the Gesellschaft and was eventually overshadowed by the focus on Gluck, the 1806 production of Mozart's *Idomeneo* should nevertheless be understood as a product of this patriotic agenda. Like the 1801 *La clemenza di Tito* and the productions of other Mozart operas in the 1790s, the 1806 *Idomeneo* was presented in a German adaptation—this time by Georg Friedrich Treitschke, one of the librettists of Beethoven's *Fidelio*. Unlike *La clemenza di Tito*, however, *Idomeneo* was not successful and disappeared after only five performances. The failure of the premiere is documented in Rosenbaum's diary:

> In the evening to the Kärntnertor Theater for the first time, *Idomeneus, König von Kreta*, an opera in three acts by Treitschke, to the music of Mozart.—Vogl as Idomeneus. I found it quite full and looked for some company to pass the evening pleasantly. . . . Never did I see a more unruly audience; not even in the Josephstadt did I see such a spectacle. After every act there was hissing; after the arias of Laucher and Marconi the hissing and pounding lasted for five minutes. Neither party gave way, and each [singer] committed the folly of stepping forward after their aria.—The opera displeased entirely, to which even the orchestra under Weigl's direction contributed its share.[26]

It is unclear who the members of the hissing and pounding parties were, or what the causes of their excitement or displeasure may have been. The poor performance of the court theater orchestra, however, is also noted by the correspondent of the *Journal des Luxus und der Moden*: "The whole thing was not properly rehearsed, the orchestra seemed half-asleep, and truly not animated by Mozart's spirit."[27]

Another aspect of the 1806 production that drew criticism was Treitschke's German adaptation, which differed significantly from the earlier Viennese reworkings of *La clemenza di Tito*. Most important, unlike Seyfried in *La clemenza di Tito*, Treitschke in *Idomeneo* replaced the recitatives with spoken dialogue. Likely seeking to imbue these dialogues with a sense of heroism and grandeur, as was expected of a German work presented at the court theater, Treitschke rewrote them in iambic pentameter. At least one contemporary reviewer—commenting on the Berlin production of Treitschke's adaptation later in 1806—complained that these poetic dialogues did not evoke the same sense of heroism as recitatives:

> The subject . . . [has] lost something through the omission of the recitatives (through which alone a work gains something definite, something whole, and by which the listener is continually sustained in a world quite other than the ordinary one)—a loss that is certainly not compensated for by the dialogue in iambs supplied by Mr. Treitschke, although it is not, in itself, unsuccessful. Heroes, such as those in this opera, can and must not speak as other people do; their language must everywhere be nothing but song, or else they annul themselves. Every listener surely feels this, even if he does not know how to account for the basis of his feeling.[28]

Moreover, Treitschke's poetic dialogues had to compensate for the meaning of the numerous arias that were excised—none of which were replaced by a new insertion, unlike in the Viennese *La clemenza di Tito*.[29] Thus, for example, Treitschke's 1806 Act 1 opened with the chorus "Godiam la pace, trionfi amore" translated as "Erhebet den Frieden, Lobsinger der Freiheit," while the recitatives and two arias that precede this chorus in Mozart's opera, Ilia's "Padre, germani, addio" and Idamante's "Non ho colpa," were compressed into Idamante's iambic monologue following the chorus.[30]

A further reason for *Idomeneo*'s less-than-ideal reception at the Vienna court theater in 1806 may have been the aesthetic status of the opera within Mozart's output at that time. Numerous commentators argued that the work deserved performance on account of Mozart's compositional mastery, while also maintaining that it was both too sophisticated to appreciate and too immature. The reviewer of the first German production of the work, in Kassel in 1802, connected its highbrow nature to its presumed Germanness but also claimed that this quality made it hard to sell to audiences:

> The opinions about the value of the music are very diverse. Connoisseurs and admirers of the composition consider it, together with *Don Giovanni*, to be the masterpiece of this great artist; the class of musicians who are more receptive to Italian melody than to German harmony find all sorts of things to carp on. They find no agreement in the style of the arias, recitatives, and choruses; the former, they say, is operatic, the latter church style. The dilettantes in the strict sense of the word, however, find the least comfort in it, for in this piece there does not occur a single theme to hum along with, and alongside the sin of its serious style the music has another to atone for, namely that it is very long.[31]

In discussing the Kassel production, the *AmZ* reviewer likewise emphasized the complexity of *Idomeneo*'s music but claimed that mainstream German audiences need to be cultivated to appreciate such a work—an attitude that the Viennese creators of the 1806 court theater production perhaps shared:

> Our theater has ventured something that no German stage has yet undertaken: to bring Mozart's *Idomeneo* to the stage. . . . To be sure, this sublime and profound music will, at first, always remain primarily for the better part of the audience; but all the more meritorious, then, for the managements, if they at least from time to time present something of this kind, so as to retain some esteem of the more cultivated, and gradually lead those who are not yet cultivated but capable of cultivation, toward something better—something that will surely succeed everywhere, if only one knows how to maintain respect and has perseverance.[32]

It is possible to imagine that the directorship of the Vienna court theater under Braun—and even more so under the Gesellschaft—envisioned productions of *Idomeneo* and later the Gluck operas as a means of cultivating the aesthetic and national tastes of the Viennese German audiences.

Contributing to the lack of popularity of the 1806 *Idomeneo* may have been the opinion that the opera was too juvenile. The Vienna *AmZ* correspondent characterized *Idomeneo* in a contradictory way: as a work in which "the Mozartian genius is already strongly and significantly expressed," but also one in which Mozart, not yet knowing the theater, "therefore often failed to be effective."[33] Similarly, the Berlin *AmZ* critic wrote:

> The music—though one cannot for a moment fail to recognize in it the great, inexhaustible artist—nonetheless also reveals the years in which it was written: namely the composer's (very early) years, in certainly overly broad elaborations and in a lack of sufficient theatrical knowledge; and, more generally, the years themselves, in certain undated elements, at least in the incidental aspects, in which opera music will always remain subject to the spirit of the times.[34]

One of the most outspoken Viennese critics of *Idomeneo* at this time was Ignaz von Mosel—composer, music critic, first biographer of Salieri, and tireless promoter of Gluck's music.[35] In an 1810 article, Mosel claimed that

Idomeneo was not one of Mozart's "best works" ("*vorzüglichsten Werke*"), the composer himself "was no longer satisfied with it in his later years," and the 1806 production of the opera at the court theater "did not please."[36] Mosel thought that *Idomeneo* "was still cast completely in the style of the old *opera seria*," in which composers considered the stage "a tournament ground" for famous singers and thus featured mainly coloratura arias and lengthy ritornellos, rather than music that would aim at "the true expression of feelings" and "proper depiction of situations." Likely under the influence of the recent Viennese Gluck productions, Mosel also wrote:

> Only Gluck had the courage to step on the hydra's head, boldly to combat the abuses of his time with deed and word (in his dramatic-musical works, and in his preface to *Alceste*), and to strive not at all for applause, but only for truth.[37]

The failure of *Idomeneo* in 1806 may have stemmed, at least in part, from the lack of ideological clarity regarding the opera's interpretation and its place within the emerging canon of Germanic masterpieces.

Germanizing *La clemenza di Tito* in 1811

Various patriotic agendas shaped the Viennese productions of *La clemenza di Tito* and *Idomeneo* in the 1810s. The 1811 production of *La clemenza di Tito* at the court theater was, according to Senici, likely intended to recapture the success of Seyfried's 1804 adaptation at the Theater an der Wien, which had remained in the repertoire until 1809.[38] At the same time, the 1811 staging also signaled a symbolic rejection of the court theater's Italian past: it adopted Seyfried's German translation from the Theater an der Wien, including his German accompanied recitatives.[39] Although the production reused Weigl's and Mayr's 1804 replacement arias, these too were now rendered in German. To diminish the opera's more archaic *seria* features still further, the only remaining da capo aria of the 1801 production, Publio's "Tardi s'avvede," was omitted.

The Germanization of the 1811 *La clemenza di Tito* was certainly prompted by the absence of an Italian company at the court theater, but it may also have been influenced by the problematic reception of Gluck's *Alceste* the previous year. The title role in *Alceste* was sung by soprano Anna Milder-Hauptmann—the leading star of Viennese opera between 1805 and 1815 and Beethoven's first Leonore—who had previously appeared as Iphigénie in *Iphigénie en Tauride* (1807), Clitemnestre in *Iphigénie en Aulide* (1808), and Armide in *Armide* (1808). Unlike these earlier nineteenth-century Viennese productions of Gluck's operas, the

1810 *Alceste* was presented by the German ensemble in Italian. Yet, *Alceste* received only four performances and disappeared from the repertoire within a month. At least one commentator attributed this failure to the use of Italian:

> It seems to us that the management made a mistake in choosing to present this opera in the Italian language, at this season of the year, and moreover almost entirely with German singers. The music is, as is well known, beautiful and full of fire and strength. Mme. Milder, as Alceste—although it was her first appearance in an Italian opera—did her utmost and was warmly received; but by the third performance the house was empty.[40]

This criticism of both language and repertoire resonates with Rosenbaum's diary, where he describes Milder's choice of *Alceste* as a "bold attempt" (27 April 1810):

> The benefit performance of Anne Pauline Milder for the first time, *Alceste*. . . . The opera bored me greatly, I did not like it, nor the ballet either. The house was not full. At the end she was called out and expressed her thanks that this bold attempt had been received with kindness.[41]

The negative response to the 1810 *Alceste* may well have contributed to the court theater's decision to abandon the previously successful Italian *La clemenza di Tito* and replace it with the German *Titus der Gütige*.

This 1811 Germanization of *La clemenza di Tito* was criticized as well, and the *AmZ* critic connected the production's failure to the inability of the German performers to present the Italianate recitatives (albeit sung in German) in a meaningful way:

> It is difficult to explain why this opera, which only a few years ago was often and gladly seen at the Theater an der Wien, has gained so little applause and attracted so few listeners at the Court Theater, unless we seek the cause partly in the unfavorable casting of certain roles and partly in the unintelligibly delivered recitatives, which make it harder for the listener to grasp the overall coherence of the work. It is true that all Italian operas are with recitatives; but the Italians make every effort to pronounce each word clearly, whereas

> most German singers, male and female, regard this type of music as a secondary matter, and believe they have done all that is required once they sing their arias, duets, etc. well.[42]

Concerns about the intelligibility of the plot in the 1811 *La clemenza di Tito* may have contributed to the decision to replace Seyfried's recitatives with spoken dialogues when the opera was revived in 1817.

Another set of critical viewpoints emerges in Mosel's review of the 1811 production.[43] Unlike in his evaluation of *Idomeneo*, Mosel acknowledges that *La clemenza di Tito* exemplified Mozart's "refining genius" ("*veredelnde Genius*"). Still, he speculates that the opera's poor reception may have resulted from "the decreasing interest in the Italian musical style," which the Viennese audience had allegedly shown for some time. Perhaps to defend Mozart's "genius," Mosel also directs sharp criticism at soprano Antonia Campi, accusing her of altering the melodic lines in Vitellia's arias to the point of unrecognizability.

Intensification of Germanocentric Attitudes in the Late 1810s

The 1817 revival of *La clemenza di Tito* was part of yet another patriotic attempt to revive older works by German composers, launched under the new directorship of the court theater, which began on 1 April 1817. Until then (and starting with Braun in 1794), the court theater had been leased to a single or multiple impresarios, but it now returned to direct state control. As Michael Jahn points out, programming decisions were firmly in the hands of Treitschke, Weigl, baritone Michael Vogl, and composer-playwright Matthias Stegmeyer.[44] The quadrumvirate's interest in constructing a patriotic canon of older works is evident from their decision to program *Don Giovanni*, *Iphigénie en Tauride*, and *La clemenza di Tito* in 1817, adding *Le nozze di Figaro* and *Die Zauberflöte* in 1818, and *Così fan tutte* and *Idomeneo* in 1819. Both *La clemenza di Tito* and *Idomeneo* were revived in the adaptations from previous years, and as before, their success was limited: *La clemenza di Tito* achieved numerous performances in its first year but appeared only sporadically thereafter, whereas *Idomeneo* remained in the repertoire for less than three months.

What had changed by 1817, however, was the critical discourse with which Viennese writers supported the performances of the two operas. Mozart and his Italian operas (together with Gluck's works) were now explicitly and without reservations presented as masterworks, as in this *AmZ* report:

> The Imperial and Royal Court Opera's effort to present to the public the finest masterpieces from home and abroad in a

> new, worthy guise was already most pleasingly demonstrated last fall in two operas, *Don Giovanni* and *Iphigénie en Tauride*. The performance of *La clemenza di Tito* . . . completed this trifecta of sublime enjoyment.[45]

An even more devotional tone appears in the reviews accompanying the 1819 production of *Idomeneo*. The anonymous reviewer for the *Wiener Theater-Zeitung* (writing under the pen name "—b—") does not even hint at suspicions of the opera's juvenile inexperience, presenting it instead as one of Mozart's most original and universal achievements:

> The composer . . . displayed in this work a maturity, a solidity, and a sureness in achieving the intended effect that stands as though it were the result of many years of continuous practice and experience. How . . . original and striking [is] every turn. . . . This is the work of the highest genius, who as such is exalted above all time and every passing taste.[46]

In the following section, the reviewer further claims that in the works after *Idomeneo*, Mozart became too conventional and thereby prefigured the lack of imagination in later generations, who prioritized pleasing audiences over creating unique artworks:

> In his later works, he has only too often asked himself, not what is most exhaustive, but rather what might be the most easily recognizable; and in this way he accustomed, enticed, compelled his contemporaries, his imitators, and the next musical generation to make the effect itself the immediate goal. Thus was formed the taste of our age, which is nothing but a sickly blossom, like an overbred carnation of which one could only wish that it might be as barren as that flower.[47]

The images of a sickly blossom and overbred carnation (i.e., ornamental, showy, but ultimately sterile), applied to the musical style typical of 1819, likely constitute a critique of the popular Italian opera of the time, especially Rossini, whose works were gaining immense popularity in Vienna between 1817 and 1820.[48] Equally striking is the reviewer's claim that the decline of later musical culture stems from Mozart's supposed compositional shortcomings after *Idomeneo*—as if Mozart's post-*Idomeneo* operas had set the tone for all later operatic compositions. This central positioning of Mozart's early works in the trajectory of musical developments leading to the reviewer's own time sharpens the patriotic and Germanocentric leanings of earlier Viennese critical discourse. It is also possible that the reviewer sought to shield *Idomeneo* from the charge that its musical style was too Italianate and not German enough.[49]

The evolution of Viennese appreciation for Mozart's *opere serie* over time is documented in Mosel's extensive essay about the 1819 production of *Idomeneo* (the first performance of which was a benefit for the mezzo-soprano Katharina Waldmüller) for the *Allgemeine musikalische Zeitung mit besonderer Rücksicht auf den Österreichischen Kaiserstaat* (General Music Journal, with Particular Emphasis on the Austrian Empire), founded in 1817 as part of the patriotic cultural campaign. Compared to Mosel's earlier views, his approach to the opera is now celebratory yet also apologetic, advocating for *Idomeneo*'s place in the operatic canon and calling for more performances despite the work's generally poor reception and its inability to compete with more recent repertoire—particularly the enormously popular works of Rossini, whose success and musical style Mosel alludes to:

> The choice of this opera does honor to the lady who selected it [Waldmüller]; and although many boxes were unoccupied, and the hall in general not as crowded as it doubtless would have been for a musical novelty in the latest fashion, it is nonetheless fine when the artist shows that his art is to him not merely "a sturdy cow that provides him with butter." Thus, too, has the Imperial and Royal Court Theater Directorate, by approving this choice and restoring to the repertoire a classical work of the highest rank, surely earned the highest gratitude of all friends of genuine music.[50]

Mosel continues with a perceptive—though also highly ideological—account of qualities of Mozart's music in *Idomeneo*. His aim is to separate Mozart as much as possible from Italian influences, while also countering the view that *Idomeneo* was merely a juvenile work:

> The music appears outdated to the admirers of the newest Italian operatic style. Leaving aside the fact that, given the period in which it was composed, this would in itself be impossible, such a judgement arises merely from the preconceived opinion—probably stemming from the knowledge that *Idomeneo* was one of the immortal Mozart's earliest works. Yet for that reason it is by no means less substantial than his other compositions; on the contrary, by virtue of the

> grandeur and the truly tragic pathos that govern the design of the whole, as well as through the masterly execution and the particularly tasteful and effective instrumentation, it occupies a distinguished place among his creations.[51]

Mosel later claims that the few passages in *Idomeneo* that might be considered juvenile are precisely those that most resemble conventional Italian music of the period:

> What may have served, though only in a very improper sense, as some slight support for that erroneous assertion are certain forms of the Italian school, which at that time had been established as inviolable law—forms that even Mozart's soaring genius did not always consider advisable to overstep, whether in order to win pardon for the new by uniting it with the traditional, or to secure for his creations—already surpassing the capacity of the age to comprehend—a certain degree of popularity through some concessions to the prevailing taste.[52]

Mosel also praises Treitschke's adaptation for excising precisely those portions he considered most like Italian opera: Arbace's two arias (No. 10a, "Se il tuo duol," and No. 22, "Se colà ne' fati è scritto"); Idomeneo's second- and third-act arias ("Fuor del mar" and No. 30a, "Torna la pace"); and Elettra's second act aria (No. 13, "Idol mio, se ritroso"). Yet Mosel acknowledges that some cuts are regrettable, implying that he did not view every excised number simply as "Italianate."[53] In particular, he laments the omission of Elettra's third-act aria "D'Oreste, d'Ajace," which he describes as "full of strength and pathos," though he nonetheless judges it dramaturgically weak because the Italian librettist placed it after the resolution of the drama.[54]

Many of the passages that Mosel regrets seeing excised from the opera are accompanied recitatives. Later in the article, he also argues that the German *Idomeneo*—and other German adaptations of heroic and tragic operas—should be performed with recitatives, since the alternation between sung and spoken delivery is "disgusting" ("*widerlich*") and "disturbing" ("*störend*").[55] Nevertheless, Mosel does not advocate for the restoration of the original Italian recitatives in *Idomeneo*. Instead, perhaps under the influence of Seyfried's earlier adaptation of *La clemenza di Tito*, he suggests that Treitschke's iambic spoken passages be set to a string accompaniment.

In their approach to the recitatives, Mosel and other commentators on early nineteenth-century Viennese productions of *La clemenza di Tito* and *Idomeneo* demonstrate highly flexible views on *Werktreue*, the fidelity to a composer's presumed original intentions, a concept that gradually became more prominent in discussions of the musical canon throughout the nineteenth century.[56] For Viennese critics, Mozart's serious operas were to be performed as representative masterpieces of a German genius, and his "spirit," often loosely defined, was to be channeled as fully as possible. Yet for the sake of making these works appear grander and more dramatic, in line with what early nineteenth-century Viennese supporters of German culture understood as Mozart's spirit, they could be substantially altered—whether by including new recitatives, excising music, or adding entirely new numbers. Treitschke's 1806 *Idomeneo* adaptation (used in the 1819 production) presents another option for reshaping Mozart's music: a substantial alteration of the famous third-act quartet "Andrò ramingo e solo." In the original composition, Idamante, Ilia, Idomeneo, and Elettra express their hopelessness and despair, and Treitschke adds a male chorus that comments antiphonally on their anguished statements:

Wie läßt man Rath und Pflicht,	How can one forsake duty and counsel,
Wann Liebe zu uns spricht?	When love speaks to us?
Eile, eile!	Hasten, hasten!
Freundes Wort lockt ihn nicht.	A friend's word does not entice him.
Ihm droht ein Grab,	A grave threatens him,
Er stürzt hinab!	He plunges downward!
Segnet ihn, ihr Götter!	Bless him, you gods!
Hört uns, lenkt von Ihm,	Hear us, turn away from him
Gefahr und Tod.	Danger and death.

The chorus was added both to the string lines that alternate antiphonally with the soloists throughout the quartet and to the instrumental postlude.[57] The effect parallels, to some degree, the interpolated choral arias that replaced numbers in Viennese productions of *La clemenza di Tito*.

Although such a reworking of Mozart's music would later seem unacceptable to advocates of strict *Werktreue*, Mosel praised it enthusiastically:

> Lastly, the quartet in the third act must be mentioned, where all four voices are balanced in the most beautiful way, each contributing its full effect to this magnificent piece of music, marked by the deepest emotion and the highest compositional

> skill. Part of the instrumental accompaniment—without the addition of a single extra note—was adapted so effectively as a men's chorus that even Mozart himself could not have withheld his approval.[58]

Mosel's enthusiasm for this substantial reworking of Mozart's quartet is a striking example of how the national canon was conceptualized dialectically in early nineteenth-century Vienna. An Italian opera could be admitted into the German operatic canon on the basis of flexible and adjustable criteria that demanded both fidelity to and departure from the composer's intentions.

Conclusion

Mosel's remarks and those of the anonymous *Theater-Zeitung* reviewer are connected by a shared desperation—an anxious urge to defend Mozart's *Idomeneo* from Viennese indifference. This anxiety must have stemmed from the broader changes occurring in the Viennese theater world at the time. As Vellutini explains, after Napoleon's defeat Italian territories once again came under Habsburg administration, which initiated a reexamination and gradual reintroduction of Italian culture into the Austrian imperial identity.[59] Throughout the late 1810s and early 1820s, an intense debate unfolded in Viennese journals and official documents, in which certain intellectuals and state officials voiced concerns that "reestablishing Italian opera (and Italian arts in general) within the empire's cultural mosaic interfered with the preeminence that German culture earned during the campaign against Napoleon, a preeminence that, as far as opera was concerned, was anything but consolidated due to financially precarious grounds."[60] Between 1819 and 1821, moreover, Viennese imperial officials engaged in heated discussions about reinstituting Italian opera at the court theater and even about leasing the institution to an Italian impresario. This latter course was realized on 6 November 1821, when the theater was leased to Domenico Barbaja, an Italian impresario. These institutional transformations may have prompted Viennese commentators, most notably Mosel, to regard Mozart's Italian *opere serie*—together with Gluck's serious French works—as canonical masterworks of indisputable status.

The desperate campaign in defense of Mozart's serious operas was ultimately unsuccessful. The effusive reviews of *Idomeneo* by Mosel and his colleague stand in stark contrast to Rosenbaum's report on the opera's 1819 premiere (25 November):

> Kärntnertor Theater . . . *Idomeneo* opera in 3 acts by Mozart. . . . The first act, which included the ballet, made no impression at all. . . . In the third act a quartet with chorus was repeated—overall the opera was not successful—nor was the house full, several boxes were empty.—Neptune's appearance caused a great stench.[61]

After its disappearance from the Viennese stage in early 1820, nearly six decades passed before *Idomeneo* was revived (1879). *La clemenza di Tito* appeared sporadically in the 1820s, then likewise vanished for more than a decade (until 1849). The same fate befell most of Gluck's operas: although *Iphigénie en Tauride* was performed occasionally through 1837, it then disappeared until 1856; *Iphigénie en Aulide* did not return until 1867; *Armide* until 1869; and *Alceste* until 1885.

The first two decades of the nineteenth century were thus an early heyday of eighteenth-century serious opera at the Viennese court theater, reflecting not so much the intrinsic musical qualities of these works as the degree to which they resonated with the patriotic, Germanocentric discourse in Vienna during and after the Napoleonic Wars. Once *La clemenza di Tito* and *Idomeneo* resurfaced in new productions later in the nineteenth century, they became subjects of new interpretations, with different values and political sentiments projected onto them—but that must be a subject of another study.

NOTES

1. For a study of the ideological underpinnings of the reception of *La clemenza di Tito* in Germany around 1800, see Sergio Durante, "Mozarts *La clemenza di Tito* und der deutsche Nationalgedanke: Ein Beitrag zur *Titus*-Rezeption im 19. Jahrhundert," *Musikforschung* 53/4 (October–December 2000): 389–400. For a study of the opera's reception in Prague throughout the nineteenth century, see Martin Nedbal, *Mozart's Operas and National Politics: Canon Formation in Prague from 1791 to the Present* (New York: Cambridge University Press, 2023), 143–82 (chap. 4).

2. These productions are discussed in Martin Nedbal, "Mozart, Da Ponte, and Censorship: *Don Giovanni* and *Così fan tutte* at the Vienna Court Theater, 1798–1804," *LiTheS: Zeitschrift für Literatur- und Theatersoziologie* 11/15 (2018): 75–109, https://unipub.uni-graz.at/download/pdf/2542444.pdf.

3. These debates are discussed in Nedbal, *Viennese Opera and Morality in the Age of Mozart and Beethoven* (New York: Routledge, 2017), 155–79 (chap. 5).

4. The emergence of Mozart's operas as national icons is also discussed in Durante, "Mozarts *La clemenza di Tito*," 391.

5. Ibid., 393–94.

6. *Deutschland* 2 (1796): 271. All translations are my own.

7. Otto Erich Deutsch, *Mozart: Die Dokumente seines Lebens* (Kassel: Bärenreiter, 1961), 413 (hereafter *MDL*); see also Otto Erich Deutsch, *Mozart: A Documentary Biography* (Stanford, CA: Stanford University Press, 1966), 472–73 (hereafter *MDB*).

8. *MDL*, 422; *MDB*, 486.

9. Austrian National Library, shelfmark Cod. Ser. n. 194, Joseph Karl Rosenbaum, "Tagebuch," vol. 1 (1 September 1797–31 December 1798), 34 verso. Question marks in the quotation refer to names or words that could not be deciphered.

10. *MDL*, 423–24; *MDB*, 487–88.

11. Austrian National Library, shelfmark Cod. Ser. n. 196, Rosenbaum, "Tagebuch," vol. 3 (1 July 1800–30 April 1801), 40 recto.

12. John Rice, *W. A. Mozart: "La clemenza di Tito"* (Cambridge: Cambridge University Press, 1991), 106–7.

13. See Nedbal, *Viennese Opera*, 123–54 (chap. 4).

14. Emanuele Senici, *La clemenza di Tito di Mozart: I primi trent'anni (1791–1821)* (Turnhout: Brepols, 1997), 69–70.

15. The adaptation was published as *Titus. Eine große Oper in zwey Aufzügen, aus dem Italienischen frey übersetzt von Herrn Joseph Ritter von Seyfried, der Rechte Kandidaten* (Vienna: Schmidt, 1801).

16. Marianna Sessi started her career in the 1790s but stopped public appearances after her marriage to Franz Joseph von Natorp. Senici claims that she returned to the stage with *La clemenza di Tito*. She in fact appeared previously on 7 January 1804, as Aspasia in a new court theater production of Salieri's *Axur, re d'Ormus*. Senici is confusing Marianna Sessi with her younger sister Victoria, who indeed made her stage debut as Vitellia in *La clemenza di Tito* on 12 April 1804. Senici, *La clemenza di Tito di Mozart*, 74; and Michael Jahn, *Die Wiener Hofoper von 1794 bis 1810: Musik und Tanz im Burg- und Kärntnertortheater* (Vienna: Apfel, 2011), 203.

17. Seyfried also cut Annio's two arias and Servilia's "S'altro che lagrime."

18. Seyfried's adaptation presents a much more decisive Tito, who is determined to punish Sesto for his crimes and thus strongly differs from the more indecisive Mozartian Tito. See Senici, *La clemenza di Tito di Mozart*, 73–74.

19. See ibid., 75.

20. "Nachrichten, Wien, den 16ten April," *AmZ* 6 (25 April 1804): col. 504.

21. Senici, *La clemenza di Tito di Mozart*, 79.

22. Austrian National Library, shelfmark OA.205. See also Senici, *La clemenza di Tito di Mozart*, 84.

23. Claudio Vellutini, *Entangled Histories: Opera and Cultural Exchange between Vienna and the Italian States after Napoleon* (New York: Oxford University Press, 2025), 40.

24. See Durante, "Mozarts *La clemenza di Tito*," 397.

25. Vellutini, *Entangled Histories*, 34.

26. Austrian National Library, shelfmark Cod. Ser. n. 198, Joseph Karl Rosenbaum, "Tagebuch," vol. 5 (12 January 1803–31 May 1806), 125 recto.

27. "Ostermesse in Wien—Theaterneuigkeiten, Wien d. 17. Mai 1806," *Journal des Luxus und der Moden* 21/6 (June 1806): 371.

28. "Nachrichten, Berlin, d. 9ten Aug.," *AmZ* 8 (20 August 1806): col. 747.

29. The only documented replacement was of an unspecified duet by Weber for Ilia and Idamante's duet in Act 3, mentioned in the review of the 1806 Berlin performance.

30. No libretto was published for the 1806 Vienna production of *Idomeneo*, but the musical structure of the opera can be gleaned from the text published for the Berlin production from the same year: *Arien und Gesänge aus Idomeneus, König von Creta, Oper in drey Aufzügen von Treitschke* (Berlin, 1806). The spoken dialogues in iambic pentameter are preserved both in the manuscript prompter's libretto for the 1819 production (Austrian National Library, shelfmark Mus.Hs.32550) and the conducting score from the court theater archive (Austrian National Library, OA.53).

31. "Idomeneus von Mozart, in Kassel," *Zeitung für die elegante Welt* 2 (11 February 1802): col. 144.

32. "Kassel," *AmZ* 4 (17 February 1802): col. 342.

33. "Nachrichten, Wien, d. 31ten May," *AmZ* 8 (11 June 1806): cols. 586–87.

34. *AmZ* 8 (20 August 1806): col. 747.

35. On Mosel's views of Mozart's opera in general, see Theophil Antonicek, "Ignaz von Mosel (1772–1844): Biographie und Beziehungen zu den Zeitgenossen" (PhD diss., University of Vienna, 1962), 377–84.

36. [Ignaz von] M[osel], "Notizen," *Der Sammler* (24 November 1810): 574.

37. Ibid.

38. Senici, *La clemenza di Tito di Mozart*, 84.

39. The libretto for this production was published as *Titus der Gütige* (Vienna: Wallishauser, 1811).

40. "Nachrichten, Wien," *AmZ* 12 (30 May 1810): col. 555.

41. Austrian National Library, shelfmark Cod. Ser. n. 200, Rosenbaum, "Tagebuch," vol. 7 (1 January 1810–31 December 1813), 14 verso.

42. "Nachrichten, Wien, Uebersicht des Monats Januar," *AmZ* 13 (20 February 1811): col. 145.

43. M[osel], "Notizen," *Der Sammler* (22 January 1811): 40.

44. Michael Jahn, *Die Wiener Hofoper von 1810 bis 1836: Das Kärntnertortheater als Hofoper* (Vienna: Apfel, 2007), 19.

45. "Theater, Hof-Oper nächst Kärnthnerthore," *Allgemeine musikalische Zeitung mit besonderer Rücksicht auf den Österreichischen Kaiserstaat* (4 December 1817): col. 418.

46. "Neuigkeiten, K. k. Hoftheater nächst dem Kärnthnerthor," *Wiener-Theater-Zeitung* (4 December 1819): 580.

47. Ibid.

48. For a basic overview, see Jahn, *Die Wiener Hofoper von 1810 bis 1836*, 31.

49. See Durante, "Mozarts *La clemenza di Tito*," 393.

50. [Ignaz] v[on] Mosel, "Wiener-Bühnen," *Allgemeine musikalische Zeitung mit besonderer Rücksicht auf den Österreichischen Kaiserstaat* 3 (4 December 1819): col. 780.

51. Ibid., col. 780–81.

52. Ibid., col. 781.

53. Specifically, Mosel refers to Ilia's first aria (No. 1, "Padre, germani, addio"), Idamante's second aria (No. 7, "Il padre adorato"), Idomeneo's second-act accompanied recitative preceding "Fuor del mar" ("Qual mi conturba i sensi"), the third-act accompanied recitative introducing Ilia and Idamante's duet ("Odo? O sol quel che brama finge l'udito"), the recitative that precedes the fourth-act quartet ("Cieli! Che vedo?"), and a third-act aria with chorus for Idomeneo (No. 26, "Accogli, oh re del mar").

54. Mosel, "Wiener-Bühnen," col. 782.

55. Ibid., cols. 782–83.

56. On the evolving concept of *Werktreue* in performances of Mozart's operas in nineteenth-century Prague, see Nedbal, *Mozart's Operas and National Politics*, 17–58 (chap. 1).

57. A musical score of this adaptation is preserved in the Vienna court theater manuscript conducting score of the opera, Austrian National Library, OA.53, vol. 3.

58. Mosel, "Wiener-Bühnen," col. 784.

59. Vellutini, *Entangled Histories*, 51.

60. Ibid., 69.

61. Austrian National Library, shelfmark Cod. Ser. n. 202, Rosenbaum, "Tagebuch," vol. 9 (1 November 1817–30 June 1821), 94 verso.

PART II: DOCUMENTS

Friedrich Schlichtegroll's Biography of Mozart: An Introduction and Reevaluation

SIMON P. KEEFE

Friedrich Adolph Heinrich von Schlichtegroll (1765–1822) was a Renaissance man of the late eighteenth and early nineteenth centuries, demonstrating a diverse range of scholarly interests and expertise. Born in Waltershausen, eight miles west of Gotha in Thuringia, at the geographical center of modern-day Germany, Schlichtegroll studied law and theology at the University of Göttingen, and from 1787 taught religion, Hebrew, German, and Latin at a school in Gotha. He published on archaeology and gemstones early in his career, and numismatics later on. Once based at the Bayerische Akademie der Wissenschaften (Bavarian Academy of Sciences) in Munich as Secretary General (from 1807), he was responsible for the academy's publications, natural history collection, observatory, and chemical laboratory, also helping to popularize Alois Senefelder's lithography technique.[1] It is for his thirty-four volumes of obituaries (*Nekrologen*) published between 1791 and 1806, however, that Schlichtegroll is most famous, including an approximately 6,000-word obituary of Mozart, published in 1793.

Often using the ducal library in Gotha for research purposes,[2] Schlichtegroll began with a volume dedicated to deaths from 1790 onward. As explained in the preface to *Nekrolog aus das Jahr 1791*, volume 2, which carried the Mozart obituary, Schlichtegroll focused particularly on German deceased who "would not be known or appreciated at all or widely enough" without the obituary.[3] Influenced by the biographical dictionaries of Georg Christoph Hamberger and Johann Georg Meusel, as well as Johann Gottfried Herder's idea of obituaries inspiring readers to "continue to work for the advancement of human society," Schlichtegroll's *Nekrolog* was "a prime model for the didactic and sociocritical impulse of Enlightenment biography."[4] Selecting his individuals on merit, not according to social standing, he concentrated especially on achievements derived from hard work and exemplary character. He also wanted the obituaries to be relatable to the experiences of his readers, rather than appearing abstract.[5]

Schlichtegroll's well-known approach to gathering information for the Mozart obituary involved sending a series of questions about Mozart to a canon at Salzburg Cathedral probably familiar to him from clerical and intellectual circles, Albert von Mölk, in the hope that Mölk would either answer them himself or know someone else who could. Mölk passed them on to Mozart's sister, Nannerl, who in spring 1792 provided extended reminiscences, including from family friend and court trumpeter Johann Andreas Schachtner. Mölk then edited and wrote a postscript to these reminiscences when replying to Schlichtegroll. More correspondence ensued, with Schlichtegroll posing further questions.[6] Schlichtegroll worked closely with this material, integrating Nannerl's, Schachtner's, and Mölk's observations with his own thoughts in the process of producing a broadly chronological account of Mozart's early life.[7] We know considerably less about Schlichtegroll's interactions with Viennese sources. He wrote to the well-connected Viennese poet, writer and court official Joseph Friedrich Freiherr von Retzer around the same time as he contacted Mölk, and had not received a reply by 25 May 1792.[8] Retzer had provided Schlichtegroll with material for the obituary of the Vienna-based mineralogist, metallurgist, and prominent Freemason Ignaz von Born that appeared in the same volume of the *Nekrolog* as the Mozart obituary.[9] Retzer probably also contributed to another one in this volume, for the Tyrolean jurist, polymath, cartographer, and diplomat Joseph Freiherr von Sperges, given references in it to Retzer and his work.[10] However, the nature and content of any Mozart-related information Schlichtegroll obtained from Retzer, or anyone else in Vienna for that matter, is unknown.

In an attempt to explain the significance of Schlichtegroll's biography, I examine its reception and re-evaluate its content, orientation, and style. I then turn to Schlichtegroll's rarely mentioned addendum published in 1798, on the genesis and composition of Mozart's Requiem.

The Reception of Schlichtegroll's Mozart Biography

The importance of Schlichtegroll's obituary of Mozart, in effect as the instigator of the Mozart biographical tradition, has rarely been in doubt. Franz Niemetschek's biography of 1798 drew almost entirely on Schlichtegroll for his account of Mozart's early life; Théophile Fréderic Winckler used it for his *Notice biographique sur Mozart* (1801), helping to launch French critical reception of Mozart; and Stendhal extensively plagiarized it via Winckler in his widely read 1814 biography.[11] The anecdotes conveyed by Schlichtegroll soon acquired a life of their own, appearing regularly in a wide range of publications. For example, Schachtner's recollection of interrupting the four-year-old Mozart at work on a fiendishly difficult, technically competent concerto, spread around Europe and America in the first half of the nineteenth century.[12]

Negativity has often surrounded Schlichtegroll's biography. In the mid-nineteenth century, Barbey d'Aurevilly found it "colorless" and "dry," while Paul de Musset considered it, and other early Mozart biographies, an erroneous portrayal of "a sort of sublime madman leading a disorderly life."[13] The *Revue chrétienne* thought it "meager" and no longer necessary to read, "thank God," and *The Pall Mall Budget* "so full of outrageous inventions and so little worthy of its subject."[14] For Ludwig Nohl, Schlichtegroll was a "collector of purely historical data," and for Rudolph Procházka—favoring Niemetschek over Schlichtegroll in a partisan pro-Czech account—a biographer "coldly contented . . . with listing the bare facts," rather than conveying (like Niemetschek) "the warm and true-to-life traits of the immortal [Mozart]."[15] Bizarrely, G. Héquet in *L'Athenaeum français* even doubted Schlichtegroll's existence, regarding him as a figment of Stendhal's imagination.[16] While the Mozart biographer Otto Jahn and scholar Constantin von Wurzbach were more circumspect, their comments about Schlichtegroll retained a critical edge. Jahn considered the biography "precise and trustworthy so far as it relates to the period of [Mozart's] childhood . . . but the notices of his later years are superficial and the judgment passed upon him as a man rests upon a preconceived and unfavourable opinion which then prevailed in Vienna partly on professional grounds and which took such deep root that even at the present day I know not if I shall succeed in establishing the truth."[17] Similarly, Wurzbach found Schlichtegroll "as far as Mozart's youth is concerned, exact and reliable," but "cursory, extremely incomplete and superficial" from 1773 onward.[18] Criticisms also persist in the modern era. Peter Branscombe reprimanded Schlichtegroll for exaggerating the number of performances of *The Magic Flute* in its first year,[19] as if he would have had access to the kind of scholarly resources and infrastructure available to late twentieth-century scholars for checking information. Maynard Solomon reproached him for including the "condescending formulations" of the postscript to Nannerl's reminiscences, "whence they made their way into many influential writings."[20] John Daverio regarded Schlichtegroll's obituary as "more a collection of anecdotes peppered with random observations on the works than a genuine biography," while Piero Melograni considered its prevailing image of Mozart as child "superficially kindly but malevolent in substance."[21] Roye E. Wates found problematic "inaccurate obituary writer" Schlichtegroll's personal unfamiliarity with the composer and the towns of Salzburg and Vienna, absence of musical credentials, and "gloriously overwritten revisions [of] and interpolations [to]" source material.[22] For Lucien Karhausen, Schlichtegroll's idea that "Mozart had to pay for his genius by immaturity, weakened body growth, disordered life and self-destruction" constituted "bogus psychology" rooted in the old-fashioned, mid-eighteenth-century work of Alexander Gottlieb Baumgarten.[23] Widow Constanze Mozart's dislike of Schlichtegroll's biography, demonstrated by her purchase of six hundred copies of the 1794 Graz edition in order to destroy them, has also not helped its reception. The most plausible reason for Constanze's action, according to Ruth Halliwell, was a fear that "the picture of Wolfgang as a high earner but a reckless spender with tendencies to dissipation might damage her chances of public sympathy and charity—her claims of support were based on a picture of Wolfgang as unlucky in his finances, and in no way to be censured for the plight in which he had left his family."[24]

The most controversial aspect of Schlichtegroll's obituary is his portrayal of Mozart as a perpetual child. In this respect, Schlichtegroll followed an addendum to Nannerl's reminiscences almost certainly penned by Mölk: "Apart from his music he was almost always a child, and thus he remained: and this is the main feature of his character on the dark side; he always needed a father's, or mother's or some other guardian's care."[25] This idea immediately gained traction in the biographical arena, joining hermeneutic forces with one about Mozart's flame burning itself out prematurely.[26] It also acquired intellectual credibility through citation in the 1844 edition of Arthur Schopenhauer's influential *The World as Will and Idea*, which regarded child-like qualities as a prerequisite for genius. For Schopenhauer, "Whoever does not to a certain extent remain all his life a big child but becomes a grave, sober, thoroughly composed and reasonable man may be a very useful and capable citizen of this world, but never a genius. In fact the genius is so because that predominance of the sensible system and of intellectual activity which is natural to childhood maintains itself in him in an abnormal manner through his whole life, thus here becomes perennial."[27] While the biographical influence of Mozart as perpetual child persisted into the twentieth century, including in Alfred Einstein's and Wolfgang Hildesheimer's portrayals of a musician who "never learned how to deal with the world,"[28] critics have generally distanced themselves from it, attempting to ground Mozart's achievements in mature engagement with late eighteenth-century aesthetic, stylistic, and cultural worlds instead.[29]

A Reevaluation of Schlichtegroll's Biography

Schlichtegroll's biographical limitations and biases are obvious to a modern reader, with lopsided attention to Mozart's career up to 1775, insufficient focus on his activities in Vienna, and superficial summaries of many of his musical accomplishments. It is certainly not a well-balanced account. Twice the amount of space is devoted to the Schachtner anecdote about the infant Mozart composing a concerto, for example, as to Mozart's entire ten-year career in Vienna. Yet a carefully proportioned, late eighteenth-century biographical assessment of a recently deceased, well-traveled musician is itself an unrealistic expectation given the difficulties at that time of locating and accessing important information and sources.

While scholars unhesitatingly assume that the imbalance between Schlichtegroll's discussion of Mozart's Salzburg and Vienna years is attributable to a discrepancy in the material received from contacts in the two locations, this remains speculation in the absence of extant Viennese sources. For Cooper Clarke, Schlichtegroll recording "almost nothing about Mozart the mature man and composer living and working in Vienna" resulted in an "enforced concentration on Mozart's childhood and youth."[30] Yet other obituary biographies in the *Nekrolog auf das Jahr 1791* also emphasize childhood and youthful and early family-related activities, including those of the theologian, church historian, and biblical commentator Johann Salomo Semler, the jurist and philosopher Daniel Nettelbladt, and the German theologian and natural scientist Johann Esaias Silberschlag.[31] Schlichtegroll thus appears to be inherently interested in this biographical area. Indeed, in a footnote to the Silberschlag biography, he explains the importance of focusing on the early years of a biographized individual's life, with examples for his readership in mind:

> It requires an apology that the obituaries so often dwell on early, seemingly insignificant youthful incidents, especially on the reasons for choosing a profession. But since so very much depends on this choice for the usefulness and peace of future life, little can be achieved by generalizing, and because fathers and sons are often very worried about this subject, it seems that a compilation of many biographical accounts can be of real use to these two types of readers. . . . Not to mention that this often reveals many of the idiosyncrasies of the man whose life is being reported, as is the case with Silberschlag.[32]

It is plausible, therefore, that Schlichtegroll made an active choice to focus on Mozart's early development and to consider only briefly events after 1775 because he genuinely believed that Mozart had reached "the pinnacle of his art" by then,[33] not because at all costs he had to make an interpretative necessity out of an informational deficiency. The obituary of Mozart is substantial by the standards of the first two years of the *Nekrolog*; only seven of a total of eighty published in the first four volumes (two volumes each for deaths in 1790 and 1791) are longer than Mozart's, including those of the indisputably famous Benjamin Franklin and Emperor Joseph II. As a result, Schlichtegroll may have been reluctant to carry a more extended Mozart biography than the one he ultimately published. Rejecting significant amounts of information received from Salzburg would have been difficult, moreover, given the rich, firsthand testimonials from sources so close to the composer.[34] If Retzer was Schlichtegroll's only Viennese source as Cooper Clarke suggests,[35] it is unlikely that material from him—irrespective of the amount of it—would have been as compellingly personal as the material from Nannerl and Schachtner. We cannot assume, as Cooper Clarke does,[36] that just because Schlichtegroll used almost everything received from Nannerl, Schachtner, and Mölk, he would have done the same with Viennese materials; interpretative choices, as well as practical decisions about overall length, would have entered the equation.

Schlichtegroll wanted his biographies to be entertaining as well as instructive.[37] Thus, he needed to tell good stories as well as document exemplary lives. The anecdotes of Nannerl and Schachtner comprise much of the Mozart biography, and we know that anecdotes are important sources of information in biographies from centuries past, including for Mozart.[38] Even if Nannerl and Schachtner do a lot of Schlichtegroll's storytelling for him, he is a skilled narrator himself, as demonstrated by the highly condensed description of Mozart's final decade in Vienna. Referencing success with the musical public, the quantity and quality of instrumental music, the "equal applause" accorded to instrumental and operatic works, and the success of *The Magic Flute*, Schlichtegroll quotes Haydn's statement to Leopold Mozart (given in Nannerl's reminiscences and taken from the family correspondence in 1785): "I say to you, before God and as an honest man, that I consider your son to be the greatest composer I have ever heard of; he has taste and possesses the most thorough knowledge in the art of composition."[39] A musician of Haydn's authority and repute articulating Mozart's greatness facilitates Schlichtegroll's cursory treatment of Mozart's Viennese years because it constitutes an unambiguous statement about Mozart's achievements and status from an unimpeachable source. It also represents one of the earliest comings together of the two composers in a published text from

Mozart's posthumous period, thereby instigating a canonizing process that continues to the present day.[40] Moreover, Haydn's statement is then used as an interpretative cipher for the Requiem (acknowledged here as incomplete), as the work's virtues are said to validate Haydn's judgment.

Projected through skillful storytelling, the idea of Mozart's complete immersion in musical activities gathers momentum in Schlichtegroll's biography and is as hermeneutically significant and influential as the idea of him as a perpetual child.[41] We are told that before demonstrating musical prowess, Mozart was naturally inclined to immersive behavior as an infant, forgetting to eat and drink when deeply involved in an activity. Later, he lost all inclination for childhood games and needed musical accompaniment to everything; his ear was also "constructed entirely for music" and his soul "continuously occupied" by it. After returning from the Grand Tour of central and northern Europe, moreover, he studied constantly in pursuit of perfection.[42] In order to pack a final punch, Schlichtegroll cannily reserves the climactic manifestations of his absorption-in-music narrative until discussing Mozart's character and personality in the concluding pages. As he explains, Mozart "seemed to be someone quite different, seemed to become a higher being, as soon as he sat down at the keyboard. Then his spirit and his undivided concentration were directed at the single object for which he was born—the harmonies of tones."[43] His immersion in music also affected everyday activities: "Even his hands had so firm an orientation toward the keyboard that he rarely, and only with significant effort and fear, managed to cut his meat at meals; ordinarily he would ask his wife for the favor." Finally, when he was playing, "it was necessary to try to prevent him from forgetting himself entirely and damaging his health. From childhood on, he especially loved to play at night; if he sat down at the keyboard at 9 o'clock, he was not to be persuaded to abandon it before midnight, and, even then, one had to half compel him; otherwise he would have fantasized the whole night long."[44] These statements, especially at the end of the biography, collectively portray Mozart's mind and body designed for one activity alone—making music.

The Supplement to Schlichtegroll's Biography of Mozart

Schlichtegroll's immersion-in-music narrative helps to explain why he included the story of the commissioning and composition of the Requiem in a supplement to the Mozart biography published in 1798.[45] It completes the interpretative circle, so to speak, of Mozart dying in music just as (in effect) he was born into it. The inclusion of the story is also attributable to Schlichtegroll's fascination with a biographized individual's final days. In the *Nekrolog 1791*, attention is devoted to, for example, the progression of Semler's final illness and last theological interactions; Sperges dying with a smile on his face in conversation with friends; the poet and politician Eberhard Friedrich Freiherr von Gemmingen's painful abdominal cramps; the continued hard work and cheerfulness of Nettelbladt and Silberschlag as the end approached; and theologian Johann Franz Christoph Steinmetz's gout, dizziness, headaches, and stroke.[46] The demise of German philologist and pedagogue Johann Heinrich Justus Köppen, who, like Mozart, died shortly before his thirty-sixth birthday, elicits particularly graphic detail, including Köppen's hallucinations of a great banquet of the gods, his wife's attempts to calm him, and an ostentatious gesture of thanks to God for salvation shortly before he died.[47]

The Mozart supplement, rarely discussed in the secondary literature,[48] is translated here in full:

> Every anecdote regarding this immortal artist, no matter how small, deserves to be preserved and distributed. Page 108 in Mozart's biography in the obituary, which was developed from the papers of his sister and friends in Salzburg, mentions his famous Requiem. Now H[err] W. Wittich gives us in the *Leipz[iger] Allg[emeine] Lit[terarischer] Anz[eiger]* 1798 No. IV an anecdote concerning this Requiem, which a credible man assures us he heard from the mouth of Mozart's widow herself.
>
> At a time when Mozart was busier than ever with works that he had undertaken partly for his own enjoyment and partly for others, a man unknown to him came with the request to compose a Requiem for him. He had, he said, received the commission from a Catholic prince who wished to have it soon in order that, as he was soon approaching the end of his life, he could be present at the performance of the Requiem for his death, on the one hand to prepare for it, but on the other hand to take away some of his bitterness at the thought of it—and more statements of this kind. Mozart promises to take on this work, but stipulates three months, because he does not want to put aside his other works and wishes nonetheless to work on the Requiem *con amore*. The unknown man is satisfied and gives him sufficient assurance with 400 ducats as payment for it, although Mozart had only asked for 200.
>
> Mozart begins the work and finds that, as he continues, it occupies his mind more than any other work and gives his

> ideas a sublime momentum; it captivates him completely, and he forgets himself so much that he spends not only the day but also a part of his nights with it. His wife, who fears that this strain will be detrimental to his health, takes the score away from him and locks it in her desk. But he knows how to get it quickly back in his hands, and now tells his wife that, while he has undertaken the Requiem for someone else, he is now composing it for himself in order to leave it for her and his friends as a memento. Thus, this piece of music, unique of its kind, owes its existence to the talents of a man who worked on it with constant thoughts of himself and the end of his life, which he perhaps felt was no longer far away. And my friend, who shared this anecdote with me and was fortunate enough to hear this music performed, assured me that some passages moved him to tears. Instead of the three months that Mozart had initially allotted to this work, he finished it in four weeks, yet the Requiem is as long as the music for an opera. Shortly after completing it, he had his friends perform it at his house. Deeply moved and intensely shattered, he dismissed them, betook himself to bed in a feverish state, and the next morning at 10 o'clock was no more.[49]

W. Wittich published his account of the commissioning and composition of the Requiem on 5 January 1798, eleven months before Johann Friedrich Rochlitz's famous version in the Leipzig-based *Allgemeine musikalische Zeitung*.[50] There are informational similarities between Wittich and Rochlitz, including Mozart's feverish work, belief that he was writing the Requiem for himself, and supposed completion of the work, which contradicts Schlichtegroll's statement about the incomplete Requiem in the original obituary. (A third version in Niemetschek's biography, also published in 1798, has Mozart connect the Requiem to his own impending death but acknowledges the work is unfinished.)[51] Differences in detail, though, include the Catholic prince's commission to commemorate his own impending death (Wittich) rather than an anonymous "distinguished man" honoring a lost loved one (Rochlitz), and Mozart's fee for writing the work: 400 ducats (Wittich), two 100-ducat installments (Rochlitz). Stylistically, too, the accounts diverge. Rochlitz's intensified version includes Mozart "immediately" working agitatedly on the Requiem and experiencing fainting fits, a reference to the visiting messenger belonging to "the world beyond," and explicit identification of the Requiem as a "worthy monument to [Mozart's] name." While Rochlitz ultimately became more influential than Wittich where the Requiem is concerned, Wittich's story reappears on a number of occasions at the turn of the nineteenth century, especially in British publications.[52]

As a source of engaging biographical information and instigator of the Mozart biographical tradition, Schlichtegroll's 6,000-word obituary is one of the foundation stones of Mozart scholarship. Many of his views, including on Mozart's childishness and responsibility for his own demise, elicit little scholarly support in the modern era. Others still resonate, though, and can continue to motivate scholarly deliberation. For example, Schlichtegroll's dispassionate presentation of certain information, when viewed in relation to subsequent biographical interpretations and orientations, can inspire new biographical perspectives. Concerning the trip to Paris in September 1777 (actually March–September 1778), Schlichtegroll straightforwardly and concisely records the city's attractions as a musical destination, Mozart's distaste for French music, his composition of a symphony for the Concert spirituel as well as various other works, and his return to Salzburg at the beginning of 1779 following his mother's death in Paris.[53] For later biographers, with the family letters at their disposal, the turmoil associated with the six-month stay invariably dominates discussion, conditioning and solidifying an impression of musical failure. Yet, as Schlichtegroll's short passage on Paris begins to suggest, musical failure is an inappropriate characterization for the Parisian sojourn; both the number of works produced, and Mozart's development as an independent performer-composer instead point to musical success.[54] In addition, Schlichtegroll encourages us to think more than we have done hitherto about the relationship between Mozart's character and personality as a child and his character, personality, activities, and achievements as an adult. Schlichtegroll tells us, for example, that the child Mozart found playing for connoisseurs stimulating, and we know from the family correspondence that this continued into adulthood.[55] The similarities and differences in the stimulation received and exhibited over time, however, remains a topic for further investigation.

The continued rude health of Mozart biography in the modern era owes much to the start Schlichtegroll furnished for it more than 230 years ago. As William Stafford states, "It is difficult to write a dull [biography] about Mozart."[56] With vibrant source material, and a keen eye for good storytelling, Schlichtegroll surely would have agreed.

NOTES

1. For useful biographical information on Schlichtegroll, see Tobias Heinrich, "Friedrich Schlichtegroll's *Nekrolog*: Enlightenment Biography," *Les grandes figures historiques dans les lettres et les arts* 6 (2017): 11–12; and Rudolph Angermüller, "Friedrich Schlichtegrolls Nekrolog auf Ignaz von Born," *Mitteilungen der Internationale Stiftung Mozarteum* 35/1–4 (1987): 43–44.

2. Angermüller, "Schlichtegrolls Nekrolog," 43.

3. Friedrich Schlichtegroll, *Nekrolog auf das Jahr 1791*, vol. 2 (Gotha: Justus Perthes, 1793), iii. All translations, except those from the Schlichtegroll biography itself, which are taken from Susan Gillespie's translation, are my own, unless otherwise indicated.

4. Heinrich, "Friedrich Schlichtegroll's *Nekrolog*," 9–12, at 9, 10.

5. Ibid., 12–16.

6. For Schachtner's memories and Nannerl's own reminiscences, see Otto Erich Deutsch, *Mozart: Die Dokumente seines Lebens* (Kassel: Bärenreiter, 1961), 395–405 (henceforth *MDL*); Deutsch, *Mozart: A Documentary Biography*, trans. Eric Blom, Peter Branscombe, and Jeremy Noble, 3rd ed. (London: Simon & Schuster, 1990), 451–62 (henceforth *MDB*). For discussion of Schlichtegroll's approach, see Bruce Cooper Clarke, "Albert von Mölk: Mozart Myth-Maker?: Study of an 18th-Century Correspondence," *Mozart-Jahrbuch 1995*, 155–91. On pages 163–69, Cooper Clarke discusses correspondence between Mölk and Nannerl over her submission for Schlichtegroll's obituary, including a preliminary draft of the letter to Mölk, and on pages 169–72 addenda to Nannerl's reminiscences.

7. For a sentence-by-sentence discussion of the sources used by Schlichtegroll, including extended commentary, see Bruce Cooper Clarke, *The Annotated Schlichtegroll: Mozart's Obituary with Critical, Historical and Explanatory Notes* (St. Anton an der Jessnitz: n.p., 1997).

8. Ibid., 88.

9. Cooper Clarke, "Albert von Mölk: Mozart Myth-Maker?," 161.

10. See *Nekrolog 1791*, 127. Born and Sperges died before Mozart (on 28 August and 26 October 1791 respectively). Thus, Schlichtegroll probably approached Retzer about both of them before asking for information about Mozart.

11. See Niemetschek, *Life of Mozart* (1798), trans. Helen Mautner (London: Leonard Hyman, 1956); Winckler, *Notice biographique sur Mozart* (Paris: J. J. Fuchs, 1801); Henri Beyle (Stendhal), *Vies de Haydn, de Mozart, et de Métastase* (1814), trans. Richard N. Coe as *Lives of Haydn, Mozart and Metastasio* (London: Calder & Boyars, 1972). For more on Schlichtegroll's impact on Mozart biography, see William Stafford, *The Mozart Myths: A Critical Reassessment* (Stanford: Stanford University Press, 1991).

12. In early nineteenth-century Anglophone, Francophone, and Germanic publications, including in shortened and adapted forms, see for example *L'esprit des journaux* 30 (1801): 152–53; *Magasin Encyclopedique* 7/3 (1801): 33–34; *The Thespian Dictionary, or Dramatic Biography of the Eighteenth Century* (London: J. Hurst, 1802), n.p.; *Supplement to the Encyclopedia, or Dictionary of Arts, Sciences, and Miscellaneous Literature*, vol. 2 (Philadelphia: Budd and Bartram, 1803), 579–80; *La Belle Assemblée, or Bell's Court and Fashionable Magazine, Addressed Particularly to the Ladies* 2 (1807): 259–60; Alexandre Choron and F. Fayolle, *Dictionnaire historique des musiciens*, vol. 2: *M–Z* (Paris: Valade, 1811), 71; *The Power of Music, in which it is shown, by a Variety of Pleasing and Instructive Anecdotes, the Effects It Has on Man and Animals* (London: J. Harris, 1814), 46–47; Stendhal, *Lives of Haydn, Mozart and Metastasio*, 165–66; Rev. William Bingley, *Musical Biography; or Memoirs of the Lives and Writings of the Most Eminent Musical Composers and Writers* vol. 2, 2nd ed. (London: Henry Colburn, 1814), 155–56; John Mason, Olinthus Gregory, and Newton Bosworth, eds., *Pantologia: A New Cabinet Cyclopedia* 8 (1817): n.p.; G. F. Shaw, *The Panorama of Nature, or a Comprehensive View of Natural History and Botany* (London: R. Edwards, 1817),

130–31; *Ladies' Literary Cabinet,* series 1 (1820): 181–82; Johann Aloys Schlosser, *Wolfgang Amadeus Mozart: Eine begründete und ausführliche Biographie desselben* (Prague: Buchler and Schlosser, 1828), 16–17; Georg von Nissen, *Biographie W. A. Mozarts* (Leipzig: Breitkopf & Härtel, 1828), 18–19; W. T. Parke, *Musical Memoirs*, vol. 1 (London: Henry Colburn and Richard Bentley, 1830), 161–62; *Lives of Remarkable Youth, of Both Sexes* (Philadelphia: E. Littell, 1830), 91–92; *The New-York Mirror: A Repository of Polite Literature and the Arts* 8 (1831): 345; *The Lady's Book* 3 (1831): 266; George Hogarth, *Musical History, Biography, and Criticism* (London: John W. Parker, 1835), 239; Charles Frederick Partington, *The British Cyclopaedia of Biography*, vol. 2 (London: W. M. S. Orr and Co., 1838), 436; W. Mullinger Higgins, *The Philosophy of Sound and Musical Composition* (London: Orr, 1838), 249; *The London Encyclopedia* 15 (1839): 202–3; *Encyclopedia Britannica*, vol. 1, 7th ed. (Edinburgh: Adam and Charles Black, 1841), 585–86; *The United States Magazine and Democratic Review* 13 (1843): 465; *The Christian Parlor Magazine* 2 (1846): 323; Lydia Maria Child, *Flowers for Children*, vol. 3: *For Children of Eleven and Twelve Years of Age* (New York: C. S. Francis and Co., 1848), 60–61; M. P. Scudo, *Mozart et son "Don Juan"* (Paris: Bureau de la Revue des deux Mondes, 1849), 8; *Musée des familles: Lectures du soir* 19 (1851): 162–63; Johann Friedrich Kayser, ed., *Mozart-Album* (Hamburg: Trupp, 1856), 90.

13. For d'Aurevilly remarks, see "Mozart: Vie d'un artiste chrétien au dix-septième siècle," *Neue Wiener Musik-Zeitung* 6 (1857): 175; *Berliner Musik-Zeitung Echo* 8 (1848): 48; d'Aurevilly, *Les oeuvres et les hommes* (Paris: Henri Gautier, 1890), 7. For de Musset's comments, see *Revue Nationale et Étrangère Politique, Scientifique et Littéraire* 3 (1861): 395. George Grove makes a similar point about the "unfounded" charges of Schlichtegroll and Ignaz Arnold (*Mozarts Geist,* 1803), in *A Dictionary of Music and Musicians*, ed. Grove, 4 vols. (London: Macmillan, 1894), 2:397.

14. *Revue chrétienne* 20 (Paris, 1873): 161; *The Pall Mall Budget* 24 (1880): 299.

15. Ludwig Nohl, *Mozart nach den Schilderungen seiner Zeitgenossen* (Leipzig: Fr. Thiel, 1880), 1; Rudolph Procházka, *Mozart in Prag: Zum hundertjährigen Gedächtnis seines Todes* (Prague: H. Domenicus, 1892), 79. The latter is also given in *Bohemia* 64/3 (15 March 1891): 26.

16. *L'Athenaeum français* 3/49 (9 December 1854): 1147.

17. Otto Jahn, *Life of Mozart* (1856–59), trans. Pauline Townsend, 3 vols. (London: Novello, 1882), 1:iii.

18. Constantin von Wurzbach, *Mozart Buch* (Vienna: Josef Klemm, 1869), 112.

19. Peter Branscombe, *W. A. Mozart: "Die Zauberflöte"* (Cambridge: Cambridge University Press, 1991), 67.

20. Maynard Solomon, *Mozart: A Life* (New York: HarperCollins, 1995), 14.

21. John Daverio, "Mozart in the Nineteenth Century," in *The Cambridge Companion to Mozart*, ed. Simon P. Keefe (Cambridge: Cambridge University Press, 2003), 173; Piero Melograni, *Mozart: A Biography*, trans. Lydia G. Cochrane (Chicago: University of Chicago Press, 2007), 182.

22. Roye E. Wates, *Mozart: An Introduction to the Music, the Man, and the Myths* (Milwaukee, WI: Amadeus Press, 2010), 28, 15.

23. Lucien Karhausen, *The Bleeding of Mozart* (Xlibris Corporation [no publication location], 2011), 58.

24. Ruth Halliwell, *The Mozart Family: Four Lives in a Social Context* (Oxford: Clarendon Press, 1998), 587. Less plausibly, Melograni suggests that Constanze destroyed the volumes "because Schlichtegroll had dared to state that Mozart had not completed the Requiem." See *Mozart: A Biography*, 244. For the 1794 edition, see Schlichtegroll, *Mozarts Leben* (Graz: Joseph Georg Hubeck, 1794). This publication could have been a private commission, as Hubeck was a bookbinder by trade and apparently published nothing else. See the discussion in Ottfield Hafner, "Die Grazer Ausgabe von Schlichtegrolls *Mozarts Leben*," *Mitteilungen der Internationalen Stiftung Mozarteum* 27/1–2 (1979): 18–21.

25. As given in *MDB*, 462. On the authorship of the addendum, see Cooper Clarke, "Albert von Mölk: Mozart Myth-Maker?" 177. See also Schlichtegroll, *Nekrolog 1791*, 2:109–10.

26. See Stafford, *Mozart Myths*, 95–97; and Adeline Mueller, "Mythmaking," in *Mozart in Context*, ed. Simon P. Keefe (Cambridge: Cambridge University Press, 2019), 284.

27. Arthur Schopenhauer, *The World as Will and Idea* (1844 ed.), trans. R. B. Haldane and J. Kemp, vol. 3 (London: Truebner and Co., 1886), 164.

28. See Alfred Einstein, *Mozart: His Character, His Work*, trans. Arthur Mendel and Nathan Broder (1946) (London: Panther Books, 1971), at 40; and Wolfgang Hildesheimer, *Mozart* (1979), trans. Marion Faber (New York: Vintage, 1983).

29. For more on the "myth of the eternal child," with Leopold Mozart interpreted tendentiously as the original perpetrator of it, see Solomon, *Mozart*, 3–18. For a recent more sober and well-argued study of Mozart and childhood, set in literary and cultural context and demonstrating Mozart's important position vis-à-vis ideas, practice, and realities related to childhood, see Adeline Mueller, *Mozart and the Mediation of Childhood* (Chicago: University of Chicago Press, 2021).

30. Cooper Clarke, *The Annotated Schlichtegroll*, 4.

31. *Nekrolog 1791*, 2:4–15, 178–80, 192–93.

32. Ibid., 2:193–94.

33. Ibid., 106.

34. By far the longest obituary in the first four volumes of Schlichtegroll's *Nekrolog* is the one for Semler printed immediately before Mozart's (see *Nekrolog 1791*, 2:1–81). The quantity and quality of personal information provided by Semler himself, in an autobiography utilized by Schlichtegroll (see the footnote on page 3), may help explain the length. In addition, Semler was based in Saalfeld, only forty miles from Schlichtegroll's hometown of Gotha, so may have been known personally to Schlichtegroll, thereby facilitating further personal recollections.

35. Cooper Clarke, *The Annotated Schlichtegroll*, 92.

36. Ibid., 92.

37. Heinrich, "Friedrich Schlichtegroll's *Nekrolog*," 16.

38. For biographies in general, see Ernst Kris and Otto Kurz, *Legend, Myth, and Magic in the Image of the Artist: A Historical Experiment* (New Haven and London: Yale University Press, 1979), 11. On Mozart specifically, see Simon P. Keefe, *Haydn and Mozart in the Long Nineteenth Century: Parallel and Intersecting Patterns of Reception* (Cambridge: Cambridge University Press, 2023), 75–80.

39. *Nekrolog 1791*, 2:107–8.

40. During Mozart's life, his name appeared alongside Haydn's in advertisements for editions, as well as in Mozart's warm dedication to Haydn of his six string quartets Opus 10 for the Artaria edition of September 1785. For the latter (in English translation), see *MDB*, 250. For private documents such as letters, testimonials, and contributions to albums that bring Haydn and Mozart together during Mozart's life and soon after his death, see, for example, *MDB*, 289, 308, 419, 466. On Haydn's and Mozart's intertwined reception in the long nineteenth century from 1791 onward, see Keefe, *Haydn and Mozart in the Long Nineteenth Century*, passim.

41. For manifestations of the immersion-in-music narrative across the nineteenth century in biographical, critical, and fictional contexts, see Keefe, *Haydn and Mozart in the Long Nineteenth Century*, 66–72, 92, 113–14, 124, 135, 174–75, 220. The spirit of Schlichtegroll's narrative also inspired twentieth- and twenty-first-century musical biographies of Mozart. See for example, Georges de Saint-Foix and Théodore de Wyzewa, *W. A. Mozart: Sa vie musicale et son oeuvre*, 5 vols. (Paris: Desclée de Brouwer, 1912–46), 5; Einstein, *Mozart: His Character, His Work*; Jean and Brigitte Massin, *Wolfgang Amadeus Mozart* (Paris: Fayard, 1959); Konrad Küster, *Mozart: A Musical Biography*, trans. Mary

Whittall (Oxford: Clarendon Press, 1996); Simon P. Keefe, *Mozart in Vienna: The Final Decade* (Cambridge: Cambridge University Press, 2017).

42. *Nekrolog 1791*, 2:87, 94 (quotation), 88 (quotation), 100.

43. Ibid., 110.

44. Ibid., 110, 111.

45. See Schlichtegroll, *Supplement-Band des Nekrologs für das Jahre 1790, 91, 92 und 93*, 2 vols. (Gotha: Justus Perthes, 1798), 2:159–61.

46. See *Nekrolog 1791*, 2:74–81, 128, 156, 191, 217, 276.

47. See ibid, 173–76.

48. Cooper Clarke (*The Annotated Schlichtegroll*, 10), for example, briefly mentions Schlichtegroll's public acknowledgment in the supplement of sister Nannerl's assistance with the original obituary, but does not discuss its content.

49. Schlichtegroll, *Supplement-Band*, 159–61. My translation. As with the biography itself, I resist the temptation to correct Schlichtegroll's factual errors here, which include Mozart's supposed completion of the Requiem, and his death at 10 a.m. Leaving the Requiem incomplete, Mozart died shortly before 1 a.m. on 5 December 1791.

50. W. Wittich's account, in a communication dated Leipzig, 20 November 1797, appears as "Anekdote den verstob. Mozart betreffend," *Allgemeiner litterarischer Anzeiger* (5 January 1798), 38–39. From the second paragraph of his supplement onward, Schlichtegroll reproduces Wittich's text verbatim. Wittich may have been the Berlin-based publisher and artist Ludwig Wilhelm Wittich (1773–1832), who was in Leipzig in 1796 and traveling outside Berlin in 1797. See the biography of Wittich in Reimar F. Lacher, ed., *Künstler(auto)biographieen* (Berlin: Akademie der Wissenschaften, 2005), 138–47, at 142. To my knowledge, the only modern (and brief) discussion of Wittich's account is Keefe, *Haydn and Mozart in the Long Nineteenth Century*, 25–26. For Rochlitz's two anecdotes about the Requiem (dated 5 December and 19 December 1798), see Maynard Solomon, "The Rochlitz Anecdotes," in *Mozart Studies*, ed. Cliff Eisen (Oxford: Clarendon Press, 1991), 1–59, at 32–34.

51. Niemetschek, *Life of Mozart*, 41–44. On Constanze's announcement published in Austrian and German newspapers at the end of December 1791 and in January 1792, setting the legend of Mozart's Requiem in motion, see Simon P. Keefe, *Mozart's Requiem: Reception, Work, Completion* (Cambridge: Cambridge University Press, 2012), 14–15.

52. On Rochlitz's intensifications of the Requiem legend primarily in reference to Niemetschek's account, and influence on nineteenth-century writings, see Keefe, *Mozart's Requiem*, 16–19, 22. Further manifestations of the Catholic prince narrative, originating with Wittich and Schlichtegroll, are discussed in ibid., 19–20.

53. *Nekrolog 1791*, 2:106.

54. For further discussion, see Simon P. Keefe, "Mozart 'Stuck in Music' in Paris (1778): Towards a New Biographical Paradigm," in *Mozart Studies 2*, ed. Keefe (Cambridge: Cambridge University Press, 2015), 23–54.

55. For example from the trip to Germany and France in 1777–79, see ibid. 28–30.

56. Stafford, "The Evolution of Mozartian Biography," in *The Cambridge Companion to Mozart*, ed. Keefe, 200–211, at 211.

Obituary for the Year 1791, including Information on the life of notable individuals who died during this year. Assembled by Friedrich Schlichtegroll.

EDITED BY SIMON P. KEEFE
TRANSLATED BY SUSAN GILLESPIE

I have resisted the temptation to correct Schlichtegroll's factual errors in notes to the translated text. The significance of the biography resides above all in its historical position, reception, and impact, as well as its orientation and style. Page numbers in square brackets refer to the original German publication of the obituary in Nekrolog auf das Jahr 1791, *volume 2 (Gotha: Justus Perthes, 1793).* [Ed.]

5 December [1791].

Johannes Chrysostomus Wolfgang Gottlieb Mozart[1]

[82] Whoever, at one time or another, has felt lost in sweet sentiments among the harmonies of this great musician, admired the inexhaustible wealth of his ideas and the force with which he ruled over the realm of his art in its broad scope; thus, whoever among all the connoisseurs and friends of music must not welcome an opportunity to share something of the curious life history of this precocious, great, and original genius! Who, among all of the above, will not thank warmly and earnestly those of his friends who were witness, from early years, to his admirable talent and its incredibly swift development, thanking them for not wanting to prevent the friends of the sweetest of all arts [83] from sharing the pleasure of making closer acquaintance with the history of his childhood and youth, which—unfortunately!—is also the greatest part of the whole life history of this magician, who beautified so many a happy hour and charmed so many a sad one for them?[2]

The human being endowed by nature with such miracle-like gifts and capacities is seldom a general model for imitation by others. Just as such a person's perfections are unachievable for us, so his errors, likewise, have no bearing on our excuses. To derive useful rules for practical life as a man in general, and, by attending to examples, to approach the achievable degree of development of our [84] nature, we must not single out those rare men as our example, but rather look to spirits with middling gifts who have, however, developed these aptitudes uniformly and carefully, and whom we may hope to equal in achievement.

But the memory of those men with rare strengths and talents for specific and important skills nevertheless remains indescribably precious and important. They are phenomena that amaze us, whose faithful reproduction the investigator of human nature regards as invaluable showpieces, to which he frequently returns in order to admire in them the limitless scope of the human spirit. Among them is Mozart, a miracle of talents and their early development; one would scarcely be able to believe what is said of him if he had not been our contemporary, and if these astonishment-generating characteristics were not confirmed by so many people.

The precise correlation that exists between the fates of Mozart and his father requires mention of the latter. *Leopold Mozart* [85] was the son of a bookbinder from Augsburg but studied in Salzburg and in 1743 joined the princely chapel as court musician. In 1762, he became vice-Kapellmeister. Along with his service at court and in the metropolitan church,[3] he busied himself with teaching the violin, and with composing. In 1756, he published the *Versuch einer gründlichen Violin-Schule*,[4] which was published in a second edition in the year 1770. He was married to Maria Anna Pertl, and it is a circumstance that cannot be without significance for the close observer to know that these parents of the artist, so exceptionally well formed for harmonies, were considered in their time to be the most beautiful married couple in Salzburg.

Of seven children of this marriage only a daughter, Maria Anna, and this son (born in Salzburg on 27 January 1756) survived; the father therefore entirely abandoned the teaching of violin and composing in order to devote all the free time remaining after his work duties to these two children. The daughter, who was older than the son, responded to the paternal instruction so well that her skillfulness led to her sharing in the admiration directed at the son during the family's travels. [86] She is now married to a princely councilor in the vicinity of Salzburg, where she devotes herself wholly, in undemanding silence, to the fine duties of wife and mother. In the final years of her unmarried state, which she spent in the paternal household, she instructed some of the city of Salzburg's young ladies on the keyboard,[5] and even now one can identify the students of Nannette Mozart among all others, by their neatness, precision, and true application.

Mozart the son was around three years old when the father began to instruct his seven-year-old daughter on the keyboard. The boy had already shown his extraordinary talent. He often amused himself at the keyboard for long periods of time, seeking out the thirds, which he then always played, and demonstrated his joy at having discovered this harmony.

In his fourth year, his father began, playfully as it were, to teach him some minuets and other pieces on the keyboard, an experience that became as easy and pleasurable for the teacher as for the apprentice. For a minuet, he required half an hour of study, for a bigger piece, an hour, and was then able to play it with the [87] most perfect correctness and the firmest beat. From then on, he made such progress that in his fifth year he was composing small pieces and committed some of them to paper.

Before he was acquainted with music, given his lively temperament, he was so amenable to childish play—if only spiced with a bit of wit—that it could make him forget eating, drinking, and everything else. Overall, a loving, tender feeling was apparent in him, so that he would often, ten times a day, ask the people who were taking care of him whether they loved him? And if they jokingly denied it, his eyes would fill with bright tears. But from the time when he became familiar with music, he lost all taste for the usual games and amusements of childhood, and if these pastimes were to be pleasing to him they needed to be accompanied by music. When, for example, he and a certain friend of the family, who paid significant attention to him, brought toys from one room to another, the one of the two whose hands were empty had to sing along with a march, or play it on the violin.

[88] In these years, he was extremely teachable and whatever his father required of him he would do with the greatest eagerness, to the extent that for a time he seemed to forget everything else, even music. For example, when he learned to count, the table, the chairs, the walls, and even the floor were written full of numbers, with chalk. Overall, he was full of fire and very easily became attached to every object; thus, he would have been in danger of going astray if his excellent education had not afforded protection. But amidst everything, it was music that filled his soul and with which he was continuously occupied. He took great strides forward in it, to the extent that even his father, who was daily in his presence and could observe every step of his education, was often surprised and astonished, as at a miracle.

One character trait recounted by a witness may serve as evidence of this. As his father was returning from church with a friend, they found

little Wolfgang busying himself with a quill pen. "What are you up to there?" his father asked him.
[89] Wolfgang: A concerto for the keyboard. The first part will be ready soon.
Father: Let's have a look. This must be something nice.
Wolfgang: No, it isn't finished yet.
The father took it from him, and showed his friend some written material with notes that were scarcely legible since most of it was written over large, messy ink spots, for the child had continuously dipped the quill to the very bottom of the inkwell, and thus the pen always had to release a spot, which he wiped up with the palm of his hand and then continued to write on again and again. Both friends laughed at first at this galimatias of notes. But when the father looked attentively at the composition itself, his gaze remained stubbornly fixed on the page, until finally bright tears, tears of admiration and joy, fell from his eyes. "See, friend," he said, with emotion and a smile, "how everything is correctly notated and follows the rules; only you cannot use it because it is so extraordinarily difficult that no human would be able to play it." "But," here little Wolfgang interrupted, "for all that, it is a concerto; one needs [90] to practice it before one performs it. Look, this is how it has to go." He now began to play, but was only able to bring forth enough for them to see what his ideas had been. For at the time he had formed the concept that playing a concerto and performing a miracle must be the same thing; thus, his concerto was a confusion of mostly correct, but mostly so complicatedly set notes that it was impossible even for any master to play.

He had already come such a distance with his art that it would have been unjust of his father not to want to let other cities and countries hear this extraordinary talent. In the boy's sixth year, therefore, his father made the first trip, together with the whole family, consisting of himself, his wife, daughter, and son, to Munich, where the two children were heard by the Elector and were showered with praise and applause. After they had returned to Salzburg, with both children now becoming daily more perfect on the keyboard, in the fall of 1762, the whole family went to Vienna, where the two children were presented to the Imperial Court.

[91] Kaiser Franz, in jest, told the son among other things that "it was no big deal to play with all one's fingers, but to play with only one finger on a concealed keyboard—that would frequently earn admiration." Instead of being taken aback by the impertinent remark, the child immediately played with one finger as nicely as is possible; he also pulled the lid over the keys and then played with such remarkable skill as if he had practiced it at length.

Even as a child, the praise of adults did not make the kind of impression on him that elicited pride. Already in those years, when he had to perform for people who had no understanding of music, he played nothing but trifling little pieces. By contrast, when connoisseurs were present, he was invariably all fire and attention, and for this reason it was often necessary to keep things concealed from him, and to present his distinguished listeners as artistically knowledgeable. Once, when the six-year-old sat down to play for Kaiser Franz, little Mozart asked the Kaiser, "Isn't Herr Wagenseil here? He should come; he understands it." Thereupon, the Kaiser asked Mr. Wagenseil to take his place near the keyboard, at which the little Mozart then suggested, "I will play [92] a concerto of yours; you must turn [pages] for me."

Until now, he had only played the keyboard, and given the unprecedented skill with which, for his age, he had mastered this instrument, it seemed as if one could not risk asking the boy also to play other instruments. But the spirit of the harmonies that lived in his breast far exceeded all expectations and all instruction. He had brought with him a small violin that he had been given in Vienna. Shortly afterward, soon after the family returned to Salzburg, Wenzl, a skillful violinist and a compositional beginner, came to Mozart the father and asked the latter for his recollections of six trios that he had written during the Mozart family's absence.

Schachtner, a court trumpeter still living in Salzburg whom the young Mozart especially loved, happened to be present. "The father," so this reliable witness explained, "played the bass line on the viola, Wenzl the first violin, and I was supposed to play the second. Little Wolfgang asked to be allowed to play second violin instead. But the father rejected [93] his childish request because he had not yet received any proper training on the violin and thus could not possibly produce anything good. The boy responded that to play second violin one probably did not need to have learned it first; but his father, half annoyed, asked him to leave and stop bothering them. The boy began to cry bitterly and ran off with his little violin. I asked whether he could be allowed to play with me, after all. Finally, the father consented, and said to Wolfgang, 'Well, so only play with Herr Schachtner, but so softly that you cannot be heard; otherwise, you must leave at once.' We played, and young Mozart played the violin alongside me. But I soon noticed, to my amazement, that I was quite superfluous. I quietly put my violin aside and looked at the father, who, at this scene, had tears of stirred and admiring tenderness roll from the paternal eye down his cheeks. Wolfgang played all six trios through in this way. After completing them, and thanks to our applause, he became so emboldened that he claimed he could also play the first violin. As a joke, we made an attempt and had to laugh heartily when he played this as well, albeit with nothing but wrong and irregular fingering. [94] But, after all, at least in such a way that he never had to pause."

More and more, it was now evident that his ear was constructed entirely for music. With gentle feeling, he noticed the finest differences in tone; and every discordance, every cacophony not softened by consonance automatically felt to him like torture. Thus, in this period of his childhood and almost up to his tenth year, he had an unconquerable fear of the trumpet when it was played alone without other music, and when such an instrument was merely held in front of him it had exactly the same effect on him as if a person presses a loaded pistol against someone else's heart. His father wanted to free him from this childish fear and once, despite his entreaties, ordered a trumpet blown in his direction. But at the very first tone, he turned pale and fell to the ground; probably he would have had a fit if it had not stopped.

Around this time, he once played Schachtner's violin, belonging to the still living old friend of the Mozart household. He praised it for its soft tone, on account of which he always referred to it as the "butter violin." A few days later, [95] young Mozart was amusing himself on his own violin when the elder gentleman arrived. "How is your butter violin?" was Mozart's quick question, before continuing with his fantasy. Finally, he paused briefly and then addressed Schachtner: "If only you had left your violin tuned the way it was when I played it last time; it is half a quarter tone lower than mine there." Everyone chuckled at this precise description; and the father, who already knew of several examples of this child's extraordinary feeling for tonality, and of his memory, had the violin brought out, and to everyone's astonishment the claim proved absolutely accurate.

Despite new daily evidence of people's admiration and astonishment at his great talents and skillfulness, this by no means made him egotistic, proud, or headstrong; instead, he was an exceptionally obedient and accommodating child. He never expressed displeasure at an order from his father; and if he had already spent the whole day having to play for listeners, he nevertheless played for all and sundry as soon as his father wished it. He understood and followed every sign from his parents, and his devotion went so far that he did not presume [96] to eat or accept even the smallest thing without their permission if someone offered it.

In June of the year 1763, in other words in the boy's seventh year, the Mozart family took its first big trip outside Germany, which as a consequence vastly broadened the fame of the precocious artist. They went to Munich, where the young Mozart played a violin concerto before the Elector, already preluding off the top of his head. In Augsburg, Mannheim, Mainz, Frankfurt am Main, Koblenz, Aachen, and Brussels, they either provided musical academies for the public, or played before various princes and other personages, to exceptional applause.

In November, they arrived in Paris, where they remained for twenty-one weeks. They were heard in Versailles before the royal family; there, the son also played the organ in the chapel, in front of the entire court. For the public they gave two large academies in a private space. In this world, as one may easily imagine, they felt very much at home. Immediately on their arrival, an image of the father and the two children was engraved on copperplate, and they generally received very respectful treatment. [97] It was here, too, that Wolfgang Mozart completed his first two works and made them public. The first he dedicated to Madame *Victoire*, the second daughter of the King; the other to Duchess *Tessé*. Both pieces were published in Paris. He was seven years old at the time.

On 10 April 1764, they traveled via *Calais* to England, where they remained until the middle of the following year. On the 27th of that month, the children were already playing before their Majesties; similarly in the following month, when the son also performed on the King's organ. Here, the listeners all valued his organ-playing above his clavier-playing. Now they gave a benefit or a grand concert for their own profit, in which all the symphonies were composed by the son; then another one to support the maternity hospital. Following a dangerous throat infection that brought the father to the edge of the grave, and that he survived in *Chelsea*, they returned to London, where they again played before the royal family and distinguished members of the nobility.

Based on the plentiful applause they received in Europe's greatest capitals, it is natural to think that the children, and above all the son, [98] did not merely remain at the level they had already attained, but continued further to advance their education. Thus, the two children now played concerts for two keyboards everywhere; the son also sang arias with the greatest feeling. In Paris, and also in London, people presented the son with various difficult pieces by Bach, Händel, Paradies, and other masters, which he not only played by sight but also immediately repeated in the appropriate meter and as nicely as could be. When he played before the King, he took a simple bass theme and overlaid it with an excellent melody. Joh. Christian Bach, the Queen's teacher, sat young Mozart on his lap and played a few measures; then Mozart would continue. Thus, always taking turns, they played an entire sonata together with such precision that anyone who was not watching them would have had to believe that the piece was being performed by a single individual. During this stay in England, and in the following eighth year of his life, he composed six sonatas, which he had engraved in London and dedicated to the Queen.

In July 1765, they again crossed over to *Calais* and traveled through Flanders, where Wolfgang often played the organs of the cloister churches and the cathedrals. In The Haag, [99] the two children, one after the other, had to survive deadly illnesses. Only four months later were they fully recovered, after which the first task of the son was to compose and publish six sonatas for the keyboard, with a dedication to the Princess of Nassau-Weilburg. At the start of the year 1766, they spent four weeks in Amsterdam, before traveling back to The Haag to celebrate the installation of the Prince of Orange. For this celebration, the son composed a *Quodlibet* for all instruments, along with diverse variations and some arias for the Princess. After having played frequently for the heir apparent, they returned to Paris, where they stayed for two months. During this time, they paid two visits to *Versailles*, went via *Lyon* to Switzerland, and spent time with the Prince of Fürstenberg in Donaueschingen. In Munich, the Elector sang a tender theme for Mozart the son, for the latter to complete at once and put it down on paper. This he did without using a keyboard or a violin. When he was done, he performed it and was rewarded by the astonishment and admiration of the Elector and everyone present. Finally, after an absence of more than three years, they arrived back in Salzburg at the end [100] of the month of November 1766.

They now remained in Salzburg until fall of the following year, and Wolfgang Mozart, through his persistent study, strode ever closer to the goal of perfection that he would reach so soon. In the year 1768, the children played in Vienna before Kaiser Joseph, who charged the young Mozart with composing an *opera buffa*. It was called *La finta semplice* and earned the praise of Kapellmeister Hasse and of Metastasio, but was not performed after that. In gatherings with Kapellmeisters Bono and Hasse, the poet Metastasio, the Duke of Braganza, Princes Kaunitz, and others, the father always asked to open up with the very best Italian aria, and the son, in the presence of all these people, composed accompanying music with full instrumentation. At the dedication of the orphanage church, he had composed the daily office, the *Offertory*, and a trumpet concerto, and conducted this solemn music as a twelve-year-old boy in the presence of the imperial court.

They spent the year 1769 in Salzburg again, until in December the father, accompanied only by his son, undertook a trip to Italy, but only after having been named court concertmaster with the Salzburg court orchestra. In [101] Innsbruck, they gave an academy at Count Künigl, where Mozart played a concerto *prima vista*.[6] Given the admiration he had earned in other countries, one can easily imagine how very welcome his appearance was in Italy, where music flourishes as if in its own soil and musical art is considered one of the foremost merits. In Milan, he received great applause in the House of Firmian and also composed various pieces. After having received the *scrittura*[7] here for the first opera for Carnival 1771, they traveled on further in March 1770. In Bologna, Mozart found an enthusiastic admirer in Father *Maestro Martini*, a great expert in counterpoint. The latter, along with the other kapellmeisters, was completely beside himself when Mozart, for every fugal theme that Martini wrote down, produced the corresponding *riposta* in *rigore modi* form,[8] and immediately performed the fugue on the keyboard. In Florence as well, this heightened the admiration of the city's music director, *Marchese Ligneville*, himself a powerful exponent of counterpoint, who put before the young artist the most difficult fugues and themes, which the latter proceeded to read straight from the page. In Florence, Mozart also made the acquaintance of a young Englishman, [102] Thomas *Linley*, a boy of fourteen years and thus of the same age as Mozart. Linley was a student of the famous violinist *Nardini* and played his instrument with enchanting skill and mellifluence. The friendship between the two youths very quickly reached a high degree of tenderness; they revealed themselves in turn not as boys but as accomplished masters of their art. *Linley* also brought Mozart, on the day of their parting, a work of poetry that he had arranged to have composed for him by *Signora Corilla*. They separated with many embraces and tears and Linley accompanied Mozart's wagon all the way to the city gate.

Mozart father and son arrived in Rome during Holy Week. On Wednesday afternoon, they went straight to the Sistine Chapel to hear the famous *Miserere*. Since, as generally asserted, it is forbidden on pain of excommunication to let this music be copied, Wolfgang Mozart intended to listen to it very precisely and then write it down at home. He did that and hid the manuscript in his hat when the same *Miserere* was performed again on Good Friday, and was consequently able to make a few improvements to his document. This [103] soon became known in Rome and caused a general stir. He had to sing it to keyboard accompaniment in an academy, whereby the castrato *Christofori*, who had sung it in the chapel, was present and, through his astonishment, made Mozart's triumph complete.

In Naples, when he played in the *Conservatorio alla Pietà*, his listeners conceived the idea that the magic must be concealed in his ring; so he took the ring off, and now the amazement was truly great. He also gave a large academy there for the Emperor's ambassador, Count Kaunitz, before returning to Rome. Here, the Pope also now desired to see him, and gave him the cross and papal brevet as *Militiae auratae eques*.[9] In Bologna, he was elected unanimously as member and *Maestro della Academia filarmonica*. For this, he was locked up all alone and given an antiphon to set in four voices. He finished in half an hour and immediately received the diploma.

They hastened now to return to Milan, because the son had previously committed himself to composing the first carnival opera there. If this had not been the case, he could also have received the *scrittura* for his [104] first opera in Bologna, Naples, or Rome. They arrived in Milan at the end of October 1770. Here, the son, in his fourteenth year, composed the *opera seria Mitridate*, which premiered on 26 December and was subsequently performed more than twenty times in a row. One can gauge the general applause that this work received from the fact that the company immediately gave him the written agreement to produce the first opera for the year 1773. They now spent the final days of the carnival in Venice; in Verona he was also presented with a diploma as a member of the Philharmonic Society. And thus he finally left Italy, where he had been greeted everywhere with exceptional honor and had been given the name *il Cavaliere filarmonico*.

When Mozart, with his father, arrived back in Salzburg in March of 1771, he found a letter from Duke Firmian in Milan, who invited him, in the name of Empress Maria Theresia, to write the great theatrical serenata for the marriage of Archduke Ferdinand. Since the Empress had appointed the eldest among the kapellmeisters, the famous Hasse, to write the opera, she consequently selected the youngest of them all for the [105] serenata *Ascanio in Alba*. He took on this task and in August, with his father, traveled back to *Milan*, where throughout the marriage festivities the *Opera* and the *Serenata* alternated.

For the election of the new archbishop in Salzburg in 1772, he composed the serenata *Il sogno di Scipione*, after which he spent the winter with his father in Milan, where he wrote the previously commissioned *opera seria Lucio Silla* for the 1773 Carnival. It was performed twenty-six times in a row. In the spring of the year 1773, he was again in Salzburg.

Several trips that he made together with his father provided the occasion for completing such outstanding musical works for the Munich court as an *opera buffa*, *La finta giardiniera*, two big masses for Munich's court chapel, etc. In 1775, the Archduke Maximilian was present in Salzburg, on which occasion Mozart composed a serenata, *Il re pastore*.

The more extraordinary the inborn talent and rapid development of this great artist was, the more readers will justify the conscientious detail [106] with which the step-by-step education he enjoyed is recounted here. From now on, we can be briefer. He had now reached the pinnacle of his art and his fame had spread throughout all the countries of Europe. In whichever of the larger cities he now chose to dedicate his rare talents to entertaining the public, he was assured of universal admiration. Meanwhile, the great marketplace of all talented excellence in the fine arts, contemporary Paris, was the most appropriate place for him, since he was already known there and would find an enthusiastic public. In September 1777, therefore, he traveled with his mother to this other capital of European luxury. It would have redounded very much to his benefit if he had remained in Paris, but he had little taste for French music. When in the following year his mother, who this time had been the sole family member to accompany him, died in Paris, he gladly returned to his father at the beginning of the year 1779, after having composed a symphony for the *Concert spirituel* and some other pieces.

In November of the next year, in Munich, he wrote an *opera seria* for the [107] forthcoming Carnival, and from there traveled to Vienna, following the call of his prince, the Archbishop of Salzburg, who was in residence there. From then on, that is, from his twenty-fourth year, he lived in Vienna and entered into Imperial service. He fulfilled in a completely satisfying way the great expectations of the entire musical public, to which his admirable and early-developed gifts had entitled him, and—to say everything in a few words—became the favorite composer of his era.

To include here a complete record of all of Mozart's various works would go too far and even be superfluous, for who would not know his keyboard sonatas and concertos, his symphonies and quartets, and what lover of music would not already have them in his hands? His operas, several of which he completed in Vienna, and among which *The Magic Flute* received such outstanding and general applause that over a period of twelve months it was staged one hundred times, earned him equal applause. Already in 1785, the great Joseph Haydn told Mozart's father, who was also in Vienna at the time, "I say to you, before God and as an honest man, that I [108] consider your son to be the greatest composer I have ever heard of; he has taste and possesses the most thorough knowledge in the art of composition." This opinion, by a judge who was called upon and qualified above all others to render it, received new confirmation in the mass for the dead, the so-called *Requiem*, which Mozart composed in his final days but was not able fully to complete. The solemn and deeply moving expression that one discovers there, most effectively combined with the highest degree of artistry, moved all hearts of the audience at the performance, which was organized as a benefit for the widow and children and won the admiration of all connoisseurs.

That was Mozart the musical artist. No student of human nature will be surprised, however, if a great artist who earned the most universal admiration in this area does not appear equally great in other aspects of life. Mozart was not especially distinguished in his physical appearance, however beautiful his parents had been in their youth, as mentioned above, and whatever influence this may have had on the fortunate formation of their son. He was small, gaunt, pale, and displayed [109] nothing extraordinary in his physiognomy. His body was in constant movement; he always had to have something for his hands and feet to play with. He was passionate about billiards and usually even had a table in his room, at which he liked to amuse himself when he was alone. Even his face did not remain unchanged, but always betrayed the external state of his soul, in which the lower faculties—one of which, fantasy, made him the artistic magician he was—quite clearly weighed more heavily than the more elevated ones.

For just as this rare person in his early years became a man in his art, so on the other hand he remained—objective judgment must say this about him—in almost all other respects a child. He never learned to look after himself; he had no sense of domestic order, of appropriate use of money, of moderation and the prudent choice of pleasure. He always needed someone to lead him, a guardian who attended to domestic matters in his place, since his own spirit was always busying itself with quite different imaginary concerns and was thus bereft of all sense when it came to other serious reflection. His father [110] knew this weakness in him when it came to self-control and thus, when his own responsibilities required him to remain in Salzburg, had the son's mother accompany him to Paris. In Vienna, Mozart married Constanza Weber and found in her a good mother of the two children he fathered with her and a worthy wife who also sought to restrain him from many a foolish and wanton act. As considerable as his income was, he nevertheless, given his predominating sensuality and domestic disorder, left nothing more to his family than the fame of his name and the attention of a large public that sought to pay down the heirs' debt with gratitude for the sweet joys of Mozart's muse.

But even this ever distracted, ever playful man seemed to be someone quite different, seemed to become a higher being, as soon as he sat down at the keyboard. Then his spirit and his undivided concentration were directed at the single object for which he was born—the harmonies of tones. Even in the most fully elaborated music, he noticed the tiniest disharmony, and immediately, with accuracy and precision, said on which instruments the mistake [111] had been made and which note it actually should have been. Even his hands had so firm an orientation toward the keyboard that he rarely, and only with significant effort and fear, managed to cut his meat at meals; ordinarily he would ask his wife for the favor. At the tiniest noise during music, this otherwise so mild-mannered man became animated by the liveliest displeasure.

Music provided the primary business of his life and simultaneously his most pleasant recreation. Never, even in his earliest youth, was it necessary to encourage him to play. Rather, it was necessary to try to prevent him from forgetting himself entirely and damaging his health. From childhood on, he especially loved to play at night; if he sat down at the keyboard at 9 o'clock, he was not to be persuaded to abandon it before midnight, and, even then, one had to half compel him; otherwise, he would have fantasized the whole night long. In the morning, he would compose from 6 or 7 o'clock until 10; then he wrote nothing more all day, except if there was something urgent to be completed.

[112] As brilliant as his career was, it was equally short. He was scarcely thirty-six years old when he died. But in this brief time, he made a name for himself that will not perish as long as even a single temple to the muse of music still stands, and often, for souls endowed with feeling and gently moved by the richness and beauty of his harmonies, enthusiastic and grateful praise will still be dedicated to his memory.

NOTES

1. Mozart's first names are frequently reported differently, for example in Meusel's *Museum für Künstler* 16, page 291, but erroneously. Those given here are authentic.

2. The assembler of the obituary, since the launch of his undertaking, has never been as pleasantly surprised as by the unsolicited, interesting contributions concerning the life of this great artist, which, alongside the external circumstances, also bear within themselves the inner stamp of credibility, and subsequently have also been reviewed, affirmed, and supplemented by a number of men who knew Mozart intimately.

3. The "metropolitan church" mentioned here is Salzburg Cathedral. [Ed.]

4. *A Treatise on the Fundamental Principles of Violin Playing*. The treatise is available in an English translation by Editha Knocker, 2nd ed. (London: Oxford University Press, 1951). [Ed.]

5. Schlichtegroll's references to the "Klavier" in his biography are translated as "keyboard," accepting that he—and the sources from which he drew—sometimes may have intended fortepiano and sometimes harpsichord. When used in contrast to organ-playing, "Klavier" is translated as "clavier." [Ed.]

6. That is, at sight, or sight-reading. [Ed.]

7. A *scrittura*, in this context, denotes a contract to write the opera. [Ed.]

8. The "*riposta* in *rigore modi*" designates a strict fugal answer. [Ed.]

9. This is the Pontifical Order of the Golden Militia, more commonly known as the Order of the Golden Spur. It was awarded to Mozart on 5 July 1770 by Cardinal Pallavicini, following a Papal patent issued the previous day; Mozart was received by the Pope on 8 July 1770. [Ed.]

Mozart in the *Allgemeine musikalische Zeitung* (1798–1803): Selected Articles and Reviews

INTRODUCED AND ANNOTATED BY LISA DE ALWIS
TRANSLATED BY SUSAN GILLESPIE

How did Mozart's contemporaries view him, and are we still influenced by their views today when we listen to his music? Those with some knowledge of the music and its performance realize that it takes effort to attempt to understand it on its own terms. One could cite as a case in point Franz Xaver Süssmayr, the first to complete the unfinished Requiem after Mozart's death. There have been several attempts to improve upon Süssmayr's work since 1792, but it was his version that entered the standard repertoire and acquired its own cultural cachet. For any work, we can decide if our goal is to get as close as possible to discovering the composer's intentions—if that is possible—or whether questions, for example about style, that are grounded in cultural contexts of that time, or of our time, or both are equally relevant. In a similar sense, we can determine whether the articles that follow inform us more about Mozart and his music or more about what his contemporaries felt was important to share about him after his death in 1791. Some assessments here, such as affirmations of the Countess's pathos in *The Marriage of Figaro* or comments on the important role that Mozart gives the orchestra in his concertos, will resonate easily with the reader. Elsewhere, the analysis that important predecessors of Mozart and the Italian Renaissance painter Raphael produced sublimely dark works invites us to consider how people of bygone eras may have received cultural products in unexpected ways. The effusive praise in one review of songs that we now know are not by Mozart causes us to question our own assumptions about what genius is.

The six articles that follow about Mozart come from the first five issues of the *Allgemeine musikalische Zeitung* (*AmZ*), the important music periodical that was published weekly by Breitkopf & Härtel in Leipzig between 1798 and 1848, and later by J. Rieter-Biedermann from 1866 until 1882.

It is possible that all these articles were written by Johann Friedrich Rochlitz, the first editor of the journal; similarities in turns of phrase as well as in the views expressed make a convincing case for his authorship of all of them, although this is not certain in the absence of name designations. One of the most interesting aspects of these articles is that we find buried in the adulation lavished on Mozart's music, various criticisms that capture the cultural Zeitgeist circa 1800 in the musical capitals of Europe.

Names more famous than Rochlitz's have appeared in the pages of the *AmZ*, including Franz Liszt, Robert Schumann, and E. T. A Hoffmann. Rochlitz himself contributed better-known pieces that have been translated and commented upon elsewhere. The articles selected here are those that focus solely on Mozart and may not yet have been translated in their entirety. One challenge for us has been to render the German text as accurately as possible while aiming for a readerly experience in English. Rochlitz's sentences are long and rambling, even by the standards of their time, and it can be difficult to ascertain their meaning in his nested sentences (*Schachtelsätze*). Moving chronologically, I will present an overview of each article, pointing toward issues of interest in them.

AmZ 1: 7 August 1799, cols. 743–52

The AmZ *was initially published in a yearly cycle that ran from October of one year to September of the next. Toward the end of the first cycle, in the 7 August issue from 1799, a review appears of a publication of Mozart's complete songs with piano accompaniment. From the publisher's foreword, which Rochlitz included in its entirety in the 7 August AmZ, readers will discover that many of his articles excuse supposedly incorrect techniques by Mozart as a byproduct of his genius. In the songs presented in* Complete Lieder and Songs with Fortepiano, *the problems, according to the publisher, Breitkopf & Härtel, involve declamation and prosody—the art of setting a text properly to music. If the song contains several verses with the same music but different text, this can become problematic. But such issues, the publisher reassures us, are too minor for someone of Mozart's stature to concern himself with—in other words, text setting was not very important to Mozart. Mozart's genius means that his music is complex, preventing all but the very simplest of his songs from becoming folksongs. According to modern-day scholarship, the first five songs Rochlitz names are correctly attributed to Mozart, but almost all the other songs listed in this article are not. And although the reviewer is aware of this, at least for most of the misattributed songs—even listing their likely composers—he engages in wishful thinking about them, that perhaps they are by Mozart after all. His logic is difficult to follow: it seems that there was a different song "Die ihr des unermeßlichen Weltalls Schöpfer ehrt" that the publisher did not include with the first group of five songs. By not including it, the reviewer explains, this careful publisher must have been concerned about its authenticity. He goes on to reassure his readership (and the publisher) that the song is in fact attributable to Mozart. Recent scholarship bears this out. The reviewer concludes that we can therefore trust the publisher when he includes these other songs, whose attribution was questioned at the time and for which other people had been named as potential composers. There could be an issue around the reviewer's use of the term* "Mozartsche," *which would generally be translated as "Mozartish" or by Mozart. One could read it as "Mozartian," or in the style of Mozart. However, when he later muses upon Mozart's humor in a particular passage or on how he did not write a particular song for an ordinary singer's instrument, it becomes clear that he has wholly accepted his wishful thinking and attributed all the songs in the collection to Mozart.*

***Complete Lieder and Songs with Fortepiano*, Accompaniment by Kapellmeister W. A. Mozart, Op. 253, 19 Engraved Pages. Berlin, available at the Rellstab Bookstore and Music Printing House. 3 Rthlr.**

Anyone with three Reichsthaler should hasten to acquire these Lieder and songs. But in order that everyone may know precisely what he can expect to get for his three Reichsthaler, the reviewer may be permitted a rather detailed advertisement. The publisher's preface, in which much is clarified, reads verbatim as follows:

> Mozart's complete songs with fortepiano accompaniment appear here all printed in one volume, following the wishes of so many admirers of this composer. On a trip through Saxony, Silesia, and Bohemia in the year 1797, the editor was fortunate enough to locate ten more songs by the deceased, along with his dances and waltzes from Carnival 1791. (He also has hopes of discovering several more years' worth of these dances.)
>
> Mozart's genius was too great to submit to all the minor requirements that a song sung by untrained voices demands. Declamation, fitting the melody like a garment to the words of every verse was something he disregarded. In some songs, one must write the music for every line differently, as has been done in the comprehensive collection, for example in the song *Kühlt, o schmeichelnde Lüfte*, among others. The song *Wer wollte sich mit Grillen plagen* is a solemn choral work, more to awaken than to banish worrisome thoughts; and in a different chorus, *Blickt auf, wie hehr das lichte Blau*, the bass voices lack the sixth line of every stanza. "One finds further errors of this kind,

> which, however, are richly compensated by Mozart's immortal talent, by charming melodies, well-chosen keyboard accompaniment, and striking modulation. His melodies, therefore, will probably never become folksongs (from his operas, only the lighthearted arias of *Die Zauberflöte* and the aria *Treibt der Champagner,*[1] from *Don Giovanni,* became popular hits); but they long remain an established, charming entertainment of the refined world, of more trained vocal chords and of the more expressive keyboard players.

Thus the publisher's profession of faith in Mozart as a composer of Lieder. Five of these songs, namely:

1) *Das Veilchen*
2) *An Chloe*
3) *Trennungslied*
4) *Das Bändchen*
5) *Abendempfindung*

have long since been engraved and printed, some by Artaria in Vienna and Lau in Hamburg, and some by others. Some songs, which have been familiar under Mozart's name for several years, are said to have found other composers as their creator. For example, *Ehelicher guter Morgen* and *Eheliche gute Nacht* by Dahlberg;[2] *Vergiss mein nicht* and *Phillis an das Klavier* by Schneider;[3] *Minna's Augen* and *Das Mädchen und der Vogel* by Müller;[4] and more of this sort. But what does this accomplish? Could not Mozart also have composed these songs? And is the collection, as a result, not stronger and worth three thaler? Moreover, who knows whether it is true; at least the publisher of these Mozart Lieder must not have believed it. Why else would he not also have included with the above-named little group of five the song, *Die ihr des unermeßlichen Weltalls Schöpfer ehrt,* etc.? That he should have regarded this piece as neither a Lied nor even a small song is unlikely. Where else would the little volume have come from? That

1. "Fin ch'han dal vino." [Ed.]

2. Johann Friedrich Hugo von Dalberg (1760–1812) was a pianist, composer, and writer of fiction and nonfiction. [Ed.]

3. Georg Laurenz Schneider (1766–1855) was a composer, organist, and music director. He is known to have written "Vergiss mein nicht," but not "Philliss an das Klavier," whose authorship remains unattributed. [Ed.]

4. August Eberhard Müller (1767–1817) was a composer, organist, and conductor as well as a successor to J. S. Bach as the cantor at the St. Thomas Church in Leipzig. [Ed.]

he should have been unaware of its existence or have left it out unintentionally is—in the case of a publisher as careful as ours—impossible. So, he must surely have encountered doubts about its authenticity. This reviewer is, accordingly, happy to be able to reassure the publisher that this Lied really is by Mozart—one of his acquaintances, Herr Ziegenhagen, expressly had it composed by Mozart, and included it in his publication with the title *Lehre vom richtigen Verhältnisse zu den Schöpfungswerken etc*, in 1792 in Hamburg.[5] As far as the remaining, largely unknown and rather numerous Lieder and songs are concerned—the collection contains a total of 33 pieces—the reviewer considers it his duty to acquaint his readers with some of the most striking beauties therein. He was so entranced by the first six of them—numbers 2, 5, 6, 7, 8, and 9 of the collection—that he is completely unable to forgo mention of at least some of them. In No. 2, *Andantino*, in 2/4 time, in E major, Minna, since love and honor enchain her, and her heart has already been given away, sings:

Now, she says, although she may have lighthearted, gently flowing, and careless blood, she hates fickleness, and closes:

5. The cantata "Die ihr des unermeßlichen Weltalls Schöpfer ehrt" is indeed by Mozart (K. 619), and the text is by Franz Heinrich Ziegenhagen (1753–1806), a German spiritualist and social reformer, who also commissioned the work from Mozart. [Ed.]

What a splendid, firm, and faithful conclusion! But this does not mean everything is at an end. By no means! Notwithstanding her faithful heart, she continues, in the same melody with which the song began:

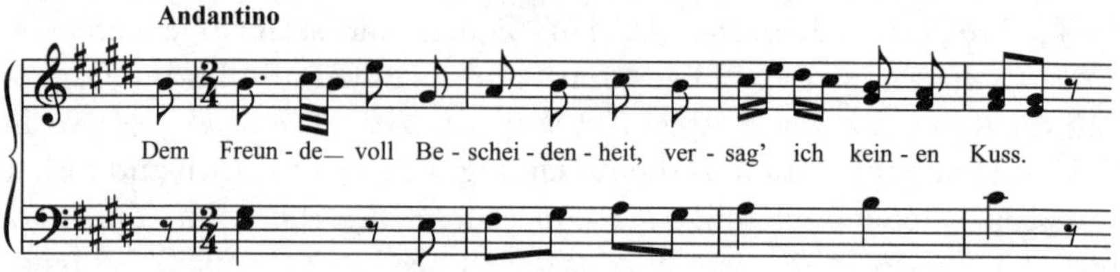

No. 5, *Gegenliebe*, cheerful and tender, also in 2/4 time and in E major—what a mischievous and naïve little thing. Just listen:

In No. 6, *An Iris*—B major, 6/8 time, naïve and gentle—the second half is especially moving:

No. 7, *Selma*, an expressive Adagio in E-flat major, in 3/4 time, is precisely the kind of piece described in the preface, where it is said that each verse must be set differently. It is a pity, however, that even with such differing underlay, most of it still simply will not fit at all. One need only examine what is meant to be sung to the following notes:

If one weren't looking directly at the printed page, one would scarcely believe that Mozart should have been so playful. More than any other, then, this particular song can serve as proof that the profession of faith laid out in the preface is completely valid. No. 8 is so original that we cannot forebear giving our readers at least the melody in its entirety:

One sees that Mozart did not write this song for any ordinary singing voice, for it extends from middle C to high A—a register to which at least the ordinary sort of throats do not readily ascend. Even more remarkable is No. 9, *Der erste Kuss*, in B-flat major, 2/4 time, tender and slow, especially on account of the conclusion, presented below, which one would almost like to describe as utterly unique,

and which becomes doubly interesting due to the perfectly analogous piano accompaniment. This reviewer would never finish if he wanted to seek out and record all the beauties and originalities of these Mozart

Lieder and songs; but he can assure readers in all honor and good conscience that all of the previously unknown Lieder and songs in this collection are not only by no means inferior to those that have been previously considered, but that the latter are so significantly exceeded by some among them that one is scarcely even in a position to comprehend how Mozart's creative genius was able to bring forth things of this kind. How bold, for example, do we not find the following opening of No. 15?

And furthermore, in the same song, the following place:

True, the Lied No. 26, *An die Tugend*, may be set to the well-known melody of a trio from *Die Zauberflöte*, but the publisher has (more than just here and there) enriched us not only with a new bass, but also with new middle voices. Please compare:

In No. 23, the piano begins like this,

and often reaches as far as *g*. In the similar No. 26, in 2/8 time, Mozart even had the fortunate idea, for those whose piano does not reach *g*, of remarking: "This voice can also be played by a flute." The *Frühlingslied* No. 31 resembles No. 8 in all respects. Two more remarkable conclusions, which in no way fall short of that in No. 9, follow. In No. 12, the daughter sings following the mother's too-late arrival:

No. 30, to be sung in four voices, closes as follows:

Like almost everything coming to us from the Rellstab company, the published edition of these Lieder, as regards both the beautiful paper and the elegant and correct printing, is comparable to the Braunschweig edition. Thus, for example, the first Lied, *Das Veilchen*, which fills three pages, includes only the following errata.[6]

Since the publisher has been fortunate enough, on his *little excursion* through Saxony, Silesia, and Bohemia, to have already found such a substantial treasure of Mozart Lieder, he certainly wishes, and with him, surely, all readers and admirers of Mozart wish, that he may decide to undertake similar and bigger trips through other provinces quite soon. The tireless enthusiasm of the publisher will surely also result in his discovering more similar treasures of Mozart Lieder and songs. In hope that he will therefore satisfy our unanimous request with the earliest possible response, we look forward with great longing to a second, third, fourth, fifth, etc., collection of Mozart Lieder and songs. Poor Mozart!

AmZ 2: 11 June 1800, cols. 641–45

In this article, from 11 June 1800, Friedrich Rochlitz juxtaposes Mozart with the Italian Renaissance painter Raffaello Sanzio da Urbino, better known as Raphael. He notes similarities in their early lives, including fathers deeply involved in their upbringings, important artistic predecessors, and shifts in artistic taste in their respective eras. But Rochlitz's primary goal is to consider the works of these two masters; he understands their contributions as stemming from a fusion of the older, darker styles with the lighter, simpler ones of their own eras.

Invention belongs to genius and execution of invention belongs to talent. For Rochlitz, the idea that Raphael without hands would still have been the greatest painter—a concept taken from Lessing's play Emilia Galotti*—applies equally to Mozart and music. Even lacking an ability to execute their ideas, their genius would have prevailed. By his lack of acknowledgment of the hard work that goes into these arts, and the development that comes about through that work, the two artists are almost fully formed from the start. At the same time, however, Rochlitz criticizes their earlier works as not yet expressive of their fully-formed genius. He reminds us that both men were mere mortals and could not achieve god-like perfection, and that they both died young, presumably due to immoderate and overly sensual lifestyles.*

6. I have excluded the errata from this translation, as the reader is unlikely to have access to this specific edition. [Trans.]

"Raphael and Mozart," by Friedrich Rochlitz

To my friend Matthisson, in commemoration of 20 May of this year.
Semper eadem natura, Seneca[7]

A parlor game calls for identifying the similarities between two suggested things or persons, and I was recently assigned this task as applied to the great men mentioned in the above title. I began in a bit of a quandary, but once I had begun, I found, to my own surprise, so much material that, even if the similarities should be merely coincidental, I consider the oddness of some of them sufficient to justify my offering them in this publication. In an honest and very prosaic manner, I must add: The events described here are, indeed, historically true; but the person who claims similarities does not thereby deny certain dissimilarities that he passes over.

Since, as regards *what* we become, so much depends on those through *whom* we became, it is noteworthy that Raphael and Mozart were the children of very fine parents. Since, as regards *how* we become something, and precisely that particular something, or rather, to what, and how, we apply what we are, so much depends on the activities of those *through whom* we have become, and what consequently gave our spirit and sensibility their first direction and nourishment, it is worth remarking that Raphael's father was a painter, while Mozart's was a music teacher and a practicing musician. Both fathers cherished and loved their arts; both eagerly participated in them and understood very well what, in them, was *right*. Both, without exactly being the possessors of high-level genius, or anything more than a well-mannered and well-constituted nature, nevertheless knew how to teach what was correct in their art to others—including their sons. And this is quite appropriate. If you have tilled the soil properly, next you add fertilizer, and only then seeds; thus, the wheat, a full, blessed crop, shoots securely forth; and yet you may well still damage it *before it forms ears*.

With eagerness and simplicity of heart, Raphael copied paintings by his father and the dry Pietro Perugino;[8] Mozart practiced following the meticulous methods of his father and the monotonous compositions of most of the composers then active in Germany.

Two great men had started to breathe a new spirit into the eras of the two children, and with almost oppressive omnipotence, to rule over the

7. "Nature is always the same." Most likely this quotation is not from the Stoic philosopher Seneca, although he did advocate living in accordance with nature. [Ed.]

8. Raphael's teacher, Pietro Perugino, and Leonardo da Vinci were both apprentices of Andrea del Verrocchio in Florence. [Ed.]

artistic world of their time. Exalted but also bleak; bold but lacking sensitive taste; powerful but without delicacy was the spirit of the two men and of their works. Michelangelo and Sebastian Bach were the names of the heroes, between whom one may perhaps be allowed to draw out not only similarities, but continuous parallels. Raphael became acquainted with Angelo's, Mozart with Bach's works, and both were so entranced with them that they completely changed—the former his manner of painting, the latter his previous manner of composing. But the somber, yet measured manner of the two great teachers' process could not be combined with the highly combustible fire of youth. Both young artists nevertheless attempted this arrangement; as a result, they both (especially Mozart) became rough, adventurous, bizarre, convoluted. Both tried a good many things in this manner, without bringing them to full completion—indeed, for the most part without even finishing them at all. Even now, works of this sort, created by them, have survived, for example Raphael's altarpiece in the Church of the Holy Spirit in Siena, and a few concertos, as well as some portions of Mozart's masses written in Salzburg or shortly thereafter.[9]

But now the beneficent, milder light of a more delicate and gentle taste arose over the eras of the two young artists. It is not that the sublime darkness of the above-named creators was scorned; their works were honored and studied. True artistic knowledge was acquired, but it was applied more selectively, following the inclination of the heart, and was aimed more at its effect, seeking to elevate the spirit through noble and sweet simplicity rather than to bend it beneath tremendous volume. Rather than having a shocking effect, as before, one aimed to move emotionally. One won people over more through cajoling rather than, as previously, through stormy conquest. The eras had to choose between imperious Minerva and mild Apollo; they opted for the latter. And now, most artists laid laurels at his feet. Leonardo da Vinci and his confreres topped the list of such painters, at least among those with whom Raphael could become well acquainted; Hasse and some Italians of the middle period[10] stood (at least among those whose acquaintance Mozart was able to make) at the apex of musicians.[11]

9. There is no altarpiece by Raphael in the Santo Spirito church in Siena. [Ed.]

10. Among these, most exceptionally, *also* a Leonardo—Leonardo Leo. Leo, who lived from 1694 to 1744 was a Neapolitan composer most known for his melodic comic operas. [Ed.]

11. Johann Adoph Hasse was an important German opera seria composer who collaborated with the influential librettist Pietro Metastasio. The Italians who influenced Mozart would certainly include the composers Giovanni Paisiello and Niccolò Jommelli, as well as the music theorist Padre Martini. [Ed.]

The great bulk of the painters in Raphael's youth, like the musicians in Mozart's, eagerly and almost exclusively imitated these new predecessors. Not so the two young men. They were too deeply moved by the spirit of earlier times, were man enough to penetrate it and hold it fast. But they also allowed the magic of the new period its rightful place and made use of what it offered that was natural, true, beautiful, and sweet. Now, in both, there awakened the free, unique genius that is heaven-sent. It moved and was nurtured in them until it stood in them, not like a growing child, but like a bold, brave, and proud man enlivened by strong, hearty nourishment and revitalized by inspiring, enjoyable draughts. And, to the main point, they themselves were now all that they could ever become. Now, all the two lacked was a large, free-spirited circle around them; opportunity that could drive them upwards and ever upwards; and art-loving patrons who would provide them with a happy existence free of care. Both found them. Raphael first in the Vatican, and later primarily in the popes Julius II and Leo X;[12] Mozart the former and the latter on the travels of his happy, vagrant, free artist's life.

And how do both now appear in their works? What is it that actually characterizes the two that is universal, always unmistakable, and most particular? *Invention*! Here the similarity of the two geniuses is too striking for me not to allow myself to spend a few minutes examining it more closely.

Invention is partly *poetic*, partly *artistic*.[13] Poetic invention provides *what* the work of art is to be; artistic invention, *how* it must become that. The former is invention of the idea; the latter, the means of achieving the thing. All invention belongs to genius. The *achievement* of the same,

12. Many of Raphael's major works are in the Vatican and were commissioned by either Julius II or Leo X. [Ed.]

13. Please allow me the following definition, since it appears to be sufficiently grounded in the matter at hand and seems to dispel many a conventional but erroneous statement, many a much lauded but empty phrase. What I referred to as artistic *invention* can also be termed "expression," but what else does one not also refer to with that term? How differently is it utilized by the painter and the musician, especially the virtuoso, in common language? But what if one would like to attend to what I am saying about the difference between poetic and artistic invention in terms of the effect of the artworks on us? Then one will find that a poetically sound work of art certainly inspires general (if not yet specific) interest in every generally cultivated person; that an artistically sound work certainly inspires a particular (precise, special, intentional) interest in every generally cultivated person. Or would one rather derive both kinds of perfection, when united with ideal performance, from some of the best-known and most splendid works of the various arts? For reflection of this kind, I propose Raphael's *School of Athens*; the Finale of the first act and the ghost scene of Mozart's *Don Giovanni*; the scenes immediately before and after the regicide in Shakespeare's *Macbeth*; or the scene in *Wallensteins Tod* by Schiller in which Max Piccolomini is pressured by the delegation of his cavalrymen.

which is to be differentiated from it, belongs to talent—about which more later. Poetic genius focuses not only on the main idea, but also on the most opportune moment and the major sensuous components that are necessary for the presentation of the idea. Artistic genius now finds the most suitable expression for it, within the boundaries of the art in which it works; it orders and treats those parts not only insofar as it serves both the expression and the presentation of the idea, but also, primarily, in that it serves to beautify what is presented and to elevate its expression.

All this is united in the true artist, but, despite that, is not yet achieved in the work of art—the artist is not yet able to make it emerge into the light of day. For this, quite a bit of skill must be acquired—by the hand and brush of the painter, by the linguistic abilities of the poet, by the musician's fingers and handling of his instruments, and so forth. This, now, is what I should like to call execution. As I have said, this is the affair not of genius but of talent and experience. Like talent in general, it is the skillfulness, the ease in presenting an appropriate external realization of what has been poetically and artistically invented—of dealing with Lessing's "recalcitrant material."[14] Without this, the genius would know how to bring forth many things, but would create nothing—at least nothing except perhaps rhapsodic, fragmentary drafts; and without the element of genius, talent would be able to produce many things, but would not create anything—at least nothing but, for example, imitations of genuinely artistic products, mannered works, and copies of a banal nature. Talent can be practiced; genius, whetted—the former as proficiency, the latter as an ability. Thus, both are perfected, but the former in quantity and the latter in quality.

Both artistic spirit and artistic skill must be united in perfection. If, however, one of the two should be more prominent, obviously it must be the former over the latter, as genius, everywhere and overall, ranks above skillfulness, as heavenly gifts outrank earthly achievements. This (I think) is what Lessing means when he says Raphael would have been the greatest painter even if he had had the misfortune to be born without hands. Similarly, one could say that Mozart would have been the greatest composer even if he had, unfortunately, not written a single note.

Now, finally, back to our main concern! But have we actually digressed from it? We are, here, probably truly in the middle of it, for

14. Gotthold Ephraim Lessing (1729–1781) was a philosopher, dramatist, and leading figure of the German Enlightenment. Johann Wolfgang von Goethe (1749–1832) was better known than Lessing for thinking about concepts or materials resisting their creator. [Ed.]

invention—consisting of a wealth, an inexhaustible wealth of it, and good fortune, unvarying good fortune in invention, both poetic and artistic—is precisely what is unique about Raphael and Mozart. It is just that through which they are what they are. For both, always exceptional, noble, beautiful ideas; and then, in addition, for the former, a world of living figures; for the latter, a world of living musical ideas, each speaking for itself—interesting, dignified, practical, and, again, each so intimately interwoven within the whole! All are limbs of *one* body and beautiful limbs of a beautiful body! All well-ordered and, now and again, presented in such a way that nothing that, in itself, can be of interest and strengthen the impact of the whole may remain concealed! And, all the while, not a single one of these limbs is poorly drawn, not a single one incorrect![15]

Through this elevated singularity of the works of both artists, which immediately wraps the *whole* person in its sweet fetters (whether that person is a connoisseur or not, so long as he is a cultivated and sensitive individual), both rose above their times; both gradually defeated the egoists who paid attention only to themselves and their own concerns, and who belittled them. Thus, they vanquished those who merely guarded the conventional, and who judged them, and the envious ones who, sensing their own incapacity, persecuted them. Through the uniqueness of their works, they achieved for themselves an eternal renown, and for their arts a new, higher level. Both founded new schools, and with them a new period of their arts commenced. I don't want to play with words, otherwise I would say more here about their most significant students, and would find it worth remarking that Raphael's greatest pupil, Iulio Romano,[16] was too *dull* and *black* in his painting, and his valiant I. F. Penni (*Il Fatore*)[17] became too wild, gigantesque, hence incomprehensible and unpleasing, etc. And I would cite some of today's significant composers who have trained themselves emulating Mozart and can be considered

15. I speak here solely of the most important of Mozart's works from his best years, i.e., so *here*, primarily of many, especially multi-voiced parts of his operas; of about five of his well-known symphonies; of most of his quartets and quintets, many of his piano concertos, and of the later (and rare) church music, and not including the works of his earlier youth, in which regard Raphael has been so fortunate that they have disappeared; this is apart from the compulsory products of some less happy hours of his later years. Here Raphael was so fortunate to be able to have his most excellent students working for him under his direct oversight and leadership.

16. Giulio Romano (1499–1546), also known as Giulio Pippi, was one of Raphael's most talented students who became an important artist in the Mannerist movement. [Ed.]

17. This should correctly read Gianfrancesco Penni, called "*Il Fattore.*" Penni earned this nickname, meaning "manager," because he played such a central role in Raphael's workshop. He and Pippi later inherited the workshop. [Ed.]

together with Raphael's above-mentioned students in these features. But everyone who cares at all about this matter already does that. I only allow myself a few select comments on those heroes themselves.

Raphael, as great as he was, and as good as he felt himself to be, constantly studied his art and sought—never resting satisfied with himself—to raise it and himself to ever greater perfection. Mozart did the same. If one did not already know this historically, even the most fleeting chronological glance at the works of the two would convince him of this fact. Raphael lived exclusively in his art and found satisfaction in it alone. He drew even in hours of rest and recuperation, drafting simple sketches that, while incomplete, were highly significant; the same applies to Mozart, and many a work that has already been included in the printed collection of his compositions and was made public in these pages for the first time[18] offers proof of that. Raphael was forced, by people and situations in the last years of his life, to deliver various great, but more pleasant and charming works than was his wont. His painting of the *History of Psyche and Galatea* did, indeed, reflect the conception of the customer, but, at the same time, did so in such a way that it was permeated with great, profound spirit; Mozart was similar in his *Zauberflöte*, *Clemenza di Tito*, and some smaller compositions.

But Raphael and Mozart, for all that, were and remained *human beings*. Thus, their works did not, in all respects, achieve the most elevated, purest, and greatest perfection. Where would one find the mortal who fulfilled everything that the immortal spirit thinks, feels, and wills for itself! Both men, now and again, appear less fortunate in what I have termed artistic execution, which will, I hope, not be confounded with what is called execution in ordinary musical language—of a thought, a movement, and so on. Raphael was weak in foreshortening, less than strong when it came to perspective; his use of colors is not always good (black shadows, red flesh), his brush frequently harsh. Similarly with Mozart: quite a few of his completed compositions are over-full, his modulations not seldom bizarre, his transitions frequently rough. He seldom writes plaintively without a few penetrating traces of concealed anger, which cannot be well described in words but are immediately felt. As far as Raphael, in these respects, lags behind soft Correggio[19] and charming

18. For example, in the sixth volume. Here we assume Rochlitz means the sixth issue of the *AmZ*, from 7 November 1798, which opens with some of his famous anecdotes from Mozart's life. [Ed.]

19. Antonio Correggio (1489–1534) was a painter of the Parma School known both for his chiaroscuro and his sensual paintings. [Ed.]

Titian, Mozart, here, is equally inferior to the Italians of the middle period, and to a few of those who are still living.

The tremendous variety among the works of both artists, as concerns their content as well as its treatment (although all have that primary character) must inspire astonishment, and would, along with their number, be almost unbelievable, especially when it comes to the masters' short lives—not quite free of certain sensual dependencies—if one did not know how the two lived solely in and for their arts, how they commenced that life so early, and how their spirit held itself aloof from everything that did not stand in quite close relation to their main work. Everything else they treated fleetingly—often carelessly; only what pertained to their primary interest was greeted with the greatest, fieriest, unabating interest. It is very noteworthy that neither Raphael nor Mozart, despite the constant drive of their spirit from one thing to the next, despite the constant pressure of new works, despite the tempting allure of advantages tied to ever new commissions, nevertheless (in their mature years) never simply cobbled their works together, treated them superficially, gave them to the world incomplete, or (if I may use this coarse but in my opinion more accurately descriptive word) simply tossed them off. Both worked quickly, but not hastily.[20] Where, in their works, one finds breaches of the conventional, of something inviolably (and probably not without reason) assumed, there it is not a question of hastiness, but of well-deliberated sacrifice of what is less essential in favor of the main thing—the effect.

I cannot pass over another beautiful trait in the character of the two artists, as well-known as it may be. Both accorded full justice to every other worthy accomplishment. Raphael, for example, always displayed the liveliest esteem for the works of his teacher Pietro Perugino and his supporter Bramante, however much his own vision and works may have outstripped theirs. (In his veneration, he even left untouched the ceiling painted by the former in the third chamber of the Segnatura.)[21] He loudly expressed his veneration of his powerful, defiant rival, Michelangelo, and supported the very significant Giulio Romano, who even surpassed the

20. With respect to Mozart, there is, here and there, an untrue rumor to the contrary. Those who promote it or can write about it as something that has been observed, must never have seen a handwritten manuscript of Mozart's. Here, even in the first drafts that he only kept for himself, *everything*—even without abbreviations, where these could occasion even the slightest misunderstanding—is written out; everything, down to the smallest *forte*, *piano*, or *crescendo*, through all the voices of the full scores.

21. The Room of the Segnatura is located in the Vatican and is the first space to have been painted there by Raphael. Donato Bramante was a mentor to Raphael and recommended him to work for Pope Julius II in Rome. [Ed.]

teacher in fieriness. Mozart too: his behavior toward Joseph Haydn, his defense of Jommelli, his veneration of Sebastian Bach and Handel, his support of and the help given to other significant younger artists are too well-known for me to need to cite individual anecdotes.

Thus, then, the two led and expended their short but densely packed lives, and each, as he approached the middle of his thirties, experienced a subtle, creeping exhaustion of his delicate body, while their spirits spiraled ever higher, but wore out the former even faster. Now, Augustin Chigi[22] convinced Raphael, and ______ ______ [23] persuaded Mozart to prepare the above-mentioned, more pleasant and charming works, and the two artists became enmeshed, for a time, through the goodwill of these customers and various circumstances, in a still more sensual life.[24] The weakened bodies became exhausted, but the spirits rose up once again, with power and majesty as never before. Both felt the chill hand of death that already gripped them; both still wanted to erect more monuments for eternity; they both chose *transfiguration*—Raphael, of the Redeemer, Mozart of the redeemed.[25] With the eagerness of those who see the specter of death hovering near them, and with the effort of those who feel "This is your last thing," both worked, and offered, the quintessence, as it were, of their most sacred feelings. Raphael's work became the first of the newer style of painting; Mozart's the first of the newer religious music; although some connoisseurs find the disposition of some parts, in both works, overly dark.

As the two artists completed these works, they died—both in the thirty-seventh year of their life.[26]

---

22. Agostino Chigi was a wealthy banker and important patron of the arts who commissioned several major works from Raphael. [Ed.]

23. We assume this person who, according to Rochlitz, corrupted Mozart as Chigi corrupted Raphael was still living in 1800, when this article was published, and so his name is not included in the text. [Ed.]

24. Chigi famously allowed Raphael's lover to stay continuously in his room, which interfered with what Raphael was working on. In Mozart's case, I do not name the particular person and do not mention that particular circumstances precisely because *goodwill* was the basis of the first.

25. Raphael's final work was *The Transfiguration*, which depicts Jesus in his glorified state. Mozart's final work was his Requiem in D Minor that sets the Latin Mass for the Dead. [Ed.]

26. This seems, in general, to be a dangerous year for great spirits who step off the beaten path of their contemporaries, and not a few besides the above-mentioned—Brutus, too, and Alexander the Great also died in this year of their lives.

AmZ 3: 8 October 1800, cols. 26–35, and 15 October 1800, cols. 51–54

The third AmZ *article is a review of a new edition by Breitkopf & Härtel of the complete works of Mozart. It appears in two parts, the first in the 8 October 1800 issue and the second the following week on 15 October. One is reminded of the earlier article on Mozart's songs, because here too, Rochlitz is convinced that depth inherent in the works is proof of their authenticity. What is particularly interesting in this review is the ranking of types of works both within Mozart's oeuvre and in more general ways. The symphony, for example, is the genre in which a composer can most freely express himself and is to instrumental music what choral music is to the category of vocal music. But the symphony is only the highest instrumental genre in its transmission of power, whereas concertos are the highest in their transmission of tenderness. As in the earlier review of the songs, Rochlitz complains about Mozart neglecting his texts and allowing incorrect declamation. He refers to Raphael again, emphasizing the timelessness of both men and their ability to surpass the achievements of others in their respective eras. The various criticisms that Rochlitz levels at Mozart's music are perhaps of most interest to the reader. Essentially, Rochlitz says that any flaws in his music, such as taking too symphonic an approach in piano works, are absorbed and taken to an extreme by Mozart's contemporaries. These other characters are Rochlitz's true adversaries then, with their exaggerations and meaningless compositions, but the person who caused the problems was Mozart. Rochlitz damningly sums up the situation in the supposed view that the French had of German music, as possessing "genius, power, and barbarism." He predicts that all this other music will fade away and that Mozart's spirit will eventually be better understood.*

Review
Oeuvres complètes de Wolfgang Amadeus Mozart, au Magasin de Musique de Breitkopf et Härtel à Leipsic

Cah. I. contenant VII Sonates pour le Pianoforte.
Cah. II. conten. douze Thèmes variés pour le Pianoforte.
Cah. III. conten. VII Sonates pour le Pianoforte.
Cah. IV. conten. VI Sonates pour le Pianoforte avec l'acompagn. d'un Violon.
Cah. V. conten. Trente Airs et Chansons pour le Pianoforte.
Cah. VI. conten. XIV différentes Pièces pour le Pianoforte.
Cah. VII. conten. IV Sonates pour le Pianoforte à quatre mains.
Cah. VIII. conten. VI Pièces pour le Pianoforte à deux et à quatre mains.

Mozart, as a poetic musical artist, not only occupies an exalted position in his own field, but is hitherto unrivaled—unique. His compositions have had not only some, but the most decisive influence on the trajectory and further development of musical art itself. And they still have and will long continue to have it—they are epoch-making in the most robust sense of the term. The undertaking to publish the entirety of all the significant and so numerous works of the Master, under such circumstances, is the first and until now the only one of its kind, at least in Germany. Consequently, it will be permissible to linger somewhat longer on each of these three points.

If one surveys the quantity of Mozartian works, one scarcely comprehends the profound depth of many of them. If one focuses on their profundity, one hardly grasps their quantity. Thus, it is natural that, before taking a closer look, one may take many of them for wrongly attributed and accept the external, historical proofs of their genuineness only with partial confidence. Upon closer inspection, this changes. The works of Mozart carry an incontrovertible, internal proof of their genuineness, which is surely no more difficult to grasp than recognizing the work of truly great painters is for those who have deeply studied their spirit and style. But the number and variety of Mozart's compositions will always provoke amazement. For, truly, there is no discipline in music, no as yet discovered form in which a musician can construct his melodies and harmonies, in which Mozart did not also and always work—admittedly with more or less good fortune.

If we now, among the plenitude of his creations, want to get to know what was most truly his own, then (it would seem) we must ask: Where did he succeed *most magnificently*—what never went awry? His works can be summarized under the following categories.

1. For the *piano*, he wrote a lot of things of an entertaining sort—polite, light, graceful, somewhat delicate. They never failed him but have been surpassed by other masters.

2. He wrote larger, more serious movements for this instrument that are very significant in every way that works of the art of music can be considered as such, and are similar in style, spirit, and artistic value to the third category.

3. His quartets and quintets, with or without piano. Now these are extremely significant almost without exception. They are of defined character, profoundly conceived, deeply felt, unwaveringly consonant, and often truly passionate. In these compositions, intended exclusively for selected smaller circles, the artist's spirit moves in a rare, strange manner, great and elevated, like an apparition appearing from another world. And if he, at moments, melts with melancholy, or trifles with the listener in a cheerful mood, they are just moments. And after that he—again, *only* for moments—rises again with bold, sometimes wild power, or writhes

in bitter, acute pain, which then seems to triumph after the victory or to perish in the struggle.[27]

4. Fourthly, Mozart wrote great *symphonies*. This is a genre in which genius may move in the freest and boldest manner, where its effect is more general (and for this very reason either moves deeply, or not at all). It can employ all musical elements as means toward its purpose (and for this very reason can easily lose its way within the mechanism of its presentation). It may be claimed that this genre is, in instrumental music, what choral works are to vocal music—it is in them that the artist most surely represents himself. Mozart's symphonies (we speak only of those from his mature years) are similar in style and spirit to the quartets, only even freer, even bolder, even richer, even more energetic—but from time to time also even wilder, sharper, and more oppressive, so that the spirit of the artist at times manifests itself more through the fermentation process than through the maturity itself. He presents more the creation that is in the process of being directly born out of chaos than the newly born creation itself.[28] Ordering and ordered reason may then, with rejection of the initially enraptured but in agreement with *subsequently* moved feelings, also find these works inferior to the most beautiful quartets of Mozart, and may, *in this case*, hand the palm branch of victory to worthy Father Haydn.

5. Fifth, Mozart wrote great *concertos*. Here he started from the only form that existed prior to him and created a new one on his own. With the sole exception of Mozart, the foundational principle of all composers in this genre (thus also the only principle to be included in the theories, and—as now—deduced in them as the only possible one) was that in the concerto the solo voice is the only meaningful voice; it is everything. The accompaniment is only *accompanying*, and exists solely to make the former more resplendent. The latter (also including ritornello, etc.) must be weakened intentionally, both in ideas and in their realization; everything of substance must be set aside, or at most obscurely and fleetingly suggested, in order to allow the solo player and his exceptionally practiced

27. So that the reader will not regard all this as empty idealism but can find it right away in a single example, one should hear Mozart's Quartet for piano, violin, viola, and cello in E-flat major, performed very well (this can only be done by individuals who, besides the necessary and considerable technical skill, also have a heart and, when it comes to music, a very maturely educated understanding). One should hear it, study it afterwards, and then listen to it again. This, by the way, is how one should treat every truly significant composition. Why? That can be discussed elsewhere. [Rochlitz]

28. One may compare, here, his well-known, truly great symphonies in E-flat major, C major (including the final fugue), and above all the one in G minor.

phrases to shine through and his performance to be all the more effective. Mozart chose and did the opposite (whether with *sufficient* grounds, this is not the place to determine). He assumed: that the concerto is the highest form that expresses more *tender* music whereas the symphony reigns supreme among those expressing *greatness*. Everything that can contribute to the achievement of this purpose must be set in the greatest possible motion; thus, *all* voices must be fully *worked through*; the soloist must merely have the foremost voice *among* them; the ritornellos must excite great expectations, and must tantalize and inspire the spirit. The *natural* charms of all the instruments in the accompaniment must also be brought to bear in striking, graceful play,[29] etc. Thus were these works created which in their nature stand almost alone, even now (despite the multitudinous swarms of imitators, who give us, as it were, only vaguely similar skeletons in place of the beautiful figures). If we now examine the character and the most consummate examples of these works, there emerges—after disregarding everything incidental—the greatest similarity in spirit, style, and sheer artistic value with the most consummate quartets of Mozart, so that what has been adumbrated there as entirely exquisite and always successful appears here, too, as entirely exquisite and always successful.

Now to vocal music. Mozart, first of all, wrote small *Lieder and songs*, to the accompaniment of the piano or a small number of instruments. In general, he succeeded quite well, some are truly excellent, and he almost never totally missed the mark, but in individual cases, one could raise more than a few objections. He wrote larger *cantatas* and, to the same extent that he gains more freedom, assumes control of greater means, and can expand more broadly, his works also become more characteristic, ingenious, original, dignified, and consequently richer in their effects, so that even criticism has less with which to find fault. He wrote *operas*—one will have to allow the reviewer, who will publicly address these in the future, when their scores are in print, to review them then in detail. For my purposes, it is enough if I mention them in sequence: *Idomeneo*, *Die Entführung aus dem Serail*, *Così*

29. It is probably not necessary to remark that Mozart, untrained as he was in the sciences and in aesthetics, did not derive these fundamental principles, did not develop and evaluate these plans (as a Gluck, a Méhul,* and a few others did with some of their successful "theatre coups"). Mozart received them as dawning consciousness from his inner feeling—the God in him. And it is quite right so. Let the educated aficionado, by contrast, seek out similar things, unique to genius, in order to enjoy them all the more richly; let the critic seek them out in order to find the harmony between beautiful Nature and underlying theory, and if it is found to derive therefrom its confirmation; or, if it should remain unfound, in all modesty to correct his theory or abandon it.

* Étienne Nicolas Méhul (1763–1817) was a French opera composer. [Ed.]

fan tutte, *Figaro*, *Don Giovanni*, *La clemenza di Tito*.[30] Everywhere, one notes that what is great, noble, bold, and powerful is most truly represented by his genius. (The *early Idomeneo*, in which the rich, powerful spirit still acts more out of fealty to itself, can be compared in this respect to the wildest of his symphonies.) He succeeded, often succeeded splendidly, in all that was gracious, fine, tender; but it never appears as pure and complete in itself as in his great achievements and his more expansive moments, when he, in his greatness, stands perfected and pure. Where he, submitting to the circumstances that often weighed him down so heavily, denied this property of his—only therein lies failure. Since we are speaking here only of the spirit that inheres in *the whole*, no attention is paid to individual excellence that contradicts what is said here, and neither is any consideration given to individual imperfections in what confirms it. To these imperfections belong the frequent neglect of the words (not the meaning) of his texts, incorrect declamation, etc., overloading of more tender vocal passages, darkening of the same by the volume of the instrumental music, and the scholarly nature of the work, etc., this last further confirming what has been said above. Finally, Mozart wrote *church music*; some of which, in the earlier years, before he reached the *height* of his learning in his travels, was not insignificant, but then, after all, not really church music. Later, there was little of it, but it was more practical; and finally, for those who can comprehend it, his heavenly *Requiem*. What shall I say about it?

Von Heldenkraft erzeugt in glüh'nder Stunde;	Of hero's strength conceived in glowing hour;
Kühn hingeworfen der Natur im Schoos,	Boldly tossed in Nature's lap,
Ob er, der Sohn, ergeben seinem Loos,	Would he, the son, surrendering to his fate,
Ersterbe, ob er zum Unsterblichen gesunde.	Perish or heal and become immortal?
Und er erwuchs, der Heldensohn. Vom Bunde	And he grew up, the hero's son. From the bonds
Des Hergebrachten reißt sein Arm sich los;	of tradition, his arm pulls free;

30. Properly understood, the following saying, which may be found somewhere (it seems to me, in Lessing) is certainly true: No painter can paint a head other than his own. As far as I am familiar with Mozart's spirit, it is most recognizable in the hours of that profound unease, so grueling for every poor mortal, in *Don Giovanni*; in the hours of that noble and serene peace, in *Figaro*; and in both united, in the Requiem.

Kühn blickt sein blaues Aug, auch schmachtend groß	His blue eye gazes boldly, and standing languidly large,
Steht er, und hört aus kaltem Richter-Munde:	He hears, out of a cold judge's mouth:
Verwegener, wühlst du auf der Menschheit Grauen?	Reckless one, do you wallow in humanity's dread?
Nur Kreuz, nicht Palme lässt dein Glaube schauen;	Your creed evokes the cross alone and not the palm frond;
Nur seine Thräne, ohne sein Vertrauen?	Its tears alone without its faith?
"Nacht deckt mich, doch vom Stern der Lieb' erhellt –	"Night encloses me, yet enlightened by the star of love
(Ihr seht den nicht) so bin ich aufgestellt,	(which you don't see) I stand
Ein Bild des Werdens überirrd'scher Welt!	A symbol of the coming of the heavenly world!

May I be forgiven for the outpouring of a soul so deeply moved, which is equally unable to gain control of itself, as to say anything better.

If one now summarizes what has been stated above, and if it is well founded, then it confirms the truth of something asserted elsewhere in these pages about what is most particular and individual in the character of Mozart, the composer: in *invention*, both *poetic* and *artistic*, riches, inexhaustible riches; and good fortune: but, in its execution, most fortunate by far in all that is great and splendid, not quite so perfect in matters more sublime.[31]

Now, such a spirit must surely have had much impact. M. certainly influenced his contemporaries significantly, even beyond his art. But speaking about that further is too far from my current intention. Also, those impacts can often only be guessed and felt in a general sense; they elude detailed evidence. Besides, it is now, more than ever, time to approach some things—over which our predecessors quarreled, but which our descendants (sooner or later) may agree upon and make their agreement known—in all seriousness. Thus, I shall pass over that and say only a few words about his *impact* on his art itself—its evolution, further development, and perfection—and *on artists*.

31. One may compare the essay "Raphael and Mozart," the 37th item in the second issue of this publication, where the above-cited concepts are more precisely described and explained.

All truly great men who walk off the beaten path, effected bad and good things. This happens not only with the good but also with the bad ones—but perception changes. They are ahead of their time, and so, evidently, their own contemporaries see more of the bad things than the good—and then just the opposite for the following generations. But because they are unrecognized in their own time, this neglect now comes to bite them again, not because of the suffering they had to endure then, but also through blind imitation even of the incidental [works] by ignorant followers. With this justification, foolish work is created by weaklings—and that is the saddest of the whole enterprise. Thus, it is everywhere, including in the artistic world. I will not provide examples of various contemporary poets, since they are each readily available to everyone. One may, however, recall, for example, that Raphael's simple greatness induced dryness, coolness, stubborn lack of charm in his contemporaries, temporarily sending them to the Romanesque School; or that Correggio's color-magic put them in the Lombard School, with empty color experimentation and stilted light-and-shadow play. But the era of great men like these quickly dissipates, while they themselves remain great and undamaged, awaiting, sooner or later, a generation that knows how to grasp their excellence, discard their imperfections, and add all of this to the general character of humanity as a whole and to all earthly life. It is these not merely chronological contemporaries on whom, thus, they have the purest effect; on them their gifts are most meaningfully bestowed. By them, only the artists' best is protected, cultivated, and enjoyed, while what is less or not at all significant disappears or is laid aside. In the same way, history is only grasped and purely enjoyed in large terms if the thousands and thousands of small details to which contemporaries are attached have disappeared and been laid aside.

Through this long detour, I have wanted to try to lay the foundation for a—now much frowned upon, heretical—word of heterodoxy that I must speak. Until now, Mozart, when it comes to art and its progress toward the goal of perfection, has caused more harm than good. The true connoisseurs and thorough admirers of his contributions, along with the few really outstanding artists of his school, will not find themselves insulted by this judgment; *they* are the exception to the rule; but here it is only possible to speak of the rule. Most of the members of this school have seized only on chance elements of the master—in part, those that are obviously deserving of criticism; only these they have held fast to, imitated, even re-created. Piano music has been invaded (and I repeat, there are exceptions) by a rough, counterproductive symphonic spirit—of which one cannot absolve several of Mozart's works in this genre—or by rich and full-seeming, pompous, pretentious cacophony that says nothing specific, and is therefore devoid of effect. This is derived from the outer covering in which Mozart enveloped the elevated spirit of various larger works of this kind, and that is taken, by its imitators, for what is fundamental. Fuller instrumental music (quartet, concerto, symphony, etc.) has become a noisy jumble of all resources, without meaningful purpose. This results in: a wearying uniformity; excessively artificial harmonies that result in a cold neglect of the melodic; an element of unceasing calculation, resulting in a lack of effect on emotion; a contradictory, bristling fragmentation and hodgepodge of ideas; a rough, wild, obstreperous running around, rampaging, raging with no clear sense of wherefrom or whereto. Vocal music also puffs itself up with similar artifice, with overloading and darkening of the song; it has melodies that hardly deserve the name melody. The words, the characters of individuals, are forgotten; and the listener who is meant to feel with them is forgotten as well. In ensembles, finales, and the like, the vocalists sing the most ordinary things—that are foolish to be singing—with a pompousness and elaboration in the instrumental parts that fail to emphasize the really significant passages and rob them of every effect. These sections are treated almost the same way in solos and arias, so that one could do without not only the text, but if need be the singer as well, and can regard the scene as a *sinfonie en programme*. The lack of accentuation, declamation, and in general the lack of educated, dignified, *individual* treatment of the words has become the order of the day and strengthens our neighbors, the French, in their verdict on our more recent great musicians: "genius, power, and barbarism." Petty incorporation of word painting, trifling imitations of Nature's own tones are not infrequently called upon to stand in for expression, or to replace it. Evils of this sort affect not only so many operas of this kind, but much church music as well, even if composed by justly famous and honored masters, etc.[32]

If someone finds the shadows of this description too dark, let him compare just one third as many works of the last three decades. By the way, with this I by no means wish to have claimed that things were better among our predecessors. It was *different* then, no doubt, but not therefore *better*. In the end, it is all the same whether everyone wants, for example, to be *Bachish*, or *Mozartish*. It will only become better when everyone wants to become what he is, and everyone who is something

32. Of the traveling virtuosos who would like to justify their lack of all education in humanities or science, who would like to justify their own excess and wantonness with a flurry of anecdotes about Mozart—of which half are truly lies, the rest exaggerated to the point of nausea—and who, in their pitiable thinking, believe themselves thus to become similar to the master, I will say nothing at all.

can be something good in his own way—not Cephish,[33] not Apollinian. Who is Paul? Who is Cephas? Who is Apollo? They are *servants*! As we are far from there, and, on the paths that are now the most well-trodden, we are more likely moving farther and farther away from there than coming closer—that is what I wished to point out.

But all that will pass and fade away, like the sapless, dry leaves of the holly oak when spring infuses new life into the powerful branches; then, Mozart's spirit will be not only more purely recognized, but also better enjoyed. Then, one will burst less often into fervent declamations in his favor, will be less adulating of every fleeting page by him, than may now sometimes occur. But one will honor what is unique about him, keep only his best and enjoy it; one will be taught, elevated, strengthened by it, and not strive to imitate it. One will forget what is less perfect in him and consign it to the mass of imperfections that exists in us all, and in even the greatest works of humans; one will not use it precisely to excuse one's own weaknesses. And in order for this to come about, the collection of his works—carefully ordered, widely distributed thanks to its reasonable price, and offered in an externally pleasing, proper way—is not an insignificant contribution. Just a few more lines on this collection itself and the compositions thus far included follow.

Conclusion
Oeuvres complettes de Wolfgang Amadeus Mozart, au Magasin de Musique Breitkopf et Härtel à Leipsic

On the arrangement of this publication and on the volumes that have appeared so far, I can be brief, since that material is very well known, based on earlier notices, by means of the widely distributed work itself, and since the greatest part by far of the included compositions have already appeared individually. The arrangement, for the most part, is as follows: Mozart's works—excepting the very early and insignificant youthful ones—are printed in three series, each of which is internally consistent and has its own numbering scheme and subscription. The first set offers small vocal pieces with piano accompaniment and all the piano pieces, with or without accompaniment by a *single* additional instrument. The second contains trios, quartets, quintets, wind ensemble music, concertos, and symphonies printed in parts. The third offers scores of the cantatas, operas, and sacred music. Each booklet in the first and third

33. The word in German here is kephisch—a reference to St. Paul, or Cephas, as he is occasionally referred to in the New Testament, hence "rocklike." We might say "Paulish." [Ed.]

volume consists of 24 to 30 sheets, bears a beautiful title vignette (most are by Kininger and Böhm), and costs 1 thaler and 12 groschen for the subscription price, or 3 thaler retail. The pieces of the second volume cannot be assessed precisely since a booklet consists of better or weaker content combined, but they are even somewhat less expensive, so that, for example, every concerto, with all the orchestral voices, costs 1 thaler with a subscription. In addition, collectors even receive the fifth booklet free of charge. At least four booklets of the piano music appear every year. The print is clear, distinct, handsome, and correct and the paper very good and strong. Certainly, everything one could wish has thus been done by the publisher. For easily understandable reasons, it could have been disadvantageous for the firm to have ordered the compositions according to the year in which they were written. Yet many a connoisseur will certainly wish, as we do, that there would be a list added at the end of every volume—a listing of its contents, including all of the compositions printed therein and the year in which they were written. This can happen even more easily since Mozart, in his later years, wrote up a complete catalogue of his works, including information on their date of composition.

The compositions in the eight volumes of *Piano Music* that have appeared thus far (information on the remaining compositions will be provided by other colleagues elsewhere in this publication) can be considered under the following three aspects:

> 1) Lesser examples, for pleasant amusement, early training, and easier practice, drawn partly from the composer's relatively early, mostly from his middle, and in a few cases from his later years;
> 2) Larger compositions, for more serious entertainment, more mature training, and more difficult practice, mainly taken from the artist's middle and later years;
> 3) Studies created by the composer more for his own sake than for the public, almost all drawn from Mozart's later years and for the most part made public here for the first time.

Naturally, the lines separating these categories—especially the first and second—often overlap, and one will not quibble with the person who would perhaps like to include in the second category some things that are here assigned to the first. The opposite case will not easily occur, since the following specifications are more likely to be too strict than too permissive.

The first of these categories offers compositions that, compared to the others, admittedly have less timeless artistic value and are more subject to the taste and fashion of the times. They will justifiably be very welcome to those amateurs who pursue music as a matter of mere amusement, light-hearted delectation, and perfunctoriness. But not solely to them. People who have been most selectively destined and armed by a benevolent Nature for *something*, and quite specifically for *excellence in it*, do and say everything, even the most common things, in their very own special way, as it aligns with their primary interest. Thus, many trifling details of Mozart's works have something about them that is quite unique, unusual, and connected—if at some remove—with his higher calling. By means of this connection, these works may also become interesting to the serious connoisseur. We consider Sonatas 1, 2, 3, 4, 5, and 7 from the first booklet as belonging to this category; 1–6 from the third booklet, of which the majority are here made public for the first time. Further, the Rondo in D major and the sonata in the sixth, Sonatas 3 and 4 for four hands in the seventh booklet, the majority of his themes with variations in the second and sixth, as well as most of his Lieder and small songs in the fifth booklet, and so forth.

Just as the second of these categories is more artistically significant and for all eras, and less for mere fashion, so Mozart's particular spirit becomes clearer, frequently brilliant here. We include some of his varied themes in the second booklet, and those for four hands in the eighth; Sonatas No. 6 in the first and No. 7 in the third, along with most of the sonatas in the fourth; plus various songs in the fifth (for example Nos. 2, 4, 7, 10, 13, and 26); various pieces in the sixth(especially the *Fantaisie* and the immediately following sonata, which belongs together with it, and the first and third rondos); the second sonata (C major) in the eighth; and, even more so, the second sonata for two players in the seventh and the first (F minor) in the eighth booklet. About all of which one could assert that they occupy a *unique* place among their kind, and so on.

Finally, the studies have the very significant historical and artistic value of the hand-drawn sketches of great painters, with which these Mozart pieces, in particular, could be compared at greater length than the space here—long since exceeded—permits. Perhaps here one should, as first among all of those included in the categories above, consider the utterly incomparable Double Sonata in F Minor, which Mozart did not make public, but originally intended for a large musical clock. The Gigue of the sixth booklet, the 1st *Fantaisie* and the fugues of the eighth belong here; and, above all, the truly great overture in Handel's—not merely manner, but also in Handel's spirit, in the sixth booklet. It is shared here for the first time from among the papers in Mozart's estate, and is, for all who are sufficiently educated to judge and enjoy it, a beautiful gift—a jewel, delectable not only for its rarity, but also for its inner worth.

AmZ 4: 1 October 1801, cols. 1–11, and 7 October 1801, cols. 23–31

The long article on Mozart's Requiem from 1 October and 7 October of 1801 sets the stage for a discussion that continues today about Franz Xaver Süssmayr's completion of the unfinished work. The author (presumably Rochlitz) criticizes Mozart's former associate's efforts in the completion, but also acknowledges that the close connection between the two men meant that even a more accomplished composer than Süssmayr would not have achieved a better result. And yet, by the end of the article, Rochlitz wishes for a "truly thorough" composer to oversee the removal of all the imperfections that can be found in the score. (We have omitted the long list of errata from this translation since they refer to specific page numbers in an edition that is not widely available.) Rochlitz notes that many aspects of the Requiem such as instrumentation, dissonances, and modulations are pathbreaking. A modern musician or scholar will be interested in the specific musical examples that stand out to Rochlitz in technically unusual or emotionally powerful ways. Our reviewer also mildly criticizes Mozart for passing through melodies and harmonies too quickly and for the shortness of many movements, all of which prevents the listener from properly enjoying the music. Of course, Rochlitz explains, it is possible that these are among the parts of the work that Mozart was unable to complete due to his premature death.

Review

W. A. Mozart's Requiem with accompanying German text. Complete score. Published by Breitkopf und Härtel Music Shop in Leipzig. (Price 6 thaler)

It is not easy, when it comes to a work like the present one, to abstain from the general effusions of praise or the communication of images of fantasy induced and enriched by the work itself. The seriousness and inner dignity of such a work of art, however, definitely require us to do so. Where it is not necessary to attract the initial attention of the public, it also creates no advantage either for the work and its creator, or for those who can put it to use. That the attention of all those who love true music—music as a matter of enduring pleasure, not fleeting stimulus—is directed toward Mozart's *Requiem* is something we may take for granted. But it is not within everyone's grasp to follow the profound spirit of the composer without a guide, and thus to acquire the full benefit and all the pleasure that it offers. To provide this guide for the person who requires it; and thus, with earnest precision and strict veneration, to ensure that the work receives its full rights, it is necessary to point to the meaning of the whole as well as to that of the individual parts of this delectable product, and, as well, since that meaning is typically explained by the words that are sung, to point, even more, to the secret means by which the expression of meaning, almost everywhere, succeeded so masterfully for the immortal Mozart, and, at the same time, to ensure, through earnest precision and honoring stringency, that this works receives what it is due—this shall be my effort in the following analysis.

But before I venture such a review of this first of its kind, unique work of art itself, I cannot but share with the readers the excerpt of a letter from Herr Kapellmeister Süssmayer in Vienna, dated 9 September 1800, to Messrs. Breitkopf and Härtel in Leipzig, along with a few comments on it. "Mozart's composition," writes Herr Süssmayer, "is so unique, and I daresay for the greatest part of living composers so unattainable, that every imitator, especially in terms of the work that it implies, would come away even worse off than the raven that bedecked itself with peacock's feathers. That the completion of the requiem that was the cause of our exchange of letters was entrusted to me came about in the following manner. Mozart's widow could very well foresee that the works her husband left behind would be sought after; death surprised him while he was working on this *Requiem*. The work's conclusion was thus entrusted to several masters; some, due to other business, were unable to take on this work, while others did not want to compromise their talent with the talent of Mozart. Ultimately, this work came to me because it was known that while Mozart was still living I had often played through and sung previously composed musical works with him, and that he had very often discussed these works' composition with me and had communicated the progress of and reasons behind his instrumentation. I can only wish that it might be vouchsafed to me, to have, at least, worked in such a way that experts may yet be able, at least, to find traces of his unforgettable teachings in it. For the *Requiem*, together with the *Kyrie—Dies Irae—Domine Jesu Christe*—Mozart has fully completed the four vocal parts and the ground bass, including their numbering; for the instrumentation, however, he had only occasionally indicated the motive. *Dies Irae* was his last verse—*qua resurget ex favilla*—and his work was the very same as in the first pieces. Starting with the verse *judicandus homo reus*, etc., the *Dies irae*, the *Sanctus*, *Benedictus*, and *Agnus Dei* are entirely newly made by me; except that I have permitted myself to lend the work more uniformity, to repeat the fugue of the *Kyrie* at the verse *cum sanctus*, etc." So much from Herr Süssmayer.[34]

34. For more information about Süssmayr's completion of the Requiem, see Simon P. Keefe, "Die Ochsen am Berge: Franz Xaver Süssmayr and the Orchestration of Mozart's Requiem, K. 626," *Journal of the American Musicological Society* 61/1 (2008): 1–65; Keefe, *Mozart's Requiem: Reception, Work, Completion* (Cambridge: Cambridge University Press, 2012). For an alternative to Süssmayer's version, see Richard Maunder, *Mozart's Requiem: On Preparing a New Edition* (Oxford: Oxford University Press, 1988). [Ed.]

That Mozart's composition for the *Requiem* is inimitable and a similar one may be not only largely but perhaps utterly unattainable for all now living composers, is something this reviewer fully believes. That perhaps, also, everything did not flow from Mozart's pen precisely as it stands there, is proven, among other things, by the in part very error-filled instrumental accompaniment. One may look, for example, at p. 45, m. 6; pp. 104 and 105; but especially p. 114, mm. 4–5; p. 116, m. 4; p. 119, m. 1; p. 120, m. 3; p. 130, m. 1; and several more. That the perfecting of this work was assigned to Herr Süssmayer, who was already acquainted with Mozart's ideas, had frequently spoken with him about them, and thus perhaps only had to write down some things he recalled, or were assigned and executed by him, was admittedly always still better than if it had fallen into the hands of a composer who was good but perhaps less familiar with Mozart and his ideas. Nevertheless, Herr Süssmayer seems to have felt very vividly how much this masterwork would have to lose due to the unfortunately much too early loss of its great creator. That Mozart placed numbers under what Herr Süssmayer called the ground bass has very much drawn this reviewer's attention, since among the very significant number of Mozart's manuscripts that he has seen directly he has found not a single one with *hand-numbered* bass. That a large part of the instrumental accompaniment would also have to be ascribed to Herr Süssmayer is quite possible, but for the fact that those of Herr Süssmayer's artistic products with which we are so far acquainted offer a rather severe critique of any claim of his more significant participation in this great work. However this may be, one owes Herr Süssmayer great thanks for every share—however small and insignificant—in the perfecting and the resulting possibility of publication of this masterpiece, to which this reviewer, then, offers thanks for his person, publicly and with his whole heart. Now to the *Requiem* itself.

The particular and unusual choice of accompanying instruments by a Mozart so extremely well acquainted with the relative advantages, imperfections, peculiarities, etc., of all the customary instruments—who must, above all and especially also in this regard, be ranked as the prime and until now unrivaled archetype of the instrumental composer—raises the expectation of something special and unusual. Probably in order to avoid everything that, in any respect, could be even remotely detrimental to the profound devotion, earnest prayer, and sublime solemnity that prevails throughout the work, he avoided wind instruments that are characterized by high, soft, and sharp tones, for example flutes, oboes, clarinets, alto oboes, English horns, and the like, and selected, alongside the usual stringed instruments, only basset-horns, bassoons, trombones, and—very sparingly but all the more intentionally, thus generating the most perfect effect—trumpets and timpani. The very first entrance of these instruments, consisting of a mere three tones at the end of the introduction, as a kind of herald of great events to come, can fully prove the correctness of this so rarely apposite comment.

Since perhaps not every reader has heard this masterpiece or has the score at hand, the reviewer inserts the introduction here in its entirety:

The theme that is introduced here in the basset-horns and bassoons is brief, but as novel in its harmonic arrangement as it is beautiful in execution; Mozart made it the major movement of the first chorus, and used it to accompany the words *Requiem aeternam*, etc. Hereupon, following the just cited examples, the voices enter in canon-like formation, namely following each other at short intervals—specifically, first the bass, then the tenor, followed by the alto, and finally the descant, thus ensuring that the figure introduced by the violins at the end of the example is retained, so that the whole takes on extraordinary power, emphasis, and solidity. Following the words *et lux perpetua lucent eis*, with which Mozart closes the first section of the chorus in B-flat major (p. 10), he employs a pleasing little episode as an introduction to the descant solo [*286], after the well-known melody of the church hymn *Meine Seele erhebt den Herrn*, whose words read *Te decet hymnus*, are arranged to be variously and interestingly accompanied by all kinds of canonic variations, inversions, transpositions in the double counterpoint of the octaves, thirds, sixths, etc., which accompany the example given above in the second measure of the figure in the first violins and the first bassoon. Now (p. 12), the choir's

bass, tenor, and alto enter with the words *exaudi, exaudi orationem meam*, then also the descant,[35] which, fortified by the unison of the basset-horns, repeats, to these words, the melody that has just been heard as a solo, and is now, as imitation of the dotted, altered figure that is also introduced in the violins, violas, and basses, especially powerfully elevated and supported. Following a conclusion in G minor, one is regaled by the repetition of that little movement in this key, which here appears even more interesting due to a small variation. Immediately thereafter, the first, or main theme is joined with the above-mentioned figure, also known as a "countersubject," as follows,

35. This is a typographical error in the *AmZ* text and should read "dann" instead of "den." [Ed.]

and thus masterfully developed. After a *so-called* "half cadence," in which A major begins as the dominant chord of D minor, there now appears, on p. 17 a very strong and in the end—pp. 25ff.—chromatic fugue endowed with many melismas, and with the following two main themes,

which, apart from the many transpositions in the double counterpoint of the octave, are shifted into double counterpoint at the octave, also on p. 21, as follows,

and similiarly on p. 24, etc. they are transposed to double counterpoint at the twelfth to the words *Kyrie eleison, Christe eleison*!

Since this reviewer is not acquainted with the perhaps very weighty reasons that may have moved the immortal Mozart here to have composed a fugue, indeed *such* a fugue, to *these* words, and since, despite all the effort he has expended on it, he has also been unable to find anything suitably satisfying, it therefore seems to him that the solemn request that is contained in the words may justify or at least excuse the contradiction in the appropriateness of this, by the way, very regular and excellently worked-through fugue. As for the perfectly missing third in the final chord, p. 28, one may pursue it in several older writers, for example Adelung, Fux, Mattheson, and, among the more recent ones, Türk on the most important duties of an organist, pp. 62–69.[36]

No. 2, *Dies irae*, is a strong, forceful chorus in D minor, arousing fright, fury, and dread. As exceptional in *this* regard, the following stand out: 1) the unusual and free treatment of the dissonant 3–4 chord:

P. 30, m. 3. 2) a similar treatment of the sixth chord:

p. 34, m. 4
3) If they are correctly marked, the syncopated notes in the bass, p. 29, mm. 2 and 4; p. 33, m. 4, and p. 34, m. 1.
4) the powerful transition from A major, as dominant chord, to F major, p. 30 at the end, and
5) the even more powerful transition from E major—similarly as dominant chord, to C minor:

p. 34 at the end and p. 35, m. 1.
6) the return to the primary key, p. 35, m. 4, etc.
7) the imitation of the descant in the tenor, p. 31
8) the following passage, repeated several times on pp. 37 and 38:

36. The reference is to Daniel Gottlob Türk, and his *On the Role of the Organist in Worship* (1787), trans. and ed. Margot Ann Greenlimb Woolard (Lanham, MD: Scarecrow Press, 2000). [Ed.]

Most prominently, however,

9) the now following imitation of that passage in all voices, p. 39, mm. 1 and 2:

10) similar imitations, pp. 40 and 41, made more splendid by a powerful accompaniment in the strings—especially the basses—and the profound modulation that emerges from it. This modulation achieves a higher level of power, among other places, through the seventh chord in the final measure, p. 40:

and through the sixth chord, p. 41, also in the final measure:

No. 3, *Tuba mirum spargens sonum*, etc., is an andante in B-flat major consisting of short solo movements through all four voices, which unite shortly before the end. Simple, beautiful, natural melodies and modulations are the striking features of this piece. For this reviewer, it is not pleasing that here the bassoon has been inserted for the solo composed for trombone. Where one has no or only really unsuitable trombonists, one must have recourse to the bassoon or another instrument in any case. But since some places in this solo include the *highest* notes of the bassoon, for example p. 43, mm. 5 and 6; p. 45, mm. 1–5, where the fullness and dignity intended for the trombone can definitely not be achieved or substituted; thus, in locations where one has trumpeters one should spare no effort to present it as perfectly as possible on this instrument.

No. 4, *Rex tremendae majestatis* is an admittedly short but excellently worked chorus in G minor that arouses astonished awe and reverence and is full of dignity and strength. The modulations (which are almost worn out due to the practice of overusing them), p. 54, m. 3, 4; and pp. 55 and 56,

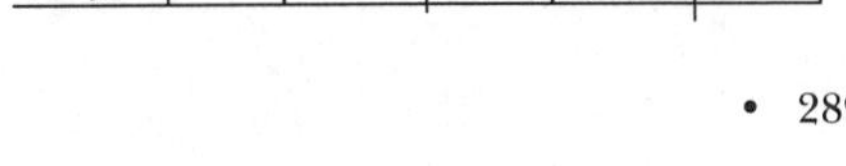

may serve the fledgling composer as examples of how, in the hands of a master, an unusual form, well-informed order, etc., transform the most ordinary, trivial things into the most extraordinary ones. One cannot possibly imagine the *Rex tremendae* expressed more emphatically and powerfully than happens here, especially p. 56, m. 5, by means of the F-minor ninth in the descant. The contrast, p. 57, m. 3, at the words *Salva me!* is masterful; whereby to this reviewer it appears necessary, in order to achieve the greatest possible degree of supplicatory modesty and complete surrender, to alter the tempo to one that is slower. As unexpected as it is new, and heightening the longing quality of the plea—and hence quite practical—comes the minor sixth in the tenor, p. 58, m. 2. Unusual and striking is the conclusion of this chorus in D minor, since Mozart particularly in this regard tends toward an almost anxious assiduousness, which he extends even to the opening and ending of entire operas, half-hour-long finales, great symphonies, and more of this sort. Should one not almost conclude therefrom that he had in mind to further develop this chorus?

Conclusion
W. A. Mozart's *Requiem with German text included*. Complete Score.

No. 5, *Recordare* is a quartet with alternating solo passages for the descant, alto, tenor, and bass in F major (probably *larghetto*, *andante*, or *andantino*; the tempo is not indicated). Full of the loveliest, most pleasant melodies made more beautiful through rich harmonies, frequent alternation in the repetition of similar ideas, and a cautious and correct application of manifold dissonances; through the extremely mellifluous figure, already chosen in the first measure, p. 59, for the cello accompaniment, in the violins, p. 60, and worked through in the canon, which dominates in the accompaniment and is retained through almost the entire piece; through the resulting unity amid greatest possible multiplicity; and through the consistency, natural connection, and mutual interlinking of various parts, the piece attains a degree of perfection that one would likely seek in vain in works of a similar kind, but that can become vividly perceptible only by virtue of the whole. This reviewer cannot forbear to present followers of Vogler's[37] system with the following excerpt from this musical work,

37. Georg Joseph Vogler (1749–1814) was a German composer, organist, teacher, and theorist. The young Mozart, in a letter to his father, refers to Vogler as an arrogant fool whose orchestra does not like him, and adds that his book would be better suited for learning arithmetic than composition. Wolfgang Amadeus Mozart to Leopold Mozart, 13 November 1777, in Wilhelm A. Gauer, Otto Erich Deutsch, and Joseph Heinz Eibl, eds., *Mozart: Briefe und Aufzeichnungen. Gesamtausgabe* (*MBA*), 8 vols. (Kassel: Bärenreiter, 1962–2005), 2:119; Emily Anderson, trans. and ed., *The Letters of Mozart and His Family*, 3rd ed. (London: Macmillan, 1985), 369. [Ed.]

which occurs shortly before the conclusion, twice, namely on pp. 75 and 76, noticeably surprising almost all members of the audience on first and second hearing, yet simultaneously affecting them in a very pleasant way. Since, on account of the less than rapid movement, one can probably not assume that the four sixth chords at "++++" actually consist just of passing notes or, as one says, occur in passing, for, even if one were inclined to admit this, one hears them all, as sixth chords, quite clearly and distinctly. Thus, this reviewer would be very curious to receive, from someone among them [the Vogler acolytes], a few satisfactory instructions and discussions concerning the appearance and possibility of that nearly common, and yet, in the terms of this system thoroughly *impermissible* and hence enigmatic enjoyment—presuming and agreeing that what pleases almost everyone, perhaps even *themselves*, cannot be bad.

No. 6, *Confutatis maledictis*, a chorus arousing shudders, fear, and horror, in A minor, in which the deeper voices, tenors and basses, supported by trombones, bassoons, trumpets, and timpani, rise up as if in struggle against the bass that is undergirded by all the strings until, after the lovely introduction, p. 80, m. 1, one is pacified and comforted by the unornamented, pleading request of the descant and alto voices, with very simple accompaniment by the violins, at the words *voca me*!, etc. But this consolation lasts only a short time; for suddenly one is moved, again, by the cursing and destruction of the damned to repeatedly amplified fear and shock. But one also, repeatedly and with growing longing, hears pleas for mercy and eternal beatitude. The highest degree of profound humility, complete devotion, etc., could probably scarcely be expressed more fortuitously than has occurred here, p. 85, by the completely new modulations, which awaken fresh, stunned astonishment and wonder, without being at all unnatural or disagreeable.[38] Those readers who are

38. The text here uses the terms "*Modulationen*" and "*Ausweichungen*," both of which are generally translated as "modulations," but this is complicated in eighteenth- and nineteenth-century understandings of the term, and could be understood as a tonicization or a less extended time in a different key area. For an extensive discussion of this concept, see Janna K. Saslaw's "The Concept of Ausweichung in Music Theory ca. 1770–1832," *Current Musicology* 75 (Spring 2003): 145–63. [Ed.]

as yet unacquainted with this great work may appreciate finding its great harmonic rarities sketched out. Here they are:

Immediately after this, the Larghetto No. 7, *Lacrymosa dies illa*, joins in 12/8 meter, in D minor, in which, among other beautiful things, especially p. 90, mm. 2–4 and p. 91, m. 1, may be proffered as a model of noble, elevated, and appropriate tone painting. In the final measure on p. 91, we find in the bass:

instead of

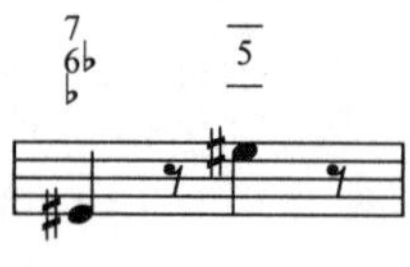

Here, on account of the following six-four chord in A, a secondary chord in A-flat evidently cannot follow; thus, it is actually the diminished seventh chord of G-sharp, with its diminished third and its diminished sixth with a suspended minor fifth. Mozart must have been a poor Voglerian, after all; for if this reviewer is acquainted with a single case in which this seventh chord with diminished third, which Vogler so strongly defended, really sounds surprising, beautiful, and yet natural, this is it. We do not want to hope that this system was familiar to our composer and that he even wrote this way intentionally.[39] On p. 92, m. 4, and p. 93, we again find a very beautiful, painterly modulation to F major, entirely expressing pious sentiment. After a brief introduction in D minor, the plea for eternal rest is repeated powerfully and urgently. With this Amen, the

39. According to the aforementioned letter, as well as others, Mozart does appear to have been familiar with Vogler's work, and just like Mozart, our reviewer is not a devotee of his theories. [Ed.]

chorus closes, via the subdominant chord, into the hard triad of D, and here, if one will, ends the first half of the *Requiem*.

No. 8, *Domine Jesu Christe*, etc. A great, strongly worked chorus in G minor, which, when it comes to complex artistry, can absolutely be set beside the first one, No. 1. The person who places particular value on canonical, contrapuntal movements, imitations, and things of this sort will be completely satisfied by the *quam olim Abrahae*, p. 106, which would assume a place of honor even among the more complex artistic works of a J. Seb. Bach, and in regard to which the same person would, perhaps, dearly regret, along with this reviewer, that the great Mozart lets us only enjoy so briefly the *ne absorbeat eas tartarus*, p. 101, and the *sed signifier sanctus Michael*, p. 104, and that he has not worked it through in a similar manner. But what if, then, this chorus were to have grown to a really fatiguing length?—A reproach that perhaps no composer ever deserved as little as Mozart, especially in his later works.—If, perhaps, this sketch even suggested a very well-calculated frugality on the part of this extraordinary musical economist? If he had been afraid that an overly extensive treatment of those passages would overtax the attention, would fatigue it, and, as a result, would weaken the power of expectation in the established promises? This reviewer, at least, believes that, by means of actual experiments and precise interrogation of the works of this incomparable artist, that he often gives more in his wise frugality than one receives from others through the greatest extravagance. And if not wrong in his thinking this reviewer has found this here, too—who will not gladly join him, and in just admiration of the detail, forget the pleasure he has purportedly been denied?—In addition to the above-mentioned extraordinarily artistic treatment of this chorus, there are also several excellent temporary modulations, among which the following, on p. 99, is exceptional for its noble tone-painting:

No. 9, *Hostias et preces*. Also a chorus, 3/4 meter, larghetto in E-flat major, of a nearly opposite character, filled with utter beauty, grace, and gentle dignity. It is only too bad, and here doubly too bad that the quite manifold, frequent harmonic beauties in this chorus follow each other in such rapid succession, or seem as if they were chasing and driving each other away, so that the listener, in the developing enjoyment of an immediately heard and experienced beauty, is moved to joyful astonishment and admiration, but at the same time—disturbed. Really, there are too many striking beauties in this chorus—too densely packed. This reviewer is far from asserting that his own individual sentiments are the only correct ones, or from offering them as a general rule. But for all that, he cannot suppress the wish that Mozart, in this chorus, without leaving anything out—which he might have preferred—could have made it at least four times as long. For in his enjoyment of the same he is like the glutton at a rapidly served table bedecked with overly numerous exquisite dishes, and who, so as not to let anything pass him by, greedily welcomes and tries everything, and in the end has properly enjoyed none of them. After a rather full conclusion in the principal key of E-flat, p. 119, the chorus begins and completes a lovely modulation in G minor, to the words *fac eas Domine*, whereupon the *quam olim Abrahae* is immediately repeated. This reviewer believes, and, after experiencing several performances, is nearly convinced that during the repetition of this *quam olim*, somewhat faster movement—but of course not exaggeratedly so—would be to good effect and appropriate.

No. 10, *Sanctus*, Chorus, 4/4 meter, D major—very slow—truly holy, full of elevated simplicity, splendor, and dignity. What mortal has proclaimed the peace of immortality and its measureless plenitude more powerfully than occurs here, by the C, rendered more powerful in unison, p. 130, m. 3, *et sequitur*. This chorus closes with a regrettably brief, lively fugue in 3/4 time, to the words *Osanna in excelsis*.

No. 11, *Benedictus*, Quartet, B major, in slow 4/4 time. Indisputably, both in the *Requiem* and overall, on account of the thoroughly light, accessible, and natural melodies and harmonies it contains, one of the simplest, most pleasing, and generally most mellifluous musical pieces. It is impossible, on account of the great unity of the whole, the almost unparalleled similarity and evenness of the individual parts, its beautiful and manifold progressions and concatenations, not to mention its several other advantages, to call out individual beautiful elements as excellent. One would have to include everything. Consequently, this reviewer is content to present his readers who are unfamiliar with it with the first alto solo:

This quartet also closes with the brief fugue of the preceding chorus—somewhat altered by its transposition into B-flat major.

No. 12, *Agnus Dei*. This chorus, in D minor, 3/4 time, also has several uniquely distinguishable beautiful elements. This reviewer is especially pleased by the noble, moving, and longing expression of the following (p. 153) heartfelt plea for eternal rest that is repeated in several keys (pp. 155 and 157):

and the outstanding modulations, p. 158, following the F major as dominant chord of B-flat, which here simultaneously also serve as introduction to the descant solo that follows and to the choruses that follow it, which, with the exception of a few entirely insignificant changes made necessary by the altered text, are copied note for note from the first chorus of p. 10, m. 2. That the fugue from this chorus, which is repeated at the end, is based on the words *cum sanctus tuis in aeternum* has already been indicated in the above-cited letter from Mr. Süssmayer. This reviewer believes that this so admirably worked fugue is more appropriate here and is even better suited to the underlying words than in the first chorus; he is just not pleased that the subject and countersubject have the same words. The author of the well-written and carefully added German text, Herr Minder, doctoral student in Theology in Hamburg, also knew to correct this flaw.

This reviewer, who has refrained from all petty criticism of small and insignificant, although—especially in the accompaniment—very numerous little defects and imperfections, for which, however, Mozart is *most probably* not responsible, earnestly wishes that in a hopefully forthcoming new edition, the work may appear under the supervision of a truly thorough composer, in order to see it entirely cleansed of these impurities. Presuming that it must be attractive to every possessor of this work to have it correct, the *most significant* printing errors follow here.

Finally, this reviewer finds it imperative to note that for the proper performance of this *Requiem* a good, sure, and strong chorus is required; above all, the descant must be excellent and adequately populated, for it might otherwise be overshadowed in the choral movements by the other singers, who have been reinforced by trombones.

AmZ 4: 2 December 1801, cols. 151–55

As indicated by the author of this 2 December 1801 review, a volume of cadenzas to Mozart's piano concertos represents a gesture toward amateurs for whom it might be difficult enough to play the concertos, let alone improvise a cadenza. The volume probably also marks a shift in musical practice whereby composed music becomes more difficult for the amateur to play and the importance of his or her ability to improvise also recedes. Cadenzas were, at least in the later nineteenth century, viewed as an opportunity for the soloist to show off brilliant technical skills. Traditions were subtly different earlier, however, as we can determine from our author cautioning that it is more important to imitate as much as possible significant modulations and themes from the concerto. He adds that one's cadenza should not just timidly imitate the larger work, indicating a difficult balance that needed to be struck. The composer of the reviewed cadenzas, P. C. Hoffmann (1769–1842), a pianist and composer from the Frankfurt area, apparently failed in this respect, and the reviewer shows in musical examples elements perceived to be unnatural and bizarre.

Review

Cadences, se rapportant aus six grands concertos pour le Pianoforte, Op. 82 de Mozart, composées et dediées à Mr. M. Clementi, par P. C. Hoffmann. A Offenbach sur M., chez J. André. (Pr. 2 Fl.)[40]

The idea of creating cadenzas to Mozart's piano concertos is fully deserving of acclaim, given that many people who perform Mozart's concertos, especially dilettantes, may find it difficult to compose such cadenzas themselves. Since, until now, no thought has been given to a work of this kind in these pages, it may be permissible to contribute something on cadenzas in general. That the word cadenza, here, may be taken in a manner that differs from the ordinary one, everyone will expect. Here, what is meant by cadenza[41] is the sort of improvisation the performer produces shortly before the conclusion of a concerto, at the point when all the instruments

40. *Cadenzas, relevant to the six great concertos for the pianoforte, Op. 82, by Mozart, composed and dedicated to Mr. M. Clementi, by P. C. Hoffmann. In Offenbach am Main, by J. André. (Price 2 florins).* Muzio Clementi was a well-known virtuoso and composer of piano music who famously engaged in a piano "duel" with Mozart at the behest of Joseph II. Philipp Karl Hoffmann was a virtuoso pianist from Mainz, who may have written the cadenzas for himself to perform. Johann Anton André was a German publisher who acquired the rights to many Mozart manuscripts from Constanze Mozart. [Ed.]

41. The German word for cadence, Kadenz, is also used to denote a cadenza. [Ed.]

cease playing, with the 6/4 chord above the *quinta modi.* This improvisation must be a series of regularly linked ideas taken from within the piece to which it refers, and must initially be so arranged that the listener, as a result, may in the shortest amount of time gain renewed overview of what has been more fully developed in the work itself. To reach this goal, the performer must: 1) proceed extremely cautiously in the choice of the ideas he wants to bring, once again, before the audience, and not, for example, grasp at insignificant figures of the accompanying instruments, merely as a way to allow his experience and his technique to shine. 2) He must seek, to the greatest possible extent, to imitate the composer in the modulation and other artful gestures, which, however, should occur freely, rather than through anxious copying. Instead, depending on the nature of the circumstances, he can work through the main idea both in the style that is free and in the one that is learned. 3) It is necessary that he play the 6/4 chord only toward the end of the cadence, in order not to have the listener believe too early that he wishes to prepare for the full conclusion; for that is easily fatiguing, and for the attentive listener it is disturbing if, at the point where his ear finally hoped to find the resting point or conclusion, the latter is again even further postponed by the performer. For just this reason, deceptive cadences must not appear too often, for as great as their effect frequently is, they nevertheless forfeit it—no longer deceiving in seeking to deceive too often—and may even elicit displeasure.

That it is not easy to compose such cadenzas (which is why they have been completely rejected by some music teachers, namely by Tosi) is true. But the challenges for the person who creates them, especially for that person who has his work published, remain inherent, and grounded in the matter itself.[42] And this is all the more so since so much that is relevant has been said about precisely this matter in well-known musical treatises (by Sulzer and Türk, among others).

If these premises are now established, then it is also established that these cadenzas of Mr. Hoffmann, while they do demonstrate expertise, nevertheless do not meet expectations. To avoid repetition, we will examine only one of them. It follows that splendid concerto in C major published by Mozart's widow. The beginning consists in a well-chosen passage for the right hand, joined in the fourth measure by the bass, which brings in an idea derived from the concerto. This idea is, however, only briefly touched upon, for in the sixth measure the composer creates a deceptive cadence on E, with a 6/5flat, and then immediately continues

42. This may concern the difficulty inherent in publishing what is generally an improvisatory form. [Ed.]

with another passage borrowed from the concerto, in B-flat major, a key he maintains continuously until the sixteenth measure. At measure 17, the composer creates another deceptive cadence, on D with 6/5flat and then, as dim6/5flat, if that were not enough, continues straightaway in B major. At this opportunity, F-sharp major, G-sharp minor, E major., etc., are also touched upon. At measure 32, the composer moves on from the augmented sixth as follows:

and then, after remaining in D minor for four measures, again briefly touches on a little episode from the concerto. At measure 36, D minor is rapidly followed by E-flat major; and at measures 58 and 59, Mr. H. seems to make a move toward A minor, but then prefers, instead, to move to C major, in which key he then, on the third page, again begins with a little passage from the concerto. After tarrying for two measures in the principal key, he begins to modulate to such a degree that one can follow him only with difficulty. A new key dominates in almost every measure. In the final line on this page, the principal key makes another appearance, and now one might believe there would be an end to the modulating. But the composer starts up again, and regales performer and listeners with passages of the following kind:

Just before the final trill, Mr. H. again picks up a figure from the concerto, which he, instead of ending it as Mozart did, extends like this:

If the composer were determined here to insert some additional measures, he would only need to continue using that figure from the concerto, since it begins high enough to move on up through 2 or 3 octaves; he would, then, certainly have arrived at the trill equally well, and even better; or, if it was necessary to modulate again, why did it not happen in the following way?

Admittedly, this continuation does not look as inventive as the other one, but at least it is cleaner and more correct. A rarity, and also deserving of mention here, is that in the cadenza filling four folio pages there is not a single modulation to the dominant. One is led all over the place, just not down the most natural path.

Mr. André declares—evidently in accordance with his well-known expertise as a publisher, not a musician—that he [Hoffmann] has composed these cadenzas "*entirely in Mozart's spirit.*" But since it may just as well be admitted now that no one played and wrote better in Mozart's spirit than—Mozart—this reviewer, who often heard that master perform concerts of his compositions, must add that these cadenzas by no means look similar to his. Mozart let his improvisations range freely in his cadenzas, but never unnaturally, in ways that were ingenious but never bizarre.

AmZ 5: 13 July 1803, cols. 689–97

Finally, we include a review of a book whose title, Mozarts Geist *(Mozart's Spirit), encapsulates a theme that all the selected articles by Rochlitz share: attempts to assess the effect of Mozart on his world and predicting his effect on the future. The book's author is anonymous, and Rochlitz does not seem aware of his identity. We know now that it was by Ignaz Ferdinand Arnold (1774–1812), an organist and writer who produced a two-volume monograph on famous composers and many novels, some of which were also published anonymously. The reviewer is positive in his overall assessment of* Mozarts Geist. *His main criticism is that others have already written on the issues that Arnold tackles and that he and others avoid subjects such as Mozart's instrumental music, which would benefit from further commentary. Rochlitz further complains that Arnold neglects to distinguish between genius and talent, which is, as we have seen, one of Rochlitz's preferred subjects. Perhaps the most interesting part of this review is when Rochlitz points out Arnold's old-fashioned (for the time) view that ghost stories and murder mysteries on the stage are an affront to beauty and morality. The time when such material was of serious concern and censored, at least in Vienna, was long gone. Rochlitz mounts a defense of such material based on the power of Shakespearean drama and the violently contrasting scenes in* Don Giovanni *arriving at an overarching unity that Arnold fails to realize. It is amusing to note that most of Arnold's novels are either ghost stories or murder mysteries. In the treatment of* The Marriage of Figaro, *both Rochlitz and Arnold avoid discussing the character of the Count and emphasize instead the ridiculousness of his obsequious lackeys. For Don Curzio this extends to an accusation of an abuse of his office. The Count—without doubt the villain of the show—is not even listed in Arnold's descriptions of each character. This deference even to fictional aristocrats was certainly pervasive in the Habsburg lands and is evident here in publications from Leipzig and Erfurt.*

***Mozart's Geist: Seine kurze Biographie und ästhetische Darstellung seiner Werke. Ein Bildungsbuch für junge Tonkünstler. Mit dessen Portrait.* Erfurt, in der Henningschen Buchhandlung, 1803. (Preis 2 Thaler, 16 Groschen)[43]**

One sees already from the title that the book offers more materials for a portrayal of Mozart's spirit than the portrayal itself. But the unnamed author, who signs the preface from Neudietendorf, has not merely compiled various materials, but, with unmistakable knowledge of what was immediately relevant here, has covered what others have said and added some things of his own. His text can also serve as an "educational book for young musicians," thanks in part to its principal contents and in part to many a good observation that the author makes in passing. That the writer spends most of his time on matters about which so many good things have already been written by others, but so quickly passes over those subjects where this is not the case (for example, Mozart's instrumental compositions), might be the most well-founded reproach that one could make about the book as a whole. We will address its components.

Mozart's biography is treated in line with Schlichtegroll's obituary and Wiemtschek's[44] well-known text. To correct several little anecdotes, such as that on p. 21, or the one recounted on p. 86, would render this review overlong. From the author's comment on the famous *Miserere*, p. 28,

43. *Mozart's Spirit: His Brief Biography and Aesthetic Description of his Works. An Educational Book for Young Musicians*. With His Portrait. Erfurt, Henning's Bookstore, 1803. (Price 2 thaler, 16 groschen). The book is now known to have been written by Ignaz Ferdinand Arnold, who also withheld his name from several other of his books. [Ed.]

44. Wiemtschek is the reviewer's misspelling of (Franz Xaver) Niemetschek, who wrote a biography of Mozart published in 1798. In 1793, Friedrich Schlichtegroll published an obituary of Mozart; see the translation and Simon P. Keefe's commentary published elsewhere in this volume. [Ed.]

it would appear that he was not familiar with it. It is a very simple choral piece, and the difficulty of grasping and writing it down in a single hearing, which the young Mozart mastered so admirably, lies in the voice leading and the harmony which are so different from modern practice—especially in their unusual modulations.[45] Emanuel Bach, p. 36 and elsewhere in the book, is confused with Sebastian Bach, otherwise one would not be able to agree with the writer on the matter at hand.[46] The second chapter, "On Artistic Talent and Genius," with special reference to M., contains many good ideas that, while they may not be new, are especially well suited to the purpose announced in the title. In this and several of the following chapters, the author could have been more concise and not repeated himself—something he does frequently—without detriment to the contents. But if he does not distinguish genius from artistic talent, then this is not a concession one should grant him, not only linguistically, but substantively as well. Genius is the gift of one's own invention; talent, the gift of holding fast to and expressing what genius has given. The two, in unity, embrace what Nature is able to bestow upon the artist, which then, must be accompanied by that person's very own individual education. The attack on Reichardt, pp.137ff., is, if not entirely unjust, very harshly expressed. The third chapter contains a description of the way M. composed, in general, where the writer warms to his subject and has even more true and good things to say. As examples one may take pp. 153, 155, and 159. There follows a characterization of melodies in Chapter IV; of accompaniment in Chapter V; of the vocal parts in Chapter VI; of the economical use of instruments in Mozart in Chapter VII. All of these deserve to be taken very much to heart by musicians in training. In Chapter IV, however, the singers might well find things to which to object. Mozart really did sometimes expect of vocalists—and not only in the pieces that he, as the author justly remarks, *was compelled* to write for specific subjects—things that may not be actually impossible, but that cannot be realized without *forceful* efforts. One must be a singer oneself to perceive this in some of his movements, which on paper do not look so bad. How difficult is it not, for example, to sing even the well-known and quite simple aria from the

45. Here, the author (Arnold) is referring to the polyphonic "Miserere mei, Deus" by Gregorio Allegri and the story that Mozart heard the piece and wrote it down from memory. [Ed.]

46. The matter being that had the muses of Vienna not entwined Mozart in their garlands at the proper time, then his music would have been in danger of falling into the style of Emanuel Bach. The author (Arnold), as the reviewer correctly points out, clearly meant J. S. Bach, and not his son, C. P. E. Bach, as the succession or order of styles otherwise would not have been correct. [Ed.]

Zauberflöte: "*Wie stark ist nicht dein Zauberton.*" The fifth chapter contains the well-founded thought, although it seems paradoxical, that in Mozart's best works there is actually no accompaniment. If only all musicians in training would follow the author's advice to sketch these works by taking out the figured bass, and, following it, working through accordingly and comparing the result with what Mozart did!—What the author says about Mozart's instrumental economy is a true statement for that time and demonstrates careful study of Mozart's scores. The nonsense that is made of Mozart's music is admittedly well known, but that it goes as far as is stated on p. 236 is something we would not have believed. The author states, literally, that in Bamberg (thus even in a city that used to have such excellent sacred music) he encountered the entire set of arias from the *Zauberflöte* and a few from *Die Entführung*, with religious text. Papageno's "*Seht, Papageno ist schon da*" had become an Easter hymn.[47] It would be quite incomprehensible how those who are in charge of the public worship of God may so completely ignore the important part played by sacred music, if one did not know how, for most people, everything that goes by the name of religion so utterly fails to come from the heart, and that, as soon as there is mention of anything that causes them any discomfort or would require effort, or even a modest inconvenience, they immediately make their most polite exit. People complain again and again that the churches are empty. Offer something that awakens the better person, something that elevates, excites, and enthralls him, and that he cannot just as well—or usually better—procure at home, and truly we will all come!

The author now comes to the "aesthetic development of the beauties of individual works by Mozart," and sets out to consider the most excellent of these in detail. It is here, however, that the above-made reproach can be most fundamentally justified: that he spends too much time on matters that have already been adequately addressed by others and spends much too little on other things, especially in the last chapters. Phrases such as that language is "too poor" for something, etc., are, after all, only phrases. If, however, one does not have the material that others have contributed here and there close at hand, and also, if a person has this, but wishes to read about some things in greater detail and to be directed to specific examples—for that person these analyses are warmly recommended. Very satisfying is the development of individual scenes from Mozart operas, for example, the first scene and the quartet in the first act, along with the sextet in the second act of *Don Giovanni*, the trio

47. Papageno's words as listed here come from Christian August Vulpius's adaptation of *Die Zauberflöte* and not from the original by Schikaneder and Mozart. [Ed.]

in the second act of *Zauberflöte*, etc. The author is equally fortunate when it comes to analyzing the musical treatment of individual characters, especially Sarastro and Pamina. But hardly anyone who has an understanding of the whole will agree with him when he rejects *Don Giovanni*, as *a whole* (with the exception of individual surpassingly beautiful elements), as a *work of art*. The basis for this judgment is found in the principles expressed on p. 249, p. 253, and particularly on pp. 326ff, according to which the author seems to see beauty and morality as entirely synonymous. In keeping with this, he also says: What is abominable should never be portrayed. Murder and ghost scenes should be banned from the theater, for with both the moral perfection of a work of art is not achieved but instead downright destroyed. Opera composers should reach an agreement among themselves not to set such murder and ghost stories. The soft tones of their lyre will be out of tune, etc. Devote your singing only to beauteous nature, never to her ugly side. Were one to want to satisfy the demands of aesthetics in the stricter sense, then characters like Don Giovanni should be neither sung about nor represented. Thus, the author sees in *Don Giovanni* only the wild surging of contrasting scenes, without their ever being elevated to the unity that floats above them and that is as little damaged by them as in a Shakespearean drama where everything is also chaotic and collapses in the end. What speaks against the author's principles, as described above, belongs to the general doctrine of art and can be disregarded all the more here, given that these very matters have in recent decades been explored so entirely satisfactorily by Kant, Schiller, and others.

Since the author is guided by the above pronouncements, it is not surprising that, in *Così fan tutte*, he also finds not an aesthetic whole, but rather a collection of individual beautiful things. How *could* he, here, keep his eyes fixed so firmly on the poor poet! Precisely here, Mozart created *alone* and had no need of a poet. But here, at least, when it comes to the individually beautiful elements that the writer praises within this in its own way also entirely unique work, he could have been more detailed and specific, because until now not very much has been said about it, and this Mozartian opera is by far less well known than all the others. He did not do it. So much the better has he dealt with *Figaro*. One will perhaps also read some passages of this chapter without reluctance. Here, the author goes through all of the characters: "In Don Curzio," he writes,

> Mozart gave free rein to his satire. Ignorance puffs itself up with the dignity of the office that has been entrusted to it, and with most solemn seriousness, delivers itself of widely

recognized, tasteless absurdities. If one looks at the D-major aria, one can hardly keep from laughing when one sees what gravitas, what musical bombast is presented by the instruments. To take revenge—what ecstasy for the wise man! And, meanwhile, in the accompaniment, things look just as confused as they are inside the head of a proudly stupid bureaucrat. People like this never puff themselves up more than when, supported by their superior position, they find an opportunity to misuse the dignity of their office against those who are weaker, as is the case in the finale of the second act. It is the penultimate movement, as the finale modulates into E-flat major, in which Mozart ridicules the gravity of this know-it-all, "illustrious" court official. The serious key is treated comically, and the melody, advancing unevenly, paints a grotesque picture of ridiculous official dignity, etc. The character of the Countess—how beautifully it is handled! Betrayed hopes, heartache, joyless days, oppressed by the jealousy of a man who misled her in love, and betrayed her! How beautifully Mozart understood how to transform the eruption of these feelings in the noble character into sublime, empathy-evoking, long-suffering endurance! How nobly and with what delicacy this part is treated! As evidence, we may cite the incomparable first aria of the second act, based in E-flat major: *Reich, o reiche mir die Schaale*.[48] Even through the noisy finales, when the maelstrom of confused feelings tears everything along with it, her character remains unchanged, well sustained throughout the entire opera. Even in the tricky situation when she agrees to the adventure that is meant to test the faithfulness of the men, she decides only with difficulty, and one feels how much inner effort this decision costs her. Among all the female characters that Mozart created, this is the most consummate and the noblest.

48. "Give, oh Give me the bowl." The Countess's aria in the second act of *Le nozze di Figaro*, "Porgi amor," does not include this line. In the German version that (the author) Arnold heard, the word could potentially refer to shawls that are used later when the Countess trades clothes with Susanna, or it could even refer to the ribbon from Cherubino, or the lost pin in Act 4. It seems that Arnold is confusing important objects in the opera and misremembering lines from the Countess's Act 2 aria. [Ed.]

And then, to continue, here is what the author says about Hannchen—most charmingly created by Mozart and generally ignored in favor of more brilliant characters:[49]

> Hannchen is the female pendant to Cherubino, and if, as a counterpart, she is presented in a weaker light, her part is nevertheless relatively developed. Her small ariette that the fourth act plays with (in F minor), is in its choice of tonality and tempo completely suited to that anxious deliberation characteristic of young girls during certain years, before they fully awaken to love. And how charmingly Mozart knew to paint her searching on the ground. (She is looking for a pin.) "*L'ho perdutto me meschina!*" The melody creeps forward only imperceptibly, repeats, and picks up the barely heard motive again like a person who is looking for something and gazes again and again at the spot his eyes have only just left, as if he must find it there and nowhere else. Only at the place where her mind turns to the count, what her godfather will have to say about that, does she feel alarm. The notes accelerate, the melody pushes forward—compared to what it had been doing—when it reaches the words *e il Signor!* But she does not find what she is seeking, falls back into her previous desolation, and ends her ariette as sadly, thoughtfully, and slowly as she began.

That Metastasio's *Titus* was abridged by Mozart should not be made the object of reproach, if only because what has been left out *can* so well be left out (and what remains, as is well known, is truly a source of trouble in a work of poetry, especially of the dramatic sort), but, even more so, because the great finale in the first act is a result of that reduction; and how can the author blame the composer, p. 357, if this opera does not have many large ensembles, since Metastasio didn't create any?[50] The discussion of *Die Entführung* is quite good, and is excellent on the subject of Pedrillo, pp. 375ff. That earlier operas that are far less characteristic

49. Hannchen is a German name used for Barbarina. Both names are diminutives for Hanna or Johanna and for Barbara, respectively. [Ed.]

50. Arnold discusses Mozart's abbreviation of Metastasio's text on pp. 357–59 of his book. The reviewer is pointing to a lack of knowledge on Arnold's part, since most of Metastasio's librettos and indeed most opera seria feature few ensemble numbers and give greater prominence to arias. Abridging the text is one thing, but the composer's role rarely involved unilaterally adding new text to the completed work of the librettist. [Ed.]

of Mozart's spirit are barely mentioned is quite correct. But when the author claims that, from Algarotti to Dittersdorf, there is "scarcely anything more to be said that would be new and good" about the essence of opera, then, after careful consideration of all that has been said by the worthy men cited on p. 400, and by so many others, we must confess that we would like to turn this sentence around: After the individual, very worthy remarks of those gentlemen, it is all the more urgent to say something new, all-encompassing, and profound that would explore the subject, since it is clear as day that most of these arguably interesting comments cast doubt on or even contradict each other, while what appears to be a consequential discussion of the whole contradicts our feelings and everyday experience. Moreover, what the writer has to say on this subject is more the suggestion of what should be provided than the thing itself, although we find individual remarks of his very apposite.

On the list of Mozart's sacred works, the cantata *Davide penitente* has been forgotten. It at least deserved to be included as a deeply learned study by the composer; and if it is not included in Mozart's catalog, which the author follows, neither is the Mass in C Major. On p. 445, the author notes that Mozart has not composed anything for wind ensemble. He must not have been familiar with the beautiful quintet that Mozart composed for Ms. Kirchgessner,[51] which was separately engraved and has now also been included in the Breitkopf-Härtel collection of piano compositions. (It is definitely not the piece that the author rightly claimed for the *Glockenspiel*.)[52] In the concluding chapters, that the author has dedicated so few lines to Mozart's symphonies and quartets—still unsurpassed by *any* composer—has already been mentioned and criticized.

In this review, we have followed the author, with attention and not without enjoyment, step by step through his entire book, not only because he has understood how to hold us fast, but also because we wanted to bring the publication to the attention of thoughtful and developing musicians. A number of incorrect expressions and turns of phrase that escaped the author, especially when he presumes to approach the higher regions of aesthetic theory (such as p. 212, or where he is led astray concerning "the

51. Marianne Kirchgessner (1769–1808) was a blind virtuoso pianist and glass harmonica player who performed concerts in most of the major European capitals. The piece is Mozart's Quintet for Glass Harmonica, K. 617. [Ed.]

52. Here the reviewer may be mocking Arnold's ignorance of the glass harmonica piece by referring to a glockenspiel piece, most likely Papageno's melody for that instrument in *Die Zauberflöte*. In general, the reviewer appears to expect more scholarly acuity than Arnold provides. [Ed.]

century's most elevated tendencies," p. 249, center), will gladly be pardoned in a musician. One attends to what he wants to say, and has often, too, said very well.

The attached portrait of Mozart seems to have been taken from the first volume of Mozart's works for the piano and has not only been enlarged but also coarsened. The original vignette was already far from being entirely accurate. But some similarity has nevertheless been retained in the image offered here, for the outlines of Mozart's face were so exceptional that, like the outlines of the heads of Frederick II of Prussia, or Socrates, they are almost impossible to misrepresent.

CODA

Understanding Mozart: The Claims of History and Philosophy

LEON BOTSTEIN

There is little risk in hazarding the guess that Mozart's name has been dropped more often than that of almost any other composer in the Western tradition of classical music. The volume of opinion and scholarship on Mozart has been astonishing and continuous since the mid-nineteenth century, starting with Otto Jahn's multi-volume biography from the 1850s. Equally astounding is the variety of myths and legends and occasional works of poetry, fiction, and drama, such as Alexander Pushkin's *Mozart and Salieri* (1830), Franz Grillparzer's poem "For a Mozart Celebration" (1842), and Eduard Mörike's prose novella *Mozart on the Journey to Prague* (1855).

Consequently, any attempt to identify the "real" or "authentic" historical Mozart, either in performance or the writing of history and biography increasingly threatens to be redundant or marginal: there are too many layers of claims and interpretations to penetrate, or easily forget. There likely will be few new major biographical revelations, no unknown masterpieces discovered, or transformative analyses beyond those already published, even about the putative Age of Enlightenment during which Mozart lived, or about Mozart's place in the subsequent periods of Romanticism and Reaction—the "Biedermeier" world—before 1848.[1] Informed commentary will still be put forward that may or may not advance our understanding. Its persistence helps sustain interest in Mozart's music.[2]

There is, however, one constant. Despite the inevitable ebbs and flows in his posthumous reputation, Mozart has remained a touchstone in the culture of the West unlike any other composer. Even in Vienna, although his operas were only intermittently staged between the 1820s and 1897, the year Gustav Mahler became the Imperial Court Opera's director, the name Mozart remained synonymous with the historical preeminence of Vienna and Habsburg Austria in the history of music.[3] The "austere" beauty of J. S. Bach's music required learning and made him a figure of veneration, but not a comparable object of widespread fascination, affection, and controversy as Mozart, in whose "sunlit" melodies everyone could bask.[4] And Beethoven—for all the sharp disputes about the man and his music, or the elaborate philosophic and literary commentary by Thomas Mann, Romain Rolland, and Theodor W. Adorno, among others—remains a more defining and coherent figure congruent with the cultural history of his times than Mozart. Mozart, as composer, personality, and symbol, has always been more chameleon-like, marked by recalcitrant inconsistencies and contradictions. He has been imagined in retrospect as a changeling for two and a half centuries, a figure whose music, image, and name nonetheless have remained popular within an astonishingly wide audience, from connoisseur and skilled amateur, to children taking music lessons, to the random person on the street. Mozart has entered our language as the synonym for exceptional musical talent and genius, much like Xerox has for photocopies.

Once it is conceded that the historical Mozart is elusive, the uses to which Mozart—or at least aspects of his work—has been put remain fascinating. Through reinvention and fantasy, he has been a mirror held up to distinct eras in history. Through Mozart, subsequent generations have expressed their anxieties and aspirations.[5]

Consider, for example, Germany both before and after its defeat in World War I. In 1913, the first edition of Arthur Schurig's two-volume Mozart biography was published by Insel Verlag. Schurig was an ardent Wagnerian. He began his biography by quoting Wagner's 1840 praise of Mozart. Wagner lauded Mozart's unrivalled success in making the specific "genius" of Germany universal, in part by appropriating and generalizing foreign influences and rendering them accessible. However, in the preface to the revised second edition, published in 1923, this brash cultural chauvinism was muted. The fortunes of the postwar Weimar Republic were at a low point. Hyperinflation, the French and Belgian occupation of the Ruhr area, the political assassinations of Matthias Erzberger and Walther Rathenau, civil unrest and uprisings such as the ill-fated Nazi "Beer Hall" putsch dominated the early 1920s.

Like Otto Jahn, Schurig was not primarily a music historian. He was a philologist and polymath who translated Flaubert and even wrote a book about the conquistador Francisco Pizzaro. But Schurig was inspired by the meticulous pre-World War I scholarship on Mozart by the French scholar Georges de Saint-Foix, an ardent Wagnerian. Saint-Foix was a perfect foil for Schurig, who was contemptuous of Jahn, himself a staunch anti-Wagnerian. Jahn glorified Mozart and his music as transcendent and immune to historical contingency. Schurig's primary purpose was to debunk Jahn and "tell the life of Mozart, without beautifying it, as it really was, free from all legends."[6] Despite his rhetorical but explicit evocation of Leopold von Ranke, who had pioneered the ideal of objectivity in the writing of history and the centrality of documentary evidence, Schurig harbored his own preconception about Mozart's character, one rooted in Schurig's allegiance to historicism and the uniqueness of discrete eras in the past, particularly when the present world seemed, by comparison, in moral and aesthetic decline. Schurig's views were uncannily in line with the opinions of Richard Strauss.[7]

For Schurig and Strauss, Mozart could most persuasively and properly be compared to the French painter Antoine Watteau (Strauss cherished the work of eighteenth-century French painters). Schurig saw Mozart and Watteau as singular in their respective fields. Their art was an evocation of a bygone age, the ancien régime, an age of moderation during which human "desires" caused by "suffering" were transfigured into beauty by art. In Mozart's historical period, the aesthetic realm had not been disfigured by "great pain" but revealed in a "noble and sensual beauty": the graceful transformation of the everyday that aligned with moral virtue and the civilized mores of a vanished past.[8]

This view of Mozart and his music did not align, however, with the opinion of the preeminent music critic of the Weimar era, Paul Bekker, a prolific writer now best remembered for a path-breaking book on the symphony and monographs on Beethoven and on Mahler's symphonies. In 1926 Bekker published a volume of essays for the general reader based on radio lectures: *Musikgeschichte als Geschichte der musikalischen Formwandlungen* (Music History as the History of the Transformation of Musical Form). He took a markedly different approach to Mozart reflective of a sense of stability and increasing prosperity in Germany. The radical right appeared to be in retreat, inflation was under control, and the country's international standing was on the rise.[9]

Bekker opened his Mozart chapter with the following argument:

> In the overall assessment of music in the eighteenth century, we have observed that it was predominantly *German* music. Within this music, its center—the location of intense concentration—shifted. It moved from north to south. Bach and Handel were Saxons, Gluck a Franconian, Haydn an Austrian, Mozart a Salzburgian of South-German origin, Beethoven a Rhinelander. Beginning with Gluck, they all moved to Vienna.
>
> Vienna became the world capital of music. But the music that emanated from there is *world music*. As the idea of the freedom of the individual and natural rights gradually

> became the focus of thought and action, it could only develop within itself toward an ideal image of humanity. Once the *person* starts to feel human and acknowledges that fact, the only possible goal becomes the community of *all* humanity. The God-fearing person searches for a community of faith, the patriot for the national community, and the individual for humanity. Persons of this kind, the *seekers of humanity*, were at that time all Germans of greatness, not only the musicians but also the poets and philosophers. Even though they were individuals highly conscious of their singularity, and focused on the cultivation of their own particularity, the higher justification of their subjectivity rested in striving—in the terms of the era—to serve humanity. We may approve of this idea or reject it. We may think the ideas they articulated utopian or the only right way to live. But we must recognize that we can only understand the *creations* of this generation by accepting this premise. Only through the shaping of two contrasts—personality and humanity, both striving toward the other—did they achieve the monumental scope of an idealism that made room for the development of the most personal and, at the same time, the most universal art. This art fused the profane with the sacred, and absorbed differences of religion, of race, of nationality within it. At its center stands the free artist as the priest of humanity, as the herald of wisdom and beauty, as the messenger of eternal peace.[10]

Bekker, like Schurig, had no use for legends and beautification. Unlike Schurig, however, he did not use biography as a means of understanding music, nor did he regard Mozart as emblematic of a distinct period of history. Rather, something about Mozart was directly pertinent to the present historical moment, in politics and in contemporary art. Immediately following his opening statement—more of a sermon than an explanatory argument—Bekker expressed his conviction that to define Mozart narrowly as a representative figure of the historical past was in fact to underestimate the true significance of his music and the function of the aesthetic in history. Mozart transcended the Rococo. What rendered Mozart important to nineteenth-century Romanticism and twentieth-century Modernism was a pervasive and consistent humanism that undermined the corrosive modern ideologies of nationalism, particularly in Germany. Bekker reversed Wagner's chauvinism by challenging modern nationalism's legitimacy and historicism's priority over normative human ideals contained within Mozart's command of the writing of music. Becker wrote:

> Mozart once was considered an artist of the Rococo, but what was understood then as Rococo was simply a delicate, gracefully decorative style. He was celebrated as an artist of beauty and grace, of restrained balance and smooth classicism, and his music as light and serene, beyond all that is crude. Anything problematic, any struggle, or the Faustian had no place in this music; it was woven out of sunlight, fragrant scents, a delightful smile.[11]

Bekker wanted to debunk this historicist trivialization of Mozart by following the long line of writers, like Jahn, who sought to communicate a profound, transhistorical Mozart. This line of argument had been advanced by comparing Mozart not to a contemporary eighteenth-century painter but to a painter whose greatness and value had been widely accepted as normative. Bekker accepted what by the early twentieth century had become a well-worn cliché: the comparison between Mozart and the Renaissance artist Raphael.[12]

Bekker's ambition was to illuminate Mozart's unique understanding of the full range of human nature, including Faustian ambition, darkness, the raw, the rough, and the cruel. Mozart's music revealed music's unique function and power: to communicate a sympathetic, empathetic, forgiving but honest account of the fallible human character. In defiance of the conceits of history as a science, Mozart's music transcended history by remaining comprehensible as truthful (including the experience of suffering and pain), normative, and universal.[13] As Karl Barth, one of the leading mid-twentieth-century Protestant theologians, observed in 1959: "Mozart makes music, knowing everything from a mysterious center, and thus he knows and keeps the boundaries on the right, and on the left, upward and downward."[14]

In light of Bekker's fate as a German Jew—and the fate of Europe less than a decade after 1926—the recognition at the core of his opening statement is heartbreaking. It was a desperate expression of hope about the politics of the moment and revealed the fragility of the brief respite from the chaos of the early 1920s. Mozart's music exemplified moral goodness. Its validity was universal and defied the differences that led humans to violence. Music reinforced what Karl Marx in 1844 had termed the consciousness in each person of their status as a "species-being," thereby transcending the fatal and ultimately false divisions of religion, national identity, politics, and race, without sacrifice to a sense of individuality or the subordination of the individual to mass conformity. Music, so Bekker hoped, particularly Mozart's, represented an art form that, after the devastation of World War I, was humanity's most promising shared means of peaceful spiritual renewal.

It was essential, then, to illuminate Mozart as not being merely a brilliant representative of a distinct historical period or group. Bekker's intent—to show how Mozart defied the taste and stylistic limitations of his era and reconfigured them in service of a universal normative discourse. Mozart's achievement was rooted in the extensive philosophical discussions around the centrality of the aesthetic during his lifetime.[15] That philosophical tradition clarifies Mozart's ambition and achievement, as well as his success in commanding and captivating a wide public in a manner singular in music history. That belief took hold initially with the nineteenth-century comparison between Mozart and Raphael.

Mozart and Raphael

The first prominent articulation of a parallel between Mozart and Raphael was Friedrich Rochlitz's 1800 essay in the *Allgemeine musikalische Zeitung* (*AmZ*, contained in this volume). Rochlitz seized on striking biographical similarities as his opening premise. Both had fathers who were their teachers and mentors. The young Raphael's role in sustaining his family after his father's death provided an analogue to Mozart's financial contribution to his family as a child prodigy. More to the point, both were prolific in disparate genres and both died young, leaving one monumental work—considered by many their greatest—unfinished, only to be completed by disciples. In Mozart's case, it was the Requiem, first completed by Franz Xaver Süssmayr,[16] and in Raphael's case, *The Transfiguration* (Figure 1). Most of *The Transfiguration* turned out to have been finished by Raphael himself, but until the twentieth century, expert opinion credited Giulio Romano, among others, with the task.

Rochlitz identified their shared personality traits, including generosity to colleagues, speed and intensity of work habits, and the ambition to introduce a new aesthetic into the practice of religion. Above all, both Mozart and Raphael embodied artistic perfection, creating beauty through a total command of form and a disarming inventiveness and directness. They both evoked the gentle and noble and communicated a delicate "sweet simplicity," all without superficiality or the denial of the tragic. Both exhibited a harmonious Apollonian genius capable of creating a universal ideal of the aesthetic that elevated even the darkest aspects of human emotion and experience.

Rochlitz's comparison struck a chord. "No parallel seems to me more justified than the one between Mozart and Raphael," Otto Jahn concluded

Figure 1. Raphael, *The Transfiguration*, 1519–20.

at the end of his Mozart biography. Both artists shared and realized "noble beauty." Their art resolved in "pure harmony." Goethe was also a proponent of the comparison. He thought their achievement, aesthetically and ethically, could never again be matched.[17] Goethe's closest musician friend, Karl Friedrich Zelter, underscored the symmetry between Mozart's musical originality and genius, and his kindness and capacity for virtue and love—the virtues they attributed to Raphael.[18]

One reason this comparison maintained such resilience was how widespread familiarity with both artists had become, particularly after 1815. In Mozart's case, this came through music that amateurs with moderate skills could enjoy playing; the wide popularity of tunes from his operas; the regular presence of the last three symphonies in the concert repertoire; and the outsized fascination and familiarity with the Requiem. The technological progress in producing inexpensive black-and-white reproductions, particularly of religious scenes, favored the clarity in line and elegance of form in Raphael's work.

Particularly significant was the perception of a direct spiritual and religious power in Raphael's various depictions of biblical scenes that hung, throughout the nineteenth century, on the walls of the educated bourgeoisie, including reproductions of *The Transfiguration*. Raphael's Madonnas seemed human, accessible, and free of excessive piety and neoclassical idealizations.[19] Raphael and Mozart captivated novices, connoisseurs, and aristocratic patrons alike, and reassured members of a growing middle class interested in acquiring cultural literacy, *Bildung*.[20]

Rochlitz and Bekker stressed the "universal" in Mozart and Raphael. Their work responded to a quest for spiritual uplift, individual freedom, and a self-awareness of dignity that could be satisfied by learning and the aesthetic realm, but not in political life.[21] This idealization functioned as a clear but tacit critique of contemporary culture and mores. Music and painting allowed viewers and listeners a personal connection with a religious experience at once modern and yet consistent with the inherited rituals of Christianity, particularly Catholicism.[22]

In the Requiem, Mozart gave piety and belief intense expression through music. The work's psychologically accessible subjectivity offered a justification for claims of individuality, liberation, and autonomy, just as Raphael gave Christ a recognizable human character transfigured into luminous and graceful beauty in works suffused by the palpable dynamism in the depiction of the human figures surrounding Jesus.[23]

An unexpected confirmation of the resilience of the parallel between Mozart and Raphael can be found in Alexander Pushkin's "little tragedy" *Mozart and Salieri,* one of four verse plays written in 1830, two of which deal directly with Mozart and would famously be set to music—*Mozart and Salieri* (1897) by Nikolai Rimsky-Korsakov and *The Stone Guest* (1879) by Alexander Dargomyzhsky. In the first scene of *Mozart and Salieri*, a poor old and blind fiddler is playing a tune from *Figaro* ("Voi che sapete") to the horror of Salieri and the delight of Mozart. In the face of Mozart's laughter, Pushkin has Salieri exclaim, "I don't find it funny when some worthless dauber makes smear and drips on Raphael's Madonna!" explicitly identifying Mozart's music with the greatness of Raphael (and, subsequently, Dante).[24]

Salieri, whom Pushkin's Mozart admires—just as Pushkin's Salieri reveres Mozart—nevertheless succumbs to envy and poisons Mozart in the name of both earthly and heavenly justice. Salieri's defense is his love of music and his tireless devotion to the craft and its practitioners. The pursuit of beauty as a central dimension of culture cannot tolerate the disturbance created by the unique and daunting magnetism of a Mozart. A figure such as Mozart undercuts those who like Salieri lovingly work to sustain the art form of music for an appreciative and cultivated public. Salieri is appalled that Mozart's music survives the crudeness and distortion of its rendition by the blind violinist.[25] Not surprisingly, the Requiem plays a decisive role in Pushkin's play, an indication of the influence of Rochlitz's emphasis on this score as emblematic of Mozart's—and Raphael's—significance in spearheading a compelling path to spirituality and religion through music and painting.

Through the Raphael comparison, Mozart emerged as the key protagonist of a unique modern aesthetic achievement, the music of the mid- and late eighteenth century. Its essence was both the expression, if not creation, of a modern sensibility, and also the reinvention and renaissance of a moral equivalent in music of the secular, pre-Christian classical past that had become, in aesthetic terms, normative and exemplary. The Greek and Roman classical heritage dominated the eighteenth century in the plastic arts, poetry, and drama; this led in turn to a veneration of the Renaissance that was credited with the rediscovery of antiquity.

In music, Gluck, Haydn, and Mozart were elevated to solve a hidden paradox. They functioned as faux-surrogates for an actual historical and ancient Classical heritage in music. They became models for how Classicism in music could be emulated by imitating contemporaries, a circumstance unique to music. Mozart became the center of a mythic Classical norm and first among equals, reflective of music's contemporary status as modernity's answer to antiquity's superiority. In the absence of authentic ancient Greek music, Mozart's music became both the "Classical" foundation as well as a harbinger of musical Romanticism, and therefore both universal and marked by a distinctive individual German character, as E. T. A. Hoffmann would claim twenty years after Mozart's death.[26]

The Renaissance, Classicism, and Modernity

Raphael's relevance to the way Mozart was understood throughout the nineteenth century was sustained by the turn to Italian Renaissance art by German painters and sculptors in two successive movements. The "Nazarenes" decamped to Rome in 1810, returning home after the revolutions of 1830. In that group were Johann Friedrich Overbeck, Friedrich Wilhelm Schadow, Peter von Cornelius, and Philipp Veit. For the Nazarenes, Raphael was no mere exemplar of formal virtuosity whose emulation was justified. He was an ideal as a man and artist whose character and sense of vocation demanded admiration. After the revolutions of 1848, the Nazarenes were followed by "German-Roman" painters, who included Brahms's close friend Anselm Feuerbach and Arnold Böcklin, the most celebrated artist in German-speaking Europe at the time of his death in 1901. The common thread between these two movements was the hovering presence of Raphael.

The German-Romans were in search of a neoclassical ideal relevant to contemporary life and found it in the Renaissance. For musical Romanticism—not just among Germans such as Hiller, Mendelssohn, Schumann, and Brahms, but also for Chopin and Berlioz—Mozart defined what it meant to be an artist, the power of the aesthetic, and the incontestable norms of beauty and perfection. The irony, once again, was that Mozart became simultaneously authentically Classical and its modern reinvention. That explains Mozart's importance to the composers who were contemporaries of the German-Romans: Brahms, Bruch, and Reger.

The most compelling case for the linkage between Mozart and Raphael, and the foregrounding of the Renaissance as the decisive period of history for the politics and culture of the nineteenth century came through in the life and work of Jacob Burckhardt. His two most widely read works were *Culture of the Renaissance in Italy* (1860, rev. 1869) and *Der Cicerone* (1855), a popular and unsurpassed guidebook to Italian architecture, sculpture, and painting. Burckhardt, a Swiss, was also an accomplished amateur musician and active as a singer in choral societies. Mozart's music represented the ideal realization of music's aesthetic potential. As one of Burckhardt's biographers put it, "Just as Raphael was the high point of painting, Mozart was the pinnacle of music . . . Mozart was his musical Raphael."[27] How does this juxtaposition inform the historical prism through which we hear and make sense of Mozart? The answer lies in Burckhardt's concluding sentences in his Raphael section in *Der Cicerone:*

> The eye takes in the divine beauty of most of the compositions as if they were self-evidently so just by themselves. That is what brings Raphael so much closer to us than all other painters. There is no screen between him and the expectations of all past and future centuries. He requires the fewest concessions or assistance from premises and assumptions. He fulfills his mission, whose spiritual axioms—without his complicity—lie very far away from us, in a manner that makes them seem close to us. The soul of modern humanity, in the arena of the beauty of form, has no greater master and protector. . . . The highest personal quality of Raphael was . . . not an aesthetic virtue, but ethical: namely the great integrity, and the strong will, that at every moment propelled him toward the beauty that struck him at that moment as the highest beauty he could see.[28]

We are so accustomed to considering music history as an auto-poetic process, as a self-contained dialogue between past and future confined exclusively among musicians, that we overlook clues from outside of music to help us understand how and why some works and some composers from the past resist obscurity and oblivion. Burckhardt's Raphael mirrors the way Mozart has been understood since 1800. His music seems exemplary—as Pushkin makes Salieri realize—consistently human and contemporary, despite the fact that his aesthetic style and spiritual ambitions betray their specific historical context. Not only did his music retain its reputation as normative in formal terms, but it remained captivatingly beautiful and appealing, without being predictable, despite sustained exposure.

As the author of a popular turn-of-the-century biographical account of the lives of the crucial "trinity" of Classical composers put it, in Mozart's music "lives, forever, a spirit of the immortal freshness of youth, of inner truth that elevates the name of Wolfgang Amadeus Mozart above all change. Into the most distant times his genius will astonish and ennoble our hearts."[29] Mozart was more than a towering figure in music history, just as Raphael was for Burckhardt more than a great painter. The formal virtues of his canvases mirrored ethical virtues. Both embodied how the aesthetic dimension can be the cause and expression of a universal ideal of the ethical, bypassing both the political and the linguistic. In 1815 Zelter described to Goethe how Mozart's Requiem had inspired a discussion about the parallels between color and pitch and the capacity for synesthesia as a criterion of the possibility and validity of aesthetic norms. Mozart realized in music a "true" objective beauty immune from historicist criticism.[30]

This fusion of Mozart's ethical character with the universal validity of his realization of form and beauty in art merged readily with the early fascination and popularity of the Requiem. It lent Mozart an aura of piety, construed within the structure of the German Catholic Enlightenment (and its reaction after the death of Joseph II) as practiced and encouraged in the Habsburg Empire, especially within its German-speaking provinces. Mozart's reputation as pious but not sanctimonious, neither an aristocrat nor a member of the increasingly wealthy "second society," as a man of the people, made him better loved and more recognized across social and economic classes than any other composer, Bach and Beethoven included.

Leopold Schmidt's popular 1856 etching, *The Apotheosis of Mozart* (Figure 2), based on a canvas by Johann Nepomuk Geiger, a court painter of portraits and historical scenes, makes this point. It was produced to celebrate the composer's one hundredth birthday. Widely distributed, it appeared in newspapers and as the cover illustration of sheet music. It luxuriates in an extravagant historicism and resembles a Baroque altarpiece composition with neo-Renaissance elements.[31] A figure, presumably Mozart, is at the center, playing the organ looking upward toward heaven. At the top is a glowing cross. At the margins are venerable musical figures, weeping angels, and, at the bottom, cherubs. The composer has become analogous to a priest, the purveyor of the expression and transmission of faith and saintliness through music—Franz Liszt as he imagined himself fondly (and absurdly).[32]

Eduard Mörike's novella *Mozart on the Journey to Prague* appeared in 1855, in anticipation of the centenary of Mozart's birth.[33] Its account is poetic, sophisticated, and resolutely secular. It portrays a gentle, divinely inspired but human individual without pretense and affectation, free of snobbery or social aspiration. Profundity and acute understanding of human nature and moral clarity are contained in a figure whose ease and humility make him the object of universal admiration, despite the recognition of the power, human insight, beauty, and brilliance in the music and argument of *Don Giovanni*—whose subject is desire, privilege, betrayal, cruelty, and the punishment of moral impunity and depravity. It is to this opera's triumphant premiere in Prague that the composer and his wife, a happy couple, have set out.

The synthesis of genius, innocence, and the quotidian, despite Mörike's weaving of symbolic meaning into the narrative, is rendered without a hint of the trappings of sainthood at the core of *The Apotheosis*. Among the many lasting virtues of Mörike's novella was one that appealed to Ludwig Wittgenstein: the use of words with economy, poetry, and grace to evoke the making of music, its effects, and its mechanisms and experience.[34] The

Figure 2. Leopold Schmidt, *The Apotheosis of Mozart*, 1856.

contrast between these two competing mythic idealizations would persist. They plagued the debate over the design of a Mozart monument in Vienna that started in 1888 and resulted in Viktor Tilgner's 1896 monument, a statue that was moved to the Burggarten after World War II.[35]

Mozart's early death (although hardly exceptional in his era) helped advance such posthumous mythmaking. His death, and his writing a Mass for the Dead (a parallel to Raphael's dying before completing his depiction of Christ's Transfiguration), had become enshrined as a tragic coda to his life since the 1790s, as if his premature exit from life was an ethical challenge. The Requiem required future generations to complete it, not merely with music that imitated Mozart's style but by each listener through spiritual and ethical emulation. This imperative elevated the significance of musical culture as an arena distinct from organized religion and politics, both realms with limited freedoms.

For composers in subsequent generations, Mozart emerged, as Burckhardt hoped Raphael would, as a guide (if not a conscience) regarding the essential interplay of aesthetic and ethical norms in modernity. As a model of how the aesthetic and ethical must cohere, Mozart hovers over the music of Brahms, Tchaikovsky, Ravel, Stravinsky, Schoenberg, Berg, Philip Glass, Francis Poulenc, and György Kurtág—even Wagner.[36]

As with Raphael, the aesthetic-ethical construct of Mozart was favored by those who held a skeptical view of the historical markers of modernity: mass democracy, modern nationalism, competitive industrial capitalism, imperialism, and above all, materialism.[37] For them, the virtues of moderation, balance, restraint, humility, human kindness, simplicity, the love of inquiry, honor, and the search for truth and beauty were mirrored by Raphael, Mozart, and European culture until the French Revolution of 1789. These were increasingly at risk.[38]

Not surprisingly, Burckhardt was, like Brahms and his friends such as the music-loving surgeon Theodor Billroth, similarly pessimistic about the future and consequently skeptical of Wagnerian aesthetics and influence. A Mozart-Beethoven contrast also thrived in the years around the Mozart centenary, and points to the distinctive character of the philosophical discourse that surrounded Mozart's career.

Mozart's Philosophical Heritage

The Raphael-Mozart comparison that began in earnest in 1800 derived plausibility from patterns of belief inherited from late seventeenth- and eighteenth-century discourses on the interrelationships between epistemology, ethics, and aesthetics. Mozart biographers, with few exceptions—the most persuasive being Georg Knepler—echo Schurig's view that "philosophical studies lay distant from the Master. For that he had neither the inclination nor the proper context nor the required universal and scientific education [*Bildung*]. He approached sophisticated problems as an untroubled man of nature. He was no methodical scribbler."[39]

Those who demur from this Romantic image of Mozart as carefree and unconcerned with critical reflection or philosophical and theological questions point to his correspondence, the operas and sacred works, friendships, participation in the Masonic movement, and the formal characteristics of his music. Taking sides in this complex web of biographical scholarship is not necessary. Mozart lived in a momentous period of political change that included the American and French Revolutions, the critique of Enlightenment conceits, the revival of spirituality and mysticism, and the onset of reaction against the assumption that equality, freedom, and fraternity represented the rational goal of history. His operas alone defy the image of a naïve lack of critical engagement with rationalist philosophy and politics.

There is reason, therefore, to appropriate a detail, no matter how insignificant, from Mozart's life to construct the terms of debate that surrounded him as he sought to make a career across Europe, then in Salzburg, and finally in Vienna. The personal library Mozart left at his death contained a volume by Moses Mendelssohn (Felix's grandfather), *Phaedon, or On the Immortality of the Soul*, a three-part work first published in 1767. How this book came into Mozart's possession is not known, nor if he, or his father, an enthusiastic reader and autodidact, ever read it. Yet it is reasonable to speculate why they might have been in sympathy with its claims.[40]

Mendelssohn opens with a reference to "proofs" drawn from a musical concept: the "harmony of moral truths." The work, a meditation on Plato's *Phaedo* and the death of Socrates, imitates Plato's dialogue form. For Mendelssohn, harmony is linked to "order and beauty," whose "pleasure . . . arises from the united impression of their constituent parts." A work of art involves both reason and feeling.[41] The immortal soul requires "the sensual feeling of various things, but also generates ideas of beauty, order, symmetry, and perfection." The aesthetic inspires "feelings with which the thinking being is impressed," aligning sentiment and emotion with reason. Beauty and the sublime "lift" humans beyond their "transitory" physical state, while "order, concord and symmetry serve not only for his rational amusement, but dispose the powers of his mind to that proper harmony which is conducive to their perfection" in the soul. These aesthetic virtues produce "affability, exchange of sentiment, and the maturity of all the moral virtues which kindle the heart to friendship, the soul to intrepidity and fire the mind with the love of truth." Mendelssohn concludes: "The faculty of feeling" belongs not to the body but to an "unperishable" essence tending toward "perfection" and "endless progress" that finds its expression in the aesthetic. His agenda for the aesthetic links the experience of art, in all its forms, to the engagement of feeling, sentiment, and sensual pleasure that align, as beautiful, with human reason with respect to knowledge, moral virtue, and the truth of the divine and nature itself.

In his 1761 *Philosophical Writings*, music is the art whose beauties are felt through "inarticulate sounds." In music sounds appear in a "sensuous" arrangement: the individual sounds combine in harmony with the whole, define the relation of the parts to the whole and the parts to one another, using forms of imitation. All inclinations and passions of the human soul make themselves known by means of sound. Music is able, therefore, to represent the multiple parts of beauty, either successively or alongside one another. The linear or "successive" aspect of music is called "melody," and alignment in music is "harmony."[42] The key distinction of music for Mendelssohn is that music, based on "inarticulate sounds," is not a language and consequently not imitative of nature. It cannot "indicate the concept of a rose, a poplar tree and so on, just as it is impossible for painting to represent a musical chord to us." Instead, music opens an imaginative, rational path to meaning, grounded in the senses through which humans "beautify" sound, just as they transform movement into dance and music into perceptible harmonic patterns.[43]

Mendelssohn's three key insights—1) expression, feeling, and sentiment are essential to the aesthetic experience; 2) these can be reconciled with reason; and 3) music is by definition not "articulate" and therefore untranslatable into word or image but capable of communicating and realizing beauty in a dynamic manner still compatible with reason—fit well into his notion of the soul and its immortality as metaphysical realities. His arguments were responsive to and influential in the intense debate within the German-speaking world between 1750 and 1800, the period in which Mozart lived and died, about the nature of art, its connection to reason, and the meaning of beauty and the sublime.

At stake in these debates was the contrast between the Greco-Roman past and modernity, and the limits of knowledge, particularly empirical and positivist methods that lent support to realism as a superior aesthetic strategy. Mendelssohn's forays into these debates followed the influential essay by Johann Joachim Winckelmann, *Thoughts on the Imitation of the Works of the Greeks in Painting and Sculpture* (1755), and Gotthold Ephraim Lessing's even more famous 1766 reply, *Laocoön: An Essay on the Limits of Painting and Poetry*; Kant's *Critique of Judgment*, published in 1790, and Friedrich Schiller's writings, notably his *Letters on the Aesthetic Education of Man* (1794).[44]

Winckelmann inspired a new age of neoclassicism, arguing for a modern emulation of the ancients that located nobility within reality, and thereby expressed an aesthetic idealization capable of transcending mere imitation. His main example was the ancient Roman masterpiece, the

Laocoön statue, in which the transformation of the subject's agony and suffering achieved "noble simplicity and quiet grandeur," reconciling pain with the evocation of nobility through aesthetic form. For Winckelmann, sculpture and painting could elevate the mundane and catastrophic to the noble and grand and serve as an inspiration to human aspiration.[45]

Winckelmann made a powerful impression on the young Goethe, who in his 1805 essay, "Winckelmann and His Age," would express criticism of contemporary Romanticism and its privileging of subjectivity and the illusions of realism. Goethe reasserted a new neoclassicism and heralded its objectivity.[46] For Goethe, beauty, in Winckelmann's formulation, did not depend on reason in the sense of mathematics or calculation. Rather, a true aesthetic sense bypassed rationality strictly understood. Therefore, truth in beauty not expressed in language, but through sound and sight was possibly a more direct and powerful path to moral truth and ethics.

Lessing's rebuttal sought to reverse Winckelmann's hierarchy of the poetic as inferior to sculpture and painting. He stressed the static nature of the visual arts—its limitation to a single moment in time—as opposed to the capacity of poetry and drama to capture the dynamics of time and space. With the success and popularity of Viennese Classical composers—Gluck, Haydn, Mozart, and Beethoven—writers, including Schiller's friend Christian Gottfried Körner and later Franz Grillparzer, extended Lessing's argument and proposed music, not just poetry or drama, as superior to the plastic and the literary arts. Mendelssohn similarly alluded to music's superiority as the art of modernity, seeing it as the most promising medium of aesthetic idealism—of beauty and the sublime—precisely on account of its reconfiguration of the experience of time.[47]

At the same time, among Mendelssohn's central convictions was the coherence between reason and sentiment: the aesthetics of beauty and the sublime, and the requirements of form were said to be consistent with epistemological and moral truth. Kant disagreed: Music was a "free" art independent of words and images but therefore self-referential and potentially arbitrary in terms of form. "In the judgment of reason," music was of "less worth" than "any other of the beautiful arts." Mendelssohn seized on music's unique character to suggest the very opposite.

In this discourse on the aesthetic, a recognition of the potential social power and political implications of musical culture emerged. The aesthetic experience of music, alone or in groups, was significant precisely because of the ambiguity and indeterminacy of its meaning. It could offer a greater experience of freedom in a temporal framework, despite lacking an evident correspondence to words or images. Given the absence of political agency or rights, even in the short-lived era of "enlightened despotism" under Emperor Joseph II, music was harder to control or regulate. If there were, indeed, "too many notes," then why?

During Mozart's lifetime, the prestige of the aesthetic encountered through music gained momentum. It could stimulate and sustain the idea of human freedom and autonomy. As Kant argued, morality was profoundly contingent on ideas of freedom, particularly the spiritual and psychological self-consciousness of freedom. If the idea of freedom was dependent on both thought and feeling, and its engagement by the autonomous individual, then music, poetry, and theater could play a decisive role as the proper guides and instruments of moral action and judgment. Kant, however, doubted the power of music in this regard.[48]

Enter Beethoven

Helping to spur the intense philosophical speculation during Mozart's lifetime was the striking growth in a critical mass of literate individuals. In the Austrian sphere the coincident modest and gradual (albeit episodic and conditional) relaxation of monarchical control over daily life, of movement and expression—the Josephine reforms of the Church, the advocacy of German as the language of education and public administration notwithstanding—created opportunities and spaces for social interactions, in Masonic lodges, reading groups, as well as public and semi-public theatrical and musical events.[49] The educated elite on the continent knew the philosophical debates that were underway in England, whose economic progress and public freedoms preceded and exceeded those elsewhere in Europe, including France. Lord Shaftesbury, Adam Smith, Frances Hutcheson, Edmund Burke, and David Hume, alongside Jean-Jacques Rousseau, Denis Diderot, and Jean d'Alembert, influenced the German-language discourse on aesthetics between 1750 and 1800. England remained an object of envy and a place of opportunity for public musical life throughout Mozart's career. Its allure would only grow, particularly after Mozart's death, as the lives of Haydn and Beethoven attest.

It is no surprise then that Schiller, in 1799, turned his attention to the consequences of the growth of amateurism in the arts. He grasped its importance for the development of the individual and social groups committed to the arts, above all in music and dance. Although he regarded amateurism (*Dilettantismus*) as dubious and pernicious, in music its benefits far outweighed its liabilities. In music, amateurism helped develop a collective sensibility and seriousness of purpose. But most of all, music created bonds among people from different classes and encouraged conversations beyond matters of individual self-interest. Indeed, musical and choral societies would be in the vanguard of the revolutions of 1848. Schiller was equally prescient about its dangers. Amateurism could readily make the participatory public more resistant to the new and unfamiliar, and among more passive listeners, self-satisfaction could degenerate into snobbery.[50]

Our capacity to understand Mozart as a historical figure, as well as his uniqueness in music history, has been impeded by the explosive appearance of Beethoven after 1791. Beethoven's prominence throughout the nineteenth century lent Mozart the aspect of a precursor. Even the perceived parallelism between Mozart and Raphael became more persuasive—especially to pessimists and skeptics about the political and economic directions during the early nineteenth century—as a way of framing an antidote to the expanding and often untethered enthusiasm for Beethoven.

A competing comparison between nineteenth-century modernity and the Renaissance came into being. An affinity between Beethoven and Michelangelo was put forward. Burckhardt, who revered Beethoven, developed the notion that the valorization of the individual and individualism was what made the Renaissance the era in which the "modern" was born. But an affinity to Michelangelo went too far. He had none of the ethical virtue and admirable moderation and calm of Raphael.[51] The Michelangelo-Beethoven pairing became more compelling in the 1860s and 1870s, since it fit with Wagner's 1870 self-serving construct of Beethoven as *the* pioneer in music as a progressive dramatic art, the composer who paved the way for the music of the future—the total work of art—and therefore the obsolescence of instrumental forms such as the sonata and symphony at which Mozart excelled.

For most of the nineteenth century, however, there were three different Beethovens. The first was the virtuoso, the protégé of Haydn's, and the culminating master of Classicism in music. That was followed by the "Romantic" Beethoven, exemplified by his heroic period, the composer of the *Eroica* and Fifth Symphonies, *Egmont*, and *Fidelio*. Here was something startling and new.[52] And last was the "late" Beethoven of the Ninth Symphony, the *Missa Solemnis*, and the final piano sonatas and string quartets. Appreciation of that third period would develop strongly during the second half of the century, primarily among advocates of a music of the future such as Berlioz, Liszt, and Wagner.

Even before "late Beethoven" became familiar enough to make a difference, the linking of Haydn, Mozart, and Beethoven, with the periodic inclusion of Gluck as a starting point and Schubert as an end-point, as music's "Classical masters" became commonplace.[53] Nonetheless, it did not impede a rift in the understanding and appreciation of Mozart vis-à-vis Beethoven by midcentury.

This rift was not surprising. The boundaries between the Classical and Romantic traditions of music are fungible. Romanticism is understood as having begun in the 1770s, the era of *Sturm und Drang* exemplified by Goethe's *The Sorrows of Young Werther* (1774) and the symphonies of Haydn from the late 1760s and early 1770s. The decisive watershed, foundational to the characterization of Romantic aesthetics in music, was the publication of E. T. A. Hoffmann's essays on Beethoven's music. Essential to the representation of Beethoven as the quintessentially Romantic artist was the idealization of an exceptional creative genius who shunned social conventions and whose originality challenged the prevailing standards of form. Beethoven's middle period revealed an overwhelming emphasis on emotional expressivity and explicit confessional intent. Romanticism privileged the composer's distinctive subjective perspective. This fit well Beethoven's second and third periods.

At the same time, Beethoven and the first generation of Romantic composers never entirely abandoned the assumptions and procedures of the Classical era elaborated and perfected by Haydn and Mozart. Among musicians, amateurs, and listeners, Romanticism in music, well into the era of Wagner and Brahms, remained tied to Classical precedents even when explicit deviation or rejection occurred. Gluck, Haydn, Mozart, and early Beethoven became comparable to the challenge presented to writers and painters by Greek and Roman models in literature and the plastic arts. Beethoven was acknowledged as the last of the great Classical composers, lending his work a Janus-faced significance. He extended the past and pointed to the future, much in the way Michelangelo was understood to have been a harbinger of new approaches to painting and sculpture. As a result, a diffuse differentiation between Beethoven as a leading new voice and Mozart as representative of a Classical past gained currency.

Already during Beethoven's lifetime, however, elements of a new Romanticism were located in Mozart's music. The Requiem, certain instrumental orchestral and chamber works (often in minor keys), and the most famous of his operas, notably *Don Giovanni*, were understood as compatible with Romanticism. This coincided with an open split between advocates of Classicism in the arts, strongly articulated by Goethe in his later years, and the Romanticism of the generation of Jean Paul Richter. Beethoven was thought to have challenged inherited boundaries of form and appeared to defy traditional criteria of formal coherence, clarity, and moderation—objective aesthetic norms associated with Mozart. The synthesis of reason, sensibility, and emotion that all humans might cultivate, the ideal pioneered by Moses Mendelssohn, seemed discredited, as was much of Schiller's theorizing about the role of art as an instrument through which liberty and goodness could be advanced. Beethoven's presence did not, however, undermine the conception of Mozart as an exemplar of aesthetic norms expressive of and responsive to emotions but rooted in the link between the true, the good, and the beautiful.

Beethoven thus represented a new, largely individualistic ideal of art for those few elite souls who were truly capable of responding to the aesthetic. Aesthetic understanding through music became associated with the capacity by a privileged few to withdraw from a troubled social and political reality. As Wackenroder wrote in 1797, "I close my eyes in the face of all the conflict in the world and remove myself calmly into the land of music as one might into the land of belief where all our doubts and our sufferings disappear in a sea of sound . . . and where all the fears in our hearts are healed finally through quiet comfort."[54]

These political implications of Romanticism need to be understood within the context of the political events of Mozart's last years and Beethoven's life. These include the American and French Revolutions, the subsequent Reign of Terror in France, the advent of Napoleon, the emergence of German nationalism after 1806, Napoleon's defeat, and the restoration of monarchical absolutism after 1815 that persisted well into the 1830s and 1840s. Ironically, the Romantic movement succeeded in elevating music as the most powerful art of the era. It justified a quietism that permitted individuals to experience a form of inner emigration from the collapse of any plausible belief in the progress of history toward a rational politics that would result in external and internal freedom and moral happiness.

Two contemporary voices at midcentury—with radically different perspectives—helped shape the image of Mozart through an explicit contrast with Beethoven. Franz Grillparzer was the most renowned Austrian dramatist between the mid-1830s and the mid-1860s. Outside of the German-speaking world, he is remembered for the oration he wrote for Beethoven's funeral in March 1827. Despite their personal relationship, Grillparzer had severe reservations about Beethoven's music and its influence. For him, Mozart remained the ideal of what music should be. Since music touched the emotions directly and bypassed the faculty of reason necessary in the other arts to understand errors, inconsistencies, and disturbances to the integrity and beauty of the aesthetic form, music's formal stability and consistency had to be immediately perceptible through one's senses and emotions. Shakespeare was entitled to toy with imperfection, but Mozart's boundary, as the ideal musician, always remained "the beautiful." Mozart inspired an emotional awareness of the good through the formalist imperative to foreground beauty and the sublime. This constraint confirmed an absolute refusal to countenance ugliness.

For Grillparzer, the essence of music was different from that of poetry. If poetry lends substance to the spirit, music spiritualizes the sensual and sensory. Writing in 1834, he identified four deleterious consequences for art in Beethoven's works, despite their undeniable greatness. The first was the mix of noise and dissonance that disturbed the refinement and correctness of human hearing. Second, Beethoven's lyricism transgressed the concept of order and coherence and undermined the unmediated perception of the logic of the whole. Third, Beethoven diminished the values of pleasing but profound sonorities and the objectivity of aesthetic spirituality, balance, and perfection. Finally, Beethoven privileged what was merely interesting, powerful, shattering, and intoxicating at the expense of the beautiful. That final reversal of values was most harmful to the art of music.[55]

Mozart, however, represented for Grillparzer the embodiment of music as an autonomous art form in which listeners encountered and intuited infinite meaning. That made music the art of modern times, superior to anything literary or visual inspired by classical antiquity. In an 1842 poem celebrating Mozart, he too compared the composer to Raphael, a divine cherub who expressed and protected "true art," creating a "second world," one just as real and substantive as the world we live in, but one that required an unerring sense of proportion and balance.[56]

Grillparzer's life was saturated by music. He was an accomplished and enthusiastic musical amateur who envied a composer's relative freedom in the contemporary political context, the Metternich era, one of strict censorship. Censors, after all, could not make head or tails out of instrumental music, but they could spot or construe criticism, lack of patriotism, or disloyalty to the dynasty in plays and poems. Grillparzer maintained his public position as a senior civil servant but stopped writing for the theater after 1838, dismayed by the lack of artistic freedom. Despite his increasingly reactionary political disposition, as well as an innate pessimism and skepticism, the aesthetic, the civic, and the ethical remained linked for Grillparzer. He continued to cling to the ideals of a politics of reason rooted in the universal centrality of freedom and civic duty. His style reflected a loyalty to Classicism reminiscent of the late Goethe.[57] Grillparzer was not inclined to privilege passion and subjective Romantic or nationalist ideals.[58]

During the same era, Nikolaus Lenau, an inspired Romantic poet, and by all accounts a superb violinist, took a somewhat different tack. He venerated Beethoven; hearing *Fidelio*, Lenau felt transported as if in a storm, to wild and sublime cliffs and dark forests in a journey that ended in infinite love and joy. There could be no more divine spirit than Beethoven, whom he credited for helping him craft his own poetic language.[59] Lenau had no interest in Mozart, whose music he considered irrelevant to the human condition in contemporary life. Not even the Requiem persuaded him that

Mozart was capable of writing music of profundity and gravity equal to Beethoven: "The human breast harbors a foundation of suffering and pain that Mozart absolutely never grasped, that however Beethoven not only knew, but understood so well that he could reproduce them in sounds." Beethoven was Lenau's sole "master"; he "wanted no Gods other than him."[60] The key document of Lenau's Beethoven obsession was his poem "The Bust of Beethoven" (1841).[61] Evoking Winckelmann and Lessing, he observed that Beethoven transfigured the suffering of the "soul" through the aesthetic in music. Beethoven's "great love" embraced everything and everyone, synthesizing the old world with the new for all "eternity."[62]

Lenau's invidious contrast between Mozart and Beethoven was taken up later in the century with greater philosophical seriousness by August Halm, a theorist, teacher, and composer, an older contemporary of Bekker's, and a strong advocate of Anton Bruckner's music. Halm considered Mozart inferior to Beethoven in strategies of musical transformation, the musical procedures that create an "inaudible" music that "is the meaning of the sounding element." Music at its best should generate an "'idea" perceivable by the mind. Mozart lacked the inner vigor that could lend sounding events a metaphysical significance as a sonic experience—the "inaudible" meaning—a component vital to all great music. The advocates of the superiority of "pure" instrumental music in the age of Bruckner and Mahler believed that such spiritual meaning generated by sounding events was essential to music's purpose.[63]

Halm accepted the basic premise of Wagner's 1870 Beethoven essay that construed Beethoven as a prophetic voice in the integration of the theatrical, linguistic, and visual. Through the organic dynamism of his forms, Beethoven pointed to the expansion and transformation of instrumental music beyond the formal scope of conventions such as the sonata form. Mozart, in contrast, failed to generate "dynamic coherence" and passion, relying on static patterns of thematic contrast and repetition. In Halm's view, Mozart did not make music a pathway to profound spiritual thought in a manner that vindicated a power unique to music.[64]

Goethe and *The Magic Flute*

We associate Goethe frequently with Beethoven but Goethe admired Mozart far more. He first heard Mozart in Frankfurt as a child when Leopold brought Wolfgang and Nannerl for a concert in August 1763. Mozart was seven, and Goethe fourteen.[65] He believed Mozart's music had a creative power that would ensure its presence in subsequent generations: "A phenomenon like Mozart will always remain a miracle that cannot be explained. But how else can the divinity create miracles . . .

through extraordinary individuals whom we behold in awe and wonder but can never grasp where they come from."[66]

Mozart's *The Magic Flute* helped shape Goethe's outlook after the spectacular appearance of *Faust, Part I* in 1808.[67] In 1807, he published a fragment, a sketch for a sequel to Mozart and Schikaneder's German-language Singspiel.[68] Goethe ran the court theater in Weimar from 1791 to 1817. His tenure included 270 performances of operas by Mozart: eighty-two of *The Magic Flute*, sixty-eight of *Don Giovanni*, forty-nine of *The Abduction from the Seraglio*, thirty-three of *Così fan tutte*, twenty-eight of *La clemenza di Tito*, and twenty of *Figaro*.[69]

Goethe placed three figures on an equally unapproachable elevated plane as artists and personalities: Raphael in the visual arts, Shakespeare in literature, and Mozart in music.[70] What distinguished Mozart, Goethe noted in 1831, was his inborn talent, his unmatched transhistorical divine gift that could not be acquired or influenced. Goethe's Mozart exhibited precisely the qualities Pushkin had assigned to him. Through his musician friend Zelter, Goethe learned of the links between Mozart and J. S. Bach. Zelter believed that both had a "mystical" genius that enabled their music to drive, in the temporal frame of performance and listening, the collective sensibility from "brightness and surface lightness toward an increasing self-recognition of darkness."[71] Goethe considered music an inborn gift that bypassed the intellect and was, nonetheless, like the capacity for language, universal. This quality accounted for its unrivaled power in human life.

Goethe posited that disciplined restraint was a requisite for beauty and the sublime to be evoked through music. Mozart's music represented the ideal realization of disciplined restraint through form and structure. Mozart achieved this in a manner that permitted originality and the full range of human expression to be present in a single work of art.[72] Form must be self-sufficient and complete. Only then can aesthetic transformation of emotion and passion, even in their extremes, be accomplished, generating a permanent, powerful object of contemplation and reflection. Goethe's notion is reminiscent of Winckelmann's and Lessing's praise of *Laocoön*, and was echoed by Mozart in a letter to his father in 1781: "Order, and balance," an end point of form, should never be sacrificed by overstepping the limits of structural logic, or veering toward "disgust," and therefore "offending the ear" thereby depriving the listener of the "pleasure" music must inspire.[73]

Mozart's Requiem may have fascinated Zelter, but Goethe's attachment was centered on Mozart's operas.[74] He supervised *Don Giovanni*'s 1797 Weimar production and many commentators have remarked on a resemblance in formal structure and coherence between Da Ponte's libretto and Goethe's *Faust, Part 1*, particularly the role their "happy endings" play. Each is an example of the aesthetic transformation of evil and, for some characters, the possibility of redemption (or at least survival), in contrast to the evident unreality of such redemption and justice in real life.[75] Mozart's opera was, for Goethe, an example of "an intellectual-spiritual creation" of "demonic" genius that exhibited a single formal dynamic arc, as if produced in a single "breath."[76]

But it was *The Magic Flute* that most captivated Goethe. Like Joseph II, he had long been interested in the Singspiel genre.[77] *The Magic Flute* was the hit of Weimar's seasons during the mid-1790s, as it was elsewhere in Europe. Goethe recognized that its unique combination of high art and popular appeal vindicated the power of German-language opera as a genre. The symbolism of the libretto impressed him.[78] Most significant, though, is that he attempted in 1795 to write a sequel and sought to recruit the composer Paul Wranitzky to compose the music. Wranitzky declined. Goethe abandoned the project as a potential theater piece and published his fragmentary poetic sequel.

Goethe's fragment puts weight on the allegorical aspect of Schikaneder and Mozart's work. The symbolism of wisdom, reason, and reflection as opposed to anger, passion, violence, and revenge, is enhanced by extensive scenic descriptions and stage directions.[79] Goethe uses the characters from the opera, opening with Monostatos and the Queen of the Night. A chorus plays a large role in a plot that revolves around the attempted kidnapping of Tamino and Pamina's child. Papageno and Papagena also make an appearance in this theatrical resumption of the battle between the forces of death and darkness and those of light and life. Parallel to the presence of irreconcilable scenic elements, such as fire and water and dark and light, is a more nuanced fascination with the dynamic interplay and porous boundaries between opposites: principled loyalty and self-interest, good and evil. Sarastro, the Speaker, and a pilgrim all signal the resilience of the forces of light and goodness. At the end, the Queen of the Night and her guards descend from the clouds, separating fire and water. The child, whose name is "Genius," eludes death and escapes to freedom: "By darkness of the night born, in glory and state, yet lost by the powers of malice and hate . . . yet safe from all ill, the child liveth still!"[80]

Goethe, like Mozart, was a Freemason. He extended the allegorical structure of Mozart and Schikaneder's mix of magic and neoclassical dramatic gestures, poetic simplicity, and moral symbolism. The influence of Masonic practices and ideas is evident throughout. The emphasis on theatricality in the Masonic rituals was celebrated by Mozart's contemporary Johann Pezzl, who wrote, "Whatever one wishes to believe, the initiation ceremony in the

Masonic orders is the most shattering, imposing, sublime of any spiritual and secular ceremonies I know." This sensibility shaped Schikaneder and Mozart's masterpiece of musical theater and Goethe's fragment.[81]

But the link between Mozart, Goethe, and Freemasonry becomes most apparent in the writings of Adam Weishaupt, the founder of the Bavarian *Illuminati* and the author of a 1788 philosophical manifesto against Kant's epistemology and concept of reason.[82] Weishaupt claimed that enlightenment required not individual freedom to reason, but an organized, hierarchical structure akin to enlightened despotism, in which a secret elite order made the rules. Kant's conception of reason led to the triumph of pure subjectivity and unbridled individualism that undermined conscience, calm, and all sense of spiritual happiness. Subjectivity, skepticism, and relativism were untenable. A subjective system based on Kant made all judgment of experience incapable of determining the truth value of human action. There can be, Weishaupt argues, no human understanding in a world without anything objective. In such a world, it is impossible to attach productive and charitable meaning to experience and knowledge.[83]

Weishaupt's notoriety should not obscure an essential link between Freemasonry and Goethe and Mozart. Freemasonry represented a utopian social structure that places reason, alongside ritual, at the center of morality.[84] Key to what he called the "kingdom of truth" is an aesthetic that matches the "eternal and indestructible" world of truth in poetry and music. A didactic opera, a form of theater, becomes an ideal medium for enlightenment. Aesthetic understanding, including of the temporal arts of music and dance, requires the capacity to extract meaning from the acts of listening and watching; it also demands a language that makes claims on behalf of knowledge. But the unity of truth—that is, of objective truths—is a synthesis of the moral, epistemological, and aesthetic.[85] The formal properties in a musical composition of expression and affects, with words, sounds, and gestures, offered the most persuasive transfiguration of evil and suffering: they are neither denied nor made impossible to confront because of unmediated ugliness and horror. This was the ideal that Mozart's operas came to represent for Goethe—a universal, objective, and complex but complete realization of ideal beauty, understood as truth, including harsh realities.

During the mid-1870s, the decade when liberalism in Central Europe began its long decline, the residue of Masonic optimism and Schiller's moral and aesthetic didacticism continued to thrive, albeit more as clichés, alongside a growing philosophical skepticism and historical pessimism. Mozart's *Magic Flute* and Lessing's final work, the play *Nathan the Wise* from 1779 (regarded as a precursor of *The Magic Flute*), came to represent the last hour of secular Enlightenment optimism and the possibility of a rational path to human freedom and moral virtue.[86]

Lessing had become disillusioned with Freemasonry, just as he was with organized Christianity. Ethics and morals consistent with Christ's teachings in the Gospels needed to be based on reason, not ritual and superstition. But he clung to the ideal of secular rationality as a source for human conduct and the likelihood that it could be conveyed through the aesthetic, in the theater, in what David Friedrich Strauss, in 1877, called "lyrical-didactic" drama.[87] *Nathan the Wise* was its finest example. However, Strauss was cautious about the impact on modern audiences of both Lessing's drama of tolerance with its critique of the conceits of the three Abrahamic religions, and of Mozart and Schikaneder's magical and musically translucent music theater. By 1877, the allure of Wagnerian sonorities and expressive chromaticism and Wagner's grandiose philosophical apparatus marked by a Schopenhauerian pessimism had enraptured the contemporary audience.

Mozart's *Magic Flute* and Lessing's *Nathan the Wise* therefore came across to the contemporary audience as quasi-religious and old-fashioned. They demanded "reverence" since they could no longer engender genuine emotional attachment. Even though these works, along with their ideals, had lost touch with reality, Mozart still presented an exception:

> Maxims on which today's ethical and religious educational attainments rest, give the drama before our eyes an aura of the sacred, and impart in the receptive spectator a mood of reverence. Therefore, one might easily miss that gripping impression a truly radical work makes, just as one might overlook the manifold characterizations within the serene sounds of Mozart's "Magic Flute" or the effervescent passion found in the melodies of his "Don Giovanni." In these two final works, that of the poet and that of the composer, however different they may otherwise be, a spirit is revealed that has broken through to clarity and peace, a soul perfected within itself, a spirit that has overcome every inner turbidity. Consequently, no external disturbance will really affect it. They are works beyond which no higher achievement was possible for the geniuses who created them; works already bathed in that transcendent light into which their creators soon after passed in death.[88]

Strauss cautioned that these were aesthetic visions of a world in which contradictions appear to have been resolved and the struggle for justice already won. The contemporary moment in history required more than such an illusion. "Pleasure" without action, and mere aesthetic "perceptions" could no longer suffice if indeed "freedom" was to conquer "servitude" and "mankind" come out of the twilight and join the struggle. Mozart's uniqueness lay in his resistance to the fate of obsolescence.

Approaching the Modern: Wittgenstein and Kürnberger

One of the curious conceits to emerge from the centrality that musical culture assumed during Mozart's lifetime and the long nineteenth century was that music—whether understood as an autonomous arena of aesthetic expression or as a component of heterogenous genres, such as song or opera—was essential to the cultivation of a sense of freedom and morality. The fact that political freedom was not a reality and wide disparities in wealth and status were the norm made the idea of inner spiritual freedom and its expression alluring. Inner sensibilities, even experienced in public, became plausible surrogates for freedom of speech and movement and political agency. Music, abetted by the Wagnerian appropriation of philosophical thinking, made listening to opera something akin to reading a novel. For a public that extended well beyond the boundaries of connoisseur and amateur (*Kenner und Liebhaber*), music achieved a status as perhaps the most independent personal means of self-understanding and spiritual reflection.

No twentieth-century philosopher pondered this possibility as acutely as Ludwig Wittgenstein. He came from a fabulously wealthy Viennese family that was deeply musical. His mother and sister were accomplished amateur pianists, and his brother Paul became a respected professional pianist, especially after World War I, during which he lost his right hand.[89] All the Wittgenstein siblings were amateurs and the house was legendary as a gathering place for the musical elite of Vienna.

In both his early work, in the *Tractatus* (1921) and his later writings on ordinary language and its uses, published posthumously as *The Philosophical Investigations* (1953), music figures prominently in Wittgenstein's effort to understand language. "A theme is not a medley of notes," he wrote in the *Tractatus*, just as "a proposition is not a medley of words." He went on to speculate how music alone communicates meaning. He probed the ambiguity of what constitutes music in the first place: "The gramophone record, the musical idea, the score, the sound waves: all stand in an inherent relation of depicting to one another, the same relation of depicting that exists between language and the world. They all share a logical structure."[90]

For Wittgenstein, Mozart's music was free of the pretentions and obsessions of modernity. It did not express irony, particularly the "irony of fate," as Beethoven's did.[91] Wittgenstein claimed in 1949, "Fate plays no role of any sort. That is not the concern of this music." He made fun of the idea that this was so because Mozart was not much of a reader. He concluded, "But if Mozart found no great *tragedy* in what he read, does that mean he did not encounter it in his *life*? And do composers never see anything except through the spectacles of poets."[92] Wittgenstein thought that Grillparzer's focus on the "beautiful" created mischief when applied to music written after Mozart. However, beauty in Mozart was beauty not tainted by pessimism.[93]

Since Mozart's music resisted these qualities, it could be understood, because it communicated a "logical plan" and succeeded in defining the "musical idea" that connected music to life and "the world." Ideas, a common logic, and a sense of completeness—the formal elements of unity in a musical work, its aesthetic properties—became an autonomous means to convey moral and ethical meanings, perhaps even truths—all convictions of Mozart's key philosophical contemporaries and his Masonic brethren. Mozart was the embodiment of formal perfection, harmony, and symmetry, without sacrifice to life's complexity and suffering. Music's potential to convey meaning and insights that could indeed influence judgment and action toward moral betterment seemed vindicated.

This idea had been eloquently expressed in 1848 by an eminent Viennese-born writer, Ferdinand Kürnberger, whom Wittgenstein admired. Kürnberger participated in the 1848 Vienna Revolution. He was imprisoned for his role in the 1849 Dresden Revolution (which forced Wagner to seek refuge in Switzerland) and returned to Austria in 1852, well before the Austrian defeat at the hands of the Prussians in 1866. He was outspoken and critical of the evident alliance between capitalist speculation and liberal pieties. He used journalistic criticism as a vehicle of political criticism, which earned him Karl Kraus's encomium as Austria's "greatest political writer." Kürnberger perfected the feuilleton, the short newspaper essay, a Viennese specialty.[94]

The belief that language, wittingly and unwittingly, was the bearer of ethical content through style, usage, and precision was central to Kraus. Ethics and aesthetics were intertwined, and certain artists at the turn of the century were inspired to argue on behalf of a radical break from Romanticism and its illusions of realism, as well as from the deceptions and vulgarities of contemporary journalistic jargon and prose. The modernist innovations of the architect Adolf Loos and Gustav Mahler were justified by ethical absolutes connected to formal aesthetic practices that respected the inherent and distinct integrity of the logic and limits of music and architectural design. A movement within fin-de-siècle Viennese modernism (that included Arnold Schoenberg) sought to reconnect art, ethics, and truth in ways evocative of Mozart's era.

Kürnberger distilled the legendary Winckelmann-Lessing debate into the simple claim that the art of the ancients took inspiration from the body—physical beauty in nature—and made sculpture their representative art. The modern age turned to the "soul," making true modern art lyrical, musical, painterly, in short: "Romantic."[95] With more than a touch of irony, Kürnberger took aim at the stylistic excesses of modern Romantic prose and music. He said that "three words" were all he needed to explain the difference between the ancients and the moderns, especially to those "thoroughly and completely" educated. The "three words" assertion regarding the limits and economic imperative in language use found its way into the *Tractatus* as its motto: ". . . anything we know, and have not just heard roaring and rushing, can be said in three words."[96] What links Kürnberger to Wittgenstein is not only Kraus, but Kürnberger's contrarian views on nineteenth-century progressive conceits about music's expanded expressivity.

The primary source of Kürnberger's reputation was his 1855 novel *Der Amerikamüde* (The Man Tired of America). The novel was a thinly disguised version of the life and reminiscences of Lenau. A controversy still lingers about matters of plagiarism and appropriation.[97] Moorfeld, a poet and the novel's hero, goes to America, and like Lenau, ultimately returns to Europe. But before he does, he pays a visit to New York, where he encounters Lorenzo Da Ponte, now elderly.[98] Overwhelmed to meet Mozart's famed librettist, he proceeds to laud his achievement and laments the absence of culture among Americans. *Don Giovanni* is declared the ideal realization of opera. Since music "requires passion and affect" and "drama motivates passion and affect," and since motivation is an operation of the intellect which works against passion, the operatic text bringing forth great music must be the one that short-circuits language, the instrument of the intellect. After all, Moorfield declares, "Is not music, the sole free-standing art with which we, on our own, surpassed the art of antiquity, and with which we created our Laocoöns, our Illiads without requiring any model precedents. . . and is not *Don Giovanni* the greatest flowering of this musical art, the sweetest and most powerful ambassador of the heart of modern humanity."[99]

Kürnberger, writing a few months before the Vienna revolution of 1848, reaffirmed that music was modernity's equivalent of Winckelmann's idealized classical antiquity. Music also stood above poetry, Lessing's ideal, as the greatest of the arts in modern times. Kürnberger distanced himself from the by then shopworn contrast between Mozart and Beethoven, but like Grillparzer, held Mozart up as the key representative of a foundational and normative Classical ideal for music. Mozart realized music's expressive and emotional power in a manner that would always seem objective and normative.[100] The qualities of Mozart's music, its variety, its ease and clarity, its sonorities, and, above all, the poise of its form all define musical beauty in a manner that coheres with ethical and moral truth. Such truths, Kürnberger believed, eluded words, as Wittgenstein also suspected.

If only everyone "could read music," Kürnberger lamented, freedom might be finally realized in everyday life.[101] Music was for Kürnberger the purest and most resilient source of hope. Hope demanded a system of communication, but perhaps not necessarily, as Wittgenstein suggested, a language in the ordinary sense of the word.[102] Learning to read music, being able to hear Mozart's music in one's head through its notation, would make music—the art of sentiment and ethically sound rationality, as Mendelssohn suggested—a universally accessible human attribute. To hear music in one's head could be a path to liberty, equality, and fraternity, a world governed by reason—the Enlightenment's unfulfilled utopia. Kürnberger's tongue-in-cheek parody articulated what justified, for Bekker, the moral and aesthetic universal humanism he claimed on Mozart's behalf on the eve of humanity's greatest betrayal of the good and the beautiful.

Kürnberger touched on all the familiar virtues of Mozart's music. It offers "life-bearing creations" and "wonderment and the pleasure of eternal instruction." In his operas, Mozart equaled the whole moral and aesthetic legacy of antiquity. Despite the abstruse character of musical syntax and notation, music does much for the "moral imagination": "One *Figaro* renders ten moral systems unnecessary." Music, as realized by Mozart, represented more than the modern equivalent of antiquity's superiority in the visual arts and literature: "Yes, the works of our music compensate us for the works of the ancient chisel . . . and a poet seeks in vain to attain the laurels of a Homer, a Sophocles, a Pindar."[103] Music could be the modern means of collective moral betterment.

Kürnberger's advocacy of music and Mozart in particular was suggestive of the overarching humanism and universality expressed by Bekker in the 1920s. This conviction survived the catastrophe of World War II. In the nuclear age, in the midst of the Cold War, Karl Barth wrote an essay about his "faith in Mozart." Barth was not a trained musician, but he listened attentively to Mozart every day. "What I owe you," Barth wrote, "frankly, is this: Whenever I listen to your music I feel led to the threshold of a world which is good and well ordered, in sunshine and thunderstorm, by day and night. This you have repeatedly given me, a human being in the twentieth century. Courage (not haughtiness!), tempo (not exaggerated tempo!), purity (not boring purity) and peace (not complacent peace). . . . I am convinced that our century, which is becoming more and more obscure, especially needs your help."[104]

For Barth, that help resided in the "pure" music Mozart so uniquely produced within a coherent, albeit eclectic, eighteenth-century manner. Mozart's acceptance and mastery of the historical specificity of his ear allowed him to write music that "is identical with the original sound of music as such . . . in its timeless form." That is "why it is so difficult or impossible to define what is typically Mozartian."

For Barth, in Mozart's works, "happiness and pain, good and evil, life and death have all been perceived in their reality as well as in their limitation." Mozart had achieved freedom through his exclusive devotion to the objective inherited norms of music. That allowed him to write music that has "no shallowness, but no abyss, either"; Mozart "takes everything seriously. However, he never lets himself go nor does he allow himself to go beyond proper limits. He only says within limitations how everything is. Thus his music is beautiful, comforting, moving. I do not know of any other music which I could characterize in this way. Mozart is universal."[105]

Let us hope that future generations will share Barth's recognition of what has made Mozart unique and universal, not just for the centuries that have passed, but for the one we live in, and which we will endure.

NOTES

1. Among the most provocative reassessments is Jonathan I. Israel's *The Enlightenment That Failed: Ideas, Revolution, and Democratic Defeat, 1748–1830* (Oxford: Oxford University, 2020), particularly its discussion of theology, philosophy, and the politics of toleration and freedom. See esp. 29–33, 403–8, 595–633.

2. A fine example is Ivan Nagel, *Autonomy and Mercy: Reflections on Mozart's Operas*, trans. Marion Faber (Cambridge, MA: Harvard University Press, 1991).

3. See W. E. Yates, *Theatre in Vienna: A Critical History, 1776–1995* (Cambridge: Cambridge University Press, 1996), 143–44.

4. These specific contrasts come from J. V. Widmann, *Johannes Brahms in Erinnerungen* (Berlin: Paetel, 1898), 16.

5. See Gernot Gruber, *Mozart and Posterity*, trans. R. S. Furness (Boston: Northeastern University, 1994).

6. Arthur Schurig, *Wolfgang Amade Mozart: Sein Leben, seine Persönlichkeit, sein Werk*, 2 vols. (Leipzig: Insel, 1923), 1:16–20 and 26–33.

7. As is well known, Strauss, Germany's greatest living composer, identified strongly with Mozart, particularly after World War I. See Willi Schuh, "Strauss at Eighty," in *Richard Strauss and His World*, ed. Bryan Gilliam (Princeton, NJ: Princeton University Press 1992), 290.

8. Schurig, *Wolfgang Amade Mozart*, 1:5–33.

9. See Konrad H. Jarausch "Die Krise des deutschen Bildungsbürgertums im ersten Drittel des 20. Jahrhunderts," in *Bildungsbürgertum im 19. Jahrhundert*, ed. Jürgen Kocka, vol. 4 (Stuttgart: Klett-Cotta, 1985), 180–205.

10. Paul Bekker, *Musikgeschichte als Geschichte der musikalischen Formenwandlung* (Berlin and Leipzig: Deutsche Verlags-Anstalt, 1926), 149–50. Emphases in original.

11. Ibid., 150–51.

12. Bekker also accepted the concomitant contrast between Mozart and Beethoven, but he demurred on the obvious Renaissance parallel that linked Michelangelo to Beethoven. He put Rembrandt forward as Beethoven's closest equivalent in painting.

13. Mozart, from childhood on, was a genuinely international figure, fluent in many languages, including English, and at ease everywhere in Europe. Like C. P. E. Bach, a composer he deeply admired, Mozart was a proponent of music as a medium of expressiveness and sentiment and freedom in structure. Like Bach, Mozart observed the politics, theology, and ideas around him, as *Così fan tutte* amply proves, but he was not a writer, either of treatises or autobiography, nor a friend of philosophers like Moses Mendessohn and G. E. Lessing.

14. Karl Barth, "Wolfgang Amadeus Mozart," in *Religion and Culture: Essays in Honor of Paul Tillich*, ed. Walter Leibrecht (New York: Harper & Brothers, 1959), 76.

15. A similar argument against the appropriation of eighteenth-century composers into the nineteenth-century nationalist narrative was expressed by Karl Friedrich Zelter in a letter to Goethe on 26 September 1830. In *Briefwechsel zwischen Goethe und Zelter*, ed. Max Hecker, 3 vols. (Frankfurt: Insel, 1987), 3:358–59.

16. For the Requiem and its completion, see Simon P. Keefe's excellent volume, *Mozart's Requiem: Reception, Work, Completion* (Cambridge: Cambridge University Press, 2012), as well as Christoph Wolff, *Mozart's Requiem: Historical and Analytical Studies, Documents, Score*, trans. Mary Whittal (Berkeley: University of California Press, 1998).

17. Otto Jahn, *W. A. Mozart*, vol. 4 (Leipzig: Breitkopf & Härtel, 1859), 626, 634, 720.

18. Zelter to Goethe, March 1829, in *Briefwechsel*, 3:153. Rochlitz's essay on Mozart and Raphael was translated into English in the influential journal *The Harmonicon* in 1830; see Simon P. Keefe, *Haydn and Mozart in the Long Nineteenth Century: Parallel and Intersecting Patterns of Reception* (Cambridge: Cambridge University Press, 2023), 64.

19. See Werner Busch, "Die fehlende Gegenwart," in *Bildungsbürgertum im 19. Jahrhundert*, ed. M. R. Lepsius, vol. 3 (Stuttgart: Klett-Cotta, 1985), 299.

20. See Frank Büttner, "Bildungsideen und bildende Kunst in Deutschland um 1800," in ibid., 259.

21. See Hans Erich Bödeker, "'Die gebildeten Stände' im späten 18. und frühen 19. Jahrhundert: Zugehörigkeit und Abgenzungen, Mentalitäten und Handlungspotentiale," in *Bildungsbürgertum im 19. Jarhundert*, vol. 4:21.

22. See Elizabeth Kramer, "The Idea of Transfiguration in the Early German Reception of Mozart's Requiem," *Current Musicology* 81 (Spring 2006): 73–107.

23. In the years after Mozart's death in 1791, the aesthetic debate in German-speaking Europe took a sharp polemical turn, however, sparked by Wilhelm Heinrich Wackenroder in *Outpourings of an Art-Loving Monk* (1797). The idealization of Raphael was countered by a negative comparison to Albrecht Dürer. Wackenroder called for a new era of German art, a nascent Romanticism that favored alternatives to neoclassicism and the Italian Renaissance. He extolled the power of nature, subjectivity, national sentiment, and realism with respect to past and present. But despite the enthusiasm that greeted Wackenroder's criticism, the veneration of Raphael and the aesthetic perfection attributed to his art never vanished from the consciousness of nineteenth-century German painters and sculptors and their public.

24. Alexander Pushkin, *Mozart and Salieri*, in *The Little Tragedies*, trans. and with critical essays by Nancy K. Anderson (New Haven: Yale University Press, 2000), passim.

25. A touching account of the old Salieri, still full of music, was communicated by Zelter to Goethe in 1819. Zelter to Goethe, 29 July 1819, in *Briefwechsel*, 2:34. As Anna Akhmatova suggested in the 1920s, Pushkin was inspired to write his "little tragedy" by his admiration for and envy of Adam Mickiewicz, the Polish poet famed for his spontaneity, theatricality, and gift for improvisation. Mozart was Mickiewicz and Salieri was Pushkin. But the real meaning of the "little tragedy" was that the same hard work and dedication that Salieri put into composing were essential for Mozart and Mickiewicz as well. The great poet Osip Mandelstam, Akhmatova's contemporary, also identified with Salieri. He argued that Pushkin's point was that for the divinely inspired artist, there is no conflict: both hard work and inexplicable inspirations and impulses are required for great art. Mozart and Salieri merely represent the two essential "stages of creative work; but they are not separated in time, they are both present continuously, complementing each other. They have a common and indivisible path." Nadezhda Mandelstam, *Mozart and Salieri: Osip Mandelstam and Anna Akhmatova: An Essay on Poetic Creativity*, trans. Robert A. McLean (Ann Arbor, MI: Ardis, 1973), 32–34, 89, at 91.

26. E. T. A. Hoffmann, *Schriften zur Musik: Aufsätze und Rezensionen* (Munich: Winkler, 1977), 35–36, 66–67, 297–301.

27. Max R. Schneider, *Die Musik bei Jacob Burckhardt* (Basel: Amerbach, 1946), 72, 89–90, 102.

28. Jacob Burckhardt, *Der Cicerone: Eine Anleitung zum Genuss der Kunstwerke Italiens* (Leipzig: Körner, n.d.), 884. Author's translation.

29. Gustav Höcker, *Das grosse Dreigestirn: Haydn, Mozart und Beethoven in biographischen Erzählungen* (Glogau: Flemming, 1890), 259.

30. Zelter to Goethe, 26 April 1815, in *Briefwechsel*, 2:454.

31. It is unabashed *kitsch*, in a manner more deftly realized by Hans Makart in his designs for the 1879 *Festzug* in Vienna for the Silver Anniversary celebration of Franz Joseph and Elisabeth.

32. Karl Schawelka, *Quasi una musica* (Munich: Mäander, 1993), 212–13.

33. Eduard Mörike, *Mozart auf der Reise nach Prag* (Berlin: Insel, 2015).

34. Martin Alber, "'Jetzt brach ein ander Licht heran . . .': Über Aspekte des Musikalischen in Biographie und Werk Ludwig Wittgensteins," in *Wittgenstein und die Musik: Briefwechsel Ludwig Wittgenstein—Rudolf Koder*, ed. Martin Alber (Innsbruck: Hayomn, 2000), 150.

35. Ludwig Speidel, "Das Wiener Mozart-Denkmal," 18 March 1891, in *Wiener Feuilletons* (Vienna: Böhlau, 1989), 71–75. On the controversy surrounding Tilgner's Mozart statue at the time of its commission, see Simon P. Keefe, "Commemorating Musicians in Vienna," in *Vienna: A Musical History*, ed. Keefe (Cambridge: Cambridge University Press, 2026), 40–42.

36. Burckhardt, not surprisingly, was skeptical of Wagner. See Schneider, *Die Musik bei Jacob Burckhardt*, 115–16.

37. These trends were exemplified by the rise of the United States after the Civil War with its unchecked embrace of money as the exclusive criterion of value in life.

38. Mozart himself extolled the virtue of moderation. See *Mozart: Briefe und Aufzeichnungen, Gesamtausgabe*, ed. Wilhelm A. Bauer and Otto Erich Deutsch, vol. 3 (Kassel and London: Bärenreiter, 1971), 245–46, letter from 1782; and Neal Zaslaw, *Mozart's Symphonies: Context, Performance Practice, Reception* (Oxford: Clarendon Press, 1991), 531.

39. See Schurig, *Wolfgang Amade Mozart*, 2:402–12 and 454. See Georg Knepler, *Wolfgang Amadé Mozart*, trans. J. Bradford Robinson (New York: Cambridge University Press, 1997).

40. See Leo Strauss, "Introduction to Mendelssohn's Phädon" (1932), in *Leo Strauss on Mendelssohn*, ed. Martin D. Yaffe (Chicago: University of Chicago Press, 2012), 29–49.

41. Moses Mendelssohn, *Phaedon; or The Death of Socrates* (Gale Reprints), viii, 132, 164, 198–99; the German text can be found in *Phaedon, oder über die Unsterblichkeit der Seele (Phaedon, or about the Immortality of the Soul)* in *Moses Mendelssohn's Schriften zur Metaphysik und Ethik sowie zur Religionsphilosophie*, ed. Moritz Brasch, vol. 1 (Leipzig: Leopold Voss, 1891), 131–268.

42. Moses Mendelssohn, *Philosophical Writings*, trans. and ed. Daniel O. Dahlstrom (New York: Cambridge University Press, 1997), 179.

43. Mendelssohn, *Philosophische Schriften* (Berlin, 1761) 86–93; also see his "On the Main Principles of the Fine Arts and Sciences," in *Philosophical Writings*, 169–91.

44. See Paul Guyer, *Reason and Experience in Mendelssohn and Kant* (Oxford: Oxford University Press, 2020); and Frederick C. Beiser, *Diotima's Children: German Aesthetic Rationalism from Leibnitz to Lessing* (Oxford: Oxford University Press, 2011), 156–282.

45. Johann Joachim Winckelmann, *Gedanken über die Nachahmung der griechischen Werke in der Malerei und Bildhauerkunst* (1756) (Berlin: Hoffenberg, 2016), 20–21.

46. This essay can be found in English translation in Matthew Bell, ed., *The Essential Goethe* (Princeton: Princeton University Press, 2018), 881–903.

47. For an elegant discussion of the sublime and its relation to beauty, notably the work of Burke and Kant, see Elaine Sisman, *Mozart: The "Jupiter" Symphony* (Cambridge: Cambridge University Press, 1993), 13–20. For Kant, beauty "moves" the mind through its representation, whereas beauty inspires "restful contemplation." See also Zaslaw, *Mozart's Symphonies*, 520–32.

48. See Kant, *The Critique of Judgment*. There is obviously a major shift in the post-Kantian era, particularly in the case of Arthur Schopenhauer. But this subject has been traversed extensively, particularly with respect to Schopenhauer's influence on Wagner. See Leonard Krieger, *The German Idea of Freedom* (Chicago: University of Chicago Press, 1972).

49. Karl Vocelka and Anita Traninger, eds., *Wien, Geschichte einer Stadt*, vol. 2: *Die frühneuzeitliche Residenz*, series ed. Peter Csendes and Ferdinand Opll (Vienna: Böhlau, 2003), 110, 342, 351, 398–405, 525–43.

50. *Schillers Werke: Nationalausgabe*, vol. 21: *Philosophische Schriften 2* (Weimar: Böhlau, 1962), 60–62, and the Anhang, „Schemata über den Dilletantismus," 342–63, 398–405, 507–42; also vol. 20: *Philosophische Schriften 1*.

51. A discussion in Goethe's home in 1829 centered on the ongoing debate over the relative virtues of Raphael and Michelangelo. Johann Eckermann, *Gespräche mit Goethe*, ed. Fritz Bergemann (Frankfurt: Insel, 1981), 345–46.

52. As late as 1851, upon hearing Beethoven's Fifth Symphony for the first time, Anselm Feuerbach described himself as possessed and "thoroughly shaken" as never before. Feuerbach, *Ein Vermächtnis* (Linz: Genius, 1912), 66.

53. For discussion of the Haydn-Mozart-Beethoven triumvirate in nineteenth-century critical writings, see, in particular, Keefe, *Haydn and Mozart in the Long Nineteenth Century*, 14–16, 50–66, 86–92, 147–53.

54. Quoted in Hans-Günter Ottenberg, *Die Entwicklung des theoretisch-ästhetischen Denkens innerhalb der Berliner Musikkultur von den Anfängen der Aufklärung bis Reichardt* (Leipzig: VEB Deutscher Verlag für Musik, 1978), 85.

55. See Franz Grillparzer, *Sämtliche Werke*, ed. August Sauer, vol. 3 (Stuttgart: Gotta, 1893), 206–16.

56. Franz Grillparzer, "Zu Mozarts Feier" (1842), in *Sämtliche Werke*, ed. August Sauer, vol. 1 (Stuttgart: Gotta, 1892), 59–61.

57. Consider the play *Die Jüdin von Toledo*. Written in the 1850s and produced posthumously, it is often compared to Lessing's *Nathan the Wise*.

58. Owing to the advocacy of Heinrich Laube, the "Young Germany" politician of the 1840s who became the guiding spirit of the Viennese stage, Grillparzer's early theater works experienced a revival in the 1850s and 1860s. Their popularity helped ensure Grillparzer's high reputation at the time of his death. See Steven Burns, "Best Readings: Wittgenstein and Grillparzer," in *Wittgenstein Reading*, ed. Sascha Bru, Wolfgang Huemer, and Daniel Steuer (Berlin and Boston: De Gruyter, 2013), 153–70.

59. Despite sympathy for the 1836 oratorio *Paulus*, Mendelssohn's music struck Lenau as superficial. For Lenau, music of the early Romantic composers never touches the soul deeply enough to cure suffering. It leaves the listener unfulfilled by its attempt to console with trivial sentimentality. See Nikolaus Lenau, *Werke and Briefe: Historische Gesamtausgabe*, ed. Antal Mádl, vol 5/1 (Vienna: Deuticke, Klett-Cotta, 1989), 97 (letter of 22 July 1831) and *Werke und Briefe*, vol. 6 (Vienna: Deutick, Klett-Cotta, 1995), 15 (letter of 25 May 1838).

60. See R. H. Thomas "Lenau and Beethoven," *Music and Letters* 18/4 (1937): 374–79.

61. Nikolaus Lenau, *Werke and Briefe: Historische Gesamtausgabe*, vol. 2: *Neuere Gedichte und lyrische Nachlese*, ed. Antal Mádl (Vienna: Deuticke, Klett-Cotta, 1995), 273–75. The poem references the symphonies, particularly the Ninth, the *Coriolan* Overture, and indirectly, *Christ on the Mount of Olives*.

62. Lenau, *Werke and Briefe*, 2:273–75.

63. August Halm, quoted in Lee A. Rothfarb, *August Halm: A Critical and Creative Life in Music* (Rochester, NY: University of Rochester Press, 2009), 50.

64. Ibid., 79–86.

65. H. Voelcker, *Die Stadt Goethes* (Frankfurt: Hauserpresse, 1932), 334.

66. Goethe to Eckermann, 14 February 1831; quoted in Robert Spaethling, *Music and Mozart in the Life of Goethe* (Columbia, SC: Camden House, 1987), 13.

67. On 12 February 1829, Eckermann expressed the hope that *Faust* would ultimately be set appropriately to music. Goethe replied, "That is completely impossible. . . The music ought to have the character of *Don Juan*; Mozart should have composed it." Eckermann, *Gespräche mit Goethe*, 365. Eckermann was astonished that Goethe had heard the young Mozart perform.

68. Johann Wolfgang Goethe, *Gedenkausgabe der Werke, Briefe und Gespräche*, ed. Ernst Beutler, vol. 6 (Zurich: Artemis, 1949), 1091–118. See also the translation by Eric Blom, "'The Magic Flute, Part II,' by Johann Wolfgang von Goethe," in *Music and Letters* 23/3 (1942): 234–54; and Markus Waldura, "'Der Zauberflöte Zweyter Theil': Musikalische Konzeption einer nicht komponierten Oper," *Archiv für Musikwissenschaft* 50/4 (1993): 259–90.

69. Wolfram Huschke, *Musik im klassischen und nachklassischen Weimar* (Weimar: Böhlau, 1982), 28–39, 191.

70. Eckermann, *Gespräche mit Goethe*, 350, 720.

71. Zelter to Goethe, 26 July 1826, in *Briefwechsel,* 2:488.

72. This sentiment is quite similar to Grillparzer's view. It has remained central to twentieth-century reception, as is the Mozart-Shakespeare comparison. As Hofmannsthal put it in 1891, Beethoven was the "rhetoric" of the soul, Wagner its "feelings." But Mozart was "more." He was realization of the "sensual beauty of form itself," which made him the equal of Shakespeare. Hugo von Hofmannsthal, "Die Mozart-Zentenarfeier in Salzburg," in *Gesammelte Werke: Reden und Aufsätze 1* (Frankfurt: Fischer, 1979), 517.

73. *Mozart: Briefe und Aufzeichnungen,* 3:162.

74. Eckermann, *Gespräche mit Goethe,* 585 and 707.

75. See Spaethling, *Music and Mozart in the Life of Goethe,* 119–21. See also Matthew Bell, *Goethe: A Life in Ideas* (Princeton: Princeton University Press, 2025), 440.

76. Spaethling, *Music and Mozart in the Life of Goethe,* 113, quoting a letter to Eckermann from 1831.

77. One of the earlies encounters Goethe had with *Die Entführung* was in Italy in September 1786, when he attended a performance of a dreadful pastiche. Goethe, *Tagebücher,* ed. Wolfgang Albrecht and Andreas Döhler, vol. I.1: *1775–1787* (Stuttgart and Weimar: Metzler, 1998), 227.

78. Goethe even made drawings for the 1796 Weimar production. And he adored the catchy tunes Mozart gave Papageno and Papagena.

79. Johann Pezzl, *Schatten und Licht: Epilog Zu den Wienerischen Freymaurerschriften* (Sydney, Aus.: Wentworth Press), 11.

80. See the translation and articles by Blom and Waldura cited earlier, and Spaethling, *Music and Mozart in the Life of Goethe,* 123–49 and 175–232.

81. Johann Pezzl, *Faustin, oder Das Philosophische Jahrhundert* (1785) (Kessinger's Rare Reprints). Knepler made a strong case for Pezzl's influence within Mozart's circle, through his *Candide*-like novel from 1783, *Faustin, or The Philosophical Century.*

82. Adam Weishaupt, *Ueber die Gründe und Gewisheit der Menschlichen Erkenntniss: Zur Prüfung der Kantischen Kritik der reinen Vernunft* (Nuremberg: Brattenaurische Buchhandlung, 1788). On Weishaupt, see Jan Swafford, *Beethoven: Anguish and Triumph* (New York: Mariner Books, 2014), 73–74.

83. Weishaupt, *Ueber die Gründe und Gewisheit der Menschlichen Erkenntniss,* 127–31, 148–69.

84. Chev. Hadrien Majoie, ed., *The Collected Works of Adam Weishaupt,* vol. 1: *The Illuminati Writings,* trans. Paul Ferguson (Malta: Malta Minerval Editions, 2025), 178–80.

85. See Nicholas Till, *Mozart and the Enlightenment: Truth, Virtue, and Beauty in Mozart's Opera* (New York: W. W. Norton, 1992), 270–319.

86. See Gotthold Ephraim Lessing, *Nathan the Wise, Minna von Barnhelm, and Other Plays and Writings,* ed. Peter Demetz (New York: Continuum, 1995), xxv and xxvi; see also Hannah Arendt's Foreword in the same volume, vii–xx.

87. David Friedrich Strauss, *Lessings Nathan der Weise: Ein Vortrag* (Bonn: Emil Strauss, 1877), 59.

88. Ibid., 60–61.

89. Paul Wittgenstein commissioned much of the finest music for piano left hand from composers such as Erich Wolfgang Korngold, Maurice Ravel, Richard Strauss, and Sergei Prokofiev. A rare photograph, in the possession of the author, shows Wittgenstein's mother and sister playing piano four-hands.

90. Ludwig Wittgenstein, *Tractatus Logico-Philosophicus,* Foreword by Marjory Perloff, trans. and introduction by Damion Searls (New York: Liveright, 2024), 45 (4.014). See Sandra Laugier, *Wittgenstein: The Senses of Use,* trans. Daniela Ginsburg (Chicago: University of Chicago Press, 2025), 18–19.

91. Byron Adams correctly observes that *Così fan tutte* has no shortage of irony, but it is not the "historical irony" characteristic of Nietzsche's generation, to which Wittgenstein was referring. Conversation with author.

92. Ludwig Wittgenstein, *Culture and Value*, ed. G. H. von Wright, with Heikki Nyman, trans. Peter Winch (Chicago: University of Chicago Press, 1980), 81e–82e.

93. See Wittgenstein, "Lectures on Aesthetics," in *Lectures and Conversations: On Aesthetics, Psychology, and Religious Belief*, ed. Cyril Barrett (Berkeley: University of California Press, 2007), 2–3.

94. Edward Timms, *Karl Kraus, Apocalyptic Satirist: Culture and Catastrophe in Habsburg Vienna* (New Haven: Yale University Press, 1986), 33–34. Otto Erich Deutsch, noted for his superb editions of documents pertaining to Schubert, Mozart, and Handel, also edited modern editions of Daniel Spitzer and Ferdinand Kürnberger, great Viennese prose writers of opinion and commentary. Both Spitzer and Kürnberger were particular favorites of Kraus, whose publication *Die Fackel* (The Torch) was greatly admired by Wittgenstein, Schoenberg, and Alban Berg. See *Portraits of Wittgenstein,* ed. F. A. Flowers III and Ian Ground, vol. 2 (London: Bloomsbury Academic, 1999/2016), 1042

95. Ferdinand Kürnberger, "Opposition to the Erection of Monuments," in *Literarische Herzenssachen*, vol. 2 (Munich and Leipzig: Georg Müller, 1911), 312. The full article can be found on 310–42. See also Wolfgang Kienzler, "Wittgenstein Reads Kürnberger," in *Wittgenstein Reading*, 335–54.

96. Wittgenstein, *Tractatus Logico-Philosophicus*, 1.

97. See George Abraham Mulfinger, *Ferdinand Kürnbergers Roman "Der Amerikamüde": Dessen Quellen und Verhältnis zu Lenaus Amerikareise* (Philadelphia: German-American Annals Press, 1903).

98. This occurred around the time Da Ponte, encouraged by Clement Moore, author of "The Night Before Christmas," recruited him to found a department of Italian at Columbia University.

99. Ferdinand Kürnberger, *Der Amerikamüde* (Vienna and Cologne: Böhlau, 1985), 528–29. The scene in the novel follows quite closely Da Ponte's own memoir, which concludes in 1830, eight years before the librettist's death. Toward the end, Da Ponte writes, "Italian opera, which in the eyes of every civilized nation of the world, is the noblest and most pleasurable of all the many spectacles of human intelligence ever invented." And *Don Giovanni* is "the best opera in the world." Indeed, Da Ponte organized the American premiere on 26 May 1826. See *Memoirs of Lorenzo Da Ponte: Mozart's Librettist*, trans. Elisabeth Abbott (New York: Dover, 1967), 3:262–72.

100. Kürnberger, *Der Amerikamüde*, 532–35.

101. Ferdinand Kürnberger, "Ich möchte lesen lernen" (I Should Like to Learn to Read) (9 January 1848), in *Literarische Herzenssachen*, 2:345–50.

102. Wittgenstein, *Philosophical Investigations*, 174.

103. All quotes from the Kürnberger essay in Appendix 1.

104. Barth, "Wolfgang Amadeus Mozart," 62–78.

105. Ibid., 62–63, 65, 67, 68, see also 73.

APPENDIX 1.

Ferdinand Kürnberger, "Ich möchte lesen lernen" (I Should Like to Learn to Read) (9 January 1848), in Kürnberger, *Literarische Herzenssachen*, vol. 2 (Munich and Leipzig: Georg Müller, 1911), 345–50. Translated by Susan Gillespie

If only I were a prince, so that I might immediately and directly have an actual example realized by Order of the Cabinet! The *actual* example; for commentary, in its impotent language, is truly as weak as a straw. My fantasy is so far removed from contemporary sentiment that I must fear receiving, already from an editor himself--at the source--a rejection of "such an impractical opinion." And then what? Did I say "prince"? Oh, if only I were a member of a commission for the adoption of a new curriculum, or even only the friend of such a member: I would not rest, and like old Cato, with his *Ceterum censeo*, I would press every day for my proposal: that in the schools one should teach the young people to read. Teach them to read? What do you mean? Don't they already learn that? What kind of mad idea is this? What should be the first and most prominent subject in every school, the basis of all public instruction in all schooling and education? Who would not have learned to read? Perhaps the author himself, so that he now has to express the wish for it in his odd title? Ah, yes! The author himself!

Recently I visited a house; there was a publication on the table—a German book. I leafed through it and did not understand a single line. Then I asked a boy, who had fortunately—not in school, but at home—learned to read, if he would read it to me. The child did so, and began to declaim, accompanied by rhetorical flourishes of his hands. I listened and pricked up my ears. It was a poem set by Beethoven! Reading that is something I did not learn in school. There, we learned only the alphabet, not the notation of music. I can read the *Cracow Calendar*; I can read the note on the door; I can—unfortunately!—read the tailor's bills and the importunate notes of aging coquettes. Only not the language of the gods, the handwriting of the angels, the works of Heaven, my adored, passionately beloved, joyous music of the heart and soul. That was never taught to me! I mastered it on my own, thoroughly, in hours without number!

This, in heaven's name, is no small matter. To leave not less than half of all of the greatest that the spirits of human history have ever thought and felt lying in a form that is not made accessible through general instruction, in letters and hieroglyphics that do not speak to me or mean anything, is a loss, an educational deficit that can only make one weep. There are, after all, no griffons and dragons guarding harmonic theory and figured bass from us. Let those learn who wish to learn. The teachers are there, and opportunities by the hundreds. Should we simply let each seek his own pathways to it? I beg your pardon! I am not someone who takes breakfast at noon. And how few people do! For someone who has completed his studies, the schoolyears are in the past. Everyone is fortunate for whatever he has managed to pick up through schooling. It can never be enough. Whatever he can later manage to find with additional efforts is extremely uncertain—extremely precarious. As a rule, it is little enough.

But are there not, then, opera houses, concerts, conservatories? Are these not like permanent art exhibitions of music, where all the old images do not just hang side by side, but are presented chronologically, one after another? One after the other—oh, yes! Very much one *after* the other. That is the rub. Now I take my Shakespeare down from the shelf as often as I feel like it. What if someone who was now unable to read were to have to wait patiently until King Lear were to appear, like a comet, on stage once again in our earthly vicinity? Or, more importantly, Julius Caesar, Henry IV, Faust, Tasso, etc., etc.? I would say thank you very much! And yet—does not this musical *prix fixe* menu have something displeasing about it: the monotony of the same thing, the absence of anything different, the lack of a voice in choosing, and the absolute tyranny of taste? If the scores of the two Haydn oratorios, of Mozart's three principal operas and the *Freischütz* were to suddenly vanish from this world, I might be able to produce them all by myself, from memory—not to speak of the march and chorus of the departure from the ruins of Athens, or any another standard piece—or several others that swim across the surface of all the public announcements like musical ducks. But who, in this circumstance, especially if he were a member of the younger generation, would ever hear the masterpieces of Bach, Hess, and Graun; operas of Gluck, Cherubini, Martini, Domenico Cimarosa, or Pergolesi; *Oberon* and *Euryanthe*; or the whole panoply of vocal and instrumental pieces by Beethoven?

Ceterum censeo . . . This is why I wish that I had learned to read. This is why I wish that the knowledge of musical notation should be considered an educational tool that is just as essential as using the alphabet to write. This is why I wish that, at public expense, a broad, public avenue be constructed that would lead—as in the case of the other arts—to the temple of musical art, instead of having every individual discover his own path through the thorns and rocky outcroppings, costly tolls and bridge duties.

Is there, then, a dearth of public music schools? What about the conservatories? How many thousands of students do they not educate? They produce fodder for orchestras—mere fodder, "Mr. Sound"; nothing but fodder for orchestras! No, that is not what I mean. Music should be no mere professional bread-and-butter discipline. It should not therefore displace other fields of instruction; it should not take entire possession of a man. Let him who wants to become a virtuoso on some instrument or other do so. But reading—learning to read music? Ah, if only we all wanted to do so! I imagine this matter along the lines of many North German schools that, alongside classical subjects, include vocal instruction as a principal subject. When I let my imagination dwell on these factual examples, they make it clear that this does not even appear to be so very impractical. Yes, indeed! Why should a Sebastian Bach have handed his students at the Thomas Church, between Kirsch and Schrevelius,[1] nothing but the delicious flora of the muse Polyhymnia?

If I seek, in my thoughts, to include the whole assemblage that emerges from among the images of the beautiful within the domain of music, my gaze grows giddy, my breast expands to embrace the heavens, and a boundless bliss lifts me beyond humanity. Form after form, character after character, a host of life-bearing creations pass before the mind—creations that can be the source of a Nestor's age of wonderment and the pleasure of eternal instruction.

Indeed, I can assert, brashly, that I owe as much to the teachings of Mozart as to those of Goethe. Every artistic nature will locate in each of them a richness of aesthetic invention that rivals Potosi's worth[2] in silver. Susanna, Zerlina, Doña Anna, Doña Elvira, the Queen of the Night. What female characters! Don Juan, Osmin, Figaro, Papageno, Sarastro—what brilliant, original, thoroughly perfected human types! For years now, when, in the quiet sunshine of a walk in the fields, or circling the ramparts in a heavy evening fog, I become immersed in solitary musing, they are my friends, my companions. They shape me, instruct and teach me, and display, as the sculptures of antiquity did for Winckelmann, their finest, most immortal, beautiful features. This, now, is the scope of three or four operas! Where are the boundaries of the terrain that remains? What is encompassed by the contents of the art as a whole? What rich treasures suffer, in dusty repertories, an ignominious oblivion, hidden from sight as if buried, like the gods and heroes of the ancient world, under the ruins and ashes of Italy. Thought gets lost in eternity in the course of this reflection, and a forest of musical statues rises up within the

1. Theodorus Schrivelius (1597–1549) was a Dutch poet and teacher at the Latin School in Haarlem. His students included Rembrandt, among many other painters. [Trans.]

2. The reference is presumably to the town Potosi, Bolivia, which from the fifteenth century on was famous as the site of one of the world's largest silver mines. [Trans.]

century from Händel to Meyerbeer, resembling the wealth of statues and monuments that reflected the rays of the Greek sun. Yes, the works of our music compensate us for the works of the ancient chisel. In music, we moderns are what the ancients were in the plastic arts. We may compare music—this art—as boldly as no other, with theirs. In the written arts, we have learned from the ancients theoretically and practically. The visual arts evolved by drinking the milk of antiquity. In music we possess the great, the most elevated virtue of artistic performance—uniqueness; in music, we have, from its earliest inception to its greatest perfection, developed the ideal of the beautiful from within ourselves as autonomously as the Greeks' chisel did from within themselves. A poet seeks in vain to attain the laurels of a Homer, a Sophocles, a Pindar; the sculptor despairs when confronted with Laocoön, Apollo, Venus, Hercules, Niobe. Only the musician has never shed tears of emulation in the presence of a Greek model. He owns his Don Juan just as Phidias does his Jupiter. And should we not be led to understand our own and most independent art the way the schoolboy gains the understanding of books? Who does not know that for a Greek his sculptural masterworks were one of the most prominent means of education? Which permitted the most ordinary Greek, without further knowledge and scholarship, to uplift his soul in the daily contemplation of his ideal. He refined his senses and ennobled his character. Did he not become a better, greater human being? True, he made use of an inborn, quintessentially human means—the eye. But why should it not be worthwhile for us, with application of time and effort, with deliberate, structured study, to make use of *our* means and render the study of music an essential part of public education?

Oh, I do know wherein my great misconception seems to lie. In music, the concept of beauty may not be as easy to construct in a philosophically fruitful manner as in the other arts. And it is of little or no significance for intellectual education that one cannot take something home from music as confidently as the student in *Faust* wants to do with the sciences. But what does that prove? The aesthetics of music may, admittedly, less easily allow the mind to absorb the abstraction from specificity, from factual, material knowledge and learning. However, one reads *Faust* because it is written in words, and the word entails a fixed concept in a way that the tone does not. And one reads the Medici Venus because it is written in lines, and the line, given its strict measurable nature, produces a solid external form in a way that music does not. Very well! Let the lecturer in musical aesthetics be perplexed by the lack of definitions, descriptions, formal analyses, and conceptual development. What if he should produce a treatise on the Champagne Aria, with citations on the piano that elude the language of words, and resist the transparent evidence of logic? What if he merely brings a heaven of premonitions down into the lecture hall; or if he only enflames the imagination to warmer, although unspecific imaginings of the beautiful; or if he only proclaims to our emotions the divine that he cannot make fully clear to the mind? His student, it is true, will not know anything. But is knowledge, then, its own purpose, or, rather, is the goal the ennoblement of character, improvement of the human heart; the refinement of customs, and an increase in the enjoyment of life? And what would lead more surely to this result than music? What makes it possible to feel the beautiful, the elevated, the purely human more immediately than music? It does nothing for the intelligence; but for the moral imagination—everything. And if it does nothing more than to make one happy—would that be beneath the seriousness of the state's purpose? Oh, no! The happy man is also the good man. All crime lies solely in the lack of joy. One Figaro renders ten moral systems unnecessary. This, now, is unfortunately all too cheerful, much too sensual, and much too Greek in its thinking! Right? The serious gentlemen respond with nothing but a smile. What? One should grow wise without the dictionary and the encyclopedia, and be able to educate oneself without logic? In school, one should develop the spirit for sweet melodies, and give a lecture on Zerlina? Yes, yes, yes! You do want to have an impact on sensibility, after all, for is it not the locus of all morality, rather than the intelligence? Well, then, there you have an art that achieves this immediately, without making the long detour through logic. Why should it be less relevant than others? Because it is also more charming than others? Oh, no! Finally, no! Become agreeable, you professors, all you privy councilors—become gracious! As the sainted Ludwig Börne said.[3] Until this happens, by the way, I want nothing more than to have given reign to a fantasy, and want nothing more than to have wished—modestly—that I had learned to read.

3. Karl Ludwig Börne (born Judah Löw Baruch, 1786–1837) was a German-Jewish political writer and satirist, who is considered part of the Young Germany movement. [Trans.]

Index

Note: Page numbers followed by "n" and "t" indicate chapter endnotes and tables, respectively; page numbers in italics refer to figures and musical examples; throughout the index, WAM refers to Wolfgang Amadeus Mozart.

Index of Works

Index of Names and Subjects

Contributors

Dorian Bandy is Associate Professor of Musicology and Historical Performance at McGill University's Schulich School of Music. He is the author of *Mozart the Performer: Variations on the Showman's Art* as well as of numerous articles and book chapters on seventeenth- through nineteenth-century music. An active performer, he has released six solo or chamber CDs, and in 2024 he was awarded the Marjorie Weston Emerson Award by the Mozart Society of America.

Leon Botstein is Leon Levy Professor in the Arts of Bard College and the author of several books and editor of *The Compleat Brahms* and *The Musical Quarterly*. The music director of the American Symphony Orchestra and The Orchestra Now (TŌN), he is principal guest conductor of the Jerusalem Symphony Orchestra, where he served as music director. He has recorded works by, among others, Schoeck, Honegger, Szymanowski, Hartmann, Dukas, Foulds, Bruckner, Chausson, Richard Strauss, Mendelssohn, Popov, Shostakovich, and Liszt. He is founder and co-artistic director of the Bard Music Festival and served as president of Bard for fifty-one years. His work has been acknowledged with awards from the American Academy of Arts and Letters, Harvard University, government of Austria, and Carnegie Foundation.

Lisa de Alwis is a musicologist at the University of Colorado, Boulder, who specializes in late eighteenth- and early nineteenth-century Viennese music and culture. Her recent work includes a chapter in the *Cambridge Companion to The Magic Flute* (2023) and one in the forthcoming *Eighteenth-Century Opera and Ballet: Essays in Honor of Bruce Brown* from University of Rochester Press. She currently serves on the Mozart Society of America board and leads the Global Seminar *Voices of Vienna* through the University of Colorado.

Susan Gillespie has translated Theodor W. Adorno and many other authors of philosophical and musicological works, as well as fiction and poetry. Her book-length translations include *Corona: Selected Poems of Paul Celan* and *The Correspondence of Paul Celan and Ilana Shmueli*, which was a finalist for the National Translation Award. Gillespie has worked as fundraiser for the New York Zoological Society, the New York Public Library, and, finally, Bard College where she served first as Vice President for Public Affairs and Development and then as Vice President for Special Global Initiatives. In 1998, she founded the Institute for International Liberal Education.

Austin Glatthorn is Lecturer in Music at the Royal Northern College of Music, Manchester. A musicologist and cultural historian investigating musical life in early modern Europe, his publications include the monograph *Music Theatre and the Holy Roman Empire: The German Musical Stage at the Turn of the Nineteenth Century* (2022), as well as articles in *Eighteenth-Century Music*, *Journal of Musicology*, *Music & Letters*, and the *Journal of War & Culture Studies*. His work has been recognized by the Mozart Society of America's Marjorie Weston Emerson Award and *Music & Letters*' Centenary Prize Competition. Together with Estelle Joubert, he is currently editing the *Cambridge History of German Opera to the Early Nineteenth Century* and serves on the board of *Eighteenth-Century Music*.

Edmund J. Goehring is Professor of Music History at the University of Western Ontario. He writes on aesthetics, historiography, and criticism, especially as they bear on Mozart. His most recent book is *Mozart, Genius, and the Possibilities of Art* (2024), and his essays have appeared in the *Cambridge Opera Journal*, *Eighteenth-Century Music*, *Film International* (on Martin McDonagh's *In Bruges*), *Logos*, *Publications of the Modern Language Association*, and *Studi Verdiani*. More recent publications, in *Poetics Today* and *Music Analysis*, offer critiques of scientific reductions of the arts. He has received grants from the NEH and SSHRC, and his book *Coming to Terms with Our Musical Past* (2018) won the Marjorie Weston Emerson Award from the Mozart Society of America.

Simon P. Keefe is J. R. Hoyle Chair of Music at the University of Sheffield and President of the Royal Musical Association. He is an elected life-member of the Akademie für Mozart-Forschung at the Internationale Stiftung Mozarteum in Salzburg. He is the author of five books, including *Mozart's Requiem: Reception, Work, Completion* (2012), which received the Marjorie Weston Emerson Award from the Mozart Society of America; *Mozart in Vienna: The Final Decade* (2017), and *Haydn and Mozart in the Long Nineteenth Century: Parallel and Intersecting Patterns of Reception* (2023). In addition, he has edited ten volumes, including, most recently, *Vienna: A Musical History* (2026).

Edward Klorman is Professor of Music at the Mead Witter School of Music, University of Wisconsin–Madison. His publications include *Mozart's Music of Friends: Social Interplay in the Chamber Works* (2016), which received major awards from ASCAP, the Mozart Society of America, and the Society for Music Theory; and *Bach: The Cello Suites* (2025). An accomplished violist, he has performed as guest artist with the Borromeo, Orion, and Ying quartets and with the Lysander Trio and was founding co-artistic director of ChamberFest Canandaigua. Klorman has previously taught at The Juilliard School, Manhattan School of Music, McGill University, and the Aaron Copland School of Music.

Martin Nedbal is Professor of Musicology at the University of Kansas. He is the author of two monographs: *Mozart's Operas and National Politics: Canon Formation in Prague from 1791 to the Present* (2023), and *Viennese Opera and Morality in the Age of Mozart and Beethoven* (2017). He is also the translator and editor of *The Published Theoretical Works of Leoš Janáček* and a co-editor of *A History of Music in the Czech Lands* (2025) and of Jan Löwenbach's *Bedřich Smetana: A Study of His Life and Work* (2026).

Jessica Waldoff is Carol and Park B. Smith Professor of Music at the College of the Holy Cross in Worcester, Massachusetts. Her research focuses mainly on issues of dramaturgy and representation in opera. She is the author of *Recognition in Mozart's Operas* (2006; paperback edition, 2011) and many essays on the music of Mozart and Haydn. She is also the editor of *The Cambridge Companion to "The Magic Flute"* (2023) and has written essays for a number of opera houses and festivals, including the Royal Opera House at Covent Garden (London), La Monnaie (Brussels), the Gran Teatre del Liceu (Barcelona), the Cleveland Orchestra's Mandel Opera & Humanities Festival, and the Salzburg Festival. She is a past president of the Mozart Society of America.

VOLUMES PUBLISHED IN CONJUNCTION WITH THE BARD MUSIC FESTIVAL

Brahms and His World
edited by Walter Frisch (1990)

Mendelssohn and His World
edited by R. Larry Todd (1991)

Richard Strauss and His World
edited by Bryan Gilliam (1992)

Dvořák and His World
edited by Michael Beckerman (1993)

Schumann and His World
edited by R. Larry Todd (1994)

Bartók and His World
edited by Peter Laki (1995)

Charles Ives and His World
edited by J. Peter Burkholder (1996)

Haydn and His World
edited by Elaine R. Sisman (1997)

Tchaikovsky and His World
edited by Leslie Kearney (1998)

Schoenberg and His World
edited by Walter Frisch (1999)

Beethoven and His World
edited by Scott Burnham and Michael P. Steinberg (2000)

Debussy and His World
edited by Jane F. Fulcher (2001)

Mahler and His World
edited by Karen Painter (2002)

Janáček and His World
edited by Michael Beckerman (2003)

Shostakovich and His World
edited by Laurel E. Fay (2004)

Aaron Copland and His World
edited by Carol J. Oja and Judith Tick (2005)

Franz Liszt and His World
edited by Christopher H. Gibbs and Dana Gooley (2006)

Edward Elgar and His World
edited by Byron Adams (2007)

Sergey Prokofiev and His World
edited by Simon Morrison (2008)

Brahms and His World (revised edition)
edited by Walter Frisch and Kevin C. Karnes (2009)

Richard Wagner and His World
edited by Thomas S. Grey (2009)

Alban Berg and His World
edited by Christopher Hailey (2010)

Jean Sibelius and His World
edited by Daniel M. Grimley (2011)

Camille Saint-Saëns and His World
edited by Jann Pasler (2012)

Stravinsky and His World
edited by Tamara Levitz (2013)

Franz Schubert and His World
edited by Christopher H. Gibbs and Morten Solvik (2014)

Carlos Chávez and His World
edited by Leonora Saavedra (2015)

Giacomo Puccini and His World
edited by Arman Schwartz and Emanuele Senici (2016)

Chopin and His World
edited by Jonathan D. Bellman and Halina Goldberg (2017)

Rimsky-Korsakov and His World
edited by Marina Frolova-Walker (2018)

Korngold and His World
edited by Daniel Goldmark and Kevin C. Karnes (2019)

Nadia Boulanger and Her World
edited by Jeanice Brooks (2020)

Rachmaninoff and His World
edited by Philip Ross Bullock (2022)

Vaughan Williams And His World
edited by Byron Adams and Daniel M. Grimley (2023)

Berlioz and His World
edited by Francesca Brittan and Sarah Hibberd (2024)

Martinů and His World
edited by Aleš Březina and Michael Beckerman (2025)